ROUGH QUARRIES, ROCKS AND HILLS

John Pull and the Neolithic Flint Mines of Sussex

by

Miles Russell

with contributions from
Julie Gardiner, John H. Pull, C. E. Sainsbury, Arthur Voice and Sally White

Bournemouth University
School of Conservation Sciences
Occasional Paper 6

Published by
Oxbow Books, Park End Place, Oxford OX1 1HN

A CIP record for this book is available from the British Library

ISBN 1 84217 054 6

Front cover: John H. Pull emerging from a gallery within Shaft 27 at Cissbury in 1954
(© Worthing Museum and Art Gallery)

This book is available direct from
Oxbow Books, Park End Place, Oxford OX1 1HN
(Phone: 01865-241249; Fax: 01865-794449)

and

The David Brown Book Company
PO Box 511, Oakville, CT 06779, USA
(Phone: 860-945-9329; Fax: 860-945-9468)

and

via our website
www.oxbowbooks.com

Bournemouth University School of Conservation Sciences
Occasional Paper 6

Series Editor (Archaeology): Timothy Darvill

ISSN 1362 - 6094

Printed in Great Britain by
The Short Run Press
Exeter

In Memory of John H. Pull,
his family, friends and team of flint mine volunteers 1922–1956

Contents

Preface

I first encountered the work of John H. Pull in the early 1990's, whilst conducting research into Neolithic Sussex with fellow archaeologist John Wallis. This investigation inevitably led us to the hills behind the modern town of Worthing where distribution maps indicated the presence of four major areas of Neolithic flint mining: Harrow Hill, Blackpatch, Church Hill and Cissbury.

Finding early excavation reports for the sites of Harrow Hill and Cissbury proved relatively easy, with published texts appearing in *Archaeologia*, the *Journal of the Royal Archaeological Institute* and the *Sussex Archaeological Collections* (e.g. Curwen and Curwen 1926; Holleyman 1937; Lane Fox 1869a; 1869b; 1876; Harrison 1877a; 1877b; 1878; Willett 1880). Frustratingly, there seemed to be few texts relating to the mid twentieth century work at the mine sites of Blackpatch, Church Hill and Cissbury, with just one report appearing in print (Goodman *et al* 1924). Discovery of a book entitled *The Flint Miners of Blackpatch* (Pull 1932) helped supply detail for one particular excavation, though it was clear that this work was not a detailed site report, rather a popular summary of some of the more important discoveries. Worse, many later commentators when referring to this particular text appeared highly critical or disparaging of the information and how it was presented.

A chance visit to Worthing Museum in late 1991 proved a revelation. Here the principal curator, Dr Sally White, presented us with an entire excavation archive, chronicling a whole range of archaeological investigations conducted at four areas of prehistoric mining, Blackpatch, Church Hill, Cissbury and Tolmere, between 1922 and 1956. Here were details concerning the examination of at least twenty-one mine shafts, six quarry pits, twenty-two flint working areas, two possible henge monuments, areas of associated settlement and some twenty-four mounds, most containing elements of human burial. Here were sections and profiles of mine shafts, whole plans of mining areas, detailed drawings of galleries, plans and sections of barrows, pits, ditches and postholes, illustrations of pottery, antler picks and flint tools of all shapes and sizes, all inked up and ready for publication. Here were site notebooks, hand written texts, specialist reports and typescripts. Here were photographs, reports on environmental data and, of course, the finds themselves in store rooms, cupboards and museum cases. All the note books, inked drawings and the majority of flint tools all possessed the same distinctive monogram of the project director: 'J. H. P' - John Henry Pull.

To say that we were amazed would be an understatement. None of this material appeared to have ever been used or widely referred to in print and certainly none of the information had ever been discussed or disseminated amidst a wider audience.

The story, as it began to unfold, of just how the data had accumulated and why it had remained unpublished and ignored by the archaeological establishment for so long appeared to be every bit as interesting as the archive itself. We decided that something should be done with this mass of information, but what?

I have been back to Worthing Museum many times since 1991, and each time have been surprised by the wealth and quality of data that survives within the John Pull archive. The nature and survival of the material demands attention and its absence from mainstream archaeological literature in the latter half of the 20th century is unforgivable. It has always been my intention to publish the results of Pull's work so that the thirty-four years of field and excavation data can finally make some contribution to our understanding of activity in Neolithic Britain. I hope that this has now, in part at least, been achieved.

Miles Russell
25th June 1999

Acknowledgements

This work would not have been possible without the help of Dr Sally White, Principal Curator of Worthing Museum and Art Gallery, who not only introduced me to the Pull archive, but also allowed constant access to the material and helped answer some of the more obscure questions relating to John Pull and the Worthing Archaeological Society. Grateful thanks must go to her and to Mrs Beryl Heryet, daughter of John and Alice Pull, for allowing me to use and publish the archive in this way. Thank you also to Liz Pye at The Institute of Archaeology, University College London and Dr Julie Gardiner, of Wessex Archaeology for permitting me to use significant parts of their unpublished postgraduate work (Pye 1968 and Gardiner 1988), especially with regard to chapter 8 of this present publication.

Acknowledgement must also be made here to Tim Darvill, Dave Field and Glynis Laughlin who read a large number of early drafts of this report and were able to correct the countless errors in spelling and grammar. It goes without saying that any mistakes that remain are entirely my responsibility.

I have, during the course of compiling this work, benefited from discussions, encouragement, criticisms and conversations with a number of friends and colleagues. In particular I would like to thank the following people for their help in shaping the feel and content of this text over the last nine years: Con Ainsworth, Barbara Alcock, Mike Allen, Kevin Andrews, Martyn Barber, Maureen Bennell, Martin Brown, Chris Butler, Jeff Chartrand, Tim Darvill, Roger Doonan, Damian Evans, Dave Field, Andy Fulton, John Funnel, John Gale, Julie Gardiner, Oliver Gilkes, Francis Healy, Beryl Heryet, Robin Holgate, George Holleyman, Alex Hunt, Ian Kinnes, Gina Koester, George Lambrick, Glynis Laughlin, Mark Maltby, John Manley, Fiona Marsden, John Mills, Ian McGuinness, Dave McOmish, Al Oswald, Janet Pennington, Roy Plummer, Lawrence Pontin, Liz Pye, Andrew Reynolds, David Rudling, John Roles, Derek and Jane Russell, Rob Sands, Paul Smith, Madeline Sarley, Gale Sieveking, Jeff Spencer, Gareth Talbot, Mark Taylor, Peter Topping, Gill Varndell, Alex Vincent, Jon Wallis, Sally White, Keith Wilkinson, Andrew Woodcock, Emma Young, the many generous members of the Worthing Archaeological Society, the staff of the National Monuments Record in Swindon and Worthing Museum (who coped with my increasingly bizarre requests for data), all at Oxbow Books, especially David Brown and Julie Choppin and the many archaeology undergraduates at Bournemouth University who have experienced lengthy field trips to the Sussex mine sites to hear about flint extraction processes, when a short talk in a warm lecture theatre would probably have been more welcome. I hope now that it all makes some sort of sense.

A huge thank you must go to my wife Bronwen, who has been an inspiration throughout, and to Megan, who made a sudden and dramatic entry to the world just as this text was coming to a conclusion. Bron will be pleased to discover that Neolithic flint mines no longer figure so prominently in my life, whilst Megan will no doubt be surprised to learn she has a father.

The story of the Neolithic mines in central Sussex is of course really the story of one man: John H. Pull. To him, his family, his colleagues and team of ever-eager volunteers between 1922–1956, I dedicate this book.

LIST OF CONTRIBUTORS (1990–99)

Dr Julie Gardiner,
Wessex Archaeology,
Portway House,
Old Sarum Park,
Salisbury,
SP4 6EB.

Dr Miles Russell,
Archaeology,
School of Conservation Sciences,
Bournemouth University,
Fern Barrow,
Poole,
Dorset,
BH12 5BB.

Dr Sally White,
Worthing Museum and Art Gallery,
Chapel Road,
Worthing,
West Sussex,
BN11 1HP.

Abbreviations

Acc.no.	Accession number
Ant.J.	Antiquaries Journal
Arch.	Archaeologia
Arch.Cant.	Archaeologia Cantiana
Arch.J.	Archaeological Journal
BAR	British Archaeological Reports
BM	British Museum
BU	Bournemouth University
CBA	Council for British Archaeology
cm	centimetre(s)
CUP	Cambridge University Press
Cur.Arch.	Current Archaeology
ESCC	East Sussex County Council
ft	feet
g	gram(s)
ha	hectare(s)
HMSO	Her Majesty's Stationery Office
kg	kilogram(s)
km	kilometre(s)
m	metre(s)
MARS	Monuments at Risk Survey
mm	millimetre(s)
MPP	Monuments Protection Programme
MS	Manuscript
MSFAT	Mid Sussex Field Archaeology Team
NGR	national grid reference
NMR	national monuments record
OD	Ordnance Datum
OS	Ordnance Survey
p.	page
PRO	Public Records Office
RCHME	Royal Commission on the Historical Monuments of England
SAS	Sussex Archaeological Society
SEAS	South Eastern Archaeological Services
SMR	sites and monuments record

Sur.AC	Surrey Archaeological Collections
VCH	Victoria County History
WM	Worthing Museum
WSCC	West Sussex County Council

A Note on Measurement

Analysis of the 1922–56 excavations at Blackpatch, Church Hill, Cissbury and Tolmere has meant dealing with a large body of imperial measurements. The urge to alter such data to fit within the metric system was at times considerable, however it was felt that as this current work was an attempt to bring together as much original information as possible, in the form of text and illustrations, then such editorial reform had to remain small scale and unobtrusive. Thus where imperial measurements are directly referred to by Pull, Sainsbury or Voice within their reports and drawings, these have been retained; metric measurements are used only within the discussions and overall conclusions. In order to ease understanding for those unfamiliar with the imperial system, and to allow modern readers to make their own calculations and cross-comparisons, a table of conversions is here appended.

Table of Conversion
To convert to metric, multiply by the factor shown.
To convert to imperial, divide by the factor shown.

Length	
miles: kilometres	1.609
yards: metres	0.914
feet: metres	0.305
inches: millimetres	25.4
inches: centimetres	2.54

Area	
square miles: square kilometres	2.59
square miles: hectares	258.999
acres: square metres	4046.86
acres: hectares	0.404
square yards: square metres	0.836
square feet: square metres	0.092
square feet: square centimetres	929.03
square inches: square millimetres	645.16
square inches: square centimetres	6.451

Mass	
tons: kilograms	1016.05
tons: tonnes	1.016
Hundredweights: kilograms	50.802
Quarters: kilograms	12.700
stones: kilograms	6.350
pounds: kilograms	0.453
ounces: grams	28.349

Volume	
cubic yards: cubic metres	0.764
cubic feet: cubic metres	0.028

Capacity	
gallons: litres	4.546
quarts: litres	1.136
pints: litres	0.568

1
Introduction

'Rough quarries, rocks and hills whose heads touch heaven'
(W. Shakespeare, Othello I, iii, 140)

The South Downs

Standing on the crest of the South Downs today is an exhilarating experience. The great swathe of the Weald stretches below you, towards Surrey, Hampshire, Kent, London and beyond. Behind you lies the sea and the great continental landmass of Europe. At either side the green, whale-backed hills and gentle valley systems stretch out, seemingly forever.

The chalkland ridge of the South Downs flows across Sussex and eastern Hampshire and represents the major topographic feature of central south eastern England. Chalk is a white, permeable rock supporting no surface water. Buried deep within it are horizontal seams of nodular and tabular flint, a vital raw material used by humans for building and tool manufacture for millennia. The western limits of the South Downs are traditionally marked by the river Test, to the west of Winchester, which drains out into Southampton Water and the Solent, though geologically the chalk continues further to the north east and west. The eastern limits of the South Downs are more emphatically marked by the sheer white cliffs of Beachy Head, to the west of Eastbourne in East Sussex. The northern face of the Downs is characterised by a fearsome escarpment, dominating the low-lying sands, sandstones and clays of the Weald. At its southern edge, the Downs merge more subtly into the Sussex and Hampshire coastal plain, now heavily developed. Seven major river systems, the Cuckmere, Ouse, Adur, Arun, Lavant, Meon and Itchen, cut through the South Downs, draining southwards to the English Channel. These river systems have the effect of dividing the chalkland ridge into a series of discrete blocks.

Human intervention

The Downs may to some appear as an untouched, natural landscape, but human interference, in the form of building, deforestation and agricultural production have helped shape the land for thousands of years. Iron Age hillforts, Bronze Age barrows,

Neolithic enclosures, World War Two gun emplacements, Medieval mottes, prehistoric, Roman, Medieval and Post Medieval fields and hedgerows, modern reservoirs, roads, farms and houses; all periods of recent human existence have played their part in this shaping of visible form. Arguably this modification began around six thousand years ago with the removal of surface vegetation and the construction of new and dramatic forms of monumental architecture. Specific areas of land were at this time enclosed with great circuits of ditch and earthen ramparts. Deep vertical shafts were dug to extract subterranean flint. Large earthen mounds containing human bone, were constructed. This was the beginning of the period known today as the Neolithic or 'New Stone Age'.

Early Neolithic monumental forms such as the enclosure, the flint mine and the long barrow, altered the way in which certain areas were visualised, perceived and understood by human populations. Monuments enhanced the importance of specific places, generating a framework of shared human experience and imposing a new order upon the land. Anyone crossing the chalkland ridge around 4000 BC would have found their movement gradually curtailed and increasingly controlled. The landscape was no longer wild. Familiar places were changing and their significance and meaning were being rewritten in new and more permanent ways.

Archaeological investigation

Neolithic monuments have long been the target of antiquarian and archaeological examination. Long and Round barrow mounds were the first prehistoric sites to be investigated on the South Downs, in the sixteenth, seventeenth and eighteenth centuries, but it was not until the early nineteenth century that there was any concerted attempt to record and publish excavation data (e.g. Horsfield 1824). In the late nineteenth century, investigation focused upon the downland flint mines of Cissbury and Church Hill (e.g. Lane Fox 1875; Harrison 1878; Willett 1880). Further investigation of Neolithic mines and enclosure sites began in the mid 1920s (e.g. Pull 1923a; Goodman et al 1924; Curwen 1929a; Williamson 1930; Curwen 1934; Holleyman 1937). A second major burst of excavation and survey took place from the mid 1970s with the arrival of the first professional archaeological units and organisations. Much of this later work has been characterised by specific research programmes, though in recent years, archaeological units have concentrated more upon developer-funded rescue excavations and non-destructive survey programmes.

Given the quantity of research conducted into Neolithic monuments in the nineteenth and twentieth centuries, one may assume that the understanding of such sites has never been better. Unfortunately this is not the case. There remains a great quantity of unpublished or poorly understood archaeological information left out of the current debate. Unpublished reports, often languishing in museum stores or private residences, have traditionally been treated with disdain by the archaeological community. This is unfortunate, for it implies that certain theoretical models are based upon a very limited data pool. Ignoring unpublished data or archive information will, with the exclusion of large amounts of primary material, serve only to prejudice theories concerning past human behaviour patterns. The validity of examining, recording and synthesising unpublished data, be it derived from museum stores, library archives, county Sites and Monuments Records or private collections, must surely no longer be in doubt.

The present work

The report before you now details one of the last, great unpublished excavation archives relating to fieldwork conducted on the Neolithic monuments of the South Downs. This particular excavation programme ran for over 34years, from 1922 to 1956, and was centred upon four areas of Neolithic flint mining at Blackpatch, Church Hill, Cissbury and Tolmere. All work was conducted under the direction of one man: John Henry Pull. The mass of illustrative and textual data presented here has been taken from Pull's original excavation archive, preserved within Worthing Museum, with the full permission of the copyright holders Beryl Heryet, Worthing Museum and the Worthing Archaeological Society. The intention throughout has been to present the bulk of this information as objectively as possible, without significant editing or alteration. Much of what you are about to read is therefore the original work of Pull

Figure 1. Location map of West Sussex downland sites referred to in the text. Solid circles indicate main areas of excavation: 1 = Blackpatch (1922-32); 2 = Church Hill (1933-9 and 1946-52); 3 = Tolmere (1949); 4 = Cissbury (1952-6). Open circles indicate other excavations and surface collection surveys: a = Myrtlegrove; b = Strawberry Patch; c = High Salvington; d = Mount Carvey.

and his collaborators C. E. Sainsbury and Arthur Voice, and I have clearly noted where my own comments and observations intrude. In this way I hope that those who disagree with my point of view, or who wish to produce alternative interpretations of their own, can at least find the primary dataset without first having to disentangle it from my own form of subjective interpretation.

There was a temptation to present the work of John Pull at Church Hill, Blackpatch, Tolmere and Cissbury as a series of distinct, if interrelated, excavation reports within recognised international, national or county-based archaeological journals. The possibility for repetition of primary source data was, however, thought to be considerable, and it was felt that in order to place the sites within their regional and chronological context, all information should be presented within a single publication. This, in turn, presented concerns regarding the full artefactual assemblage derived from the 1922–56 excavation programme, which, in an ideal world, would closely accompany the site reports. To publish the cultural assemblage in full together with the feature discussion could however create a report so lengthy as to be almost totally indigestible.

It has therefore been decided that the majority of specialist contributions, thoughts and essays relating to the artefactual assemblage will be presented within a separately published companion volume (Russell in Prep). Experiments in separating site results and interpretations from artefact reports have worked well in the past (c.f. Barrett, Bradley and Green 1991; Barrett, Bradley and Hall 1991), and I make no apology for attempting to do the same here. In fact, the separation of site and specialist reports has allowed more room for discussion and has also, in the case of the companion volume, allowed the inclusion of additional data relating to the cultural assemblage from little known nineteenth century flint mine excavations. The companion volume to this report will therefore contain detailed analyses of the lithic, ceramic, faunal, environmental and geological remains, but will not repeat detailed information relating to context or feature interpretation.

For the purposes of this particular publication, summaries of the main artefacts, as recorded by Pull and discussed at length by later writers (e.g. Clarke 1970; Curwen 1954, 96–141; Evans, Jones and Keepax in Mercer 1981, 104–111; Gardiner 1988, 1207–49; Gibson 1982, 155–6; Longworth 1984, 275; Musson 1954; Pye 1968; Smith 1956, 187; Wainwright 1971, 251, 287), are supplied at appropriate points in each site report. A summary catalogue of surviving flint material from Blackpatch, Church Hill, Cissbury and Harrow Hill has been presented within this publication as Chapter 9, so as to facilitate a comparison of the quantity and range of stone tool types recorded from the Worthing group of mines. The remainder of this current volume sets out the life history of John Henry Pull (Chapter 2), the excavation methodology employed throughout the investigation of the Blackpatch, Church Hill, Cissbury and Tolmere sites (Chapter 3), and a detailed summary of the major features at each site (Chapters 4–8). More information relating to specific aspects of the 1922–56 excavations may be found in the appendices. The overall significance of the excavation findings is summarised in Chapter 10.

2
John Henry Pull: a Biography
by Sally White

'Far from where people dwell he cuts a shaft, in places forgotten by the foot of man; far from men he dangles and sways. The earth, from which food comes, is transformed below as by fire; Sapphires come from its rocks, and its dust contains nuggets of gold. No bird of prey knows that hidden path, no falcon's eye has seen it. Proud beasts do not set foot on it, and no lion prowls there. Man's hand assaults the flinty rock and lays bare the roots of the mountains. He tunnels through the rock; his eyes see all its treasures' (JOB 28, 4–10)

Figure 2. John Pull standing at the base of Shaft 1 at Blackpatch, indicating the entrance to gallery vi, in October 1922. Gallery vii lies at the centre of the photograph, whilst gallery i is positioned at the extreme left. Note how only the area of the shaft itself has been exposed during the course of this excavation (© Worthing Museum and Art Gallery).

During the first half of the twentieth century a number of gifted and enthusiastic amateur archaeologists were at work in Sussex. Most of them were affluent professional men like the Drs E. and E. C. Curwen. John Pull was one of the most gifted of amateur archaeologists, but he had a very different background to that of people like the Curwens, and never fitted into to the archaeological 'establishment'. Pull spent nearly forty years investigating the archaeology and geology of the South Downs (figure 2). He excavated more flint mines and working areas than any other archaeologist in Britain and was meticulous in recording the results of his work. He was also, by all accounts, 'a most loveable character'.

The early years

John Henry Pull was born on 25th June 1899 in Tarrant Street, Arundel, West Sussex, where his father, Albert Pull, was foreman in charge of the plumbing and sanitary engineering part of the restoration programme at Arundel Castle. In 1906 John Pull and his parents moved to Walthamstow in North London, where he was lucky to have a schoolteacher who encouraged his skill as an artist and his interest in nature. Pull proved to be a talented watercolorist with a sharp eye. His daughter Beryl possesses a series of sketchbooks which belonged to him as a teenager in which he drew and painted the birds and plants that he saw around him.

Albert Pull wanted to run his own business and in 1910 the family moved to Worthing, where they lived above his ironmongers and plumbing shop at 9 South Farm Road. John Pull was enrolled at St Andrews Boys School where he finished his formal education. In 1914 his sister Jessie was born at the family home. By now John Pull had transferred the interest that he had developed in the countryside around Walthamstow, to a deep and abiding fascination and love of the South Downs. As well as a delight in what the Downs offered visually, he wanted to learn about their geology and archaeology. For the rest of his life, one of the most outstanding aspects of his work was the determination to give as rounded a picture as possible of whatever subject he was working on.

After he left school, one of his uncles got him a job at Woolwich and in 1916 he volunteered to join the army and became a private in the Rifle Brigade. Although he was later offered promotion, he refused it because he did not wish to order soldiers to go on duties which would probably lead to their death. During the war Pull was gassed and captured by the Germans. Later he managed to escape and, just before the Armistice, he was being sheltered by nuns in an Ursuline Convent at Mons in Belgium. He only discovered that the war had ended when he reached the Dutch border and was advised by the border guards not to enter Holland as it would take longer to be repatriated from there. When he was safely back in England he wrote and thanked the nuns for their help. They were delighted to hear that he was safe and told him that of all the soldiers they had helped, he was the only one to contact them later.

Back in England Pull's parents wanted him to join his father's plumbing business, but although he gained some skill as a plumber, this particular career did not interest him. For a number of years he supported himself by selling gramophones and records from his father's shop. In 1925, after a five-year courtship, he married Alice Quelch, whom he had met when she and her parents had moved to Worthing. Together they had a daughter, Beryl. Unfortunately, Pull's gramophone business did not survive the recession.

By this time it was clear that for John Pull, work was simply a means of earning enough to support himself and his family and enable him to spend as much time as possible exploring the Downs. In the late 1930s he joined the Post Office, which in those days liked to recruit ex-servicemen who then became Civil Servants. For a few years Pull was one of the temporary Post Office staff who were stood off and re-employed annually so that they had fewer rights as employees. During the Second World War he became an established member of staff.

In some ways being a postman suited him. Being gassed had left his chest damaged and his health benefited from the outdoor life. He was also, at this time, the Post Office locksmith for the Worthing area, often being called out when keys were lost or locks got jammed. He found time to do general repairs on people's household appliances as well. The hours he worked as a postman left him with plenty of time to pursue his hobbies which by now included geology, archaeology and teaching himself Latin.

Blackpatch: 1922-32

In 1922 Pull had discovered a series of interesting looking pits on land owned by the Duke of Norfolk at Blackpatch, to the north of Worthing. With the Duke's permission he began to excavate what proved to be his first flint mine. He reported the results of this first season's work to the Worthing Archaeological Society and, after agreeing that the project was too big for one person, asked the Society's members to help. They also voted a small sum of money towards the excavation expenses. Pull began to supervise the excavations on behalf of the society in August 1922 (figure 3).

At the 1923 Annual General Meeting of the Worthing Archaeological Society Pull read out part of his report on the excavations, hoping that the Society would publish

Figure 3. Volunteers and members of the Worthing Archaeological Society engaged in the clearance of galleries ii and i of Blackpatch Shaft 1 during 1922. Spoil is here being shovelled into wicker baskets before being hauled to the surface and dumped against the edges of the excavated area (© Worthing Museum and Art Gallery).

Figure 4. A guided tour of Blackpatch Shaft 1, provided by the Worthing Archaeological Society to members of the Brighton and Hove Archaeological Club and Sussex Archaeological Society, in May of 1923. Such visits, which appear to have deliberately excluded Pull and his colleagues, served only to widen the schism between established archaeological societies in Sussex and the new breed of working class enthusiast (© Sussex Archaeological Society).

the full version. By this time, however, the Society had set up an Earthworks Sub-committee, consisting of Eliot Curwen, Dr Millbank Smith, Messrs Goodman and Lovell with Worthing Museum Curator Marian Frost as secretary. They decided that Pull's report was not good enough and, as a first step, wanted him to agree to someone else re-drawing the flints that he had illustrated. When the Committee met again in June 1923 they had Pull's response. He had laid down four conditions relating to the Blackpatch report: that his text should be published intact, that he should retain the right to peruse the printer's proofs, that the report should be published under his name, and that only his drawings should be included within it. The Committee, on behalf of the Worthing Archaeological Society, declined to publish his report.

Bearing in mind that Pull had been responsible for identifying the site, initiating and directing the excavations and recording the results in great detail, what followed seems bizarre. At the instigation of Dr Curwen, the Worthing Archaeological Society appointed Curwen, C. H. Goodman and Marian Frost to draw up a report of the Blackpatch excavations. The Society also used Curwen and Goodman, rather than Pull, to take members on tours of the site (figure 4). In November 1922 the Earthworks Sub-Committee decided that the Worthing Archaeological Society should publish a summary of their report in the Society's *Annual Report* and that they should submit a fuller, illustrated version to the Sussex Archaeological Society for publication in their annual journal, the *Sussex Archaeological Collections*.

In December the editor of the *Sussex Archaeological Collections*, L. Salzman, told Pull that Dr Curwen was preparing a report about Blackpatch, which led Pull to write in

Figure 5. John Pull engaged in the clearance of gallery i, Shaft 2 at Blackpatch in 1924, shortly after the removal of support by the Worthing Archaeological Society, who by then had transferred resources to the nearby site of Harrow Hill (© Worthing Museum and Art Gallery).

protest to the Worthing Archaeological Society. He again offered them a copy of his report which they once more refused to accept. In February 1924 Herbert S. Toms, Curator of Brighton Museum and a highly respected figure in museums and archaeology, resigned from the Worthing Archaeological Society in protest of their treatment of John Pull. Salzman tried, unsuccessfully, to persuade Pull to collaborate in Curwen's report of his work at Blackpatch. In due course the report by E. and E. C. Curwen, C. H. Goodman and M. Frost was published in volume 65 of the *Sussex Archaeological Collections*. Pull resigned from the Worthing Archaeological Society, bitterly hurt by his treatment. His interest in archaeology survived however, and he and his colleague C. E. Sainsbury continued to excavate at Blackpatch until 1932 (figure 5). The Worthing Archaeological Society transferred its interest and energy to the Curwen's excavations on the neighbouring flint mines of Harrow Hill.

Pull may have come into conflict with the local archaeological establishment but he was not without admirers both in Sussex and further afield. In 1932, with admirable promptness, he published the results of ten years work in a book entitled *The Flint Miners of Blackpatch*, with a foreword written by Sir Arthur Keith. Keith's admiration for Pull is evident and, describing their first meeting, he notes his amazement that anyone so young and who had 'to earn his bread and butter by the labour of his hands' could be such a 'finished draftsman'. *The Flint Miners of Blackpatch* was well received by reviewers in both local and national newspapers. The reviewer in the *Manchester Guardian* for 17th October 1932, for instance, described Pull as 'a young archaeologist of discernment and enthusiasm' and added that 'when the author is expounding and tabulating the results of his researches his book is in every respect a model of what such archaeological records should be'.

Church Hill: 1933–52

When he had published the results of his work at Blackpatch, Pull did not waste any time before moving on to other sites. A brief exploration of Cock Hill was followed by seven years work on the mines at Church Hill, near Blackpatch, where he worked again with C. E. Sainsbury. Although Marian Frost, the Curator of Worthing Museum had been one of the group that had rejected Pull's Blackpatch report, her deputy at the museum, Ethel Gerard, was always one of his supporters. When she became one of the editors of the *Sussex County Magazine* she used her position to publish several notes about Pull's work at Church Hill.

After the start of the Second World War, Pull was an early member of the Post Office Unit of the Local Defence Volunteers. He later moved to the Intelligence Unit which was based at Muir House in Broadwater, though what his precise duties were here remained a secret. At some point he became a corporal in the Home Guard. After the war he resumed his work at Church Hill, gathering around him a group of committed young men from all sorts of backgrounds who had just come out of the services. Work continued at Church Hill until 1952 (figure 6).

While working at Church Hill in the late 1940s, Pull realised that there was a lack of any technical training for young people interested in archaeology. Together with

Figure 6. Arthur Voice, to the left of the picture, engaged in the removal of chalk rubble fill from a gallery within Shaft 4 at Church Hill in 1946 (© Worthing Museum and Art Gallery).

George Holleyman, Philip Burstow and Major Roper, he arranged a series of lectures which took place between February and April 1949. Their aim was to build up an able and willing team of trained 'senior scholars' and others who would be available to help on excavations. These lectures proved to be a real success with 25 people attending the first. Pull was always willing to share his knowledge and interest and had an approachable manner which helped him to stimulate enthusiasm for archaeology in other people.

In 1947 Ethel Gerard persuaded Pull that the time had come to rejoin the Worthing Archaeological Society. He did so, somewhat warily. By this time, however, the membership was more varied and open in outlook and he was welcomed, finding many supporters and fellow enthusiasts within the Society. The following year he became a member of the Committee and in 1952–3 he was Chairman of the Society, having been nominated by Ethel Gerard. He remained a member of the Society, and of the Sussex Archaeological Society, for the rest of his life.

Cissbury and after: 1952–60

In the 1950s Pull spent several years working on the flint mines just outside the southern entrance of Cissbury hillfort before moving to help in the excavation of the Long Down mines. Many people still talk of visiting the Cissbury excavations and of being inspired to learn more about archaeology through listening to Pull enthusing about his work. At this time the well-known archaeologist V. Gordon Childe used to stay at Warnes Hotel in Worthing to convalesce, and John Pull and his friend Con Ainsworth visited him there to discuss archaeology and to show him the latest finds from the excavations.

It is John Pull's interest in archaeology which has had the most lasting impact, but he was also fascinated by geology and learnt enough about chemistry, physics and geology to lecture on these successfully. He was very proud to have been invited to lecture to the British Association on his work. In 1949 he completed a book entitled *The Story of Flint*, with an enthusiastic foreword by Miles Burkitt, then lecturer in archaeology at Cambridge, which was aimed at prehistorians and geologists alike. Sadly the work was never published, though the manuscript is held by Worthing Museum. Pull's interest in fossils led him to a new hobby in later years, when he acquired a stone polisher. He devoted himself to this new interest with the same concentration he did to his other hobbies and amassed a considerable collection of polished stones from the Downs and elsewhere.

As a civil servant John Pull had to retire in 1959 at the age of 60. A few months later he took a job at the newly opened branch of Lloyds Bank in Durrington on the edge of Worthing. On 10th November 1960 there was an armed raid on the bank during which John Pull was shot and killed. For his family, the tragedy of his death was compounded by the wave of publicity which followed. His killer was one of the last people to be hanged in England.

Pull's death shocked the town and his fellow archaeologists and geologists. The then curator of Worthing Museum, Len Bickerton, had known him for some eleven years and, at the end of a letter of sympathy written to his widow, he sums up the

Figure 7. John Pull holding a Neolithic antler pick, at the base of Church Hill Shaft 7 in 1952. Behind him can be seen the southern and south eastern undercuts, the south eastern still largely filled with chalk rubble (© Worthing Museum and Art Gallery).

reaction that almost everyone who knew Pull had had to his death: 'For me the loss is that of a friend, modest, unassuming, intensely practical and purposeful. A man whom I have been glad to know and from whom I have learned much'. The Worthing Archaeological Society decided to commemorate Pull's contribution to Sussex Archaeology by holding an annual lecture in his memory. The first Pull Memorial Lecture was held on 14th November 1961. Lady Wheeler was booked as the speaker, but had to back out at the last minute due to her daughter's illness. Her place was taken by Norman Cook, Keeper of the Guildhall Museum in London. The John Pull Memorial Lectures continue to this day and being asked to present one is still considered to be a great honour within Sussex.

John Pull's family and the Duke of Norfolk deposited all the finds from his excavations, as well as the extensive paper archive, in Worthing Museum where they make up the bulk of the exhibits in the flint mining display. When he began his investigation of the flint mines at Blackpatch, for the simple reason that they intrigued him, Pull can have had no idea that he was starting his life's work (figure 7), or that he would make so great a contribution to archaeology. He lived long enough to see archaeology begin to open up to the public, but it is a great shame that he was unable to participate in the great expansion and generation of interest which took place in the 1960s and 70s. He would have revelled in it.

3

An Excavation Methodology for Flint Mines

'So, in the end, above ground you must have the Haves, pursuing pleasure and comfort, and beauty, and below ground the Have-nots, the Workers getting continually adapted to the conditions of their labour'.
(H. G. Wells 1895, The Time Machine)

Excavation and spoil removal

A methodology for the successful exploration of Neolithic mineshafts and related surface areas was devised by John Pull and his colleagues during the course of the 1922–3 season at Blackpatch and modified only slightly over the years that followed (See Appendix 1). First a detailed plan of the relevant surface depression of the backfilled shaft was created, before the area was divided into equal-sized quadrants along the cardinal points of the compass. Soil was then removed one quadrant at a time so that continuous section drawings, running both north–south and east–west, could be compiled through shaft infill. Pull was very keen to record the full nature of all mine deposits, reasoning that the abandonment and subsequent infilling of empty shafts were phases of

Figure 8. Looking down to the excavated floor level of Shaft 27 at Cissbury in 1953. Note the clipboard and pen for recording context information, the small hand-picks, the rope, bucket and broad bladed, short handled shovels for removing chalk rubble, as well as the rope ladder designed to provide a means of entry and exit to the working area (© Worthing Museum and Art Gallery).

Figure 9. A dramatic way of removing spoil from the lower levels of a mine shaft as demonstrated at Blackpatch Shaft 1 in 1922. The basket of rubble is attached to a rope and pulley system and will reach the surface of the pit once the volunteer holding the other end of the rope has hurled themselves into void below. The relative success of this extraction method is not recorded, though presumably the risk of injury from falling rubble, poor landing at the bottom of the shaft, collapse of the pulley system or collision with the basket on the way down, was considered to be low (© Worthing Museum and Art Gallery).

Figure 10. A pit-floor-level-view of the winching gear used to extract rubble from Shaft 27 at Cissbury in 1953.

activity which could prove just as important as the initial cutting and extraction of raw materials (Appendix 2).

The majority of other archaeological features encountered at the mine sites, including the pits at Tolmere and the round mounds at Blackpatch, were also excavated in quadrants so that two-way sections could be drawn. The quadrant excavation method was not always utilised and at Tolmere experimentation with different techniques of examination is evidenced at Barrow A, where the round mound soil was removed in a series of parallel strips running north – south. A more careful method of trial trenching and test pitting was also often employed at the mine sites to investigate the nature and potential of buried features prior to larger scale investigation (e.g. Barrow 1 Blackpatch – Section A, Shaft 18 at Cissbury).

Figure 11. An attempt to remove a single block of chalk, noted as weighing between "3 and 4 cwt" (152.4 – 203.2 kg) from Shaft 1 at Blackpatch in 1922 using the rope and pulley system. It is not known whether this particular attempt proved successful, though the evidence here would not appear promising (© Sussex Archaeological Society).

Figure 12. The 'pithead' of Shaft 1 at Blackpatch late in 1922, showing the hoisting rope, pulley and supporting tripod as well as the general spread of freshly excavated chalk rubble surrounding the feature (© Worthing Museum and Art Gallery).

Spoil was removed from shafts with shovels and buckets, and from the longer galleries with a trolley and rope system. Access into the mine was being provided by ladders of wood or rope (figure 8). The excavation of deeper holes necessitated the construction of hoisting apparatus in the form of a wooden tripod, erected directly over the excavated area, supporting a rope and pulley system (figures 9 and 10). Once in place, buckets and baskets of rubble, and in some cases individual blocks of chalk, could be hoisted directly from excavated area to the ground surface above (figure 11). Spoil seems to have been deposited fairly close to the lip of some shafts (figure 12), and the collapse back of rubble must, at times, have been a constant source of worry, especially as few excavators ever appeared to wear protective headgear.

Recording practice

A full series of field survey diagrams, feature plans, profiles and sections were drawn by Pull for each excavated mine site, the majority of drawings later being inked-in ready for publication. Though these drawings are meticulously detailed in the amount

Figure 13. John Pull recording the dimensions of the excavated area and the relative position of artefacts recovered from the fill of Shaft 27 at Cissbury in 1953 (© Worthing Museum and Art Gallery).

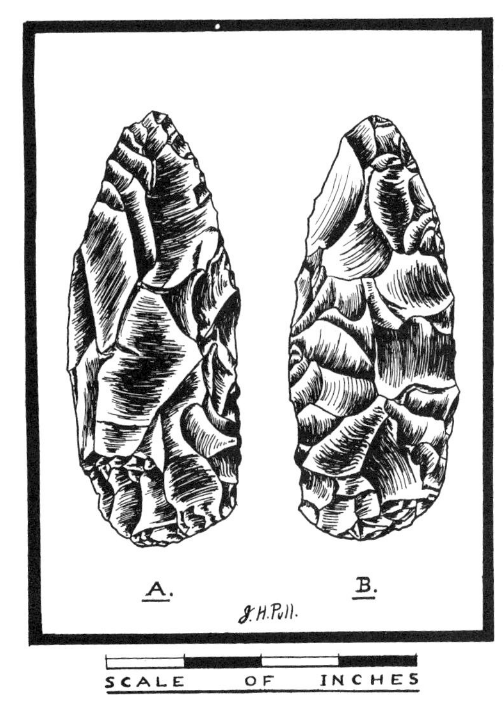

Figure 14. Flint axe roughouts found in association with human remains in Shaft 1 at Church Hill as drawn by John Pull in 1933 (© Worthing Museum and Art Gallery).

of contextual data recorded upon them, one criticism that could be levelled is that the full extent of the excavation generally went unrecorded. In the absence of defined trench edges for the plans for Church Hill, Blackpatch, Cissbury and Tolmere, it is often difficult to see just how extensive an area of the subsurface was originally revealed in the course of the 1922 and 1956 examination. Non-appearance of trench boundaries is, in this particular instance, not too insurmountable a problem, but it does mean that certain specific inked-in features, for example the barrow-mounds of Blackpatch, are often left floating in a frustratingly intangible white void of time and space.

Section and profile drawings were made by Pull for most excavated mine galleries during the period of fill removal. Special care seems to have been made to ensure that the walls of each gallery were not unduly damaged by modern digging equipment in order to better record original areas of tool-marking. Drawings of certain artificial markings on the walls were made, while plaster casts of the most prominent examples of antler pick impressions were also taken. Occasionally certain areas of the chalk wall appear to have been sawn-up and removed for storage in Worthing Museum.

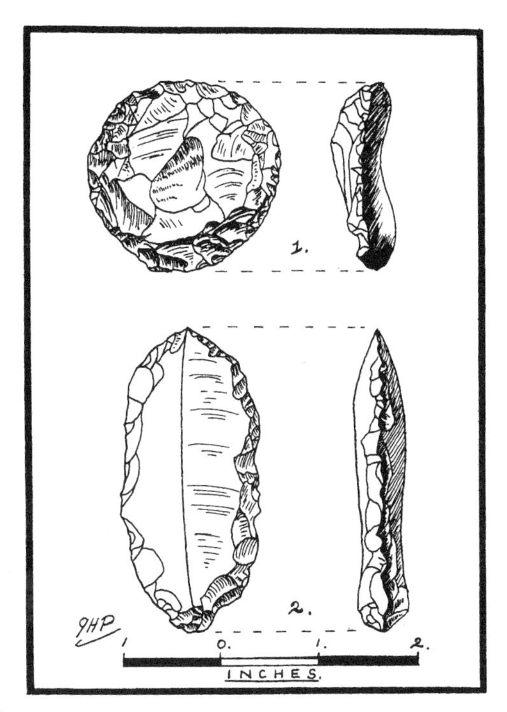

Figure 15. A discoidal scraper and oval knife/scraper hybrid from layer 3, Church Hill Shaft 4 as drawn by John Pull in 1947 (© Worthing Museum and Art Gallery).

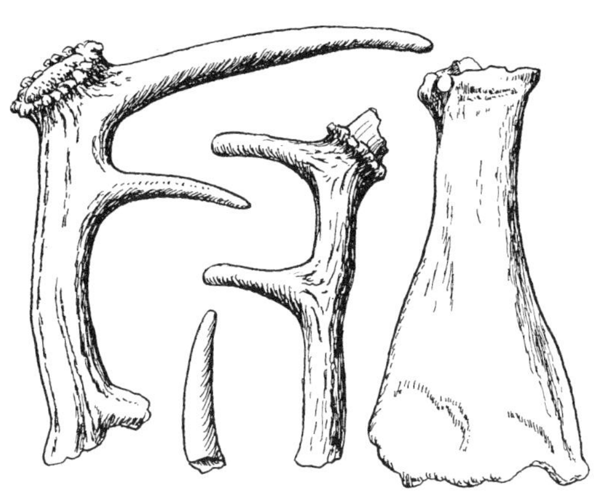

Figure 16. Two antler picks, an antler tine punch and an ox scapula shovel from the basal levels of Shaft 7 at Church Hill as drawn by John Pull in 1952 (© Worthing Museum and Art Gallery).

The relative positions of all artefacts encountered during the emptying of mine shafts was recorded by measuring down from a fixed point, usually a steel rod, set at the central point of shaft fill (figure 13). As shaft excavation continued, such datum points were often transferred into a fixed position within the exposed wall of the mine. As well as recording depth and context for artefacts, the approximate location of finds within the pit was further recorded by using points of the compass, set out as a clock face in hour and half hour intervals with north set at twelve o'clock which, in Pull's words, were due to 'the hours of a clock being much more familiar and easier to remember than the lesser divisions of the compass' (Appendix 1). This technique of three dimensional recording proved so successful that it was retained throughout the later examination of pits and shafts at Church Hill, Tolmere and Cissbury.

All artefacts found during the course of mine shaft excavation, including land mollusca, charcoal and all manner of geological specimens, were recorded in a series of site notebooks. A selection of flint and pottery artefacts was also later illustrated by Pull (figures 14, 15 and 16). The absence of sealable finds bags meant the majority of artefacts, especially the worked flint, had the site name, feature number, layer number and date of discovery written directly upon them in pencil, prior to their removal from the excavation site. These details were more often than not later rewritten on the relevant artefacts in black indelible ink. Pull was keen that all artefacts and ecofacts extracted from features during the course of the excavations were reported upon in some detail. Much of the flintwork Pull described himself, though few of the detailed catalogues appear within the Worthing Museum archive. Much of the remaining finds assemblage was farmed out by Pull to other authorities (e.g. letters 13, 15, 18, 19, 20, 29: Appendix 5) a series of specialist texts being compiled for the final excavation report that unfortunately never saw the light of day.

Site security

As work was conducted by volunteers on a strictly episodic and part-time basis at weekends or on occasional weekday afternoons (some shafts could take anything up to two years to completely clear and record: Appendix 2), prevention of accidental damage or deliberate vandalism to the workface, in the absence of the excavation team, was considered paramount. Despite the fact that the majority of open shafts were surrounded by a wire fence, creating a small compound within which the tool hut was often positioned, Pull thought it prudent to ensure that the entrances to unexcavated basal galleries were never left exposed so that the 'removal, defacement or contamination of evidence by casual visitors' could be minimised. That some form of illicit disturbance was at times encountered, is evidenced by Pull's comment that some 'youthful and mischievous intruder' had made a series of makings into the chalk face at the entrance to galleries 4 and 5 in Shaft no. 1 at Blackpatch while the excavation volunteers were away (Appendix 1). Some of the 'soot-marks' noted from the gallery systems of Blackpatch Shaft 2 may also have originally have been the result of such illicit nocturnal investigations.

In a further attempt to avoid unauthorised disturbance, it was felt necessary to ensure that each gallery should, if possible, be completely exposed, explored and recorded within the confines of a single working day. Such time restrictions could of course lead to severe logistical problems, as was notably the case at Cissbury where, during the examination of a gallery in Shaft no. 27, a human skeleton was unearthed (Appendix 3). The human remains, revealed at around 7pm on Wednesday 27th May, were carefully, if hurriedly covered with chalk rubble to prevent unwanted disturbance and to ensure that a more detailed examination could be conducted later. At 4pm on the following Friday (29th May), Pull and his colleagues returned to Shaft 27 to resume the excavation. A more complete idea of the time and working constraints imposed upon the excavators during the course of this particular afternoon can be gleaned from Pull's working report (Appendix 3), where he notes that, once the bones had been fully recorded, the decision was made to remove them:

> Two hours of daylight were now left to us in which to get the bones out, wrapped and packed up ready for removal. We accomplished this final part of our task in an hour and a half, all the time expecting the shaft wall to cave in upon us...The whole task of getting this skeleton out of its precarious position in the mine to a

> place of safety was one of the most gruelling I have ever experienced (Worthing Museum Acc. No. 1961/1586).

Nevertheless, by 10.15pm that evening the skeleton had been lifted and safely deposited in the stores of Worthing Museum, Pull characteristically adding to his typescript report that 'England's oldest miner, and one of Worthing Borough's first inhabitants, had had his first motor car ride'.

Health and safety

Removal of chalk rubble from the narrow galleries themselves could be difficult and dangerous at the best of times. The original miners, working at the restricted and dimly lit workface within galleries, may not have experienced too great a problem with regard to the stability of the overhanging rock, given the limited amount of time each gallery may have been left open before abandonment or backfilling (though the skeleton from Shaft 27 at Cissbury could of course provide a different story). Pull and his team were, however, working within underground voids left empty for some 4,000 years and, in places, it was clear that serious amounts of subsidence and roof collapse had occurred, adding to the hazardous nature of gallery examination. Hefty timber and steel props can be seen supporting the roof of excavated galleries in a number of working photographs (figures 17 and 18), though how effective these

Figure 17. Timber pit props erected in order to support the entrance of a gallery, shown here still choked with rubble, in Shaft 27 at Cissbury in 1953 (© Worthing Museum and Art Gallery).

Figure 18. A complex series of timber and iron posts erected within the lower levels of Shaft 24 at Cissbury in the spring of 1956, following the severe frost and snow falls of the previous winter. The danger of keeping excavated shafts open for long periods of time is well illustrated here. The unstable nature of the rock face in this pit convinced Pull that "it would be unwise to attempt to clear this underground area" and Shaft 24 was finally abandoned and backfilled late in 1956, bringing the examination of the Worthing mine series to an end (© Worthing Museum and Art Gallery).

Figure 19. The dangers of examining subterranean gallery systems are well illustrated in this picture taken in 1922, during the initial clearance of Shaft 1 at Blackpatch. Here the feet of a volunteer can just be made out as they disappear into the cramped space of a gallery, still partially filled with chalk rubble (© Worthing Museum and Art Gallery).

Figure 20. The removal of chalk rubble within the confined space of a Shaft 27 gallery, heavily supported with timber pit props, at Cissbury in 1953 (© Worthing Museum and Art Gallery).

would have been in the case of a sudden and catastrophic roof collapse, is debatable. Hard hats and breathing apparatus do not appear to have been in regular use until the commencement of the Cissbury excavations, though repeated reference is made to the availability of first aid kits.

Even without the health and safety considerations, the clearing and recording of basal galleries by the excavation team could prove laborious, dangerous and time consuming, especially if the gallery in question was choked with rubble (figures 19 and 20). A vivid depiction of the restricted space available within the galleries is provided by Edmond Venables, who, in his 'Salute to the Late Mr J. H. Pull' in the Selborne Notes for the *West Sussex Gazette*, describes a visit by the Littlehampton Natural Science and Archaeology Society to one of the recently opened mines:

> The longest [gallery] was pointed out to us, and one of our members got down on hands and knees and crawled into the entrance to that gallery. His heels had just vanished when he reappeared, evidently thinking he had seen enough. Feeling that this had rather spoilt the occasion, and knowing that the gallery was reasonably safe, I entered the same tunnel, which was so narrow that my shoulders rubbed against the walls on either side, while the roof was so low that I could not proceed on hands and knees but was forced to crawl along on my chest. Behind me came a doctor on holiday from India, and behind him came Frazer Hearne.
>
> The gallery ran for 60 feet into the hillside, and at the far end was a tiny round room, just large enough for me to turn round but not for my companions to do so.

> Therefore, they had to wriggle out backwards, and, while I do not suffer from claustrophobia, I was scared pink that they might become wedged in the confined space. When wearing an ordinary jacket, it is one thing to go forward, but quite another thing to go backwards. I was particularly apprehensive about Frazer Hearne, for he was the most burly of the trio and he was wearing a rough tweed plus-four suit, and I had horrible forebodings that his jacket would ruckle up from the hem and that he would be trapped in the narrow tunnel.
>
> I do not mind admitting that it was a relief to stand once more in the sunshine outside the gallery. Yet I had only ventured where I knew Mr Pull had gone before me and explored the ground. Frankly I admired him for being the first man to venture into those dark recesses since the last miner wriggled out of the galleries for the last time (Venables 1960).

A similar feeling of the difficulties experienced by those excavating the basal galleries, as well as the excitement inherent in being the first to explore these subterranean workings, is provided by Elliot Curwen:

> The floor is littered with broken chalk to a depth of 12 to 18 in., leaving a space of only about 18in. between it and the roof. A long dark tunnel stretches before us...Slowly and with awe, one of the excavators creeps into the gallery, candle in hand, noticing everything, and careful to disturb nothing. He is acutely conscious that he is the first human being to enter this underground workshop for some four thousand years. Suddenly he catches sight of a row of holes cleanly punched in the chalk wall...while on the floor close by is a pick made from the antler of a red deer...the holes look as if they had only been made yesterday, fresh and clean-cut, with the chalk burred a little at the lip by the pressure of the pick. Progress along the gallery is far from easy. One must crawl on elbows and stomach, trailing useless legs over hard and angular pieces of chalk, one's fingers spluttered with candle grease. It is warm, and the silence is intensified by the tiny, far-away song of the mosquitoes who have found their way through the chinks in the chalk to this subterranean place of repose (Curwen 1930a, 18-9).

During the early years of mine examination, and certainly at Blackpatch before the intervention of the Worthing Archaeological Society, it is clear that Pull sometimes worked alone in the shafts. Later, during the excavations of 1950 at Cissbury, a series of strict working regulations controlling the activities of the excavation team appears to have been implemented:

> 1) The keys [to the site fence] shall be in duplicate and shall be disposed as follows:
> Mr J. H. Pull, 23 St Elmo Road Worthing
> Mr F. Bridle, 64 Hollingbury Gardens
> Mr J. Lucas, 71 Leigh Road.
> 2) No person shall descend the shaft unless there be one on watch at the surface.
> 3) No person shall enter the underground levels unless there be one on watch at the shaft base in charge of the signal bell and lighting system battery box and one on watch from the surface.

4) No person shall descend the shaft unless the ladder is secure and the overhead haulage gear is stationary.
5) No person shall enter the underground levels unaccompanied by the superintendent or his deputy and all working underground must wear a helmet and carry each his or her own pick, personal lamp, candle and matches.
6) No visitors shall be admitted within the fence to the shaft or underground unless accompanied by the superintendent or his deputy and must carry a special permit from Mr J. H. Pull.
7) A first aid box must be taken into the underground on each and every occasion any party enters and this must be brought out when work is finished and hung in the cabin.
8) All ropes, tools and working apparatus shall be examined and checked by the mine superintendent each time they are brought into use.
9) No person shall leave the fence or cabin unlocked on cessation of work.
10) Remember it is better to be safe than sorry (Worthing Museum Acc. No. 1961/1586/A).

The need to clearly state excavation procedure may have been due to the increased awareness of potential hazards at the mines, earlier photographs of the Church Hill and Blackpatch excavations show that serious risks were at times taken by those emptying the shafts. The fact that the Cissbury excavations were conducted upon Worthing Borough land close to one of the most popular tourist sites on the downs, may also have helped formalise the safety considerations at the work place. Certainly the health and safety of the visitor to the excavations appears to have been foremost in the mind of the Borough Engineer for Worthing, Mr G. H. Kempton, who, after visiting the excavations of 1953, wrote to Pull to say that he was:

> a little concerned to see the temporary form of fencing which has been erected...I assume that you will be putting up a more substantial fence for the protection of the public before the hole is deepened sufficiently to make it dangerous (Appendix 5, Letter 26).

Pull, in his notebook covering the 1953 excavation season, notes that nine days after Mr Kempton's letter, on the 28th March, a chain-link fence was delivered to Cissbury to replace the, presumably now rather weather beaten barbed wire fence that had been brought back into service from the Church Hill excavations (figure 21).

The increased numbers of people visiting the Cissbury excavations and entering the opened mine shafts on a legitimate basis as guests of the excavation team, may have necessitated the writing of a formal disclaimer, in case of accident, injury or defacement of the workface:

> I/we the undersigned herewith acknowledge that neither the Worthing Archaeological Society or any member thereof, nor the archaeologist in charge of the Cissbury flint mine excavations, or his deputy, will be responsible for any accident or damage either to person or to clothing, nor for loss of personal

Figure 21. Shaft 27 at Cissbury, looking north west towards Church Hill. Here the excavation, still in its initial phases, is screened from public access by a metal chain-link fence, replete with warning signs (© Worthing Museum and Art Gallery).

> possessions on entering within the precincts of the fencing enclosing the excavations or in descending any open shaft or entering into any of the working levels of the mines.
>
> I/we furthermore agree to respect the instructions of our guide and to abstain from damaging or moving any mine gear, apparatus or equipment nor shall any mark be cut upon the walls of the shafts or levels or any portion of rock be removed therefrom (Worthing Museum Archive Acc. No. 1961/1585).

Thankfully, no serious injury ever seems to have occurred either to the excavation volunteers or the many site visitors during the twentieth century examination of the Worthing mine sites.

4
EXCAVATIONS AT BLACKPATCH, 1922–32

Blackpatch Hill (NGR TQ 094088), to the west of Findon Village, rises to 500 feet (150 metres) OD. It lies to the immediate east of the extensive flint mining site of Harrow Hill (Curwen and Curwen 1926; Holleyman 1937; McNabb et al 1996) to the north-west of Church Hill. The area of flint mining was discovered by John Pull in the early 1920s (Appendix 1), a first encounter vividly described by Pull in his book *The Flint Miners of Blackpatch*:

> Where I stood on the spur of Blackpatch my attention was drawn to what looked like a large grass-grown mound, thrusting its head above some bushes some thirty yards from the greenway. Never having been on this particular hill before, and knowing nothing of any prehistoric features which it might possess, I proceeded to negotiate the stunted junipers between myself and the mound. I found that the mound stood in a broad clearing...The whole clearing was thickly studded with saucer-shaped depressions in the hillside ranging from ten to forty feet in diameter and from one to five feet in depth...I immediately realised that I had stumbled across a hitherto unexamined, and, so far as I knew, unrecorded site which promised to be of interest (Pull 1932a, 19).

Permission to investigate the site further having been granted by the landowner, His Grace the Duke of Norfolk, a series of trial examinations began in 1922. Over the next ten years at least nine mine shafts, four flint working floors, twelve round mounds and a series of other associated features were investigated by Pull and his team of volunteers (figures 22 and 23). Unfortunately, much of the early fieldwork was conducted at a time of conflict between the archaeological 'old guard' and the new breed of archaeological, working class enthusiast, and Pull found himself being openly attacked, ignored or censured. A good example of the type of intellectual snobbery directed at Pull and his team may be seen in the letters from an individual known only as 'Antiquary' which appeared in the pages of the *Worthing Herald* (Appendix 5, letters 1 and 6).

Following the completion of work in Shaft 1 Blackpatch, a report on the excavation was written and published by members of the Worthing Archaeological Society in volume 65 of the *Sussex Archaeological Collections* (Goodman et al 1924), apparently without Pull's knowledge, consent or co-operation. As a consequence Pull ensured that, from 1924 onwards, control over all information resulting from his work at

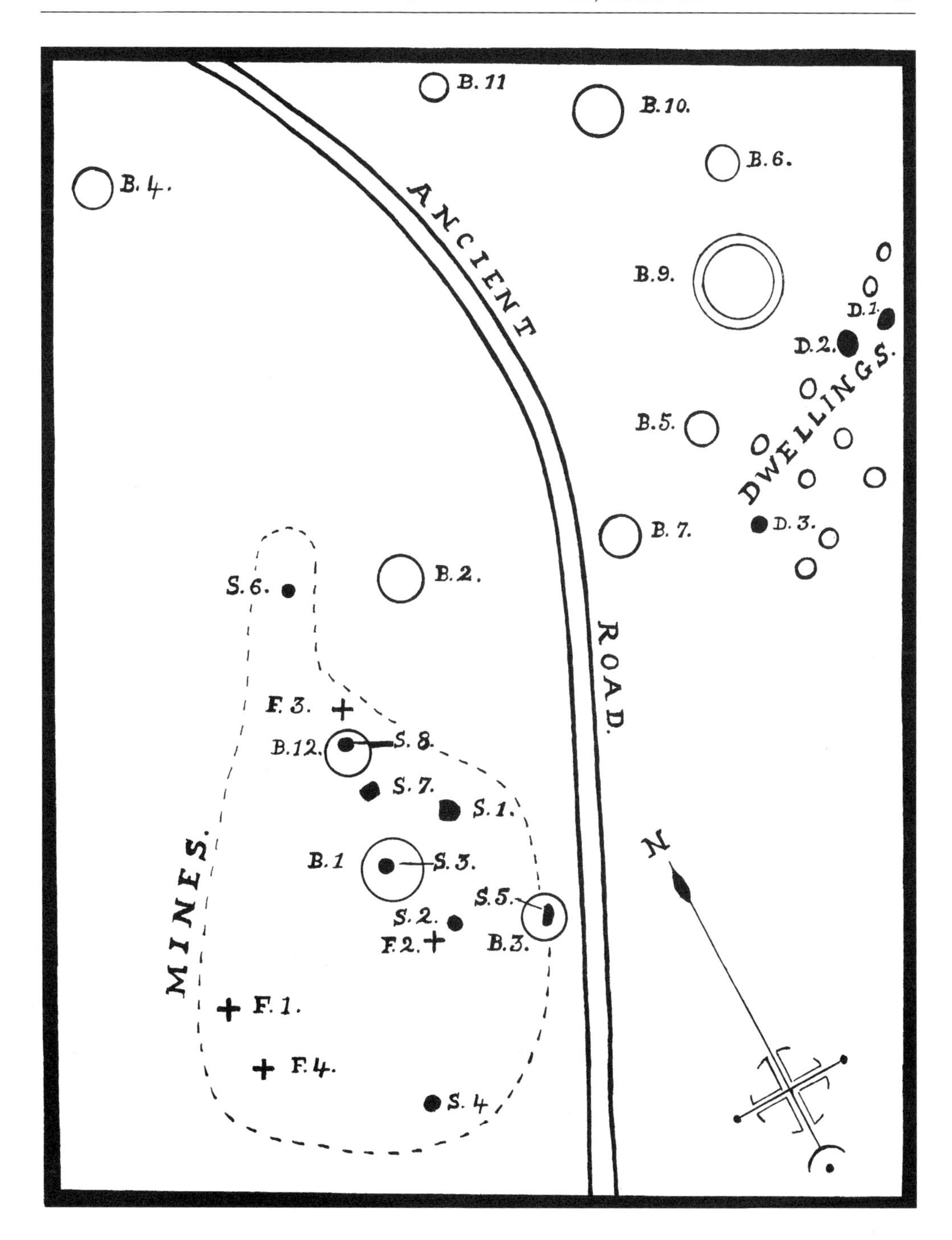

Figure 22. Blackpatch: a slightly generalised plan of the main shaft, barrow, chipping floor and dwelling site features investigated between 1922 and 1932. Note that three dwelling sites are here recorded as having been investigated (© Worthing Museum and Art Gallery).

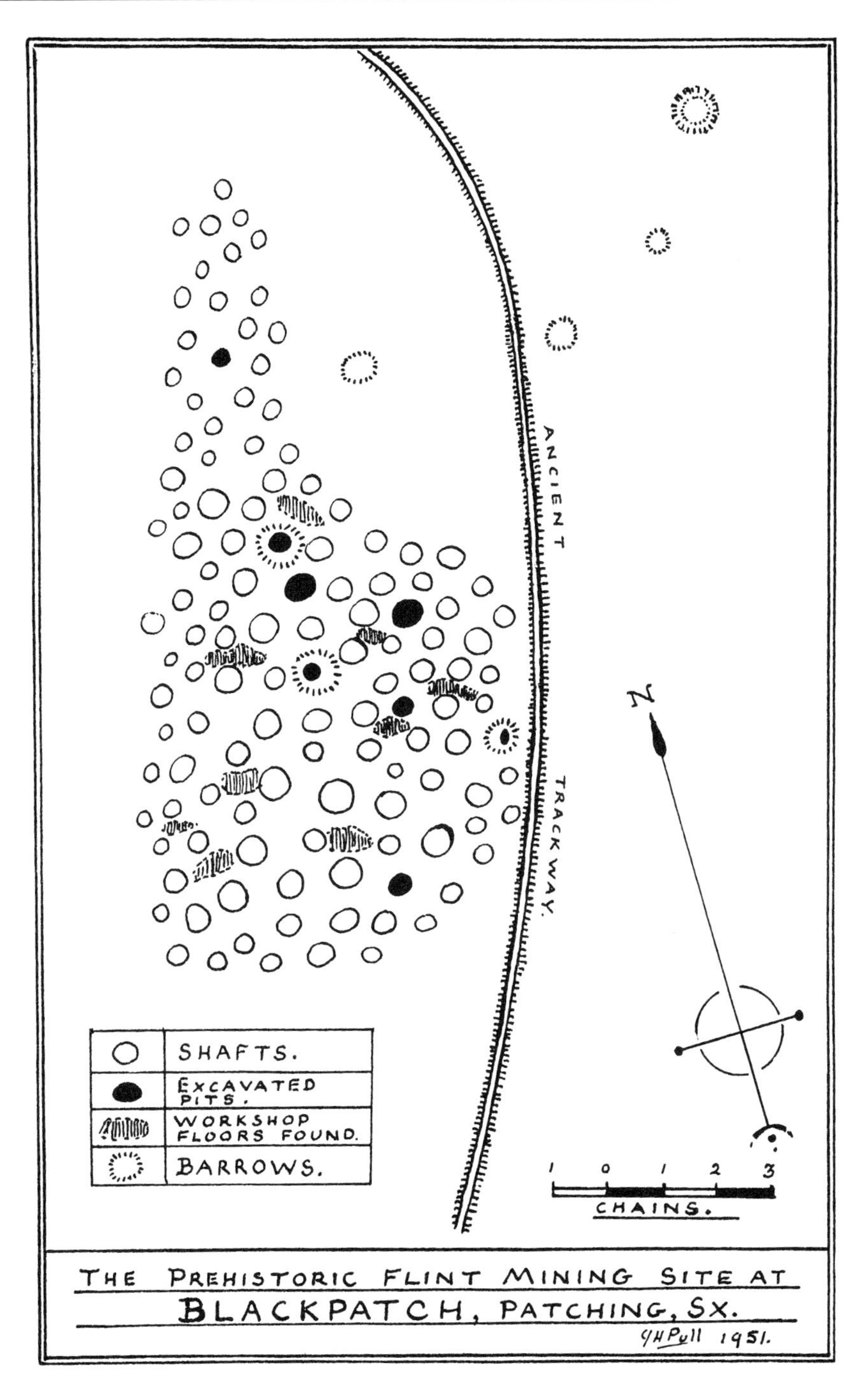

Figure 23. Blackpatch: a simplified plan of the main shafts visible as surface depressions in 1951. The positions of all chipping floors located by Pull through surface investigation are also indicated. See figure 22 for feature annotation (© Worthing Museum and Art Gallery).

Blackpatch was maintained by disseminating data through the medium of lectures, seminars and local newspapers rather than through the recognised journals of the archaeological establishment. A series of detailed and well illustrated articles chronicling the results of the archaeological fieldwork at Blackpatch written by Pull and his colleague C. E. Sainsbury, appeared in the Magazine of the *Worthing Herald*, between 1923 and 1928. A summary of the main results was later published by Pull in his book *The Flint Miners of Blackpatch* (1932a), a popular work designed for 'experts and general readers' alike (Keith in Pull 1932a, 14).

A series of unpublished typed and hand written excavation notes, lecture notes, texts, and typed page proofs covering all aspects of the Blackpatch excavations, and at all levels of detail, exist within the archive of Worthing Museum, together with photographs and inked plans and sections. It is from this that the reports which follow, concerning the examination of the shafts, barrows and 'dwelling sites', are taken.

THE MINES

Shaft 1

The examination of Shaft no 1, at the north-eastern margins of the mining area was one of the first pieces of excavation conducted at Blackpatch by John Pull. It also proved, as far as the archaeological establishment was concerned, to be his undoing. Sally White has already chronicled the crisis of 1923 surrounding the disputed authorship of the final report for Shaft 1 and the war of words that followed its unauthorised publication in volume 65 of the Sussex Archaeological Collections (White 1995; see also Chapter 2 and Appendix 1). Until now, only two versions of the Shaft 1 excavation report have been published: the text produced by the editorial committee of Goodman, Frost, Curwen and Curwen (Goodman et al 1924), which was savagely criticised by Pull and his colleagues (Letter 12; Appendix 5); and a summary of the main results produced by Pull for The Flint Miners of Blackpatch (1932a, 34-40).

A third text, concerning the discovery and examination of Shaft 1 survives in the John Pull Archive in Worthing Museum (Acc. No 61-1585A). This typed manuscript would appear to be a version of the original excavation report submitted by Pull to the Worthing Archaeological Society in 1923 for publication. As such this text must presumably represent the 'official' report alluded to by Pull, Sainsbury, Dilloway, Watkins and Bunce in their scathing attack upon the alternative site description compiled by Goodman, Frost, Curwen and Curwen (Letter 12 Appendix 5). With this in mind, the 'official' Pull text, deemed unsuitable for publication by the Sussex Archaeological Society, is reproduced in full for the first time as Appendix 1.

A comparison of Pull's text with the alternative, unauthorised version produced by Goodman et al, proves extremely enlightening. Pull's report is concerned primarily with excavation methodology, something that the editorial committee's text studiously avoids. Pull, furthermore details the nature of the shaft fill and mine abandonment, while Goodman and his collaborators prefer to concentrate more upon the galleries, their fill and associated artefacts (Goodman et al 1924). This clear textual divide presumably represents the two distinct areas of the Shaft examination that Pull's group and the Worthing Archaeological Society claimed eventual authority over, namely the initial clearance and subsequent gallery examination. Indeed Pull himself notes, in his criticism of the published 1924 text, that the non-participation of Worthing Society members, especially Goodman, Frost Curwen and Curwen, in the early stages of the mine clearance meant that their description of this particular phase of work 'must of necessity be of pure fiction' (Letter 12; Appendix 5).

Additional elements, reflective perhaps of the general atmosphere under which the Blackpatch report was originally written, and also of the then growing divisions between the mine excavators and factions within the Worthing and county-based Archaeological Societies, can be detected within the published text produced by the editorial committee. First it is notable just how much the published text plays down John Pull's role within the excavation: Pull is mentioned just twice in a forty-two page report (Goodman et al 1924, 71). The text also states emphatically that it was Goodman, and not Pull, who first discovered the Blackpatch mining complex in 1919. This point would appear to be irrelevant, unless Goodman wished somehow to emphasise right of excavation and subsequent publication by claiming first discovery, for it was Pull who first undertook excavation and survey, a point observed by Sir Arthur Keith in his foreword to *The Flint Miners of Blackpatch*:

> If any had suspected that Blackpatch was the site of an ancient flint mine, they made no attempt to verify their guess by the application of pick and spade. That was left for Mr Pull to do (Keith in Pull 1932a, 13).

It is possible that Goodman, assuming that he had found the mining site at Blackpatch first, felt that Pull was muscling in on his discovery.

According to the report published later in the Sussex Archaeological Collections by Goodman, Frost, Curwen and Curwen, the Worthing Archaeological Society took part in the Blackpatch excavations only because John Pull had appealed directly to them 'as it became clear that the labour of excavating a pit would prove more than he could undertake unaided' (Goodman et al 1924, 71). Pull (as noted in Appendix 1) supplies us with a very different version of events whereby help was offered, by implication almost out of the blue, by the Earthworks Committee of the Worthing Society. Whatever the truth of the matter (and it is possible that certain members of the Society were annoyed that Pull had been excavating in their territory without recourse to them), it is clear from the tone of the editorial committee's report, that at no time did they consider Pull to be in control of the excavation, noting that by August 5th 1922, they had completely 'taken over' the work (Goodman et al 1924, 71). As a consequence, neither Pull, nor any member of his survey team, are explicitly referred to in the acknowledgements of the published report.

One further point is worthy of note here. On one page of the *Sussex Archaeological Collections* report, an otherwise innocuous passage ends with a rather curious statement:

> no tally-marks or other purposive scratchings were observed on the walls either of the shaft or galleries, *nor were any engraved flints found* (Goodman et al 1924, 77: my italics).

The reference to 'engraved flints' appears to hark directly back to one of the main arguments used by the anonymous critic 'Antiquary' in their attack upon Pull and his colleagues in the pages of the *Worthing Herald*:

> Reference is made to an engraved flint...This discovery may be of the greatest importance, or, on the other hand, it may be the result of somebody's joke (Letters 1 and 6; Appendix 5).

'Antiquary' made the flint a point of considerable, some would say perhaps overtly aggressive, disagreement with Pull. Sly reference to the object within the report compiled by the editorial committee of Goodman, Frost, Curwen and Curwen could, if one is so minded, be taken to imply that the identity of the elusive 'Antiquary' may be within the ranks of the editorial committee itself.

A more complete overview of the nature of Shaft 1 as excavated was produced by John Pull within his book *The Flint-miners of Blackpatch* (1932a, 34–40). A series of notes, alternative page proofs and unused illustrations compiled by Pull for this book are preserved in Worthing Museum and it is from these texts that the following report is taken:

> On being emptied of its infilling the shaft was found to be roughly D-shaped in plan, its W wall being nearly straight. With a diameter of 17ft its mean depth was 10.5ft, at which depth the flint seam appeared (figure 24). The walls were vertical or nearly so, presenting neither batter nor overhang at the lip. The floor was somewhat irregular, slightly raised in the centre and sunken on the E side.
>
> 8 openings pierced the walls of the lower part of the shaft (figure 25). Of these 7 were direct entrances to galleries belonging to the shaft (see figure 2). The last was a hole broken through from the shaft into a gallery belonging to the system of the shaft to the N. The 7 gallery entrances had an average height of 2.5ft (figure 26). These radial headings which led from the shaft base varied in length from 5 to 30ft, in width from 3 to 7ft, and in no place were the roofs much more than 3ft in height (figures 27 and 28). The short galleries were choked indiscriminately with abandoned tools and chalk debris (figures 29, 30 and 31) which had entered from the shaft. The longer ones were fairly clear in some places, in others neatly stacked with chalk blocks, and elsewhere choked with masses of chalk rubble.
>
> The flint seam mined for was exposed in many places along the gallery sides at floor level (figure 32). Firmly embedded nodules had not always been extracted whole, but had been broken asunder. Careful examination of the gallery floors near these nodules showed masses of fine flint splinters, resulting from the forcible fracture. Close observation of the empty pit and its galleries produced evidence from which important facts could be gathered. It was clear that the shaft immediately to the W was older than this pit which we had excavated, for all the galleries on that side were foreshortened. Miners driving headings in that direction had soon been forced to abandon their efforts on breaking through into

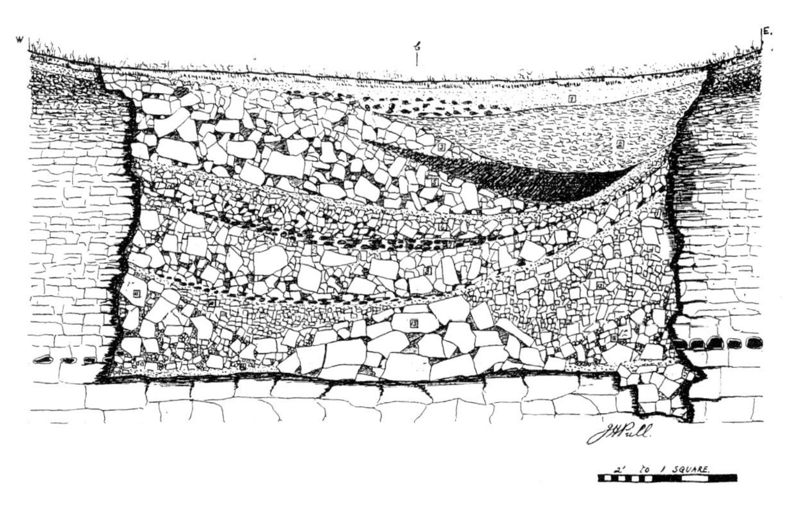

Blackpatch Excavations – Shaft No 1. 1923.
Section East & West

Figure 24. Blackpatch Shaft 1: the first section through a mine to be produced by Pull. This drawing was not used by Goodman et al for their 1924 article on the excavation of the shaft (© Worthing Museum and Art Gallery).

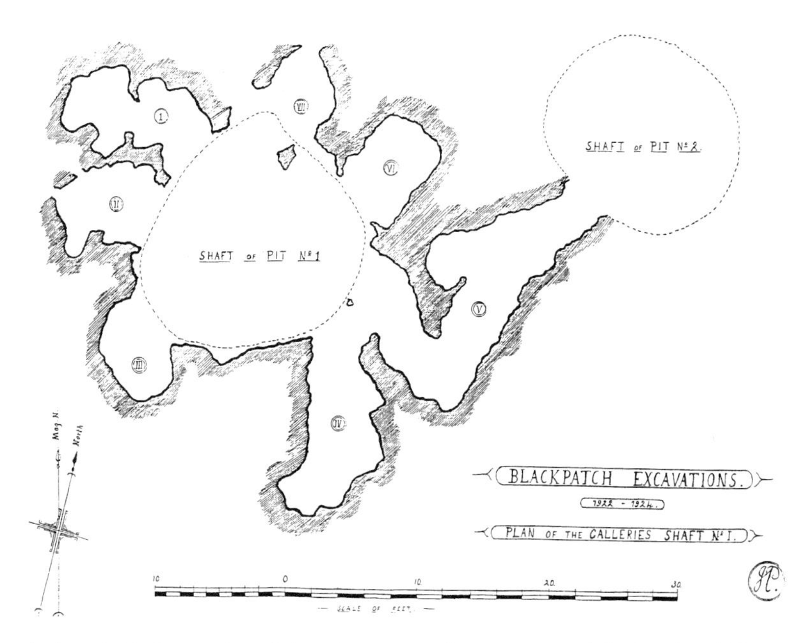

Figure 25. Blackpatch Shaft 1: a plan of the subterranean features exposed during the 1922–4 programme of excavations. There is little significant divergence between this drawing and that produced by Goodman et al for their 1924 article on the excavation of Shaft 1 (© Worthing Museum and Art Gallery).

Figure 26. Looking out from gallery v into the Shaft 1 at Blackpatch. Note how extraction here has eroded the central chalk wall support, supporting Pull's later comments (made during the examination of Shaft 2) that certain areas of Blackpatch Hill rest upon "slender isolated buttresses" (© Worthing Museum and Art Gallery).

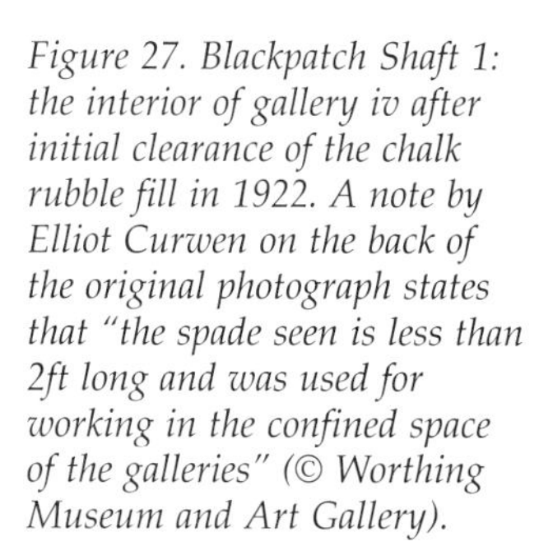

Figure 27. Blackpatch Shaft 1: the interior of gallery iv after initial clearance of the chalk rubble fill in 1922. A note by Elliot Curwen on the back of the original photograph states that "the spade seen is less than 2ft long and was used for working in the confined space of the galleries" (© Worthing Museum and Art Gallery).

Figure 28. Blackpatch Shaft 1: the interior of gallery v in 1922, looking back towards the main area of the shaft (© Worthing Museum and Art Gallery).

Figure 29. Blackpatch Shaft 1: the interior of gallery i prior to examination by the 1922 excavation team. Pieces of at least two antler picks are visible, lying on top of the rubble in the foreground (© Worthing Museum and Art Gallery).

Figure 30. Blackpatch Shaft 1: an antler pick, arrowed by Curwen, photographed in situ within gallery iv (© Worthing Museum and Art Gallery).

Figure 31. Blackpatch Shaft 1: a block of chalk that, as noted by Curwen on the reverse of the photograph, bears "several marks of blows by the antler picks of miners". The piece was photographed as found within gallery iv (© Worthing Museum and Art Gallery).

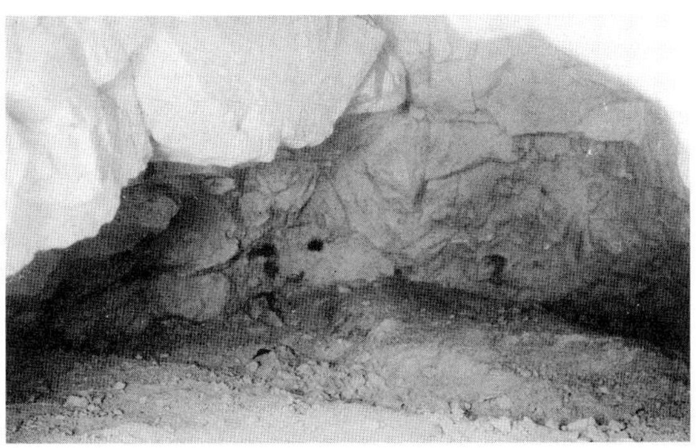

Figure 32. Blackpatch Shaft 1: the interior of gallery vi following the removal of rubble fill. Note the location of isolated nodules of flint within the back wall of the gallery (© Worthing Museum and Art Gallery).

the older galleries which had already existed there (galleries which belonged to the shaft to the W). In one instance they encountered a mass of solid rock, of greater thickness, which had been left untouched. Similar older workings had been encountered on the N side of the pit, a gallery from the pit to the N having been all but opened up by the sinking of shaft no 1.

The S wall of Shaft no 1 had no galleries driven from it. This at first seemed very curious, but from personal experience of coal mines I was able to ascertain, by sounding with a wooden rod, that the chalk wall was here very thin, and concealed galleries came toward and almost through it from the S. The presence of the shrouded galleries in this direction had, I concluded, undoubtedly been previously observed by the men operating this shaft. Consequently no attempt had been made to open up an already worked out section.

On the SE the galleries were long and fairly straight. One, entering the E wall of the shaft, proceeded for a distance of about 10ft, where it was met at right angles by a long, straight gallery proceeding from the shaft to the NE. Owing to some slight difference in levels these gallery floors formed a step at the point where they met, through the roofs and walls were cleared to an even height and width. From this it was evident that the shaft to the NE was open and working at the same time as Shaft no 1, the miners driving headings in the 2 shafts had met and perfected a clear and convenient working passage from one pit to the other. It did not seem that all the galleries of shaft no 1 were worked and cleared out at one time. Some of them were indiscriminately piled with masses of chalk rubble that had evidently been taken and deposited in them from the shaft at a time after they had been worked out.

This suggests that one or perhaps two galleries were driven at once, and when worked out became useful receptacles for chalk excavated in the process of cutting other galleries. This saved the labour of raising the unwanted chalk to the surface. Judging from the character of the lowest portion of the infilling, the large diameter of the shaft also appeared to have served some similar purpose. The shaft having been sunk and the flint removed for its base, the material excavated from its galleries had been first piled up in the centre of the pit, and then, when its earlier galleries fell into disuse, against the sides. Exhausted of its flint, and falling at once into disuse, the shaft had been artificially filled in to within a few feet of its lip.

Shaft no 1 had been artificially filled to within 3ft of its brim, with a number of layers of chalk debris which were more or less markedly stratified. Tilts of large chalk blocks were interrupted by layers of flint flakes, small chalk and one thin band of charcoal. Though it was possible from their varying thickness to detect the direction from which these various layers had been introduced into the shaft, it is unsafe to infer from this that mining operations were actively in progress in the direction indicated. For, as there was every evidence that dumps had existed on the surface about the mouth of this shaft, it is necessary to take into consideration the fact that the direction of the tilts of infilling may be due to the relative position of large dumps, which may have been fed from reverse directions to which they had discharged into shaft no 1.

> It is of interest to note that the site of shaft no 1 had been occupied as a temporary living floor after it had become sealed with rain-wash or fine silt, but before the formation of the surface soil. The living floor consisted of a pile of flint working debris, animal bones, including those of ox and pig, and, what was more curious, a quantity of lower jaws of sheep complete with their teeth. No other bones of sheep were present. Only these 12 to 15 lower jaws. Among and around this central pile were quantities of burnt stones, some very fine flint implements, including an ovate and a beautifully finished celt, also a red quartzite hammer stone. (Worthing Museum Acc No 1961/1585/B)

Few of the recorded flint finds from Shaft 1 could be traced at the time of writing, though both Pull and Goodman produced definitive lists and a full series of drawings. These can help, not only to understand what has been lost, but also just how much, if at all, the levels of recording differed between the 'official' and 'alternative' texts. In addition to the flint, three antler picks, three pick heads, three antler rakes, 18 detached tines, 10 crowns and four cut pieces of antler were recovered from the shaft (Pye 1968, 75).

Despite the controversy that surrounded the publication of the Shaft 1 results, it is interesting to note that the published report of Goodman et al does not differ markedly from the texts supplied by John Pull. Certainly the recorded measurements of the shaft and its associated galleries are broadly similar in both texts and the two plans of the mine are both recognisably of the same feature. The major discrepancy between the two reports may, as already been noted, have more to do with the different roles played by Pull's team and that of the Worthing Archaeological Society, with Pull, Sainsbury, Dilloway, Watkins and Bunce (Letter 12; Appendix 5) excavating the main shaft and the Worthing Society investigating the basal galleries.

One last point of difference between the 'official' and 'alternative' texts which should be noted is that Pull regularly concentrates upon the practicalities of mining and the mechanics of flint extraction, something which is not dealt with in significant detail by Goodman et al, while the editorial committees report, in its examination of the parallels for the mine, cites a lengthy series of references from ancient and classical literature (Goodman et al 1924, 101–4). This point, perhaps more than any other, serves to remind us of the very real divide in 1920s England between the classically educated members of the archaeological establishment and the up and coming working class enthusiasts who were, at this time, becoming more involved in their own research and investigations.

Shaft 2

> *By John Pull*
>
> Mineshaft no 2 was situated 24 yards south of shaft no 1. This pit was indicated by a slight depression nine and a half feet in diameter and 3 inches deep. Five larger depressions lay immediately round it. The upper infilling of this shaft consisted of the usual surface soil to a depth of one foot. Beneath this the fine silt or rain-wash, and the associated coarse silting at its base, attained a depth of two

and a half feet. From the coarse silting downwards, the shaft was filled to its bottom with stratified tilts or layers, of various sized chalk rubble and chalk blocks (figure 33). The surface soil yielded some Romano-British pottery, including fragments of blue provincial ware.

Emptied of its filling, Shaft No 2 differed in many respects from pit 1. Ten feet in diameter at its mouth, and almost perfectly circular, it descended, funnel shaped, its diameter decreasing to seven feet at a depth of six feet from the surface. The south-eastern portion of the upper lip of the shaft was traversed by a steep cut from the lip to a depth of three feet. This step crossed the south-eastern corner of the shaft and had a total width of five feet. At six feet from the surface a second and larger step projected into the shaft from the south, and completely bisected it from east to west. This step reduced the lower half of the shaft to a semi-circular section with a chord of four and a half feet. The maximum depth of the shaft was ten feet nine inches.

At its base it was pierced by five openings, four of these were entrances to galleries (see figure 5), and one a hole cut from the shaft in order to let light into the gallery (figure 34). The gallery entrances were of an average height of three feet and about the same in breadth. The flint seam mined for was in evidence round the base of the shaft and along the gallery walls. It was the same seam as that exposed in pit 1. The gallery system of pit 2 was very complicated. The galleries ramified in every direction, linking up shaft with shaft and gallery with gallery, both with the system belonging to shaft no 2 and with similar complicated systems of neighbouring pits, to the bases of which access was gained.

The exploration and survey of these galleries was a most strenuous task and was accomplished with some personal risk to the excavators. So much of the chalk rock had been so extensively undermined that there had been considerable falls of roof in several places. Indeed in one place the span of roof at a junction of several galleries had collapsed within three feet of the surface of the hill side, giving rise to a miniature underground mountain consisting of perhaps 100 tons of fallen chalk rock. So close and interlocked were the workings that it was realised that the whole area in the neighbourhood rests merely upon thin walls and slender isolated buttresses.

It was of more than passing interest to note that in pit 2, every gallery, where it turned at right angles to its entrance, had its walls pierced at intervals with fairly large openings designed obviously to admit daylight from the open shafts. If Shaft No 2 and the pit immediately to the east of it were open and working at the same time (and there is every reason to believe that such was the case, as many communicating galleries had been cleared out to full width and height at their junctions), then there would have been daylight enough penetrating from these shafts to operate the whole of the workings which range round the two pits, an area which contained not less than a thousand square feet of flint seam.

The single instance contrary to this evidence came from a gallery entered from Pit 2. This gallery actually belonged to the main system of the pit to the south of pit 2. It was a straight gallery, and when worked from the shaft to which it belonged would have been flooded with daylight throughout its length.

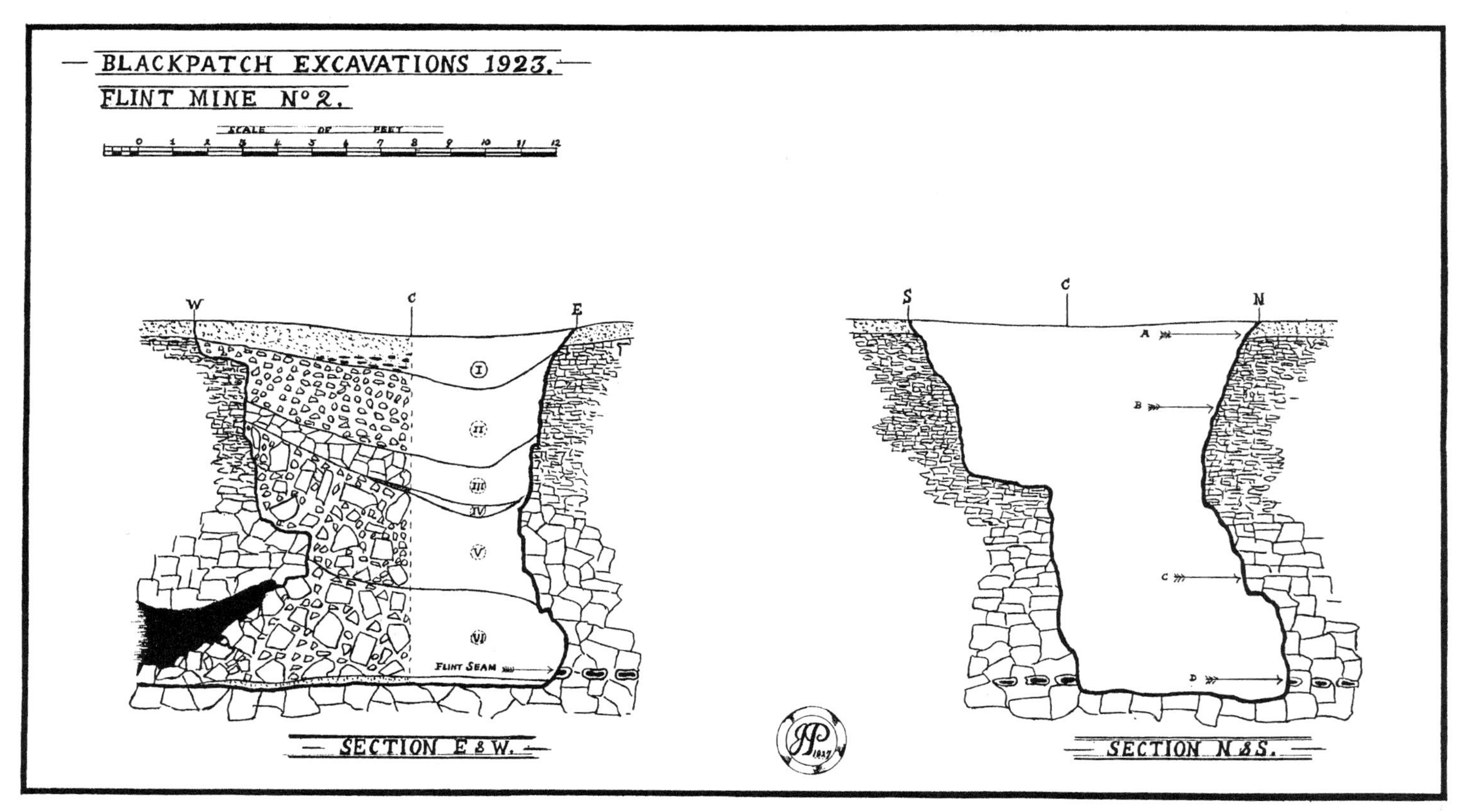

Figure 33. Blackpatch Shaft 2: a half section and profile. Note the presence of a distinct step or ledge within the northern wall of the cut (© Worthing Museum and Art Gallery).

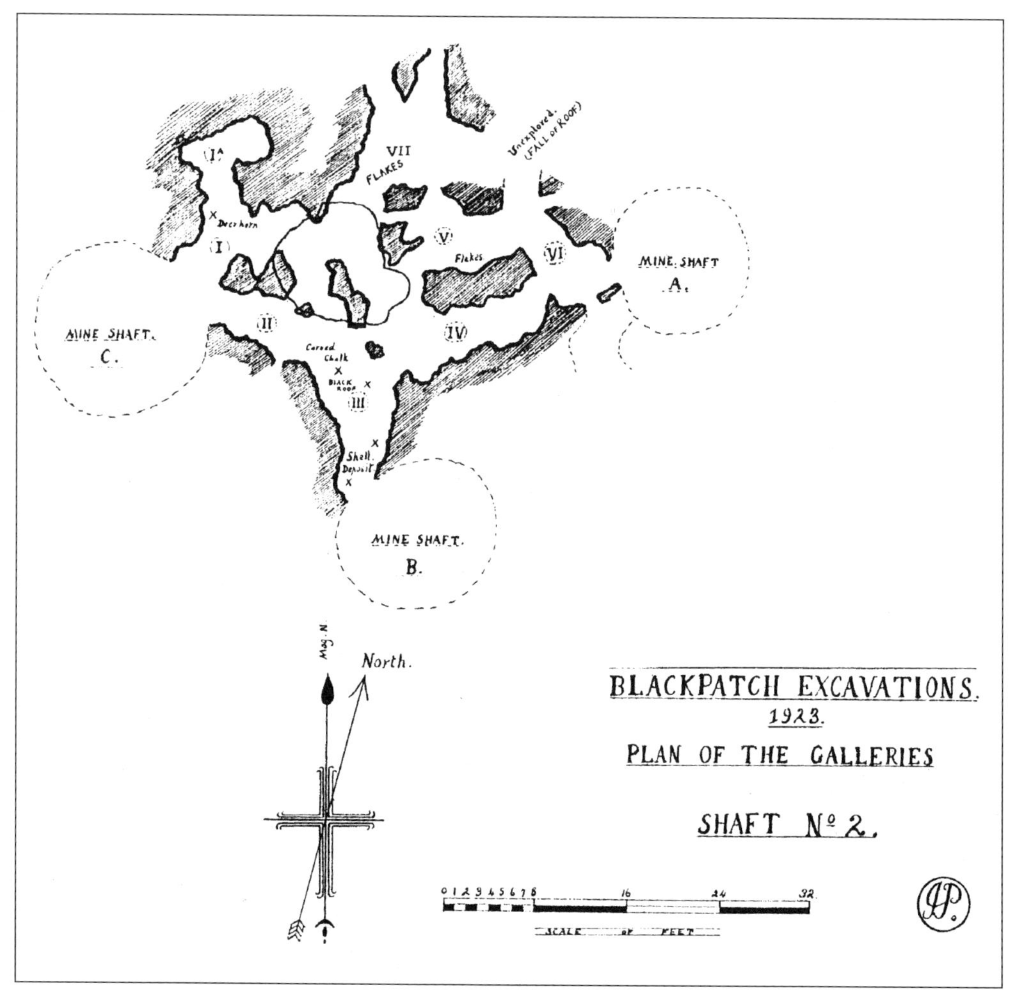

Figure 34. Blackpatch Shaft 2: a plan of the subterranean features exposed during 1923. Note the location of shell deposits, flint flakes, antler, carved chalk and charcoal-blackened ceiling (© Worthing Museum and Art Gallery).

> Halfway down it, however, there was a small, blackened smoke patch upon the chalk roof, and among the chalk rubble on its floor was scattered a small quantity of fragments of charcoal. It would appear that someone had entered the gallery at night, perhaps in search of some forgotten belonging or a tool left there during the day, and so had taken a burning brand from the fire or a blazing torch and had afterward knocked it out against the roof (Worthing Museum Acc. No. 1961/1585).

Only two axe roughouts from the excavation of this shaft appear in the archive of Worthing Museum to this day. Six distinct layers of mine fill (I–VI) are recorded on the inked section for Shaft 2, while a seventh (unlabelled), appears to indicate primary fill at the very base of the shaft. The upper levels of Shaft No 2 were partially covered, along the north-western edge, by 'Chipping Floor' No 2. Pull later observed that the stratigraphic relationships between Floor 2 and Shaft 2 suggested that the floor predated the original cutting of the mine shaft (Pull 1932a, 62).

The accompanying plan for Shaft 2 plots the rough positions of flint flakes, an antler pick (deer horn), carved chalk (possibly the result of animal gnawing activity) and a shell deposit, as well as the area of the charred roof within gallery III. The nature of this charring is intriguing, especially if it does represent evidence of some form of artificial lighting being employed at the original time of flint extraction. An alternative theory, that the material is evidence of a more recent intrusion into the mine (presumably at night or early evening), by some unauthorised individual (Holgate pers. Comm. 1995), is a possibility that should not, however, be entirely ruled out.

Shaft 3

Shaft 3, close to the approximate centre of the mining zone, was overlain by Barrow 1 and appears to have been investigated, at least partially, during the examination of that Barrow. Pull implies that the shaft was excavated to its base, or at least to the top of the basal galleries (1932a, 44), though the only certain illustration of the pit, which appears with the drawing of the Barrow 1 section, shows a shaft in which only the upper 10–15 feet had been examined. Pye, in her 1968 postgraduate thesis notes, rather enigmatically, that two galleries at the base of Shaft 3 appeared to have been 'rubbed smooth' (1968, 9) which could be taken to imply that the shaft had been completely emptied to the basal levels. Alternatively it is possible that data from another shaft had inadvertently been misidentified here. No finds from this particular period of shaft excavation have been traced at the time of writing. Whether the shaft was completely emptied by Pull and his team or not, it is clear, from the evidence of the upper fills, that Barrow 1 had been constructed immediately after the backfilling of the pit.

Shaft 3a

Shaft 3a lay to the immediate east of Shaft 3 and Barrow 1. Though never fully opened, part of the western upper fill of the shaft was investigated during the excavation of Barrow 1. This trench, reported by Pull in the November 3rd 1923 edition of the *Worthing Herald*, revealed that the topsoil, which was 18 inches in depth, covered a layer of rainwash, consisting of chalk rubble and dust. At the interface between this deposit and the topsoil were recorded '..flint implements and flakes representative of the Blackpatch industry, including a Cissbury type axe, a segmental tool and an example of the fluted cone' (Pull 1923b). Another find in this layer was the engraved flint, the authenticity of which was queried so vigorously by 'Antiquary' in the letters published in the *Worthing Herald* (Appendix 5, Letters 1 and 6).

Shaft 4

Pull notes, in *The Flint Miners of Blackpatch* that Shaft 4 was of 'similar character to Shaft 2' being 'roughly circular in plan, with vertical sides' and 'extensive ramifying galleries' which connected the feature with its immediate neighbours (Pull 1932a, 44). Unfortunately, little more can be said with regard to this pit as neither a full textual account of the nature of the feature, nor a detailed illustration (other than shaft location) appears to have survived.

Fragments of a human jaw and femur were recovered from the upper fill of Shaft 4 'one foot below the rainwash' (Pull 1932a, 56). Seven flakes, marked as deriving from 'Shaft 4, layer 8' (presumably a layer of lower pit fill) also survive in Worthing Museum. The human jaw appears to have been that of a 'very young person' while the femur is noted as having belonged to an adult. It is not known what other material was associated with these remains. Pull suggested that the bones may have been part of a more formalised burial deposit to the west of the shaft (the direction of silting), which was disturbed by mining at the time Shaft 4 had been almost completely filled.

> A shapeless dump...occupies the surface on the west of Shaft 4. It is possible that this dump represents the remains of a barrow that has been almost destroyed, or that it is merely a mining dump and not a barrow. Yet it may contain further fragments of the skeletons disturbed by the sinking of one of two likely pits, debris from which had been cast on to the dump, and, sliding into Shaft 4, had taken some of the bones with it (Pull 1932a, 56).

Given the nature of ritual deposition recorded elsewhere at Blackpatch, it would appear somewhat unlikely that prehistoric miners would so blatantly have disturbed an earlier burial deposit when sinking a new shaft. An alternative explanation of the bone could be that it originally represented part of a disarticulated deposit of human skeletal material, akin perhaps to the debris occasionally encountered within the backfill of Neolithic enclosure ditches such as at Whitehawk (Williamson 1930; Curwen 1931a; 1934a; Russell and Rudling 1996) and Offham (Drewett 1977). An antler pick recovered from somewhere within the fill of Shaft 4 gallery was radiocarbon dated by the British Museum in the late 1960s (Barker et al 1969) and a determination of 5090+/-150 BP (4350–3500 cal BC: BM–290) was obtained.

Shaft 5

> *By J. H. Pull and C. E. Sainsbury*
> This mine consisted of a shallow pit sunk into the chalk rock to a depth of three and a half feet below the natural surface. The infilling consisted of unstratified chalk rubble, slightly compacted in its upper part by water, but nowhere separately distinguishable from the material of Barrow 3 which lay directly above it (see figure 41). Quantities of flint flakes and nodules of mine flint, together with charcoal and some fragments of pig bones were recovered from the filling of the pit, as were also a few very fine flint axes or celts of Cissbury type, and some fragmentary antler picks. On the shaft floor, extending over an area of four feet,

> were a quantity of flakes and flint chippings, some of which it was possible to replace one upon the other, thus demonstrating that flint working was undoubtedly executed upon the spot. Among these flakes occurred a quantity of charred, blackened and decayed wood.
>
> The pit, when emptied of its infilling, appeared as an irregular, somewhat elliptical quarry, rather than a true shaft. It measured nineteen and a half feet north and south, by seven feet east and west. The western edge was pierced on the floor level by five shallow workings. Two of these workings could be properly called galleries. The central and northernmost were merely undercuts in the pit face, though flint had been extracted from them. Gallery 1 was five feet in length and two feet in width, and from one and a half to two feet in height. Gallery 2 was four feet in length and one and three quarter feet in width and about the same height. Both these galleries were stacked to the roof with chalk rubble throughout their length, among which were scattered many flint flakes and waste nodules. Much of the chalk rubble bore marks of the use of antler picks, though no such marks were found upon the walls. The walls of the gallery entrances were slightly rubbed on their projecting angles by the passage in and out of the mines.
>
> The flint seam mined for had been removed from the whole of the floor of the pit and galleries, but was distinctly traceable along the base of the gallery walls. Taking into account the difference in surface levels effected by the slope of the hillside, the flint seam was the same one as that worked in the shafts previously excavated by us. The galleries and workings had all been driven into the western edge of the pit, that is toward the rise of the hillside. No attempt had been made to proceed eastwards in the direction of the road. This may be an indication that the road existed as a trackway at the time the flint mining was in progress (Worthing Museum Acc. No. 1961/1585).

The small size of Shaft 5, makes it more akin to a quarry pit, such as Shaft 6 and the central pit of Barrow 2 at Blackpatch, than a flint mine per se. Pye (1968, 8) suggested that pit 5 may have been an unfinished quarry exploiting an inferior seam of flint left untouched by the majority of other shafts. That the pit was never completed is a distinct possibility, though it should be noted that, even if its original excavators had deemed the feature to be a failure, they certainly took time to replace a significant quantity of soil back into the open quarry following its abandonment. Lack of success (or perhaps the time or resources to adequately complete the task in hand) could explain the need to build a mound of structured mine debris (Barrow 3), containing ritually-charged material, over the top of the quarry immediately after its backfilling as a special deposit or sacrifice, possibly to ensure more success next time. Whether the flint located here was inferior in any way, as Pull suggests, is a matter for debate (though no flint seam is indicated at the eastern margins of the section drawing), as too is the theory that area of mining avoided an 'ancient trackway', for it may be more plausible to view the track as a later feature avoiding the cratered land surface caused by the earlier mineshafts. Of the flint and antler material recorded as having been found within Shaft 5 (Pye 1968, 75), only a single flint flake can be traced today.

Shaft 6

Pull has little to say concerning Shaft 6, situated at the northern margins of the mining area, save that it:

> possessed no galleries at all, nor had the walls of this shaft been undercut in any place. Careful sounding of the walls appeared to indicate that the pits immediately around this one (which were indicated by depressions on the surface) also possessed no galleries (Pull 1932a, 44–5).

An inked plan and section, dated 1928 and housed in the Worthing Museum archive, shows that Shaft 6 was really little more than a quarry pit (figure 35), similar perhaps in intent to Shaft 5 in that only the first flint seam encountered during the cutting of the feature appears to have been exploited. The plan indicates that the feature was roughly oval, measuring 2.4m north–south, by 3m east–west. A slight overcutting of the wall, into the flint seam, had occurred at the base of the southernmost face of the pit. The shaft, which bottomed at a depth of 1.8m, contained at least three distinct fills below the topsoil: large chalk rubble, rainwash, and a thin deposit of flints (possibly worked) at the interface between rainwash and surface soil. None of the finds from Shaft 6 can be traced today.

Shaft 7

Pull notes that Shaft 7 was of 'similar character to Shaft 2' being 'roughly circular in plan, with vertical sides' and 'extensive ramifying galleries' at its base which connected it to its immediate neighbours (Pull 1932a, 44). An inked plan of Shaft 7, which survives in the Pull Collection and was published in *The Flint Miners of Blackpatch* as plate 8 (1932a, 46), shows at least nine galleries radiating out from Shaft 7, connecting it with at least four other shafts, including Shaft 8 (figure 36). Pye (1968) notes the frequency of right-angled junctions between the galleries belonging to separate shafts here, suggesting, as Pull had indicated for Shaft 2, that these may have been designed to reflect light from the shaft into the darker areas of the working galleries. An interesting idea, this unfortunately remains untested within the Sussex mines. Pull records that a cremation deposit was observed:

> One third of the way down this shaft, between layers of chalk debris which constituted the infilling...This interment had been made in the centre of the then partly filled pit. The shaft had afterwards been further filled up with broken chalk, either discharged from some nearby mine then in the process of excavation, or from a fresh and unweathered dump on the surface (Pull 1932a, 56-8).

The burial, which consisted of 'a small quantity' of cremated human bone, charcoal and firecracked flint, did not appear to have been burnt in situ. A flaked axe (of Cissbury type), a scraper, a flint knife (all illustrated by Pull in plate 9 of *The Flint Miners of Blackpatch*), and a 'curious charm of worked chalk' (perhaps the product of animal gnawing) were found in close spatial association with the cremation and may therefore represent material placed at the same time as the human remains. The flints,

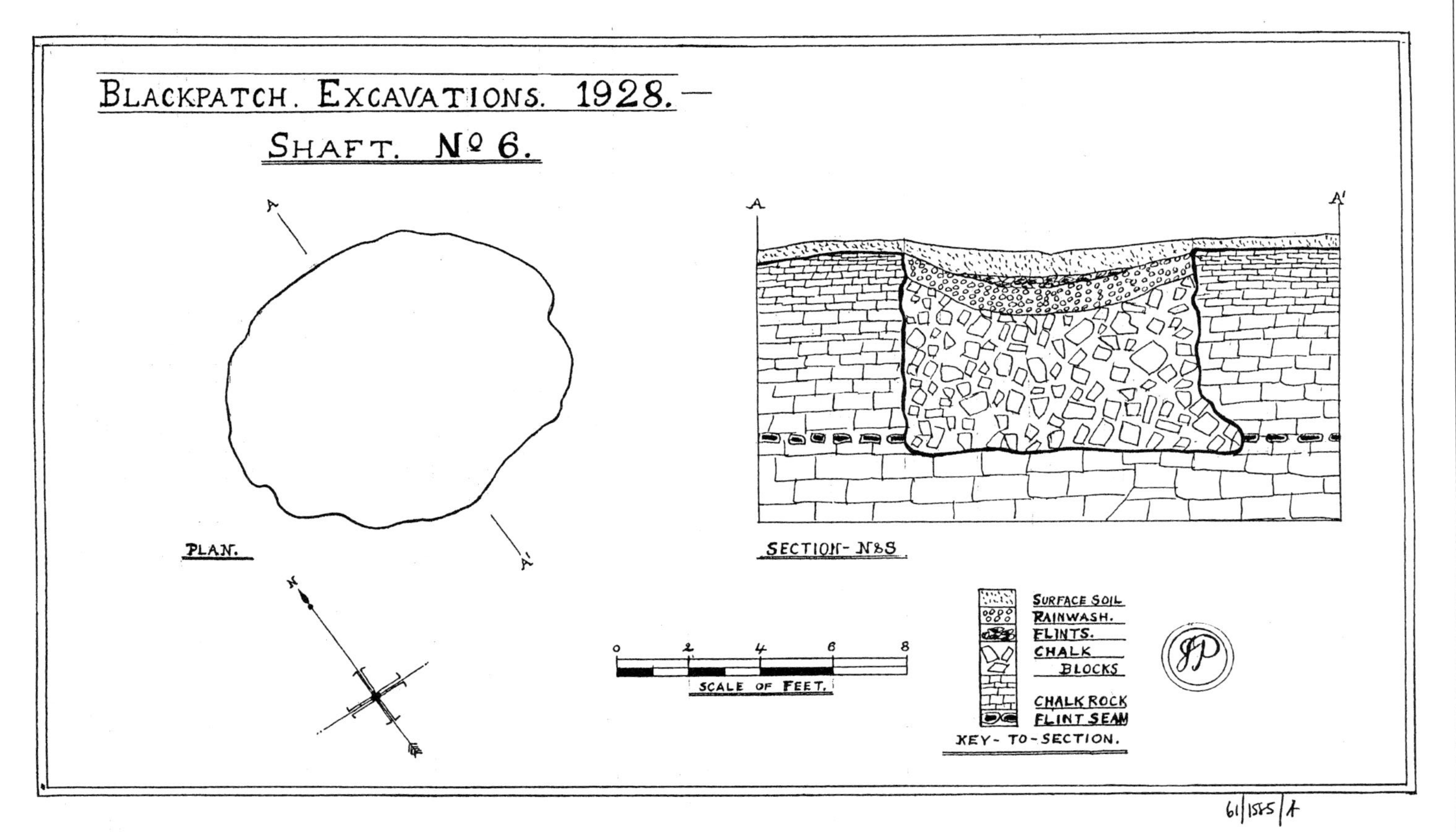

Figure 35. Blackpatch Shaft 6: subterranean plan and section (© Worthing Museum and Art Gallery).

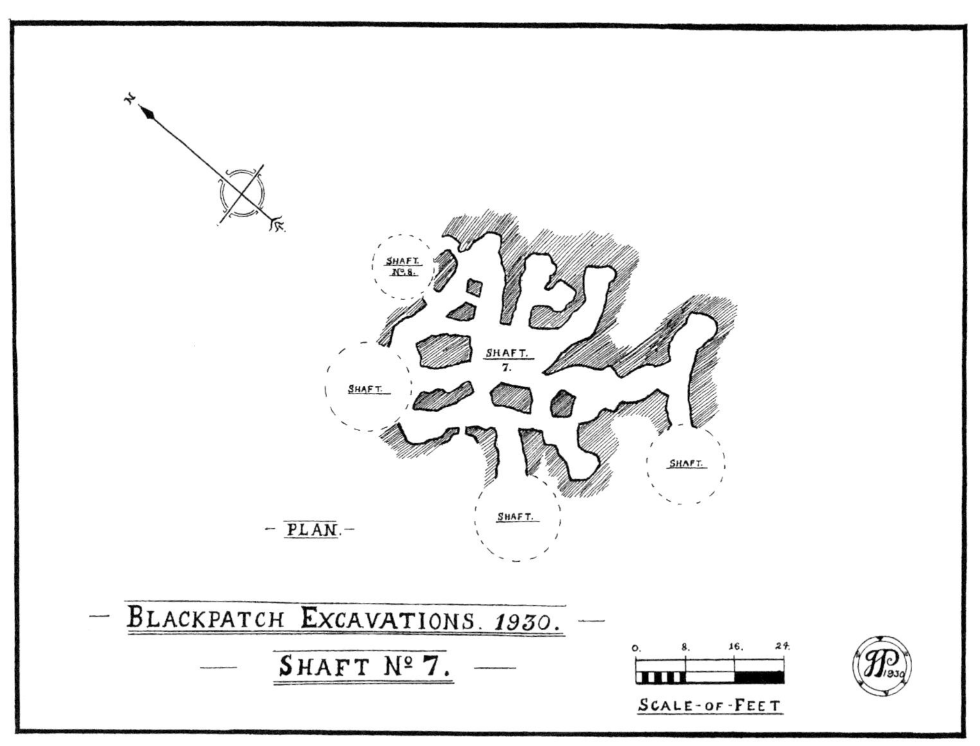

Figure 36. Blackpatch Shaft 7: plan of the subterranean features exposed in 1930 (© Worthing Museum and Art Gallery).

together with an additional three retouched flakes (presumably also from mine backfill) survive in Worthing Museum. The fact that the deposits noted above were found within layers of mine debris, displaying no obvious sign of being intrusive to the fill, would appear to indicate that they were contemporary with a period of extraction activity (Pull 1932a, 58).

Two thirds of the way down the backfill of Shaft 7 was a large area of flint working which measured around 9m in circumference and was 0.1m thick (Pull 1932a, 49). A large quantity of animal bones, 'principally ribs of oxen', was distributed across the flint working deposit, something which suggested to Pull that 'meals had been habitually eaten here by the flint knappers' (1932a, 49). This is of course assuming that the flint and bone material represents an in situ deposit and not an accumulation of secondary refuse. A further observation concerning the nature of this deposit is made by Pull:

> Along the shaft wall on the northern edge of this floor was a huge pile of raw flint nodules, awaiting treatment. These gave the impression that for some reason or other the flint-working on this floor had been suddenly abandoned (Pull 1932a, 49).

Abandonment of the working floor had, Pull theorised, occurred at, or shortly after, an extensive collapse of surface chalk rubble back into the shaft. Such a theory does not, however, explain why any flint nodules covered by such a collapse were not immediately retrieved by the miners, unless of course they were fearful of extracting material which the earth had been seen to reclaim. Alternatively, the unworked flint could represent either surplus material left forgotten on the working surface before being later covered by a collapse in the shaft wall, or the deliberate deposition of unutilised floorstone, perhaps similar in intent to the flint capping observed at Barrows 1, 3, 5, 6, 7 and 9.

Pull also notes (1932a, 108, plate 10.1, 3 and 4) that part of a large chalk cylinder of 'oval section, accurately proportioned and beautifully finished' was found close to the base of Shaft 7, while a piece of chalk carved 'somewhat like the toe of a boot' and a chalk cone 'with a twisted base' were additionally recovered from mine backfill. A further piece of modified chalk from gallery 1, was described by Pull as:

> a spherical chalk carving which appears to have been a sculpture, in the round, of a human head. Unfortunately this had been exposed to frost and the surface was slightly pitted and flaked (Pull 1932a, 108).

The sketch which accompanies Pull's description of this last piece (1932a, plate 10, figure 2) does not clarify interpretation, and unfortunately the piece cannot now be located.

Shaft 8

Pull does not refer directly to the opening of an eighth shaft (in fact he comments regularly upon the 'seven shafts opened' at Blackpatch: e.g. 1932a, 45) though 'S8' is clearly marked as having been cleared on a number of site plans produced. Furthermore, it is clear that a number of finds in Worthing Museum, including five flakes, a laurel leaf and a fragment of flaked axe, were all at some time found within the fill of Shaft 8. Pull states clearly that Barrow 12 directly overlay the infilled remains of Shaft 8 (1932a, 84), while an inked plan of Shaft 7, further demonstrates that Shaft 8 was linked to 7 by a series of north–south aligned galleries. The way in which Shaft 8 is outlined within this plan as a surface hollow would, however, appear to suggest that, though some of the galleries were traced, the shaft itself was never fully opened from ground level. The recorded flint assemblage may therefore have originated either during the basal gallery investigations, or from the removal of upper shaft fills during the examination of Barrow 12.

THE SURFACE CHIPPING FLOORS

A large number of 'Surface Chipping Floors' or flint working areas have been recorded at the Blackpatch mining site. Some areas of flint working residue have already been noted within partially backfilled mine shafts 1, 5 and 7. Presumably these areas were used either because the hollow formed by the partially backfilled mine provided some form of shelter from the natural elements, or because the mine itself, even though it was no longer in operation, was still considered to be a special or significant place. At least four distinct surface working floors were identified and excavated by Pull and Sainsbury around the mineshafts at Blackpatch, though it is not known whether the full extent of these features was ever fully defined. These have been labelled Chipping Floors 1–4.

Chipping Floor 1

By J. H. Pull

Floor 1 was situated in the extreme south-west of the mining area. Completely obscured by turf and surface soil, its presence was discovered by means of probing with a steel rod. It partly occupied a ridge between the lips of three shafts. The extent of the ground covered by the chippings measured 15 square feet. The flakes of which it principally consisted, rested directly upon the original hill surface, and amounted in bulk to several bushels. They were packed together without any matrix, and attained a maximum depth of three inches. Chipped pieces, nodules of small size and several roughly blocked out axes of Cissbury type occurred among them. It was noted that the patination of the pieces was universally a dead white on the upper face, and glossy white to grey upon the under face.

The deposition of the floor was obviously contemporary with some mining immediately to the east of it, as at that extremity it was covered by six inches of small chalk rubble which constituted a low ridge at the lip of the depression. The remainder of the floor was purely superficial, being devoid of any covering, other than four inches of surface soil and turf. It was perfectly clear that the site had been worked at one period only (Worthing Museum Acc. No. 1961/1585).

Chipping Floor 2

By J. H. Pull

Floor 2 occupied the shapeless ridge of undisturbed ground between shaft 2 and Shaft C immediately to the south-west (figure 37). The floor was found to consist of a mass of flakes and chipped pieces resting on the original hill surface. The chippings were in places packed tightly together without any matrix. As was the case with floor 1, the eastern end of this site was covered with small chalk rubble (mining debris) attaining a maximum thickness of one foot, this debris being surmounted by the usual surface soil and turf.

Resting among the flakes, which constituted the main portion of the floor, was the residue of two large hearths. The flakes in the immediate vicinity of these were thoroughly burnt, and a large quantity of burnt flints was piled upon them. The first of the two hearths occurred near the lip of shaft 2, and a few feet to the west of it were found a number of fragments of pottery. Where the western end of the floor dipped into the depression formed over the head of the mine shaft to the south-west, a number of flint implements were met with. Beyond this the floor

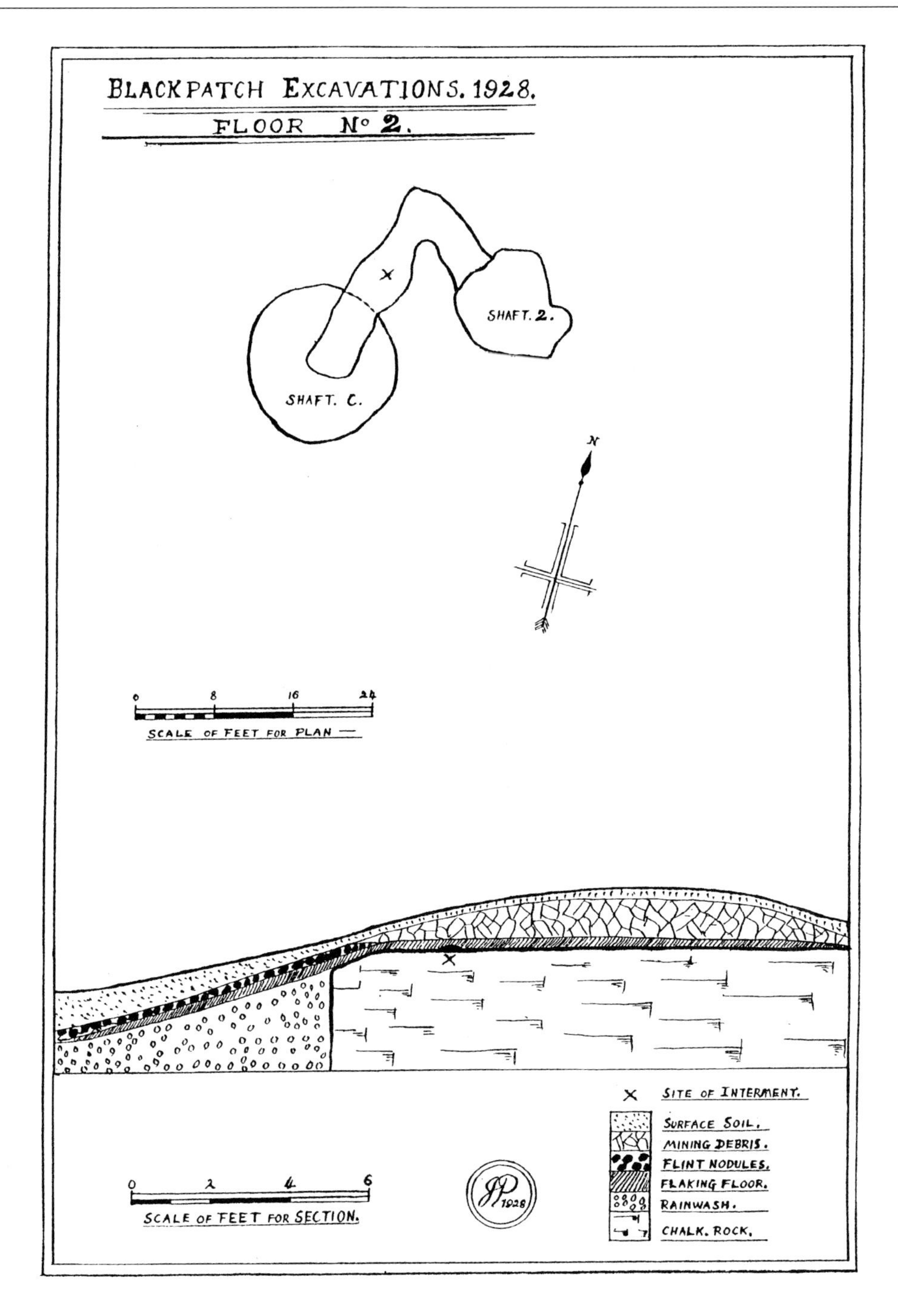

Figure 37. Blackpatch Chipping Floor 2: plan and section of the feature, demonstrating its relationship to Shafts 2 and 'C'. Note the position of the cremated interment, apparently beneath the floor deposits (© Worthing Museum and Art Gallery).

was surmounted by a second hearth. In this hearth a quantity of charcoal, and completely charred bones (at first believed to be animal, but now known to be human) were found. The rainwash in the vicinity was charged heavily with ash. Numerous bones of ox, sheep and pig were distributed near the hearth. Several more fragments of pottery were found near this second hearth. Quantities of broken nodules of mine flint surmounted the western end of the floor.

At a distance of 11 feet from the lip of shaft 2 was found a small, much worn down rubber of sandstone, such as might have been used for rubbing down bone tools. At 16 feet from shaft 2, resting on the face of the chalk rock, beneath the floor, and covering an area of about a square foot, was a deposit of thoroughly cremated human bones laid in a round heap and admixed with much charcoal. In contact with these bones were several fragments of a pottery vessel. The pottery, in this instance, was identical in paste and texture to the other fragments found on the floor. This pottery is British No 1 and of the Beaker class. To the east of and in contact with the bones was a very finely chipped celt of Cissbury type. Six inches to the south of these bones was an elongated oval implement of flint and a flint pick. One foot to the west of the bones occurred a small charm or pendant, fashioned from soft Wealden sandstone, in shape like a triangle, polished and ground to a thin edge all round. The apex, which may have, and most probably did contain a perforation for suspension round the neck, was missing.

It was perfectly clear from the absence of disturbed or inverted soils that this interment had not been introduced after the tilt of chalk mining debris, which had here covered the floor, had been deposited. It was further clear that the cremation had not taken place where it was found. Re-examination of the charred bones from the south-west hearth, 25 feet from shaft 2, revealed the fact that some of them were human, though the larger portion were animal. One is tempted to suppose that it was at this hearth that the ceremonial burning of the body had taken place, also the customary funeral feast, and that it was from this hearth that the ashes of the dead had been gathered up.

The importance of the presence of an interment after cremation beneath the undisturbed floor and overlying mine debris cannot be underestimated. Flint implements, characteristic of the whole of the flint culture at Blackpatch, together with sherds of undoubted Beaker pottery being placed with the interment, the whole being covered with a chipping floor which itself is prior to some mining in the area is if great interest, especially as the tilt of rubble over the floor was in turn covered with a thickness of surface soil and was entirely in keeping with the whole of the mining area and adjacent barrows. It is certain that the hearth at the south-western end of the floor is later than the mines shaft infilling which it covered. It is also certain that the whole of the floor and the hearth at its eastern end is earlier than Shaft 2, as it appears that it was from Shaft 2 that the mining debris which surmounted the floor had been tilted; also the floor ended so abruptly at the lip of Shaft 2, as to present the appearance of having been cut through when that shaft was sunk. We are faced with the fact that the cremated interment is undoubtedly of the same date as the flint mines (Worthing Museum Acc. No. 1961/1585).

Chipping Floor 3

By J. H. Pull

Floor 3, situated to the north of Shaft 7, partly occupied virgin ground between the lips of three pits, and partly overlay the mouth of a shaft. It was a large floor and, like Floor 1, consisted of a single layer of closely packed flakes and chippings. Among these were distributed a goodly number of flint implements in all stages of completion. This floor had also been worked at one period only.

Chipping Floor 3 also afforded some indication of the relative age of pits and dumps in its neighbourhood. The floor was certainly later than the shaft which it partly overlay. This shaft was silted up in the usual way, but the fine top silt had from the most part drifted from that side of the shaft mouth uncovered by the floor. Some few inches of silt overlay the floor in that direction. The floor was also noted to be earlier than the dump of mining debris which has been added to the bulk of Barrow 12, for the south-west edge of the floor passed a foot or two under the base of this dump. The whole of the floor was covered with surface soil and turf attaining a depth of from three to four inches (Worthing Museum Acc. No. 1961/1585).

Chipping Floor 4

By J. H. Pull

Floor 4 was situated a little to the south-east of Floor 1. This floor was similar in character to the others, and occupied a ridge of virgin ground between the mouths of two shafts. This floor had been overlaid by a low tilt or dump of small chalk rubble. On excavation it was found impossible to determine from which direction this rubble had come, but it indicated that some mining was carried on near by, after the floor had been deposited. A miner's broken pick of red deer antler lay upon the floor, whilst several incomplete flint axes, and a good one broken in two halves, were found among the chippings. Two inches of surface mould overlay the whole (Worthing Museum Acc. No. 1961/1585).

THE BARROWS

Barrow 1

Barrow 1, a prominent mound overlying Shaft 3 at the approximate centre of the Blackpatch mining area, was, in 1922, one of the first parts of the Worthing complex to be archaeologically examined by John Pull. His examination consisted of a trench, measuring 20 feet by 2 feet, being cut to the centre of the mound 'in much the same manner as one would cut a big cake' (Pull 1923b). The preliminary results of this examination, complete with section drawing, were published in the November 3rd 1923 edition of the *Worthing Herald.*

The main body of the mound appeared to consist of chalk rubble capped with 'large selected unworked nodules of mine flint'. A series of flint tools, including an engraved flint and an axe of 'Cissbury-type' were recovered from the base of the surface soil. Pull suggested, in the published article, that the mound represented the remains of a round barrow, constructed over a number of in-filled mine shafts. That some considerable time had elapsed between the infilling of the shafts and the construction of the mound, was, he theorised, indicated not only by the formation of extensive rainwash deposits in the upper levels of shaft fill, but also by the fact that the flints from the mound were 'patinated dead white' as opposed to the 'blue' coloured flakes from the shafts 'leading one to believe that they had been exposed to atmospheric actions for a considerable time prior to being included in the rubble in which they were found (Pull 1923b). No trace of a primary interment was recorded from this trial excavation.

The article published in the *Worthing Herald* was seized upon the anonymous crtic known only as 'Antiquary' for an attack upon the excavation methods employed by Pull and his colleagues (Appendix 5, letter 1). The main drive of this attack would appear to have been that the method of examination employed upon Barrow 1 was a single trench, something which 'Antiquary' considered to be as 'much an attempt at 'looting' as the old method of digging a hole in the centre and filling it in again.'. This seems hardly fair, for Pull had made it clear that his intention in 1922 had been to cut a section through the mound to examine its form and nature. In other words this was purely an assessment of the mound's archaeological potential and not a full blown excavation. Having attacked Pull's excavation technique, 'Antiquary' went on to 'protest against the statement that a heap of rubbish was a 'tumulus' or burial place, and further of the Bronze Age, without a single scrap of evidence.' (Appendix 5, Letter 6).

In retrospect the comments made by 'Antiquary' appear to be no more than the manifestation of an extreme form of intellectual snobbery, though the effect that they must have had upon the local amateur archaeological community should not be underestimated (cf. Appendix 5, letters 2, 3, 4, 5, 7, 8, 9, 10, 11). Such attacks may have been instrumental in driving Pull to further efforts, for in 1924 he was back at Blackpatch, determined to resolve any interpretational problems surrounding his earlier work. This time Barrow 1 was excavated more completely, the final results being published firstly in the *Worthing Herald* (Pull 1927) and later in *The Flintminers of Blackpatch* (Pull 1932a, 63–7). An alternative version of the 1932 text, written by Pull, is preserved within the Worthing Museum archive:

> Situated roughly in the centre of the prehistoric flint mining station at Blackpatch was a roughly circular, grass-grown mound. This mound, as judged from its large size and regular base contour (figure 38), presented an appearance quite in contrast to the shapeless heaps of turf-covered mining debris which rose between the pits in the vicinity.
>
> During the excavations of 1922, it was thought that the mound might represent a round barrow, presumably of the Bronze Age. The mound measured 43 feet east–west by 44 feet north–south, its base being quite regular. Its maximum height was five feet above the natural surface of the hill. The mound rested partly upon five sunken depressions, indicating the filled in shafts of flint mines, and partly upon the ridges of ground between the mouths of these pits. The mound appeared

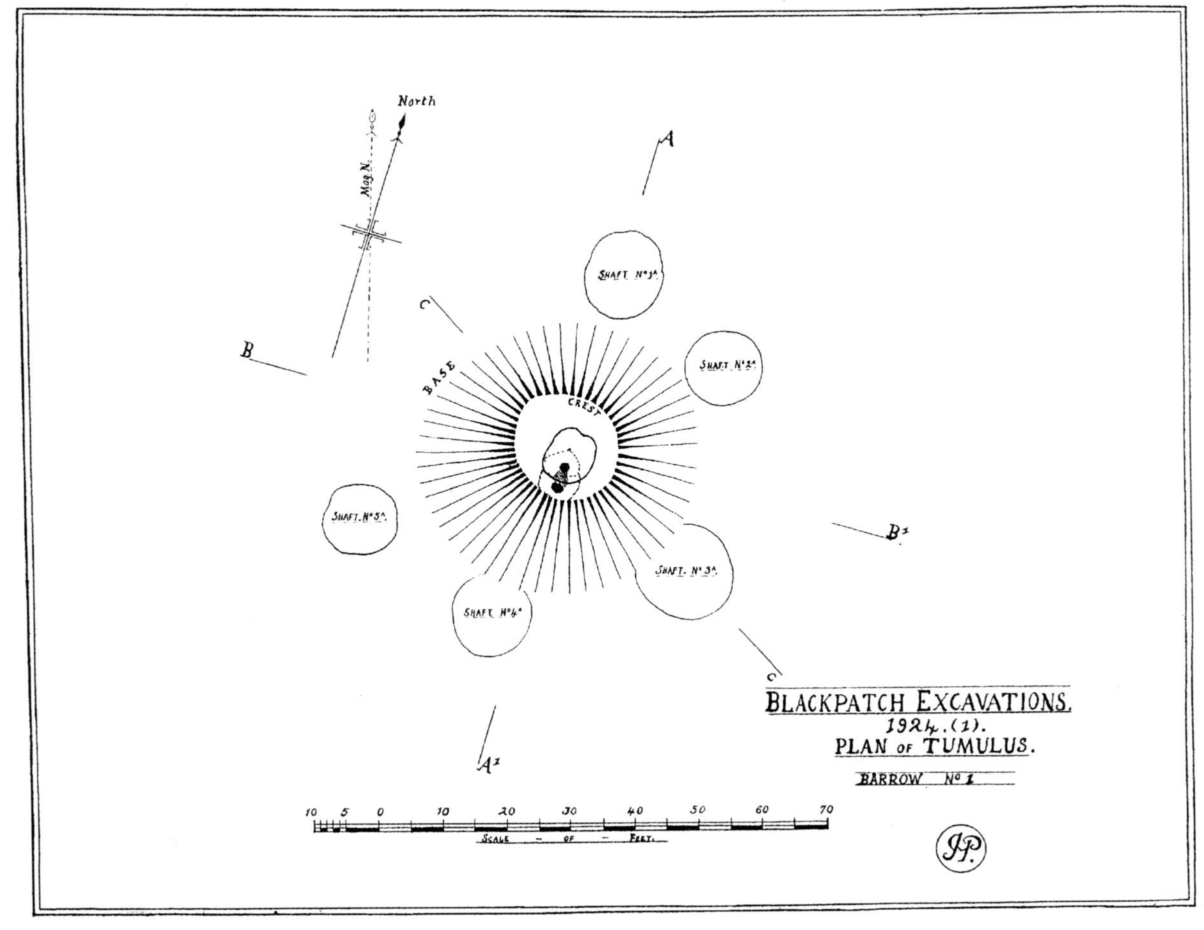

Figure 38. Blackpatch Barrow 1: surface plan incorporating subsurface detail revealed during the course of the 1924 excavation (© Worthing Museum and Art Gallery).

as a huge inverted basin, the summit being occupied over a radius of seven feet from its centre by a bowl shaped depression. The maximum depth of this depression was three feet, giving the mound's summit a cratered appearance. This sunken centre of the mound caused both the excavating party and the authorities that visited the diggings in 1922, to think that the mound had been previously excavated. In 1923, when a section was cut into the eastern side of the mound, this idea was unfortunately still adhered to. So much controversy arose, however, after the publication of the account of the digging of this section in *The Herald Magazine* that it was decided to push the matter further.

Practically the whole of the mound has now been excavated. It was found that the body of the mound was composed of all sorts of chalk rubble and blocks of chalk drawn from the prehistoric mines (figure 39). The whole of the top of the mound, including the central crater, was found to be roofed with an even layer of large flint nodules representing the floorstone mined in the area. Surface soil and rainwash (chalk silt) had accumulated in the central crater to a thickness conformable with that met with in the excavated shafts.

At a point three feet south of the mound's centre and three feet below the turf, at the bottom of the crater, was found an interment. This consisted of very thoroughly cremated human bones mixed with ashes and charcoal. Scattered among these were a great number of fragments of a large hand made and badly fired cineary urn with overhanging rim, liberally ornamented with a series of alternate horizontal and vertical lines impressed with a twisted thong. This interment was scattered southwards from the point mentioned, to the edge of the crater bottom, some seven feet and a further portion of it was found resting in the crest of the mound on a higher level, some of the charcoal and fragments of urn being only 18 inches below the crown of the mound.

In actual contact with the interment was a small flint celt or axe, and some few feet to the north of it a very fine oval flint knife and some fragments of bone, since identified as those of a species of domestic pig. To the east of the interment were found a few small rounded lumps of worked chalk of peculiar appearance, looking as if they had been stabbed all over with some sharp pointed instrument when in a pulpy condition. The reason for portions of the interment being found on two different levels is explained by the fact that the barrow had been erected over the mouths of two mine shafts, both of which had been filled in prior to the construction of the mound.

One of these mine shafts was situated immediately beneath the centre of the barrow, while the other was under the eastern portion, the dividing wall between the shaft's lips being in one place only 18 inches thick. There must have been some difference in time between the working of these two shafts, for the in-filling of the one beneath the eastern portion of the mound had evidently settled down and sunk to its maximum extent before the mound was raised over it. Further, a dump of mining debris, dividing its mouth from the body of the mound above, had been covered by a local tilt of old surface not in-situ. The barrow must have been raised above the other central shaft immediately after that shaft had been

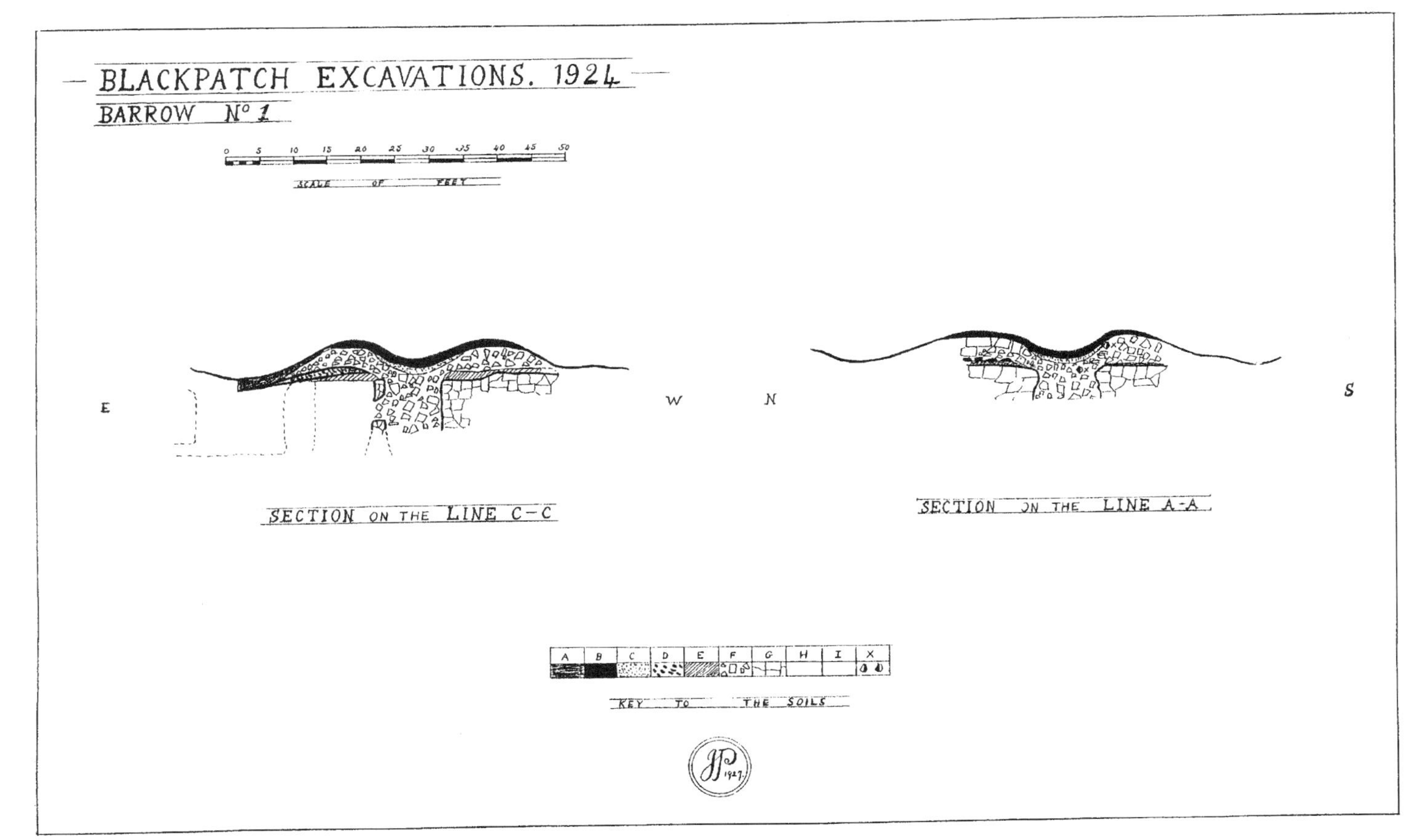

Figure 39. Blackpatch Barrow 1: two sections through the collapsed mound structure and the uppermost layers of Shaft 3 beneath (© Worthing Museum and Art Gallery).

> filled in, for it was impossible to discern where the chalk rubble, composing its in-filling, ended and the rubble, of which the mound was constructed, began. The addition of the weight of the mound, roughly in the region of 100 tons, showed no further settlement in the eastern shaft, whilst the central shaft had sunk the central portion of the mound three feet, its contained interment having settled and sunk contemporary with the in-filling. This settlement gave rise to the re-dished appearance of the barrow's crown.
>
> It seems reasonable to assume that some mining was still going on in the vicinity at the time as the barrow was erected and roofed with floorstone. The finding of a barrow containing a cremation above the shafts of the flint mines, throws some fresh light upon the vexed question of the age of the pits. From the evidence obtained it seems impossible top separate the period of interment and that of the mining activities (Worthing Museum Acc. No. 1961/1585).

The 'overhanging rim urn' noted by Pull represents the larger part of a single collared urn, identified by Longworth as being an Unclassified Series, SE Style, form BII (Longworth 1984, 275). Longworth's identification was made from John Pull's drawings (reproduced as plate 12 in *The Flintminers of Blackpatch*) as the sherds themselves had unfortunately become lost since the excavation. The present whereabouts of the human cremation, the pig bones and the 'chalk charms' (possibly representing animal gnawing activity) are also unknown. Of the recorded flint tools (Pull and Pye note the presence of at least two flaked axes, one oval knife and a segmented tool) only a single axe roughout appears to have survived, in Newbury Museum (Gardiner 1988, 1216). A second axe roughout at Newbury, marked as being from 'Cissbury', but without any clear context, could possibly represent the mis-identification of the second example found within Barrow 1.

The fact that a 'cremated interment' was recovered from within the body of mound 1 would appear to justify, at least in part, Pull's original interpretation of the earthwork feature as a place of burial. Interpretational problems remain, however, with accepting the feature as a 'round-barrow' in its own right, rather than perhaps an earthen mound containing burial or ritual artefact assemblages (not least in that the one recorded burial element could perhaps be considered too minor a deposit to have such an impressive marker mound raised over it). This may seem pedantic, but the morphological distinction between a deliberately constructed round barrow and a modified spoil heap containing burial elements is a crucial one if understanding of the range of activities conducted within the Blackpatch mining area is to be achieved.

A number of possibilities present themselves concerning the interpretation of the earthwork feature. Firstly the mound could be viewed as a barrow with a single, small scale, off-centre primary burial deposit or the burial itself could represent a secondary deposit inserted into an already existing mound of partially structured mining debris. The mound could of course represent a barrow with a secondary cremation deposit, the central burial having been destroyed by some unrecorded antiquarian examination (though Pull's comments would appear to indicate that the central depression within the mound was caused by mine subsidence and not any later digging activity). Alternatively the burial could originally have represented only one element of a larger assemblage of 'ritually charged' items (including flint tools) placed within a deliberately structured mound of rubble excavated from the surrounding mines, and capped with an unutilised deposit of floorstone.

Given Pull's comments on the differential patination of flint tools recovered from the upper levels of shaft fill and mound make-up, we must assume that at least some of the material incorporated within the mound was residual. There is no clear evidence, at least from Pull's records to indicate that the cremation and collared urn were secondary to mound creation. The balance of probability would appear to be that earthwork and burial were both contemporary, the human skeletal deposits forming only one part of a series of formal deposits placed within the structured layers of 'Barrow 1'. The fact that the body of the mound was composed of chalk rubble and floorstone debris (together with the clear absence of a quarry ditch) would appear to indicate that the earthwork was constructed predominantly from mining debris. If the mound was constructed during a phase of extensive flint extraction, then the date of this particular extraction is unfortunately unclear. It is possible that the feature was constructed in the Earlier Neolithic (assuming that the majority of flint tools recovered from within it are contemporary with construction and are not residual elements accidentally incorporated into the mound during its construction), or that the mound dates from the Later Neolithic or Early Bronze Age (assuming that the collared urn with cremation is not intrusive).

Barrow 2

By J. H. Pull and C. E. Sainsbury

This barrow was situated on the highest portion of the spur of the hill occupied by the flint mines, some 150 feet to the west of the ancient road, and at the north-east extremity of the prehistoric site. Near it, within 20 feet, are some depressions marking the mouths of filled in mine shafts. The barrow consisted of a slightly oval mound. Across the longer axis, the base of the mound measured 27 feet, the shorter axis measuring 22 feet. The sides of the mound were gently sloping, and rose to a maximum height of 10 inches above the natural surface. A little to the east of the centre, the mound was somewhat depressed and flattened (figure 40).

On removing the turf, the mound was found to consist of small chalk and soil. Unevenly distributed among this were a few large nodules of flint, also a few flints showing signs of human workmanship, and one or two flakes, all patinated dead white on all faces. To the east of the centre of the barrow, sunk into the chalk rock, was a large oval grave. The longer axis of this grave lay north by east and south by west, and measured nine feet, the shorter axis measured five and a half feet. The sides of this grave were vertical, or nearly so, the maximum depth being four and a half feet and the minimum depth two and a half feet. The bottom of the grave was flat at each end at a depth of two and a quarter feet; its centre, however, was occupied by an uneven hole, sunk deeper than the rest of the grave. This hole extended to the sides of the grave across the shorter axis.

The wall of the oval primary grave had been cut into on the east side at a point north of its centre. This penetration had been performed at a time long posterior

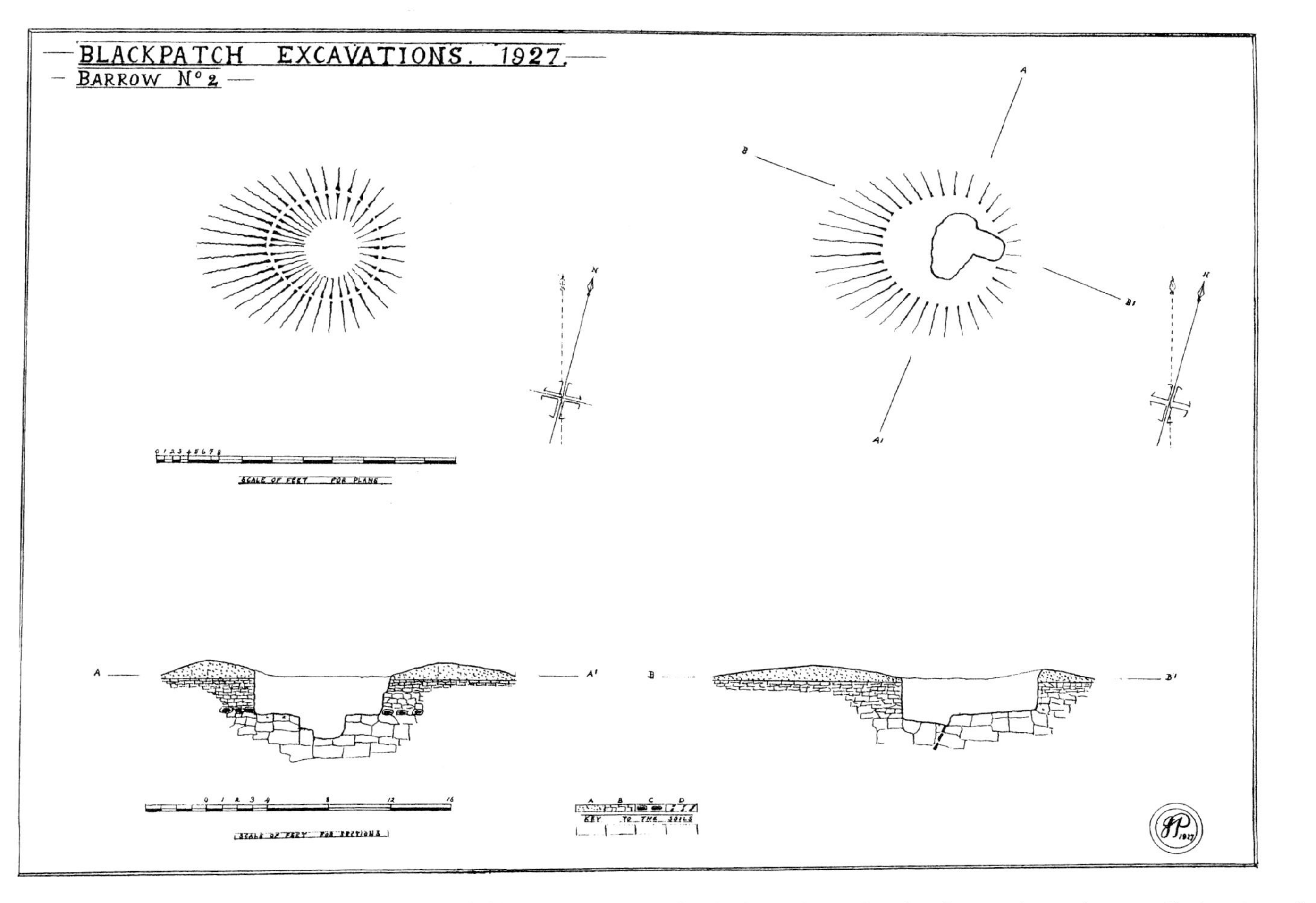

Figure 40. Blackpatch Barrow 2: (clockwise from top left) pre-excavation surface hachure plan, subsurface feature plan and two profile drawings of the internal pit (© Worthing Museum and Art Gallery).

to its original construction, a secondary grave having been made in the east side of the barrow. This secondary grave, like the primary one, had been sunk into the chalk rock. Its sides were vertical and parallel, its bottom flat and even. Its width was three feet, its depth two and a quarter feet.

Remains of three distinct interments were met with in the primary and secondary graves. That portion of the primary grave which lay to the south of its junction with the secondary grave was filled to a depth of from nine to 12 inches below the surface with somewhat compacted brown mould. In this soil, at a depth of nine inches from the turf, at the western edge of the grave, two feet south of the centre, occurred a single fragment of a human skull – the skull of a very young person. Below the surface soil, the primary grave was filled with large and small chalk rubble, the interstices between which were not filled in. In this rubble, at a depth of two feet three inches, resting against the south and east sides of the hole in the floor of the grave, were the much disturbed remains of an inhumation. The bones were well preserved, being impregnated with chalk. They consisted of a skull, several arm bones, a portion of the pelvis and sacrum, and a single phelange. These bones and skull represented all that remains of a skeleton, which had been disturbed and broken up, presumably when the secondary grave had been dug. The bones were those of a fully developed man, in the early middle period of life, the sutures being open and the skull thin. The skull is markedly brachycephalic and well filled.

The northern end of the primary and secondary grave was filled to a depth of nine inches with brown soil. Beneath this, to a depth of one foot nine inches, was small chalk rubble. Below this again, to a depth of two feet from the turf, was small chalk admixed with much brown soil. From two feet to the bottom it was filled with chalk rubble with no admixed soil. Occupying the primary grave, and partly in the secondary grave, was the much decayed but undisturbed skeleton of a fully developed man, extended at full length and lying on the back with the feet to the east. That portion of the skeleton that lay on the solid chalk floor of the secondary grave consisted of the right and left legs and feet. The upper portion of the body had lain across, and partly above, the floor of the primary grave. The bones of the upper portion of the body had gone almost entirely to decay, a few fragments of vertebrae, scapula and ribs being in position, also the bones of the left forearm and a hand, underneath which was a mass of iron scoria, representing all that remained of an iron knife. The skull and teeth were entirely missing, as were also the bones of the right arm. From the evidence obtained it would appear that the burials had been effected in the following order:

Interment 1 – An inhumation in the primary oval grave or cist at the time the barrow was raised. The skull being characteristic, without doubt, that this burial was one of the Beaker folk. The absence of any datable associated articles of funerary significance makes it difficult to assign an age to this interment. The fact that it was an inhumation in an oval grave with its long axis not orientated, and a round barrow above, certainly points towards the Early Bronze Age or Beaker period. A serrated lump of chalk found near the skull, being similar to those found near the urn in Barrow 1, seems to connect the two barrows, as does the presence of mine flint in the material of the mound.

Interment 2 – This was, judging from the small skull fragment, an inhumation, and had probably been a secondary interment in the barrow. Near the isolated skull fragment were found two small pieces of chalk, bearing stain of some small article of bronze which had entirely gone to decay. As the whole infilling of the grave had apparently been turned over, it is impossible to say whether this article had belonged to the period of the interments 1 and 2 or to the period of the third interment.

Interment 3 – This interment was undoubtedly of Saxon date, the intended grave for which had been commenced to the east of the primary grave and, as the digging of this had proceeded westward, the primary grave was broken into. The Saxon interment had been made in the manner customary to that people. The body had been laid at full length with the head to the west. The personal belongings, which in this case consisted of a typical iron knife, having been buried with the body. No subsequent disturbance of the mound had been made since this Saxon interment was sealed in it. The iron knife seems to have been a straight blade with a thick back and one keen edge, and had possessed a guard and tang: a typical Saxe, from which we are told the Saxons got their name (Worthing Museum Acc. No. 1961/1585).

None of the finds noted by Pull and Sainsbury as having been derived from Barrow 2 could be traced at the time of writing. The primary interment here is referred to in the above text, and more strongly elsewhere (Pull 1932a, 67–9) as having been a fully articulated burial disturbed by later digging activity. A problem with accepting this at face value is that though there clearly has been secondary disturbance within Mound 2 (namely the insertion of a Saxon grave), it unclear whether any primary deposit was fully complete at the time of interment. Disarticulated body parts are known from the backfill of a variety of Early Neolithic constructs, and also appear to have been recorded from Shaft 4 and Barrows 9 and 12 at Blackpatch. It is possible that 'interment 1' represents a similar type of deposit. If a primary articulated body had been encountered during the cutting of the Saxon grave, we would perhaps expect to find at least some of the earlier bone material scattered throughout the backfill of the secondary cut and not solely from the fill of the 'primary grave' slot.

Similarly the second burial, in fact only a fragment of skull, may also have originally formed part of a dismembered set of body parts, for the primary deposit need not represent the component parts of a single individual. Alternatively the fragment could represent an isolated skeletal deposit, as per the femur and lower jaw pieces retrieved from the upper fill of Shaft 4. The possibility that the isolated skull fragment could have formed part of the Saxon burial, itself missing the head, seems unlikely given Pull and Sainsbury's thoughts on the relative age at death of the two individuals represented and the lack of apparent disturbance to the later burial. In fact it is likely that the Saxon skeleton was originally interred in a decapitated state (see also Barrow 12), such deposits being not uncommon from this period (Reynolds 1998).

Where encountered, Saxon decapitation burials have usually been viewed as representing victims of warfare, though it has recently been argued that they may more plausibly indicate victims of the early English criminal justice system whereby felons were executed and buried, usually at the boundary limits of a local estate or territory (Reynolds 1988, 8). Incorporation of burials into an existing prehistoric mound may be seen as a deliberate attempt to link with the ancestral past (cf. Williams 1997), or, in the case of executed criminals, such barrows may have been viewed as a suitable resting place for the unworthy members of society who would now 'endure eternal torment from supernatural monsters' (Reynolds 1998, 9). If the Barrow 2 skeleton does represent the remains of a criminal, the inclusion of an iron 'knife' as a grave good would seem somewhat bizarre, unless of course this item was the original implement of execution. The absence of any artefactual material surviving in Worthing Museum today must unfortunately preclude a detailed discussion.

The structural nature of Barrow 2 requires some explanation, for the absence of a clear central mound makes it unlike the majority of other 'barrow' sites recorded from Blackpatch. Absence of a mound structure could be explained by the secondary Saxon burial having disrupted the upper levels of the earthwork, casting soil outwards to create the defined 'ringwork' evident in the plan. It is interesting, however, that this circular, bank-like deposit of soil, looks, superficially at least, akin to the type of spoil heap sometimes recorded from around the outer lip of a flint mine (cf. Holgate 1991, 15–16). An additional observation, with regard to the nature of the central pit of 'Barrow' 2, is worth noting here:

> It was evident that a deer horn pick similar to those used in the flint mines had been employed to dig it, for a large splinter from the point of such a pick occurred at the bottom of the grave together with a block of chalk bearing the imprint of a blow delivered from such an implement (Pull 1932a, 67).

Looking again at the section drawing produced for Barrow 2, it is noticeable, not only how deep the so-called 'grave' pits have penetrated the chalk bedrock, but also how they have been cut through a seam of tabular flint. In this context, Pull's observations regarding the antler pick marks on the walls of the cut assume more importance for it is possible that this feature, instead of a grave and barrow mound, could represent the remains of a flint quarry pit or abortive mine (similar perhaps to the quarry pits recorded from nearby Harrow Hill: Holgate 1995b) which, in its final stage of use, was backfilled with rubble and disarticulated human bone. In this particular scenario the recorded body parts from the 'primary grave' do not necessarily represent a burial (or series of burials) within a defined grave cut, but the deposition of ritually charged material within an abandoned feature.

Barrow 3

By J. H. Pull and C. E. Sainsbury

Barrow 3 was situated on the western edge of the ancient road that forms the boundary of the flint mining area. It consisted of a low circular mound, 28 feet in diameter and 1 foot in height (figure 41). Situated around it, on the north, west and south-west, were depressions presumably indicating the presence of mine shafts. The crest of the barrow was flattened, but not sunken. The whole mound

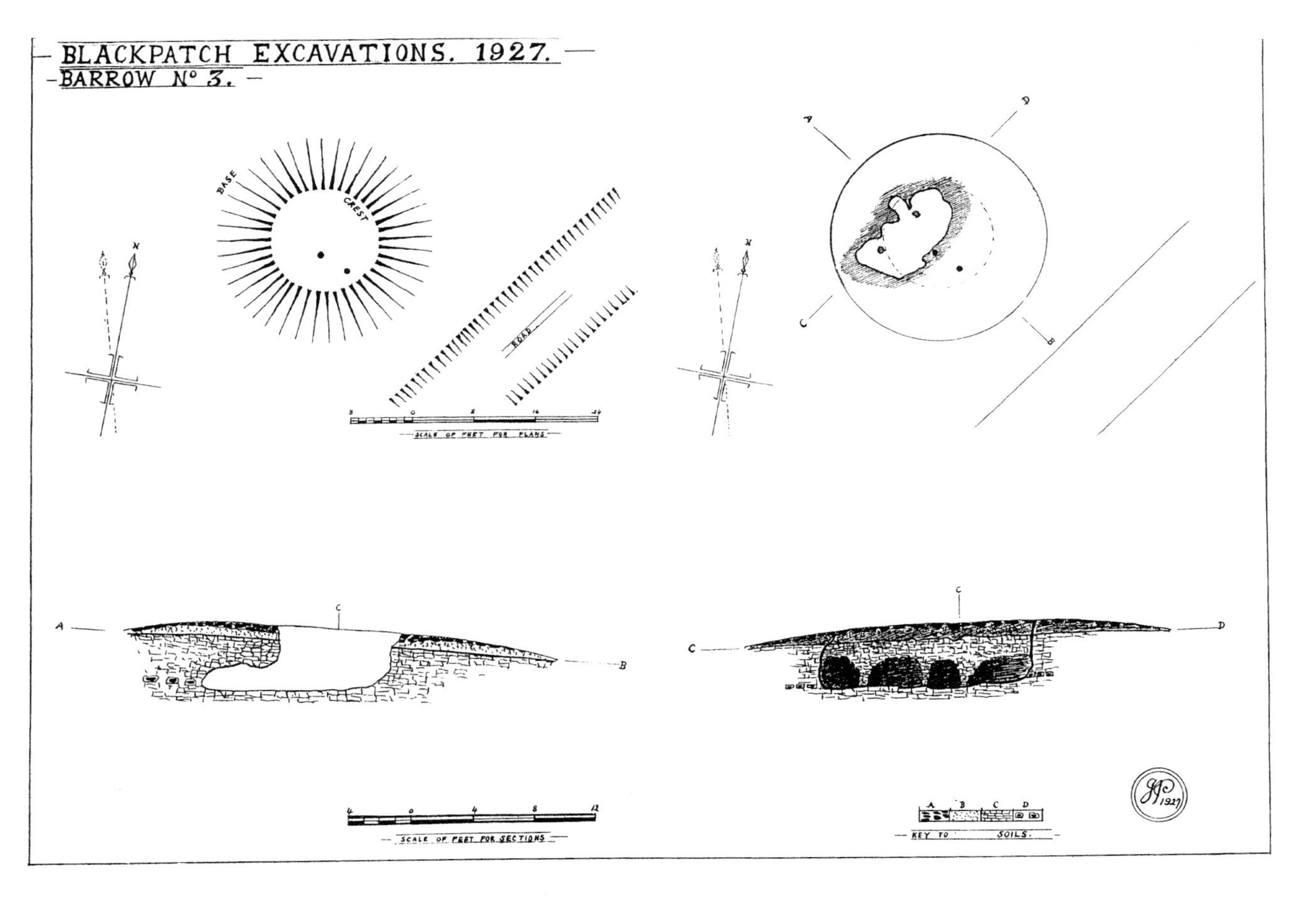

Figure 41. Blackpatch Barrow 3 and Shaft 5: (clockwise from top left) pre-excavation surface hachure plan showing the position of the two internal inhumation burials, subsurface excavation plan showing the extent of the Shaft 5 workings, profile of the northern wall of the shaft illustrating the nature of the subterranean headings and north west - south east profile. Note that the bottom left profile drawing appears to show the Shaft cutting through the body of the mound, something contradicted by Pull and Sainsbury's text (© Worthing Museum and Art Gallery).

was covered with turf moss, beneath which was a capping of very large flints. This flint covering extended over the whole of the mound, the flints of which it was composed being floorstone nodules, such as were mined in the vicinity. Many of these flints, especially near the centre, were very large indeed, weighing individually up to 14lbs. The interstices between them were filled with surface soil. The capping of flints had certainly never been disturbed since it was laid.

Immediately beneath the flint capping, over a radius of seven feet from the centre of the mound, was a mass of flint debris which appeared to be in situ. This consisted of floorstone nodules, compacted masses of flakes, fine chippings and splinters. Distributed among these were hammerstones and implements of flint in all stages of manufacture, some perfect, some unfinished and some broken in the making. In the centre of this layer of flint working debris, over a radius of some six feet, was a quantity of burnt flints, charcoal and a few burnt flakes. Although the burnt flints lay between the chipping floor and the flint capping of the mound and were limited to a central area, they could not have represented the remains of a fire or hearth in situ, as flints, flakes, chalk and soil in contact with them, showed no signs of the application of fire. These burnt flints, flakes and charcoal must, therefore, have been gathered up from some site nearby when the mound was raised.

Beneath, and in contact with, the layer of flint working waste were found the much decayed remains of three interments. At a point two feet south of the centre of the mound, and 18 inches beneath the surface, lying on a carefully constructed platform of flint nodules, was the skeleton of a very young man, the fourth molar being unerupted. The bones were much disintegrated, but it was possible to recognise their relative position. It was concluded that the body had been interred in the contracted position and was laid on the left side with the head to the north and the face to the east, the hands being up to the face. The platform of flints on which this skeleton rested appeared to have been carefully laid, the flints themselves being floorstone nodules, and slabs of tabular flint, which traverses the semi-vertical joint planes met with in the mine shafts of the area. None of the flints showed any indication of having been submitted to flaking.

To the west of the bones, behind the shoulders, was a leaf shaped arrowhead made from a flake of mine flint. The arrowhead had been worked by pressure flaking with a bone punch. A foot further to the west lay a large chopper and an ovate implement. To the north, near the head, lay a very finely finished Cissbury type axe or celt of perfect shape and workmanship. Beside it lay a more roughly made axe of the same kind. With the axes was a single tusk of wild boar. To the east of the bones lay a large rough axe of Cissbury type. Distributed among the bones were a number of dead land snails of two species, *Helix nemoralis* and *Cyclostoma elegans*. To the south and east were some teeth of Ox (*Bos Longifrons*) and Pig (*Sus scrofa*).

At a point five feet south-east of the centre of the mound, and one foot beneath the surface, occupying a space four feet square and separated from the interment previously described by about two feet of chalk and soil, was the skeleton of a young woman with unerupted fourth molars. This skeleton lay upon slightly

> compacted chalk rubble and soil and was in a somewhat better state of preservation, this being possibly due to the better drainage afforded by the material on which the body had been interred. So far as could be ascertained from the position of the bones and lower jaw, the body had been interred in the contracted position, on the left side, with the head to the north and the face to the east, the hands in this case being to the knees.
>
> Over the woman's lower jaw and teeth lay a large block of tabular flint. This slab was marked on the underside with an incomplete circle deeply incised through the crust, the incised portion being patinated dead white. The horns of the incomplete circle were to the north and the circle faced downwards on the jaw. The circle had apparently been produced by a very large thermal fracture, though whether this had been obtained by artificial means or produced by a natural agency, it is impossible to say. Its presence was undoubtedly of funerary importance and appears to be an instance of the cult of the incomplete circle or crescent so often met with and associated with ancient burials and primitive folklore. A number of large blocks of tabular flint overlay the other bones of the woman. A quantity of dead land snails of the same species as those that accompanied the previous interment were found among the bones. Immediately to the north of the skeleton, near the head, lay a rough Cissbury type axe and some teeth of ox and pig.
>
> Distributed over a wide area to the south and east of the mound's centre were the thoroughly cremated bones of a third individual. These burnt bones were scattered, some among the skeleton of interment 1, some among the skeleton of the woman, and some fragments beyond the area occupied by the flint working debris which overlay the interments. It would appear that this cremation was a contemporary interment scattered ceremonially. The three interments, over which the barrow had been raised, were all on the level of the natural contour of the hillside. Below this level, the west and central portion of the mound completely overlay the infilled shaft of a flint mine. This mine consisted of a shallow pit, sunk into the chalk to a depth of three and a half feet below the natural surface, that is four and a half feet below the apex of the barrow. The infilling of this pit consisted of unstratified chalk rubble, slightly compacted in its upper part by water, but nowhere separately distinguishable from the material of the mound above (Worthing Museum Acc. No. 1961/1585).

Few of the finds from Barrow 3 appear to have survived to the present day. Only two axe roughouts, one flaked axe and a single hammerstone exist in Worthing Museum, while the human skeletal remains appear ultimately to have become victims of the Second World War, being destroyed during a bombing raid on London in 1941 which gutted the Royal College of Surgeons where they were being stored.

Pull and Sainsbury were convinced of the stratigraphic relationship of Barrow 3, in that it had been constructed almost immediately after the infilling of Shaft 5 and very shortly before the excavation of another mine (as demonstrated by the floorstone deposit overlying the burials). Pull later emphasised this point more strongly:

> The excavation of Shaft 5 and Barrow 3 demonstrated that the pit and burial mound were contemporary. Mine Shaft 5 was worked out by the miners and filled in with unstratified chalk rubble to the lip. The infilling had settled down, but had had no time to become weathered, or for any trace of rainwash to form before the site was chosen for a burial place (Pull 1932a, 69–70).

There would seem, on present evidence, very little reason to doubt such a conclusion, though it is unfortunate that the inked section of Barrow 3 appears to show Shaft 5 cutting through the central portion of the overlying mound (apparently indicating that the mound was constructed before the mine). Pull's text states that this was not the true relationship, so the drawing must presumably illustrate the full area of shaft fill removed prior to the detailed recording of Barrow deposits in section.

Mound 3 appears very similar to Barrow 1, in that both were constructed over recently filled mine shafts and both were built predominantly from mined chalk and flint rubble, being roofed with a deposit of unutilised floorstone nodules. The only significant difference in appearance was that Barrow 1 had at some time subsided into the collapsing mine beneath it. The nature of artefact deposition within Mound 3 would however appear markedly different. Here two inhumations and a cremation were retrieved, one of the burials apparently resting upon a platform of floorstone material. If this platform is interpreted as a structural element, and not perhaps an earlier attempt at capping (perhaps of the mine itself), then it is hard to see how it may have functioned. Interpretation is not helped by the non-appearance of the platform on the inked section drawing or upon any other illustrative material from the Blackpatch excavation. Its full nature and extent is therefore difficult to gauge, but it may have performed a use only at the time of the deposition of human bodies, perhaps functioning as a ritual or ceremonial layer of good quality mine flint (perhaps a ceremonial knapping floor) deliberately returned to the soil, together with two representatives, male and female, of the then contemporary community. If this is the case, then the significance of corpse positioning, the male placed upon the flint deposit, the female away to the south-east, is unclear.

It is also uncertain how the recorded cremation relates to the two skeletons. Pull and Sainsbury seem to suggest that all three deposits were broadly contemporary. Certainly, the absence of any apparent stratigraphic disruption within the upper level of Mound 3 would indicate that the cremation was probably set down before the floorstone capping was added to the earthwork. However, the fact that at least some of the burnt bone observed within layers above the inhumations would suggest that it was incorporated after these particular burials were set down. How much later is, in the absence of clearly associated artefacts, open for debate, but it is possible that with Barrow 3 we are seeing the end product of at least three distinct phases of mound construction: the construction of a platform or layer of floorstone nodules over a newly backfilled mine and the setting out of corpses and other deposits on or around it; covering of these deposits with large quantities of waste, including knapping debris, charcoal, burnt flint and at least one cremation; the more complete covering of this deposit with mine excavated spoil including the final roofing with floorstone.

Just how many of the artefacts recovered from within and around the human remains deposits may be viewed as grave goods is also unfortunately unclear, especially as all appear to have been covered with a large quantity of knapping waste. At best the artefacts, consisting of two flint axes, a leaf shaped arrowhead, a boars tusk and ox and pig teeth around the male, a single axe and some teeth of ox and pig around the female, may only really be described as being spatially associated with the bodies. It is possible that the material in question represents the debris of some residual activity at the site of the backfilled mine (and therefore unrelated to the purpose of the mound) or even that the artefacts themselves represent ritual items, of just as much significance to the people that deposited them, as the human remains. The significance of the mound, and the problem of defining what exactly constitutes a barrow or a mound containing special items (some of which just happen to be human bodies or body parts), is discussed further under individual Barrow descriptions and also within the main conclusion.

Barrow 4

By J. H. Pull and C. E. Sainsbury

Barrow 4 was situated on the crest of the ridge immediately to the west of that occupied by the flint mines. Like Barrows 1 to 3, it was positioned on the west side of the ancient road, which traverses the shoulder of the hill. Barrow 4 was a bowl shaped barrow very similar in structure to Barrow 2, that is to say a low, roughly circular grass grown mound. Its diameter east and west was 32 feet, and north south 36 feet. Its maximum height above the natural surface was one foot. Its centre was depressed to a depth of six inches over a radius of four feet. The body of the mound was found to be composed of chalk, soil and flints, the flints predominating (figure 42).

At the centre was a large oval grave measuring eight feet by five feet, sunk to a depth of two and a half feet below the mound's centre, that is to a depth of two feet into the chalk rock below the surface of the hillside. The longer axis of the grave lay in a direction west by north and east by south. The sides of the grave were vertical, or nearly so, and its bottom roughly flat; though somewhat lower in the centre. The upper portion of the grave was filled beneath the turf to a depth of nine inches with surface soil. Below this again was a mass of loose flints, the interstices between which were not filled in. Scattered among these flints were many portions of the skeleton of a fully developed man. The bones were in a comparatively good state of preservation, but were much broken and disordered and many of them missing. The bones recovered comprised half of the pelvis, the ulna and radius of one arm, a portion of one femur, two halves of a humerus, one tooth and a small fragment of skull, several phalanges, one scapula and several pieces of ribs.

It was quite clear that the grave had at some time been opened and this skeleton, for there appeared to be the remains of but one individual, had at that time been broken up and either partially removed, or, what seems more probable, so reburied as to cause portions of the bones to come into contact with vegetable humus or other matter which would promote the rate of their entire decay. Of course there is always the possibility that the bones were disjointed and scattered

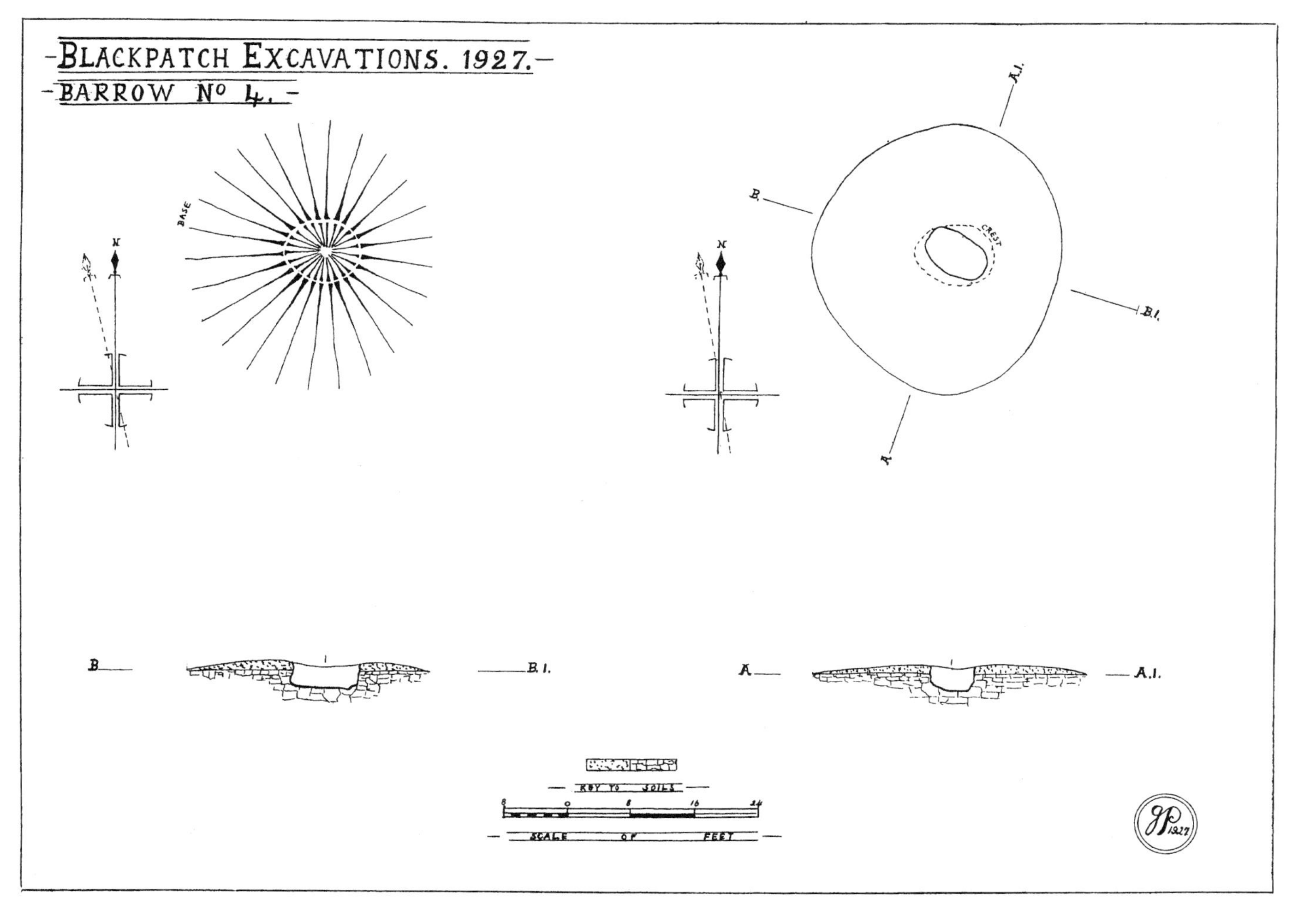

Figure 42. Blackpatch Barrow 4: (clockwise from top left) pre-excavation surface hachure plan, post excavation feature plan and two section drawings incorporating central feature profile (© Worthing Museum and Art Gallery).

> ceremonially at the time they were interred. Among the flints at the eastern end of the grave was a large triangular arrowhead made from a simple flake, the trimming having been effected by bone punch work. Also an oval knife made from a flake, with a thick back and bone punched along one edge. The tooth of an ox was lying near this knife. At the western end of the grave were several flint flakes and a rough flint knife, also struck core of mine flint to which the flakes did not fit. All these flakes and artefacts were of the floorstone quality flint evidently obtained from the mines nearby.
>
> The rough flints which formed the grave filling and structural material of the mound above were not mine flint, but rough flints which had been gathered from the surrounding hill surface. These flints differ from mine flint in their exterior surfaces through weathering and exposure. Over the bottom of the grave, to a depth of six inches, was clean small chalk rubble, which had apparently not been lifted since the primary interment was made. This rubble was devoid of any article of human workmanship.
>
> Judging from the ancient appearance of the fractures of the bones of the interment, and from the fact that such a depth of surface soil was intact above the grave, it would seem that the disturbance of the skeleton, which had lain therein, was far from recent. We cannot lay this disturbance at the door of any modern curiosity hunter, so many of whom in the past 100 years have made unrecorded excavations for the confusing of posterity. The water compacted condition of this material with which the upper portion of this grave was sealed also points to an early date for the presumed disturbance. It is of course possible that the disturbance was made by the insertion of a secondary burial in the mound, the bones of which had entirely gone to decay. It is worthy of notice that the mound was slightly elongated at right angles to the direction of the longer axis of the grave, as was also the case with Barrow 2. Like Barrow 2, the mound differed from Barrows 1 and 3 in being devoid of flint roofing and containing no burials by cremation.
>
> On the surface, a few yards to the east of Barrow 4 was found a single fragment of Beaker pottery and one of those peculiar egg-shaped serrated lumps of chalk identical with those found associated with the interments in Barrows 1 and 2. A quantity of dead land shells, including *Helix nemoralis* and *Cyclostoma elegans* were found associated with the bones in Barrow 4 (Worthing Museum Acc. No. 1961/1585).

The nature of Barrow 4 and its contents again poses a number of problems with regard to interpretation. The central burial deposit would appear to represent the disarticulated remains of a single adult male, though the question must remain as to whether this represents the condition of the body at the time of interment. Pull and Sainsbury, as noted above, suggested a variety of ways in which the skeleton could have reached this state of decay, including the possibility that it had been disjointed prior to burial. By the time Pull published the account of the excavation in The Flint Miners of Blackpatch, this interpretation had been discounted in favour of the suggestion that the whole deposit had been 'at some time been reopened and its primary interment broken up' (Pull 1932a, 73).

This is not beyond the realms of possibility, for the section drawing produced for Barrow 4 appears to indicate that the pit then containing the skeleton had been cut from, or close to, the modern ground level, making it secondary to the period of mound construction, while the mound, in section, also seems to possess the dished centre characteristic of later disturbance (It must be pointed out, however, that a similar relationship is incorrectly shown on the original drawing for the cut sealed beneath Barrow 3 at Blackpatch). Such disturbance could have resulted from either the insertion of a secondary burial or ritual deposit, since destroyed, an unrecorded antiquarian investigation, post-prehistoric flint quarrying, or the inward collapse of the whole structure. Any of these events could have disrupted the skeletal remains contained within the mound to the level recorded by Pull and Sainsbury.

Welch has suggested that the postulated secondary disturbance to the Barrow 4 skeleton could have been caused by the insertion of a Saxon burial deposit, such as that recorded from Barrows 2 and 11 (Welch 1983, 459). It seems unlikely that any such secondary deposit would have escaped modern detection however, even if damaged by chemical or agricultural erosion. Another problem with the theory of later disturbance is the total lack of post-prehistoric artefacts recovered from the central cut, though if such disruption were caused by the poorer elements of society (cf. the flint quarry pits cut by Victorian workhouse inmates at Wolstonbury Hill: Curwen 1930b), then the general absence of artefacts would not be surprising. Alternatively the central pit within Barrow 4 could be seen as a secondary prehistoric feature, cut into an existing mound of chalk rubble, specifically to inter the partial disarticulated remains of an individual (disarticulated remains being a feature within Shaft 4, Barrow 12 and possibly Barrows 2 and 9). Such an interpretation would place the remains more squarely within a Neolithic context, perhaps making them contemporary with the arrowhead, flakes and knives also retrieved from pit fill.

The body of the mound, into which the pit containing human remains had been cut, appears to have been formed, at least in part, by chalk and flint rubble. The clear absence of a quarry ditch around the mound could indicate that the rubble was derived from elsewhere on site, perhaps from a contemporary working mine or perhaps from the reuse of an existing spoil heap. No evidence of mine-flint 'capping', such as recorded within Barrows 1, 3, 5, 6, 7 and 9 at Blackpatch, was noted from Barrow 4, the material overlying the human remains being represented by nodules of surface flint. Such an observation could be taken to indicate that this structure was not contemporary with a significant phase of mining activity.

Barrow 5

By J. H. Pull and C. E. Sainsbury

Barrow 5 was situated some 200 feet to the east of the ancient road, on the crest of the spur of the hill occupied by the flint mines. It was a bowl barrow and consisted of a low circular mound 21 feet in diameter. Its total height was nine inches above the surrounding surface and its apex over a radius of four feet from its centre was somewhat flattened (figure 43). The mound itself was composed of soil and small chalk. Like Barrows 1 and 3 it was totally roofed, or capped, with a layer of flint

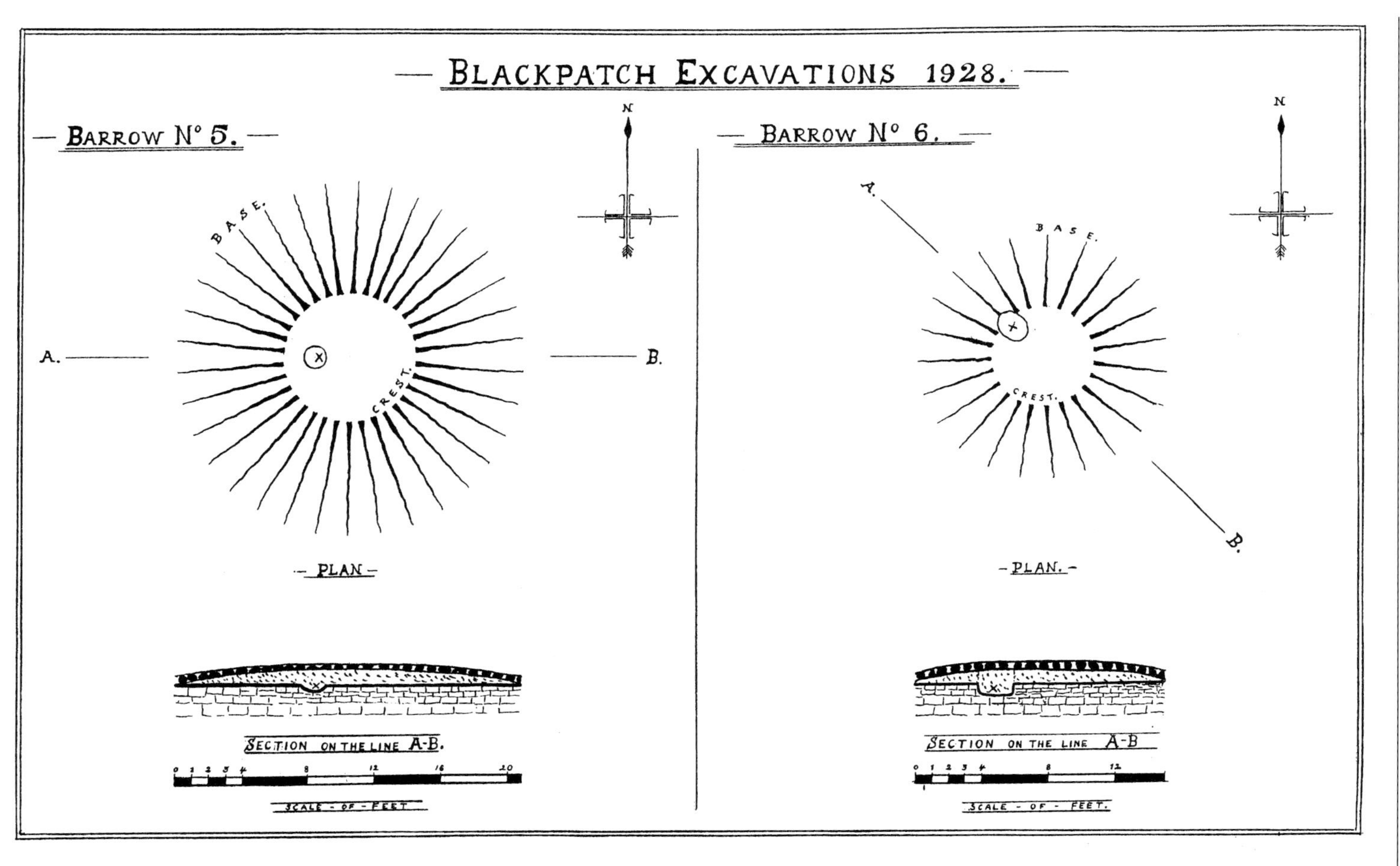

Figure 43. Blackpatch Barrows 5 and 6: pre-excavation surface hachure plans incorporating the positions of subsurface features, and sections (© Worthing Museum and Art Gallery).

nodules. The barrow had no encircling ditch nor was there any visible hollow in the hill surface anywhere near. The presence of chalk indicated that the mound had evidently been constructed from material gathered in the neighbourhood of the mines. The flint capping which covered the mound to its base had certainly been obtained from the pits, for it consisted entirely of the characteristic floorstone nodules. Thick moss and turf covered the whole.

Beneath the mound at a point two feet west of its centre was a shallow depression of natural origin in the surface of the chalk rock. This measured one foot across and was but six inches deep. In the centre of this saucer shaped cavity was an urn standing upright of cineary type with overhanging rim. The urn is very small, being but 4 and a half inches high. The rim is ornamented by a reticulated or diamond pattern set within two encircling lines, the whole pattern having been produced by the impress of twisted thong or twisted string before the clay was fired. Roots descending from the turf had penetrated and cracked the urn, but the closely packed surrounding soil had held it in position. Over the top had been placed, as a cover, a large flat flint. The urn itself was empty of soil and contained but a single flint flake struck from the outer crust of a nodule. This flake was serrated by pressure flaking the edges and had centrally upon its face a thermal fracture of three cup-shaped pits arranged triangularly so as to produce a likeness to a cloverleaf.

Many unburnt flakes of mine flint were strewn around the urn, and above its cover stone. Six inches to the east of the urn and from that point to one foot east of it, were a quantity of thoroughly cremated human bones and skull fragments, arranged in a crescent, the horns of the crescent pointing westwards towards the urn. Among these bones was a small pebble of whitish yellow quartz and a small fine flint blade with semi circular hollows worn in both cutting edges as if it had served the purpose of an arrow or spear shaft trimmer. To the south of the interment were two leaf shaped arrowheads manufactured from flint flakes and an elongated water worn pebble of black flint. The hollow in which the urn stood and the area round the bones was packed with fine soil, admixed with charcoal. The body represented by the calcined bones had not been burnt within the area of the mound.

At the centre and toward the south-west, the capping of flint nodules was covered, and also underlayed, with many flint flakes and fine chippings. These occurred for the most part in little heaps. The presence of these flakes mixed with very fine chippings and splinters which mark the final stages of implement manufacture, implies that the flaking had been effected upon the spot, both during and after the laying of the flint roofing of the mound. We have here, apparently, a definite instance of the practice of flaking flints at the burial of the deceased, a custom prevalent among the builders of the round barrows. It would appear, from the fact that the pottery urn found accompanying the interment represented by the burnt bones, but not containing any of them, though of cineary type, had been intended in this instance to take the place of either a drinking cup or a food vessel. Next probably a drinking cup was intended (Worthing Museum Acc. No. 1961/1585).

The 'overhanging rim' (or collared) urn, survives in Worthing Museum (Acc. No 570: Longworth 1984, 275). The whereabouts of the flint artefacts described by Pull and Sainsbury, unfortunately remain unknown. As with the majority of barrows at Blackpatch, it would appear that Mound 5 was constructed primarily from mining debris. Although situated some 60m to the east of the main block of recorded mines, there is no reason why excavated spoil from a mine could not be shifted any distance to a selected spot in order to create such an earthwork, especially if moving spoil proved easier than digging a new quarry ditch or pit closer to the desired site (this is of course assuming that there was not originally an area of mining in closer proximity to the mound). In any case it would appear that it was the mined debris itself that was vital for the construction of the majority of the Blackpatch barrows, especially with regard to floorstone capping. The presence of this capping, when combined with the significant quantity of knapping debris within and above mound 5, would support the argument that the structure was assembled during a major phase of prehistoric mining.

The cremation and collared urn do not appear to have been central to the positioning of the covering rubble mound, assuming, of course, that the mound had largely retained its original shape. The hollow containing the urn does not sound natural in this sense, if it were, the position of the vessel within it would be extremely fortuitous!. This may cause problems if one is looking at the mound in the sense of a conventional burial mound or barrow, but not if one is looking at the earthwork as representing a structured series of soils, obtained from the nearby mines, each containing ritually charged material, including human body parts and/or burials. It is assumed that the cremation deposit and the collared urn from Mound 5 are contemporary, with the urn perhaps representing an accessory vessel. If this is the case then a number of the flint tools within the mound (especially the Earlier Neolithic leaf-shaped arrowheads), could well represent residual elements from an earlier phase of activity. Alternatively, it could of course be that the collared urn is a secondary insertion into an existing Early Neolithic mound. Such an intrusion, if cut through the centre of an existing cremation deposit, could explain the cremation's 'horn-like' appearance. The earthwork section, when combined with Pull and Sainsbury's text, would, however, suggest that there had been no such disturbance within the upper flint capping of the mound and that cremation, urn and the mound itself were all contemporary.

Barrow 6

By J. H. Pull and C. E. Sainsbury

Situated about 100 yards north-east from the Barrow 5, was Barrow 6, a bowl barrow. It consisted of an almost perfectly circular mound, with a diameter of 15 feet, and a maximum height of nine inches. Its top was flattened over a radius of three feet from its centre (figure 43). The mound was entirely capped, or roofed, with a closely laid layer of flint nodules. These flints, which formed the exterior casing, were of floorstone quality, being derived from the nearby mines. The interstices between them were packed with surface mould and the whole covered with a thick layer of turf and moss. The body of the mound beneath the capping was composed almost entirely of flints and mould with a little small chalk. The flints that formed the body of the mound were of two kinds, some derived from the mines, and some weathered and broken, which had been gathered from the surface of the hillside. Three inches of natural surface mould existed below the base of the mound and, beneath that, three inches of chalk silt.

At a point one and a half feet north-west of the mound's centre was an oval hole sunk into the chalk rock by artificial means. The longer central axis of this hole had a direction north-west and south-east. The hole measured two feet by one and a half feet from edge to edge, and was one and a quarter feet in depth below the natural contour of the hill surface. Its sides were vertical, its bottom irregular and perforated by natural pipings in the chalk rock. The hole was filled to its surface with fine black mould mixed with large quantities of charcoal, and a comparatively large quantity of calcined human bones and skull fragments. These burnt bones represented an interment after cremation. Among the charcoal and bones in the hole were numerous flint flakes and chippings, some of which were burnt. Several small flint pebbles that had passed through the fire and a few fire reddened and burnt flints occurred among the bones, as did also a single small fragment of Beaker pottery and a bone pin. The material of the mound immediately above the cist, and over a radius of two feet from it, was composed of thoroughly burnt flints mixed with a few unburnt ones. Flint flakes, pebbles and chipped pieces occurred among these. No trace of charcoal or bones was met with outside the lip of the oval hole. Three feet to the south-east of the interment was a quantity of unburnt flint flakes and chippings, including a leaf shaped arrowhead.

It is noteworthy that no recognisable shells of land mollusca occurred throughout this barrow. This was also the case in Barrow 5. The area of marked mollusca zones appears to be limited to the confines of the mining area. The occurrence of mollusca in the barrows seems to be only in relation to burials by inhumation (Worthing Museum Acc. No. 1961/1585).

None of the artefacts recorded by Pull and Sainsbury as having come from Barrow 6 can be traced today, though illustrations of some of the flint tools were made by Pull at the time of their discovery. The absence of the material is particularly unfortunate considering the presence and apparent nature of the bone pin and Beaker sherd retrieved from 'close to' the cremation deposit.

Mound 6 bears a striking resemblance to Barrow 5 at Blackpatch. Both earthworks consist of small bowl-shaped, mine rubble mounds capped with a layer of floorstone. Both cover off-centre cremation deposits and both cremations are associated with Late Neolithic/Early Bronze Age pottery (in the case of Barrow 6 a single Beaker sherd). Pull later comments in on the 'extraordinary duplication of objects associated with the interments in Barrows 5 and 6' (Pull 1932a, 77). These artefacts (illustrated in plate 16 of the 1932a publication), appear to have been the only material directly retrieved from the 'grave' fill of either barrow and consist of two leaf-shaped projectile points, two small double-edged blades, two oval black pebbles and a firecracked flint flake.

As with Barrow 5, the cremation deposit beneath the mound may represent a secondary insertion into a pre-existing dump of mine upcast. This could explain some of the potentially earlier flintwork within the mound (unless the flint is residual), and also perhaps the off-centre positioning of the internal cremations. If the burial from Barrow 6 is secondary, something which Pull may well have been trying to indicate in the section drawing, then it is secondary only to the primary dump of mined flint, for the floorstone capping above certainly does not appear to have been significantly disturbed. This could be taken as suggesting that Barrow 5 was originally a simple dump of mine debris that was modified at some later date by the insertion of a series of special deposits (including at least one cremation) and the covering with floorstone flint. Whatever the interpretation it would seem, from the evidence of the mound capping at least, that significant mining activity was still being conducted at Blackpatch at the time the cremation burial and Beaker sherd were deposited.

Barrow 7

By J. H. Pull and C. E. Sainsbury

Barrow 7 was situated on the east side of the ancient road, 76 yards south-east of Barrow 2. It was a bowl barrow, almost perfectly circular, 20 feet in diameter and nine inches high (figure 44). It had no surrounding ditch and was flattened to within three feet of its edge. The low mound was composed of chalk and soil, and was totally roofed or covered by a single layer of large flints, which had been obtained from the nearby mines. Among these flints were several rough implements. About the centre, both above and beneath the material of the roofing, were scattered quantities of flint flakes and fine chippings. Surface soil and turf covered the whole.

At the centre of the mound was a slight saucer-shaped hollow, which had been excavated out of the face of the chalk rock. This hollow was two feet in diameter and three inches deep. Over it lay the much-decayed skeleton of a young person of uncertain sex. The body had been interred in the contracted position on the right side with the face to the east, the hands being up to the face. Before the face were two small leaf-shaped flint flakes and some fragments of a pottery vessel which had possessed on overhanging rim. The rim had been ornamented with a reticulated pattern set within two encircling lines. This ornament had been produced with some sharp pointed instrument. Behind the head were some burnt flints. Behind the back was an elongated object of carefully smoothed chalk, much worn down on one face as though by continual rubbing. A handful of pieces of sandstone and a very fine oval tool of mine flint lay with this.

None of the artefacts recovered from Mound 7 can be traced today, though as with Barrow 6, some drawings were made by Pull at the time of their discovery. One such illustration, of the collared ('overhanging rim') urn has aided identification (Secondary series, SE style, form BII: Longworth 1984; 275). The chalk cylinder may have been similar to one retrieved from Shaft 1 at Blackpatch (Pye 1968, 18).

Flint roofing is evident once again at one of the Barrow sites, but Pull does not elaborate as to whether this is a deposit of floorstone comparable with the capping noted at Barrows 1, 3, 5 and 6. The observation that 'several rough implements' (possibly axe roughouts) were recorded 'above and beneath this thin deposit' may

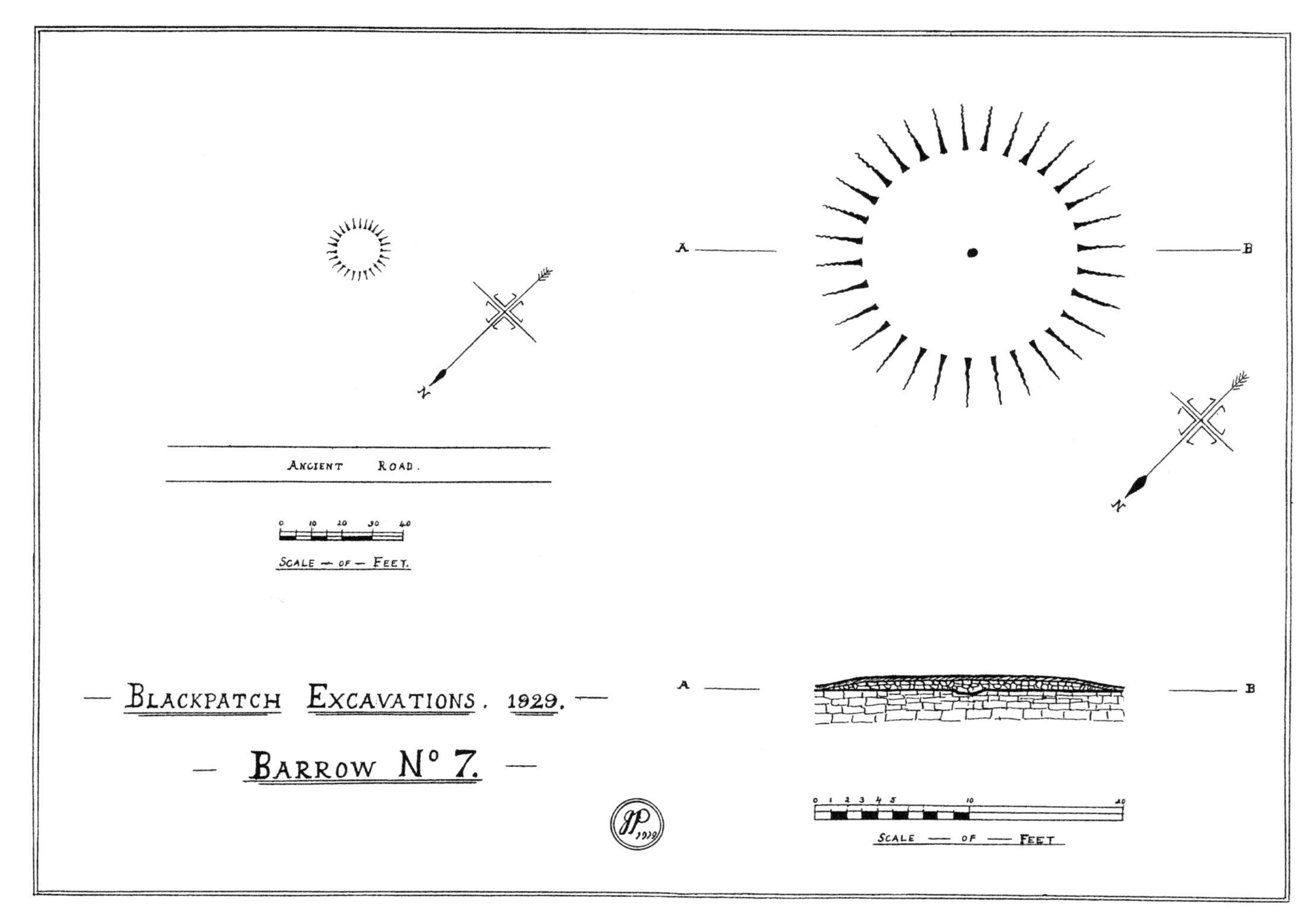

Figure 44. Blackpatch Barrow 7: pre-excavation surface hachure plans, one to the right incorporating subsurface detail (human bone deposits), and section (© Worthing Museum and Art Gallery).

argue against it being floorstone, assuming of course that the finds represent residual material scooped up with the flint. This is hardly conclusive and the recorded objects may represent evidence of in-situ knapping. The central position of the inhumation, in relation to the overlying mound, and the fact that it did not appear to be a secondary insertion through existing deposits, may suggest that mound, burial and collared urn were all contemporary. The nature of the large 'mine obtained' flints, within and covering the mound, would further indicate that both the burial and the collared urn were set down at a time of significant flint extraction.

Barrow 8

> *By J. H. Pull and C. E. Sainsbury*
> Barrow 8 was situated north-east of Barrow 2, 14 feet from the western border of the ancient road. It was, like Barrow 7, a bowl barrow 12 feet in diameter and six inches in height (figure 45). The mound had been raised over a saucer shaped excavation in the chalk rock. This hollow was six feet across, and was filled to the brim with loose chalk. Over this hollow, and within the boundary of its rim, were found the much-decayed remains of a pottery vessel. The vessel had been a very small one, four or five inches high, and had possessed an overhanging rim ornamented with a pattern consisting of a single series of inverted chevrons set within two encircling lines, the pattern having been produced with twisted thong. Some burnt flints, a scraper, a very fine oval tool and quantities of flint flakes were also distributed round the lip of the central hollow. The body of the mound consisted entirely of large flints from the mines. No trace of an interment was found, and we can only conclude that any interment that had been present, was by inhumation and had gone entirely to decay. The mound had never been interfered with and the less destructible funeral furniture had remained intact (Worthing Museum Acc. No. 1961/1585).

Of the artefacts recorded as having been retrieved from Barrow 8, only a core and a single flake appear to have survived to the present day. The collared ('overhanging rim') urn was identified by Longworth (as an unclassified series, SE style, form BII: Longworth 1984, 275) from an original drawing made by Pull (1932a; plate 12). The fact that this urn was in a bad state of preservation at the time of its discovery is suggested by Pull's later comment that it was 'very poorly fired and on drying had crumbled to pieces' (Pull 1932a, 80).

Whether the mound had originally contained a burial deposit is a matter for debate. Pull and Sainsbury have noted that if there had been an interment it may have decayed completely. Pull elaborated further when he noted that:

> the fact that the mound was constructed entirely of loose flints, originally without any matrix allowing free access to air and water, would in itself be sufficient to account for the disintegration of the bone (Pull 1932a, 80).

This may be true, but we must be wary of automatically assuming that every recorded mound site at Blackpatch would have covered human burials. It has already been

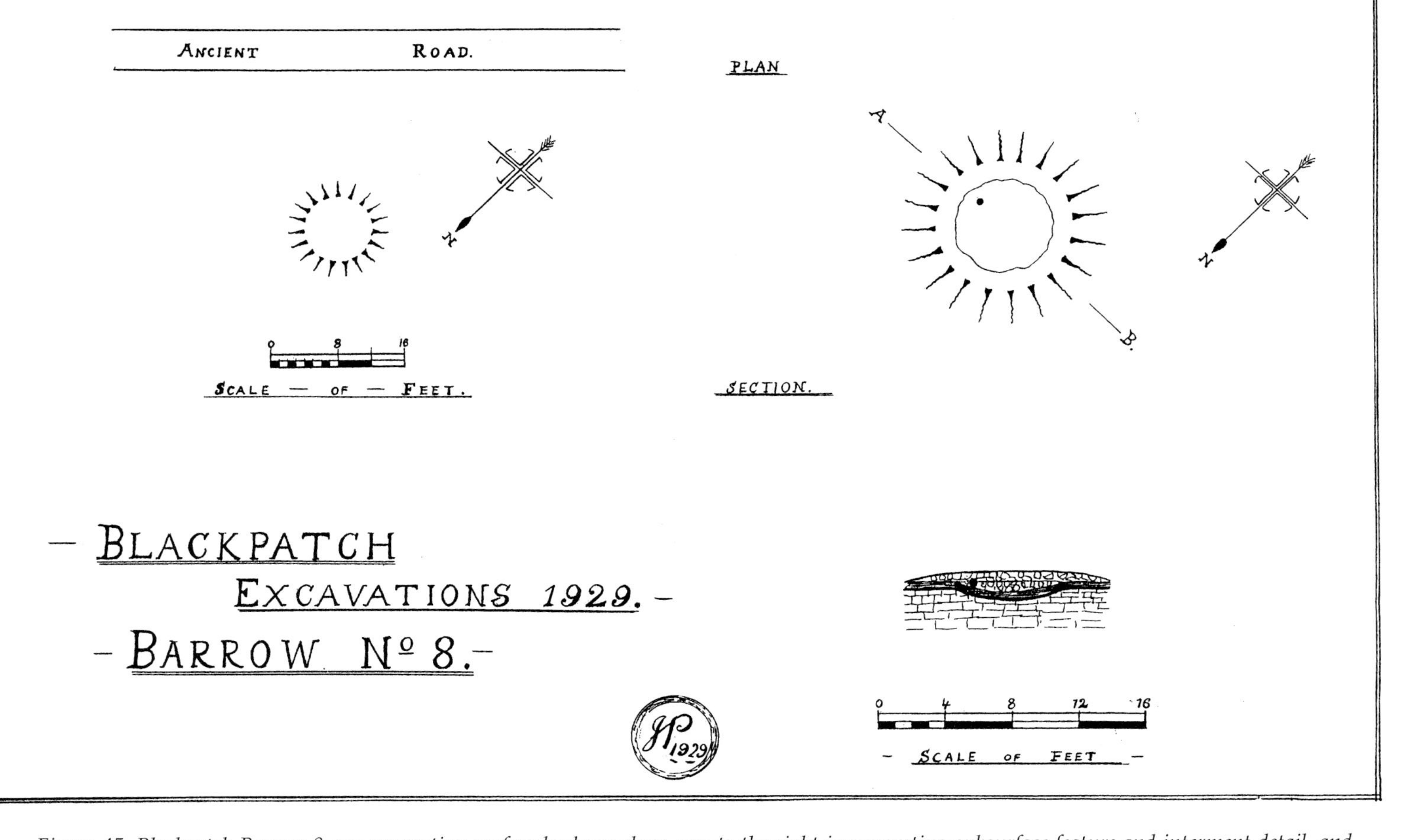

Figure 45. Blackpatch Barrow 8: pre-excavation surface hachure plans, one to the right incorporating subsurface feature and interment detail, and section (© Worthing Museum and Art Gallery).

noted that a significant number of the Blackpatch mounds are not strictly barrows, in the sense that they possessed single primary interments, but may more realistically be viewed as structured mounds of mine debris containing special artefact assemblages, some of which just happened to be burials, bodies or body parts. Absence of human remains within such a mound should not therefore create problems with regard to interpretation. Barrow 8, the smallest independent earthwork feature excavated by Pull and his colleagues at Blackpatch, may in this sense be viewed as a dump of mine flint (not apparently floorstone) set over a hollow or pit containing a significant deposit of knapping debris, firecracked flint, tools and a small collared urn.

Barrow 9

By J. H. Pull and C. E. Sainsbury

This barrow was situated on the east side of the ancient road, about midway between Barrows 5 and 6. It belonged to a class of burial monument known as ring barrows. The structure differed from the round barrows in the neighbour-hood, and was to some extent peculiar. Barrow 9 consisted, not of a mound, but of a circular area of the hill surface enclosed by a simple, uninterrupted trench (figure 46). The material excavated from this trench had been thrown outward. The space enclosed within the trench was 40 feet in diameter. It was not raised above the present level of the hillslope, nor had it been disturbed below the surface. Repeated sections disclosed its interior composition: Three inches of turf and nine inches of surface mould mixed with surface flints; below this were six inches of loose chalk representing the natural weathered face of the chalk rock.

The surrounding trench was three feet in width and one foot nine inches in depth. It had been made by digging out the natural surface of the hill down to the face of the chalk rock, the material excavated having been

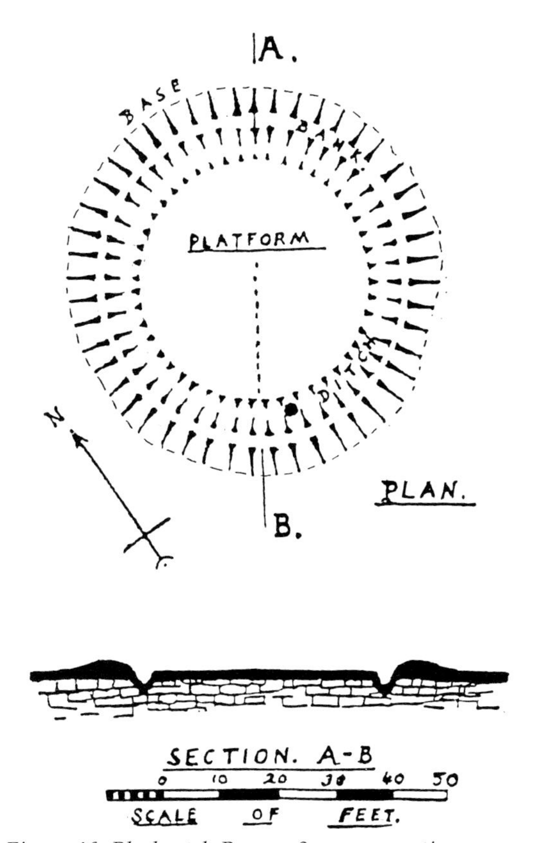

Figure 46. Blackpatch Barrow 9: pre-excavation surface hachure plan including the position of subsurface human bone deposit, and profile (© Worthing Museum and Art Gallery).

> thrown outward to form a low outer bank. This bank was 10 feet in width, thus brining the total outside diameter of the barrow up to 66 feet. The infilling of the trench was of great interest. At the bottom were three inches of chalk silt. Over this, and occupying the full width, the trench was paved with a nine inch layer of closely laid nodules of flint extracted from the adjacent mines. The interstices between these flints were packed with surface mould. The top of the trench was filled with this mould to a further depth of nine inches. The outer embankment, as one would expect, consisted of a mixture of surface mould, chalk and flints.
>
> A little to the east of the centre of the area enclosed by the ditch were found fragments of bones and teeth of ox, pig and sheep. With these bones were some burnt flints and two flint knives. In the north-west area of the ditch, beneath the flint paving, were some fragments of pottery, including the rim of an urn which had possessed an overhanging lip and had been ornamented by an impression of the finger nail. In the western portion of the ditch, also beneath the flint pavement, were found a rough celt of Cissbury type, half of another, a core, some used flakes, a flint knife, and a large quantity of flakes and chippings, all of the quality flint derived from the mines nearby.
>
> In the southern portion of the ditch, also beneath the pavement, over an area of about six feet, were some much decayed human bones, some fragments of red deer antler, three very fine scrapers, burnt stones, and fragments of a pottery vessel. This ceramic had most probably belonged to the Beaker or drinking vessel class. The fragments were highly ornamented, with a pattern of incised lines produced by the application of some sharp pointed instrument. The decayed human bones indicate the presence of an interment. The associated pottery agrees in paste texture and ornament with what has been found in the adjacent barrows. The flint implements are identical in style and workmanship with those found in the flint mines and in the dwelling sites (Worthing Museum Acc. No. 1961/1585).

Of the material recovered from Barrow 9, only three flint artefacts, a flake and two scrapers, survive within the Worthing Museum. The whereabouts of the collared (overhanging rim) urn sherds, Beaker fragments, faunal and human remains are at present unknown.

Barrow 9 is probably the most intriguing of all the mound sites investigated by Pull and Sainsbury at Blackpatch. The site, though it does contain human burial elements, is clearly not a barrow in the conventional sense. In fact the structural morphology of the earthwork, with its lack of a central mound or burial and its possession of a circular ditch with an external bank, could be taken to indicate affinities with the class of non-utilitarian Later Neolithic monuments known as henges. At least one such earthwork enclosure has been positively identified in Sussex, at Mile Oak north of Portslade (Russell in Press a) and other, smaller sites are also indicated at Itford Hill, Steyning, Playden and Cock Hill (Cleal 1982; Russell 1996a, 18–20, 22–3, 25–7). Lack of a clear point of entrance or orientation for Blackpatch Barrow 9 however, makes clear identification or affiliation impossible.

As with a number of the mounded Barrow sites at Blackpatch (namely Barrows 1, 3, 5, 6 and 7) the final phase of activity at Barrow 9 was marked by the deposition of floorstone, emphatically terminating the structure. This flint covering occurred only after the site had been in use for some time, allowing for the partial silting of the ditch and for a series of structured deposits, including flintwork, pottery and disarticulated human and animal remains, to be set down. The presence of the floorstone flint 'pavement' would suggest that the enclosure constituting Barrow 9 was contemporary with one of the major periods of prehistoric flint extraction at Blackpatch.

Barrow 10

By J. H. Pull and C. E. Sainsbury

> Barrow 10 was situated on the south face of the hill slope, overlooking Barrows 7, 8 and 9. It was a bowl barrow, 32 feet in diameter and three feet in height. The mound was composed of soil and clay with flints. It had no flint roofing. At the centre was an oblong grave, excavated in the chalk rock to a depth of two and a quarter feet below the natural surface. The grave was seven feet in length and two and a half feet wide. It was filled with clay and chalk. The longer axis of the grave had a direction east and west, and upon the bottom were the partially decayed bones of a fully developed man of middle age. The skeleton lay extended at full length on the back with the head to the west and the feet to the east. The face was looking directly upward. The left arm was extended by the side, the right was crossed over the body towards the left thigh. It seems probable that the man, whose skeleton this was, had met a violent death, for the left thigh had been completely severed half way up the shaft, the dismembered femur lying at an angle to the pelvis.
>
> This interment was undoubtedly of Saxon date. The type of grave, the position of the skeleton, and the form of the skull make that quite evident. It may be that the barrow itself was of Saxon construction and was not a mound carried over from the Beaker period. One cannot, however, be certain of this, for the centre of the mound, and for some feet to the north of the centre, showed signs of having been disturbed below the hill surface. The presence of clay, which here overlies the hilltop in irregular patches, rendered it impossible to form any opinion as to the cause or nature of the disturbance (Worthing Museum Acc. No. 1961/1585).

Although none of the artefacts recorded from Barrow 10 could be traced at the time of writing, there can be little doubt that the main burial here was of Saxon origin, Saxon graves having also been recorded from Barrows 2 and 12 at Blackpatch. Interestingly these individuals may also have either died violently or have been decapitated shortly after death, perhaps indicating victims of the Saxon criminal justice system (cf. Reynolds 1998). The question remains, however, as to whether the structure of Barrow 10 itself may also be attributed to the Saxon period. Certainly the mound appears quite unlike any of the other recorded barrows at Blackpatch, being built of soil and clay with flint rather than mined flint and chalk, a fact which could be explained as denoting some chronological variance.

Unfortunately no detailed plan or section of Barrow 10 could be located at the time of writing, so it has not been possible to verify whether the Saxon grave had been inserted into the stratigraphy of an existing prehistoric mound (such as had happened at Barrow 2) or whether both were broadly contemporary. Despite this, the comments of Pull and Sainsbury, when combined with Pull's later observation that 'nothing was found in the barrow to connect it in any way with the flint mining' (Pull 1932a, 83), would appear to be conclusive: Barrow 10 was not contemporary with the main period of prehistoric mining activity recorded from Blackpatch. One further point should be noted here, namely that though Barrow 10 seems to have been constructed after prehistoric mining had ceased, it contained no residue relating to that earlier activity. Any doubt that the quantities of knapping debris, mined flint and axe roughouts recorded from the other Blackpatch Barrow sites may represent residual elements, incorporated into significantly later mounds, would, from this evidence alone, therefore appear somewhat unlikely.

Barrow 11

By J. H. Pull and C. E. Sainsbury

Barrow 11 was situated on higher ground north-west of Barrow 10. It was a small bowl barrow, being 16 feet in diameter and nine inches in height. The mound was composed of soil and flints, and was superficially roofed with a layer of flints. At the centre, on the level of the natural hill surface, was a vessel of pottery, inverted upon a large slab of tabular flint and covered by a second. The urn had possessed an overhanging rim, and was totally devoid of ornament. It was about one third filled with thoroughly cremated human bones, skull fragments and teeth. These represented the bones of a young person. Some flakes of mine flint and a few burned stones occurred in the material of the mound. The large slabs of tabular flint, which had served as a base and cover stone for the urn, had most probably been derived from the flint mines. Such tabular flint has frequently been observed in the workings, filling semi-vertical fissures of upheaval in the chalk. One such filled fissure completely bisected Shaft 1, another occurred in the galleries of Shaft 2, while a third crossed the floor of the large Beaker grave in Barrow 2 (Worthing Museum Acc. No. 1961/1585).

None of the finds noted by Pull and Sainsbury could be traced at the time of writing. The identification of the collared (overhanging rim) urn by Longworth as a Secondary series, SE style, form BII (Longworth 1984, 275) being based upon an original illustration published by Pull (1932a, plate 12). Mound 11 appears to have been constructed predominantly of flint rubble. Pull later makes the observation that the flints in question were 'derived, in this instance, from the hill surface roundabout' (Pull 1932a, 83) which could be taken to indicate that the mound was not constructed during a significant period of flint extraction, although tabular blocks of flint were noted within the body of the structure. Without evidence to the contrary (no plan or section of the mound was located in the course of this study), it must be assumed that the inverted collared urn was contemporary with the construction of Mound 11.

Barrow 12

By J. H. Pull

Barrow 12 was the most remarkable burial mound met with at Blackpatch. Situated on the minefield between Shaft 7 and Chipping Floor 3, was another mine: Shaft 8. This shaft had an extensive gallery system at its base which communicated directly with that of Shaft 7. Excavation has shown that an interesting series of events took place after Shaft 8 had been filled to its surface with chalk rubble. No rainwash had time to form before a large barrow was erected over it. This mound was 28 feet in diameter and two and a half feet high (figure 47). The mound was composed chalk rubble, chalk blocks and waste flint derived from the pits. At the centre, and just a little south of the lip of shaft 8, the

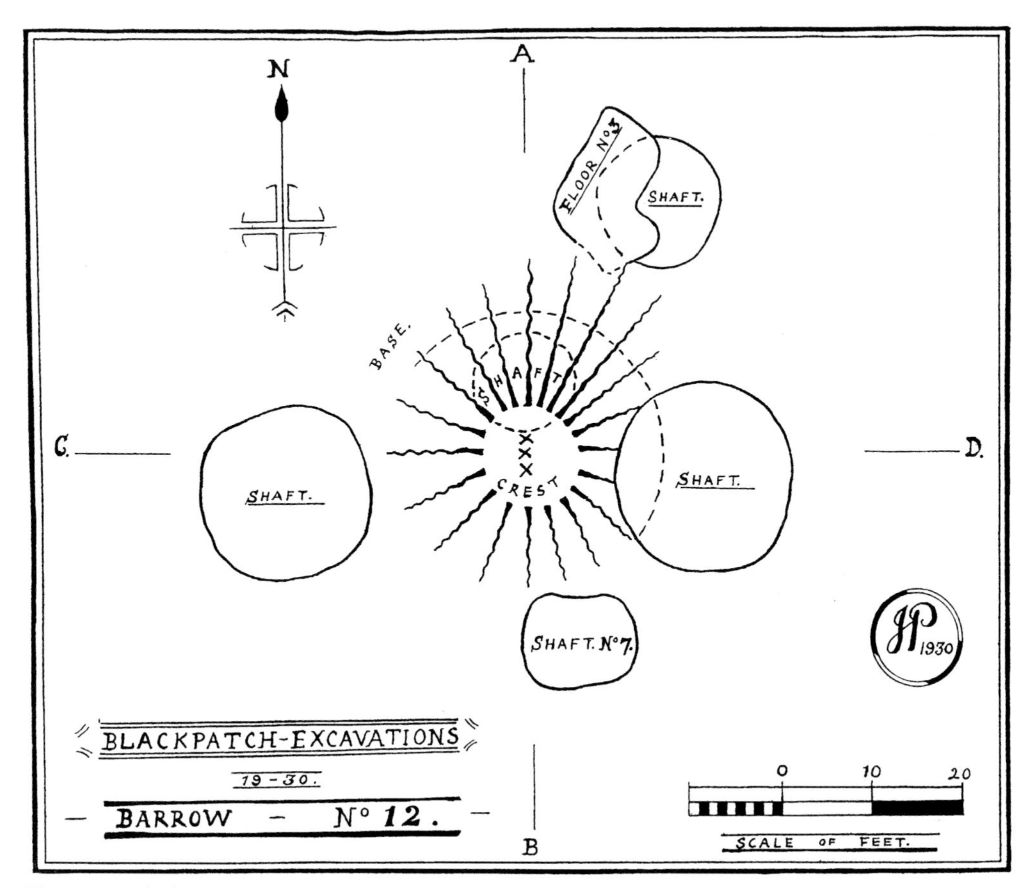

Figure 47. Blackpatch Barrow 12: surface hachure plan incorporating subsurface feature detail, showing the relative positions of three human bone deposits and the location of four mine shafts (including Shaft 8 over which it directly lies) and Chipping Floor 3 (© Worthing Museum and Art Gallery).

primary interment had been made. This was represented by a skeleton which had been laid on the right side in the contracted position, with the head to the west and the face to the south. The bones of this skeleton had been largely disturbed in order to insert a second burial.

The secondary burial was represented by the complete and well-preserved skeleton of a tall, muscular man of the Beaker type. This skeleton was crouched, lying on the right side with the head to the west and the face to the south, both hands being up to and before the face. The knees were flexed. Between the hands was a curious object – a charm of worked chalk. Behind the back were three more of these. At the feet was a flint celt or axe and a flint knife. A third interment, whether primary or secondary it was impossible to say, had been made by the folk who built the mound. None of the bones of this third interment were in situ. They were scattered throughout the centre of the mound.

After the primary interment had been made and the mound raised over it, some mining had been going on to the north, for a mass of mining debris, 10 feet in extent, had been thrown up onto the mound from this direction. This debris consisted of large chalk blocks and waste nodules of flint, the interstices between which were not filled in. This material had come from a depth, probably from a gallery. Amounting to some tons in weight, it had distended the bulk of the barrow considerably, so that on this side its former outline had become obliterated. In addition to this dump of material discharged from a mine which had been worked later than the building of the barrow, a shaft, whose circular mouth here cut away the side of the barrow to a considerable depth, had been sunk on the eastern side of the mound. There is no doubt whatsoever that this barrow was of inter-mine construction. The date of its building was later than shaft 8 and earlier than a pit to the north and another to the east.

At a far later period than of its construction, after a lapse of perhaps as long as two thousand years, Barrow 12 had been utilised by the Saxons as a burial place. Three Saxon interments were present in the upper portion of the mound. These were represented by skeletons, one to the north and two to the south of the original interments, and all of them at a higher level. These Saxon skeletons were all extended at full length on the back with the heads to the west, the hands being folded in the pelvis in each case. The Saxon skeleton which lay to the north of the mounds centre was without a skull, and it seems reasonable to suppose that the body had been interred in a headless condition. This is a circumstance previously met with at Blackpatch as Barrow 2, quite near by, contained a headless Saxon skeleton in an intrusive secondary grave. The other two Saxon skeletons in Barrow 12 exhibited two vastly different skulls (Worthing Museum Acc. No. 1961/1585).

If the stratigraphic relationships recorded by Pull for Barrow Mound 12 are correct, and there seems little reason to doubt this, then here there is direct evidence for the construction of a mound containing human body parts prior to the cutting of a nearby flint mine. In other words, Barrow 12 appears to postdate the infilling of mine shaft 8, upon which it is directly placed (as Barrow 1 and Shaft 3; Barrow 3 and Shaft 5), but predate at least two significant areas of flint extraction to the immediate north and east. It is unfortunately difficult to discuss and compare the exact structural makeup of Mound 12, due to the absence of a detailed section drawing in the Worthing Museum archive. Nevertheless, the earthwork would seem to be broadly consistent with Barrows 1–8 and 11 in that it had been built predominantly from mine waste and contained a number special deposits including, in this instance, human bone.

The exact nature of the human bone deposits appears complex, though it would seem that both articulated and disarticulated elements were originally represented. The position of the articulated skeletons, approximately central to the overlying mound, may indicate a primary placing in relation to the mound's construction. It is now almost impossible to determine whether the first skeleton, described by Pull as disturbed, had been disrupted by the insertion of the 'Beaker type' male (or by some later animal burrowing activity), or whether it had already been partially disarticulated at deposition. How either skeleton related to the bones of an apparently single individual scattered throughout the centre of the mound, is also unclear. This skeletal material could be akin to the isolated body parts recorded from Shaft 4 and Barrows 2 and 9 at Blackpatch. Alternatively it could relate, as Pull suggested, to an earlier deposit, perhaps contemporary with the construction of the mound, which had been severely disrupted by the later insertion of two prehistoric corpses or by the addition of the three Saxon interments into the upper levels of the earthwork. At least one of the Saxon skeletons appears to have been decapitated, mirroring the evidence recorded from Barrow 2 and perhaps suggesting that the three burials in question may represent a series of executions (cf. Reynolds 1998).

The relationship between skeletons and potential grave goods is (as already noted with regard to the material from Barrow 3) almost impossible to quantify, especially if the bodies in question represent deposits of equal importance to the axes, tools and chalk charms. At best we can only observe a rough spatial association between the stone artefacts and the bodies in the mound in that they were recorded from the same levels and would therefore appear to have been deposited contemporaneously. The whereabouts of artefacts derived from Barrow 12 are at present unknown.

OTHER AREAS

Several areas close to the main group of mines at Blackpatch were investigated by Pull and his team of excavation volunteers between 1922 and 1932. It would appear that these included a group of surface indentations to the east of the mines and to the immediate south-east of Barrows 5, 7 and 9. Pull and Sainsbury variously describe these hollows as representing the remains of 'dwellings', 'hut sites' or some other form of settlement structure contemporary with the main period of flint extraction. An edited version of the following text from Worthing Museum appeared in the June 1st 1929 edition of the *Worthing Herald* under the title 'The Flint miners of Blackpatch: Article 5'.

The 'Dwellings' and 'Hut Sites'

By J. H. Pull and C. E. Sainsbury

A little to the east of the spur of the hill on which the mines are situated is a short dry valley. The upward sloping end of this coombe is enclosed by a large oval earthwork of unknown origin. From this earthwork, westwards to the mines, the hill is dotted with a considerable number of dwelling sites. These are scattered widely apart and their presence is visibly indicated, sometimes by slight depressions in the turf, but more usually by the difference in depth of colouring in the turf itself.

Two of these sites have been examined. The first was a visible depression. It proved to be a shallow circular excavation with vertical sides, eight inches in depth, and 20 feet in diameter. The primary excavation had penetrated through six inches of surface soil and one foot of chalk rock. The second site was not indicated by any visible depression. It proved to be a shallow, saucer shaped excavation, 15 feet in diameter and 18 inches in depth at the centre. Both were filled with about one foot of soil, flints, and broken chalk and, below this, six inches of chalk silt or rainwash. No central hearth was indicated. In the chalk silt at the bottom were found indications of occupation. Fragments of pottery, including some pieces of an urn of cineary type, also flint flakes and implements, including Cissbury type celts, broken sandstone rubbers, animal bones and burnt flints.

In one hut circle, seven very fine flint scrapers occurred in a heap, and in the other, six chalk thong whiteners of the same description as those found at the bottom of Shaft 6. The pottery fragments were all of the same paste and texture as that recovered from the barrows and from beneath Floor 2. The presence of scrapers appears to establish the fact that dressed hides were used by the dwellers here. There is no doubt that the contents of these dwellings are contemporary with the mines and barrows; the culture betrayed by the artefacts is the same.

What form of hut surmounted the depressions is yet another matter for speculation. At present we have but little to guide us. It is certain that the removed earth and chalk was not sufficient to have formed a substantial wall round their sides, and, with the passing of time, all of it seems to have drifted back into the shallow excavations. No postholes were visible in the face of the chalk rock. It seems probable that the huts consisted of a simple scooped hollow surmounted by a series of wooden stakes leaning inwards, and covered or roofed with stretched hides, thatch, or perhaps turves. As no central hearths occurred, as has been observed in some other places, it seems certain that fires, when cooking operations were carried on, were best used in the open air. One would imagine that the dwellings indicated were of a temporary nature. When it is taken into consideration that none of the mines seems to have been exposed to severities of weather for any length of time, and that they were worked in a period of very damp climate, it seems reasonable to suppose that the site was only occupied during the few fine months of the year, winter quarters possibly being situated in some more sheltered situation. One can imagine the miners returning periodically for a few months in the summer of each year to carry on their work and to renew

> their supplies of flint implements for tribal use and barter (Worthing Museum Acc. No. 1961/1585).

The nature of the large oval earthwork, which Pull and Sainsbury describe as enclosing the upper end of the Coombe, remains something of a mystery. Pull certainly does not seem to mention it again and the feature does not appear on any map or plan of the Blackpatch site. From the brief description supplied, it does not sound dissimilar to a cross-ridge dyke or other form of later prehistoric land boundary, but, until the feature can be securely located and identified on the ground, such a comparison can be taken no further.

No detailed illustration of the dwelling sites could be located during the course of the present work, their only appearance being upon an inked sketch map of the Blackpatch complex preserved within the Worthing Museum archive (reproduced here as figure 22). The illustration appears to indicate that, contrary to the textual account reproduced above, a third hollow ('D3') had at some point been investigated, presumably following the publication of the June 1st 1929 newspaper article. This is supported by Pull's later statements where he notes that 'we have examined several of the sites' (1932a, 52–3). Just how many more were examined at this time is not unfortunately known, though Pull goes on to note that:

> Some proved to be circular excavations with vertical sides and flat bottoms, penetrating 6 inches of surface mould..and descending to a depth of from 9 to 18 inches into the chalk rock beneath. Others were saucer-shaped and of about the same maximum depth as the former. They varied in diameter from 8 to 20 feet. The infilling common to them all was purely material which had been naturally deposited (Pull 1932a, 52–3).

The scoops prove somewhat problematical with regard to interpretation, something which is not helped by the lack of artefactual material surviving to the present day. The concentration of worked flint, flint tools (including scrapers and 'Cissbury type' axes), animal bones, sandstone rubbers and pottery within and around the hollows does suggest some form of intensive activity, related perhaps to settlement or food or hide processing. Unfortunately, the absence of observed structural data, in the form of pits, postholes or hearths, precludes a precise interpretation. Pull was certainly convinced that they represented a form of domestic shelter or structure, an argument which he later elaborated.

> It is possible that the purpose behind the excavating of the bottoms of these hut floors below ground level may have been of a dual nature. Firstly, the sides of the excavation would take the outward thrust exercised by the base of the superstructure. Secondly, the absence of hearths suggests that the floors were covered by combustible material. Excavations below ground level, in addition to affording good drainage to these huts, would, if boarded over or packed with dry grass and brushwood, ensure a dry floor for the dwellers. Yet such a floor would be incapable of sustaining a hearth. This then may be the reason why dwellings of this particular class have not yielded any trace of interior hearths, though the abundance of burnt stones which have drifted into them since their decay

proclaims the presence of hearths very near to them. To these dwellings there was probably a common hearth somewhere between them, on the surface and in the open (Pull 1932a, 54).

5
Excavations at Church Hill, 1933–9, 1946–52

Church Hill (NGR TQ114083), rising to a height of over 500 feet OD, lies to the east of Findon village in West Sussex, to the south-east of the Blackpatch mining complex and north-east of Cissbury (figure 48). The earliest archaeological examination of Church Hill may have been by Colonel Lane Fox (later General Pitt Rivers), possibly in the late 1860s while he was involved in excavations at Cissbury and Highdown Hill (Lane Fox 1869b). Pull records, in the Church Hill Excavation Notebook (Worthing Museum Acc. No 1961–1584A), that a certain Colonel Margesson remembered Lane Fox investigating a number of barrow mounds 'many years ago (when he was a boy)', Margesson adding 'Pitt-Rivers found nothing as the mounds had been previously opened and looted of their contents'. No record appears to exist of any such investigations, though Pull later suggested that a series of barrows possessing dished centres visible on the south-eastern summit and north-western slopes of Church Hill were attributable to this phase of activity (Pull 1933a, 472; 1933b, 506).

It is of course possible that Margesson was wrongly attributing the work of Henry Willett who was working upon Church Hill in the late 1860s. The problem of attribution is further compounded as the full extent of archaeological work conducted in this part of Sussex during the late 1860s and early 1870s remains vague. We know, for instance, that at some of the work of Lane Fox and Canon Greenwell around Cissbury was never published (e.g. Burstow 1962) and, while Lane Fox was not in his early years known for a predilection for investigating burial mounds, his colleague at Cissbury, Cannon Greenwell, certainly was (Kinnes and Longworth 1985). Indeed Greenwell is known to have opened at least one barrow mound at Cissbury (Kinnes and Longworth 1985, 141), probably in or around 1868, and this particular piece of fieldwork could have been supplemented by an investigation of the mounds upon neighbouring Church Hill.

Ernest Willett certainly conducted fieldwork upon Church Hill sometime between 1868 and 1870 (Law 1927). Willett, who was later to excavate a shaft at Cissbury (Willett 1880), opened several of the Church Hill depressions, but appears not to have fully bottomed any of them (Law 1927, 222). Consequently, though he is credited with interpreting the depressions as representing the remains of flint extraction pits, the overall results of his work were considered disappointing as he found only 'flint

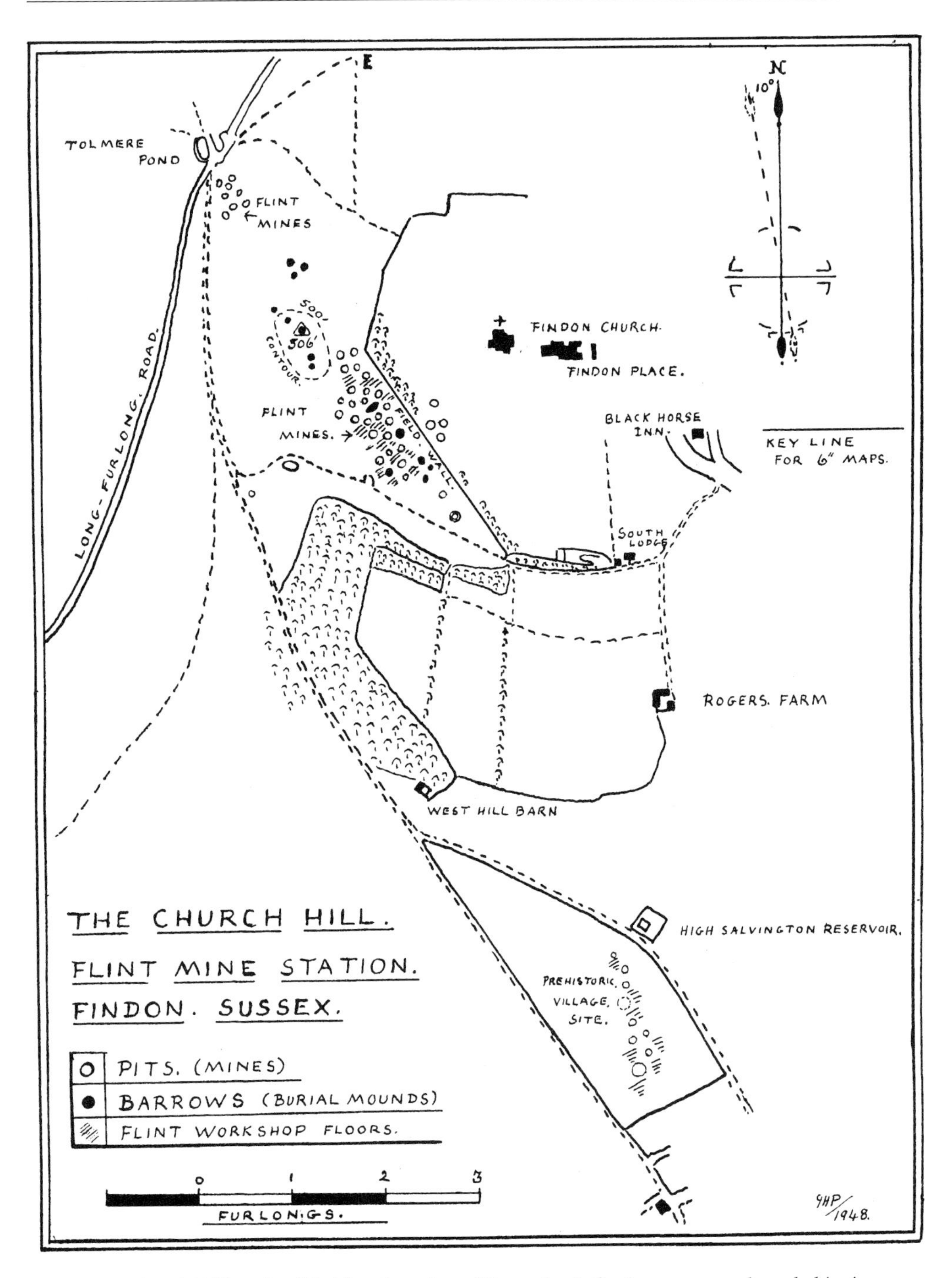

Figure 48. Church Hill: a simplified location plan of the main shafts, barrow mounds and chipping floors visible on Church Hill, Tolmere and High Salvington in 1948 (© Worthing Museum and Art Gallery).

flakes and some coarse pottery' (Pull unpublished lecture notes: Worthing Museum Acc. No 61/1584). Unfortunately no detailed record of this phase of fieldwork appears to have been made, though Pull marked two shafts on his plan of Church Hill as 'W1' and 'W2', with the intention of indicating areas investigated by Willett.

In 1922, Herbert Toms, then curator of Brighton Museum, surveyed the more prominent mine shaft depressions and spoil mounds visible on Church Hill. Toms noted the existence and extent of the site in a letter to the *Sussex County Herald* in August 1922, but it was left for his assistant, William Law, to publish the survey plan in volume 1 of the *Sussex Notes and Queries* for 1927. Some 26 shafts and four surface mounds were plotted in the course of the survey. John Pull and C. E. Sainsbury commenced a preliminary survey of the Church Hill earthworks in November 1932 (figure 49), recording 'thirty-one depressions, ranging from ten to forty feet in diameter' (Pull 1933b, 506). Excavation began on the 18th of December 1932 upon the feature later termed 'the Fire Mound'. Work on the mine shafts (figure 50) continued intermittently until the outbreak of war in 1939, with detailed excavation summaries appearing in the *Sussex County Magazine* (Pull 1933a, b, c, d, e, f). In November 1945, following the removal of military units from Church Hill, John Pull returned to the mine sites, this time being joined by his son-in-law Arthur Voice. A new survey was conducted, with Pull and Voice noting that:

> apart from the sinking of a deep revetted and sand bagged dug out in Shaft 2, and the cutting of a slit trench in the south-west of the area near Shaft 4, little damage had been done to the prehistoric site. No high explosive bombs had been dropped here, nor had any part of the hill been used by our defence units as a range for explosive missiles. A most fortunate state of affairs indeed (Worthing Museum Acc. No. 1961/1584).

Excavation commenced in 1946 with the opening of the 'Great Shaft' (Mine shaft 4) and continued, with a minor break in 1949 to investigate the site at Tolmere, until 1952. A summary report on the work appeared in volume 27 of the *Sussex County Magazine* for 1953. As with Blackpatch, a series of typed and hand written excavation notes, notebooks, lecture scripts, texts, photographs, finds reports and illustrations, providing a considerably more detailed analysis of the Church Hill fieldwork than the summary reports appearing in the *Sussex County Magazine*, survive in Worthing Museum's John Pull Collection. It is from this section of the Museum archive (Acc. No 1961/1584) that the following original texts are taken.

THE MINES

Shaft 1

By J. H. Pull

The pit chosen for examination was situated a little to the west of the centre of the mining area. This pit was indicated by a saucer shaped depression 18 feet in

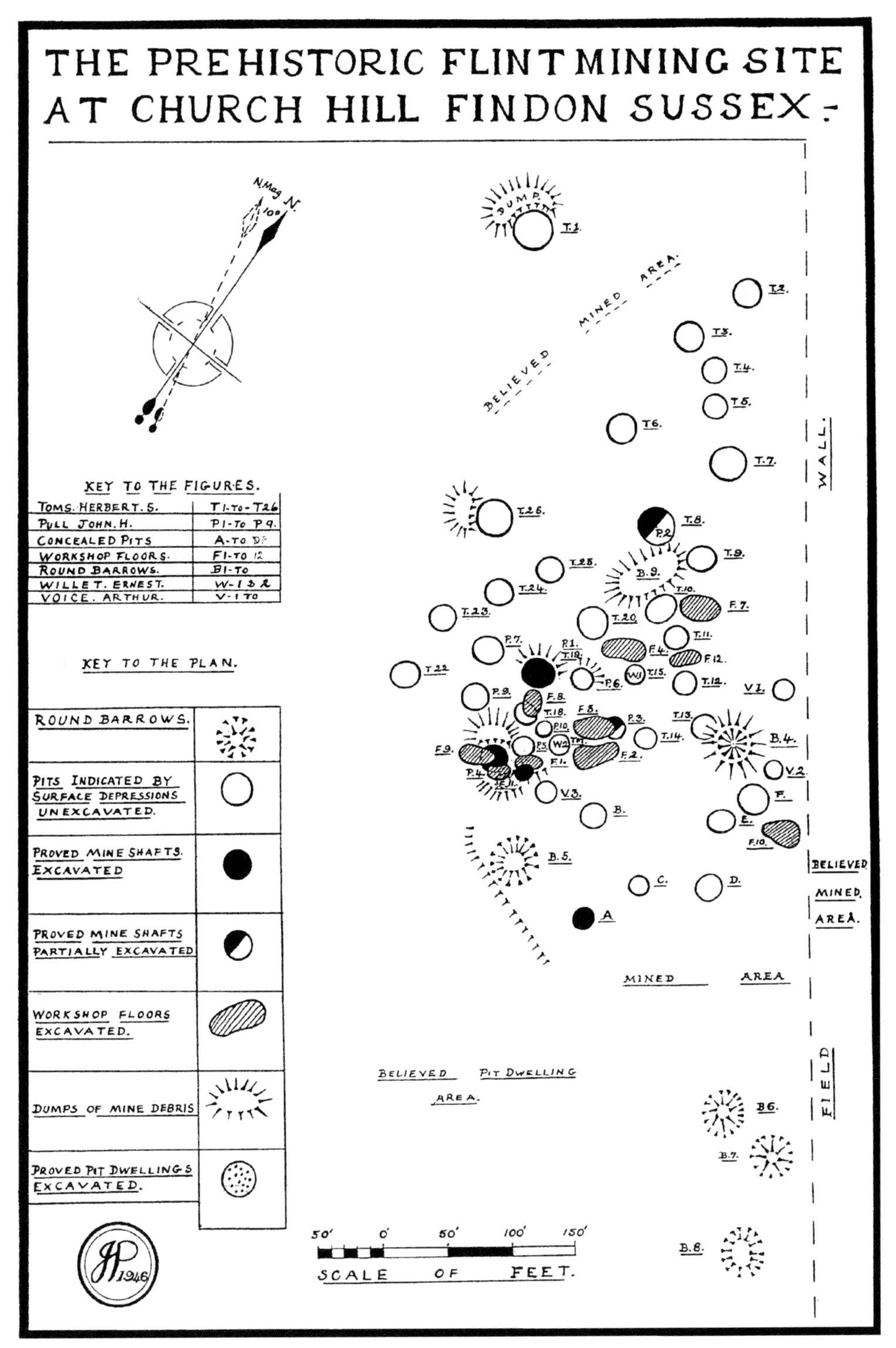

Figure 49. Church Hill: plan of the main shafts, barrows, chipping floors and other surface features visible in 1946, as well as all areas of archaeological investigation conducted up to that date (© Worthing Museum and Art Gallery).

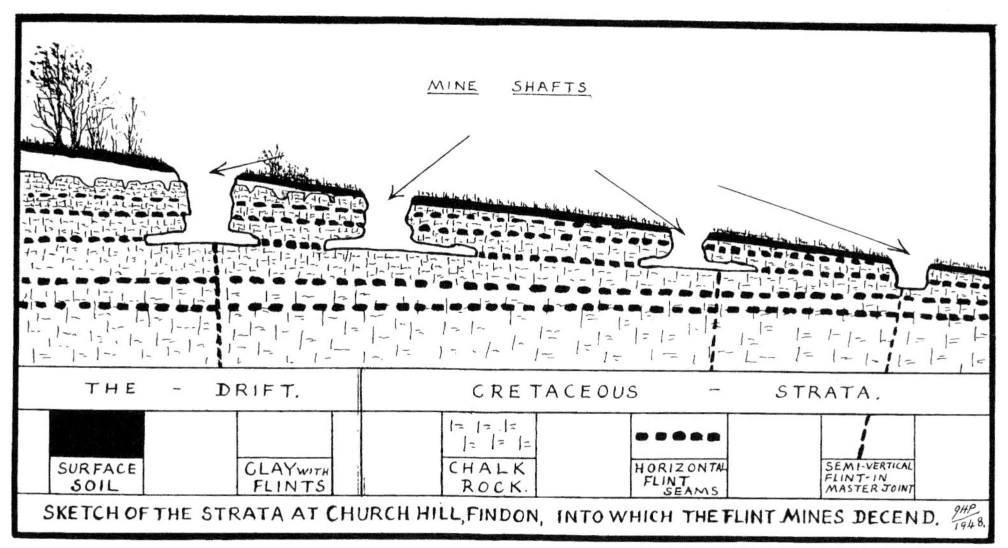

Figure 50. Church Hill: sketch to demonstrate the nature of prehistoric flint extraction on the hill (© Worthing Museum and Art Gallery).

diameter and two feet in depth. On being cleared of its infilling (figure 51), the pit shaft proved to be 17 feet across at the mouth and it descended 16 feet into the chalk rock. In plan the shaft formed an irregular rectangle with rounded corners. The sides of the pit were vertical, or nearly so, to within a few feet of the bottom, where they tapered slightly inwards. The solid chalk penetrated by the shaft was covered at the surface with a few inches of turf and soil. Below the surface soil the face of the chalk was found to be much broken up by weathering, but to below two feet from the surface the rock was very solid and in large slabs, divided by a multiplicity of horizontal joint planes and semi-vertical fissures of upheaval.

The seam of good flint sought by the men who had sunk this pit lay at the shaft base, three other seams of inferior quality having been passed through in order to reach it. These other seams lay respectively nine and a quarter, ten and a half and 13 feet from the surface. The good seam mined for consisted of a layer of somewhat large, closely packed nodules of excellent flaking quality. This seam was found to have been totally removed from the floor of the shaft. Some attempts to follow up the floor seam by driving headings had been made along the northern, western and southern walls of the pit base, but none of these headings extended for more than a few feet, nor had any of them been fully developed into what might be termed true galleries. Soundings taken of the walls of these undeveloped galleries indicated with certainty the existence of some galleries passing through the chalk from neighbouring pits to within a few feet of them. Judging from this it would seem at first that this shaft which we had reopened was of later date than the obviously galleried pits adjoining it to the north and west, but this was not the case, as the infilling of our shaft testified.

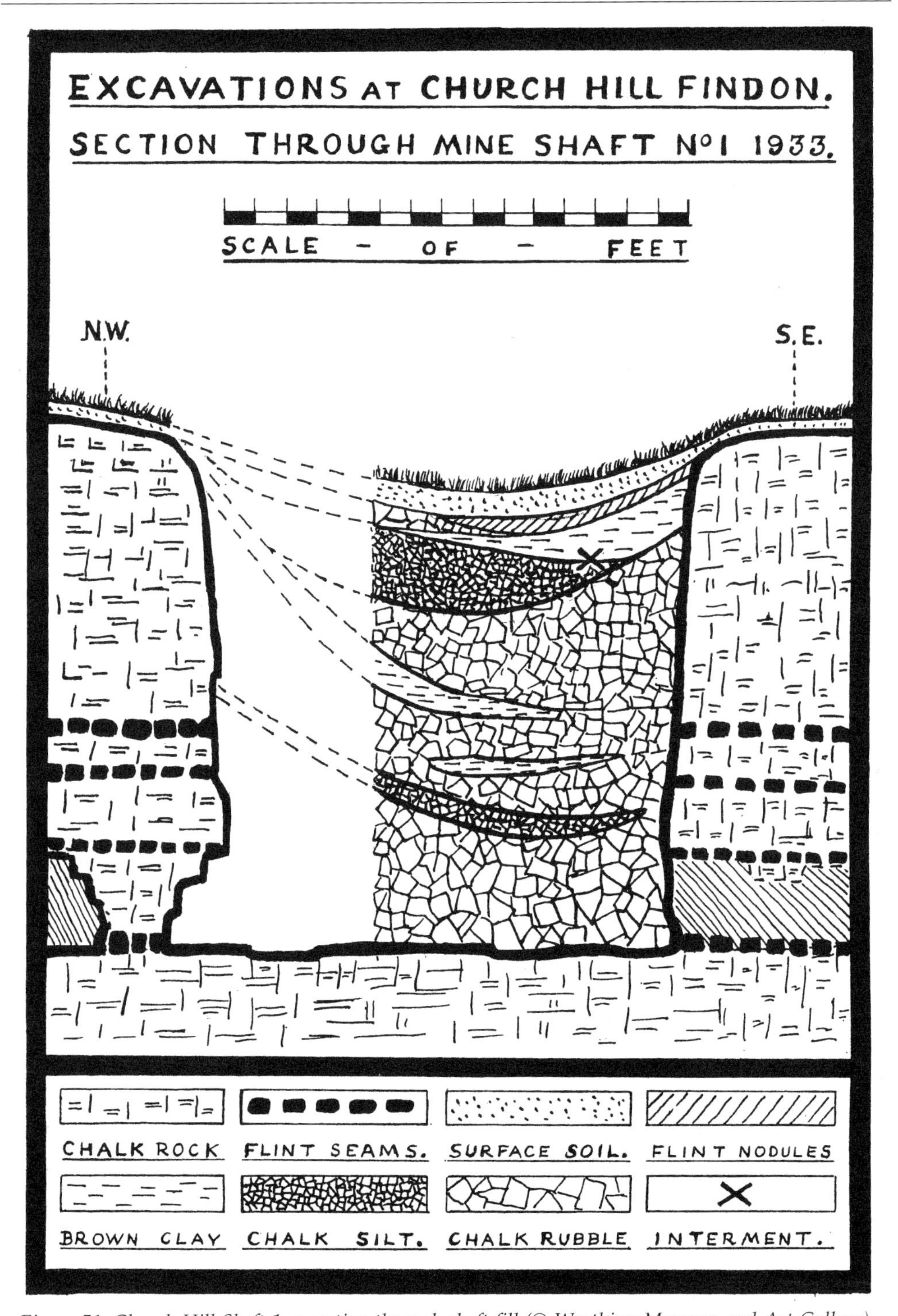

Figure 51. Church Hill Shaft 1: a section through shaft fill (© Worthing Museum and Art Gallery).

The infilling was made up of various distinct layers. Most of these layers were tilts of chalk rubble, and red or brown clay. As is usually the case on the downland flint mine fields, the shafts at Church Hill are in such close proximity that the space left upon the hill surface between the bore of the pits was never sufficient to accommodate the amount of refuse thrown up when new pits were sunk. Consequently the worked out and abandoned shafts soon became filled with tilts of this waste material removed from later mines. As the Church Hill mines are situated on the patchy and serrated edge of the deposit of clay-with-flints which caps the hill top, the presence of tilts of clay in the infilling of the shafts is to be expected, although all of the pits do not actually section the unequal margin of this overlying stratum.

At the bottom of the pit was a mixed mass of chalk rubble and chalk blocks, which appear to have been mostly introduced from the north-west. Over this rubble was a nine inch layer of naturally formed chalk silt, indicating an interval in the process of artificial infilling, during which some degree of weathering had taken place. Above this silt was a tilt of chalk rubble and chalk blocks which had been introduced from the south-east. The continuity of this tilt was interrupted midway by a thin spread of brown clay. Above this clay this particular layer of rubble yielded several chalk blocks which bore the marks of blows delivered from the miners picks, which were of red deer antler. A humanly carved piece of chalk about the shape and same size of an ordinary bun also came from this layer. On the surface of this same layer of rubble were found a number of flint implements, a quantity of primary flakes, some charcoal, and a number of mining tools made from the antlers of red deer, including an antler pick which had seen such a length of good service as to be of no further use. There was also an antler which had been cut from a slain animal, a large portion of skull being still attached. It was evidently intended to prepare this latter antler for use as a miner's pick, but for some reason this intention had never been carried into practice, and the antler had been discarded intact.

The layer just described was almost covered by a large tilt of red clay that had been thrown in from the south-west. Apart from a few scattered flint flakes, this layer was sterile of any items of human handiwork. A large tilt of chalk rubble which rested upon it filled the pit to within four feet of the surface. This rubble had been introduced from the south-east. In the surface of this layer were found a number of antler tools, including a broken and worn out pick, a very fine mallet and two punches. A quantity of good flint implements also occurred in the upper part of this layer, including a fine broad celt, a heavy well chipped pick, a large oval implement and a very fine discoid hand axe, this latter being the only one of its kind which has so far been found at Church Hill. A peculiar dagger shaped blade, well worked on both faces, and a thin blade with an oblique point complete with its haft, cut from a tine of red deer antler were also found in this layer.

Following the deposition of this last layer of infilling, the shaft and the surface around it had apparently been abandoned for some considerable time during which a heavy blanket of weathered chalk rubble and fine chalk silt had formed. This layer was highly compacted by the combined action of frost and water and contained a mass of shells of dead land mollusca. The most prevalent shells were those of the round-mouthed snail *Cyclostoma elegans*, the bush snail *Arianta arbustorum*, and *Helix nemoralis*. The Cheese snail *Helix obvoluia* was also well represented, though no single example of *Helix aspersa* occurred. After this large quantity of silt had accumulated, further activity on the part of the miners had been resumed. This is to be noted as evidence of special interest, for at Blackpatch the infilling of the seven shafts, which were reopened in different parts of the mine field, always terminated in the deep layer of silt near the surface of the pits. At Church Hill this was not the case, as the record of our exploration will now make clear.

Following the formation of the rainwash, three different vessels of pottery had been broken up and deposited on its surface. The first of these vessels represented by many fragments of the rim and body was, so far as the can be made out, a hand made, fairly large and thick, round bottomed bowl, the paste of which is black and very soapy to the touch. This vessel was ornamented over the whole surface by means of impressions made by a woman's fingertips. The second vessel represented by a flat base and thin well fired body fragments was evidently a Beaker or drinking vessel, which had been ornamented with zones of horizontal and parallel lines interposed with chevron pattern; the ornament having been deeply incised with some sharp pointed implement. The third vessel was of thick brownish ware with flint grit in the paste. The fragments show no attempt at ornament nor were there sufficient of them to enable the shape of the vessel to be made out.

At the same time, or very shortly after, these broken potsherds had been deposited, the surface of the rainwash in the shaft had been chosen as the site of an interment. This took the form of a burial after cremation. Burnt human bones together with a small quantity of charcoal had been gathered up from the funeral pyre and had been enclosed together with the blade of a flint axe within a vessel of pottery. This vessel, with its contents, had then been deposited in an inverted position in the shaft, four feet from the south-eastern edge of the pit. A second flint axe, very like the one enclosed with the bones, was deposited beside the rim of the pot, on the east side, together with a tiny bone tool. This bone tool appears to have been the very one used to produce the ornamentation on the pot.

The pottery vessel itself, when found by us, was unfortunately broken into many fragments, this being due to the settling down of the infilling of the pit below but it has been possible to completely and accurately restore it. This particular vessel promises to be somewhat in the nature of a puzzle to the experts. It is hand made and irregular, the walls are thin, the paste is mixed with flint grit, and the pot is well fired to redness in the upper part; lower down it is buff coloured and black inside, being indifferently hardened near the base, thus disclosing that it was baked in an open fire. The ornament upon it consists of alternate zones of fine dots or pits impressed with the bone point found near it. The intervals between the zones of ornament are fairly well spaced. The paste, shape of body and ornament are all in accordance with that of a zoned Beaker of

> late date (probably Abercromby's type C), but the rim is extraordinary, and seems to indicate native influence derived from some Neolithic bowls after the fashion of Later Bronze Age food vessels. Some experts think that the vessel shows Hallstatt characteristics.
>
> This peculiar burial in the shaft at Church Hill was covered by a tilt of brown clay admixed with surface soil. This had been introduced from a south-eastern direction, and was two feet in thickness at a point immediately over the interment. Many fragments of broken bones and a number of teeth belonging to at least two oxen, together with some flint implements and a quantity of flakes occurred in this layer. The layer was itself covered over on the west and south-west by a tilt of large chalk blocks which had evidently been discharged from a depth in a shaft which exists in that direction and which was evidently worked at a time after the actual covering up of burial. The blocks of chalk forming the last tilt had been prevented from badly weathering by the presence of much clay in the surface soil which covered them. The exposed surface of the clay that covered the burial on the east and south-east sides of the shaft was covered by the debris of a surface chipping floor. This debris had not been moved, it was in situ. It consisted of waste flint nodules, flakes and fine chippings, among which were flint implements in all stages of manufacture. Above all this, the contents of the shaft were finally sealed in with nearly a foot of naturally deposited surface mould, which contained such a large proportion of clay as to be very sticky when wet and very hard when dry. At the base of this surface soil were found some fragments of a Romano-British vessel of blue provincial ware (Worthing Museum Acc. No. 1961/1584).

Though some of the Church Hill finds presently reside in Worthing Museum, the current whereabouts of a significant number of flint artefacts, recorded as having derived from Shaft 1, remain unknown. Some consolation is, however, gained by the fact that, as at Blackpatch, many of John Pull's original finds drawings survive in the Worthing Museum archive. These records demonstrate that the number of axe roughouts from the fill of the shaft, when compared to other tool types, is relatively high.

The pottery assemblage recovered from the upper-most levels of Shaft 1 infill probably represents one of the most discussed elements of the Church Hill mining complex, being considered at varying times by Curwen (1954, 115–6), Smith (1956, 187), Pye (1968, 31–2), Clarke (1970, 322), Wainwright and Longworth (1971, 287), and Gibson (1982, 155–6). This is hardly surprising, for the assemblage itself is diverse, consisting as it does of Barrel Beaker, Barbed Wire Beakers, Collared Urn, Grooved Ware and possible sherds of Food Vessel and Peterborough Ware. The majority of this material, though being deposited late within the history of the Shaft 1 abandonment, clearly seems to have predated some mining activity to the immediate south-east of Shaft 1, for the assemblage, and in particular that accompanying the cremation deposit, appears to have been sealed by mining debris (a point also noted by Curwen: 1954, 115–6). This may indicate that, as at Blackpatch, flint extraction continued on into the Later Neolithic. A rough sketch in the Church Hill Excavation Notebook provides a clearer view of the fill beneath the final spread of mining debris, and the way in which it affected the structural integrity of the cremation beneath, distributing it, in Pull's words 'over space of about four feet'.

Shaft 2

Little record of the excavation of Shaft 2 could be traced at the time of writing. Pull, in a series of notes entitled 'Excavations at Church Hill, Findon' housed in Worthing Museum (Acc No 1961/1584) states that 'the second mine shaft opened was situated in the south of the area and proved to be an ungalleried pit, 10 feet deep and only about eight feet in diameter'. Unfortunately there would appear to be no further information (textual or illustrative) concerning the nature of the mine. The general plan of Church Hill, drawn by Pull in 1946 seems to indicate that Shaft 2 was only ever half sectioned, though as it would be rash to state that the pit was without galleries from an incomplete examination, it would seem probable that the feature was at some stage opened in its entirety. Two flint flakes from the shaft survive in Worthing Museum.

Shaft 3

Although Pull indicates that only six Shafts (1, 2, 4, 5a, 6 and 7) were ever excavated at Church Hill (Pull unpublished: Worthing Museum Acc. No's 61/1584 and 61/1584A; Pye 1968, 21), the 1946 inked plan of the site appears to show that Shaft 3, lying beneath Floor 3, had at some stage, been examined, albeit partially. No detailed information today exists regarding the nature of any such examination, the only noted artefact being a single flaked axe, recorded by Pye as having been 0.23m in length (1968; Appendix 1). This axe could alternatively represent an isolated find from the surface of Shaft 3, rather than the product of an excavation.

Shaft 4

By J. H. Pull and A. R. Voice

Pit 4, when emptied of its infilling, presented one of the most interesting spectacles ever witnessed by any student of prehistoric mining. The roughly circular shaft, 16 feet in diameter at its mouth and 12 feet in diameter at its base had been sunk into the solid chalk of the hillside to a maximum depth of 16 and a half feet from the surface. Four horizontal seams of nodular flint had been passed through in doing this (figure 52). Serious attempts had been made by the miners to drive high level headings in order to work the third seam from the surface and cave like excavations had been made by them on the south, west and north-west. These were six feet high and eight feet in width and from three to eight feet in depth. The fourth seam from the surface was, however, the main one. This had been totally removed from the floor of the shaft and had been followed up by driving headings or subterranean galleries (figures 53 and 54).

These galleries were from three to four feet in height, from four to seven feet in width and up to 30 feet length. Nearly all the work had been done with picks,

Figure 52. Church Hill Shaft 4: the lower fill of the shaft during excavation. Note two of the fourth seam gallery entrances, still choked with chalk rubble, and an area of third seam working, visible behind the top of the wooden ladder (© Worthing Museum and Art Gallery).

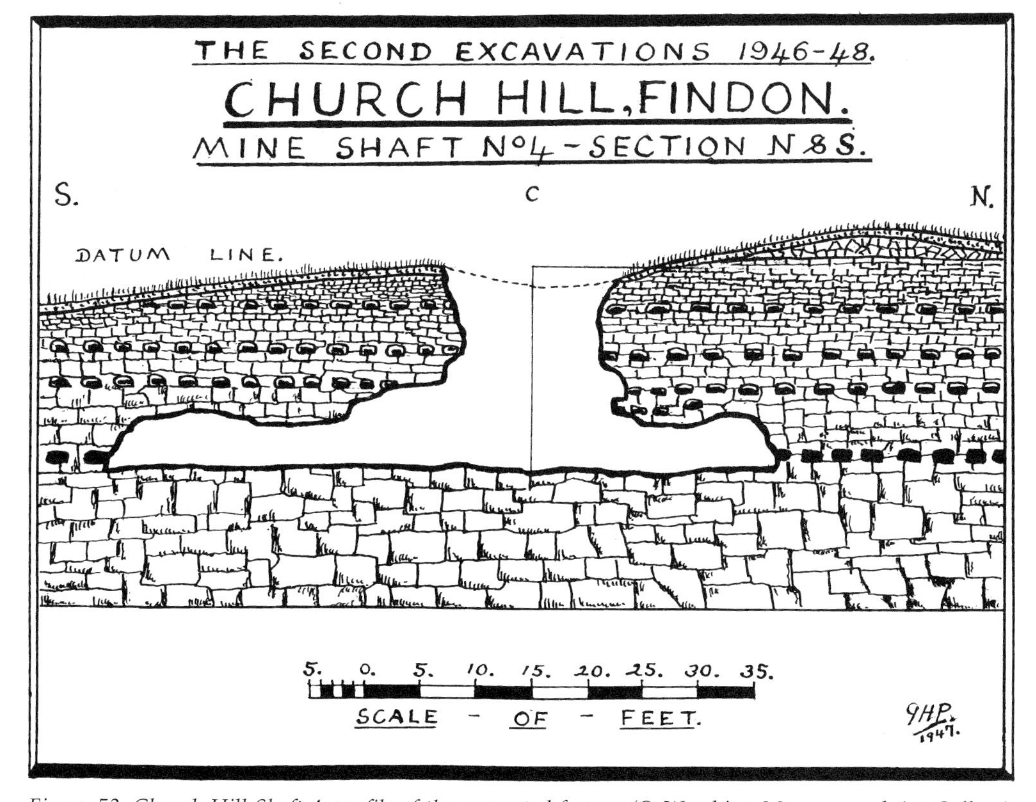

Figure 53. Church Hill Shaft 4: profile of the excavated feature (© Worthing Museum and Art Gallery).

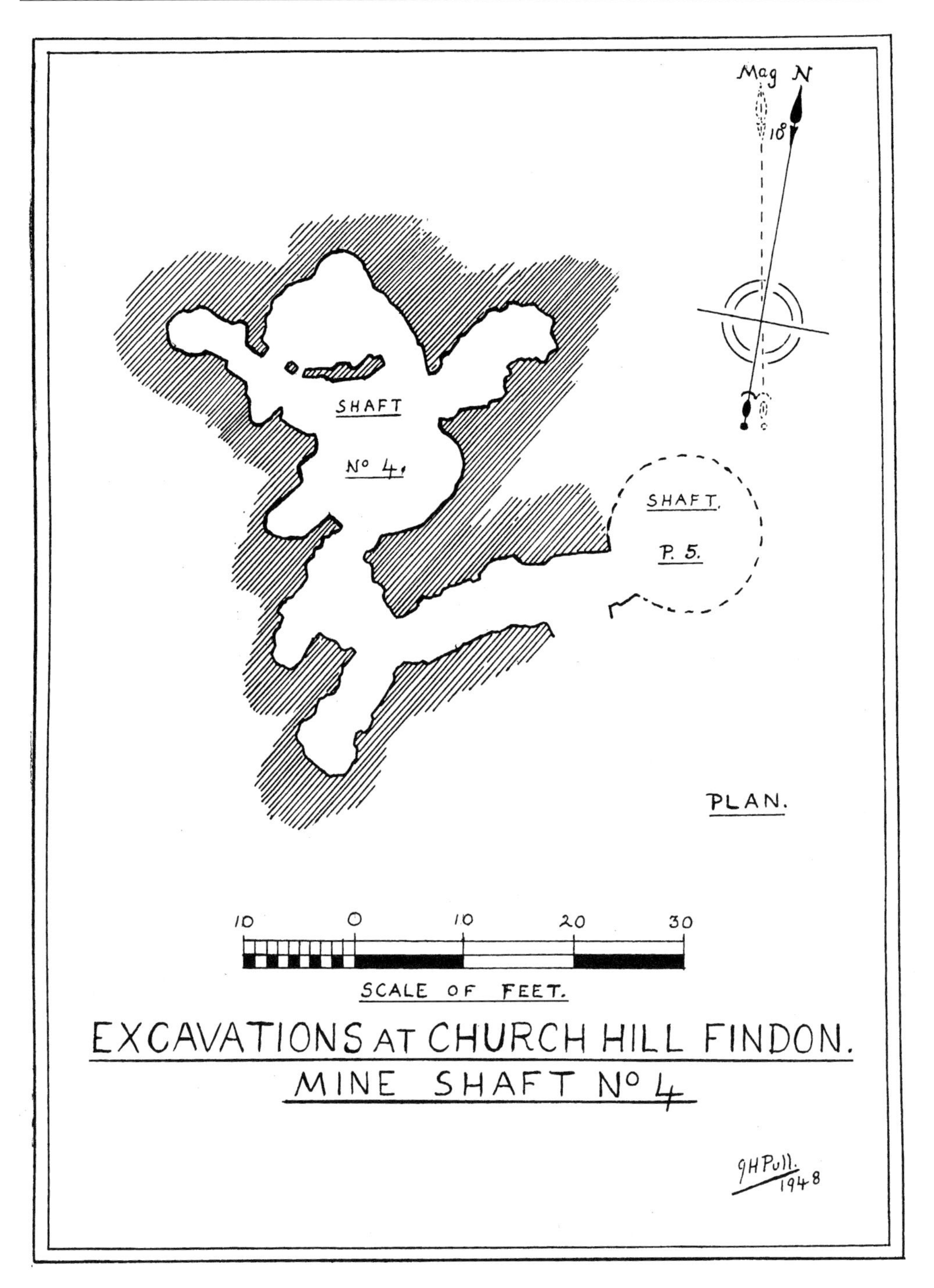

Figure 54. Church Hill Shaft 4: plan of the subterranean gallery systems (© Worthing Museum and Art Gallery).

levers and punches cut from red deer antlers and shovels made from the shoulder blades of the ox. Many of these tools of every kind were found in the shaft filling or on the gallery floors (figure 55). In one gallery, however, other tools had been used, not hitherto observed in any Stone Age Sussex flint mine. Large wooden bars with rounded ends had been driven into the chalk with heavy mauls, and where masses of rock had thus been broken away, the holes were left in long section, so effectively that it was possible to make plaster casts of the wooden punches, and to show the progress made by each successive blow. Over the heads of the galleries were found symbols cut in the chalk with antler tools: miners marks apparently, but quite incomprehensible to the excavators, and unprecedented either at Church Hill or at Blackpatch (figures 56, 57 and 58).

On the floor of the shaft was a layer (layer xv: figure 59) of consolidated chalk dust with which was admixed a proportion of splintered flint resulting from the breaking up of nodules from the base seam as they were extracted. No flint or antler tools were found over this basal layer. Covering this floor was a layer of clean chalk blocks many of them over one and a half feet across (layer xiv), the interstices between which were not filled in. this mass of chalk debris sealed the gallery entrances and choked the shaft to a distance of nine feet from the bottom. Much of the basal portion of this chalk rubble may have been filled into the large diameter shaft from its own galleries when they were being operated and may thus have represented material that had never been raised to the surface. The upper portion must have been discharged into the shaft from the surface and so far as could be ascertained from its sloping surface, must have come in from a south-easterly direction, probably from Shaft 4a, which must have been operated a little later than the pit under examination. The silt layer (Layer xiii), which lay between layers xiv and xii (which is really part of xiv) was one foot in thickness and accumulated during our suspension of excavation during the hard winter of 1946–1947.

Following the deposition of layer xiv/xii, the shaft of pit 4 had filled in to within two feet of the hill surface in the following way. On the unweathered surface of layer xii rested a deposit, nearly one foot in thickness, of flakes, chippings and waste flint marking a period when the shaft had been used as a sheltered spot in which to carry on the business of the manufacture of flint implements. A number of finished

Figure 55. Church Hill Shaft 4: an antler pick and flint blade photographed as found within the rubble of a gallery system (© Worthing Museum and Art Gallery).

Figure 56. Church Hill Shaft 4: gallery head marking 1 (© Worthing Museum and Art Gallery).

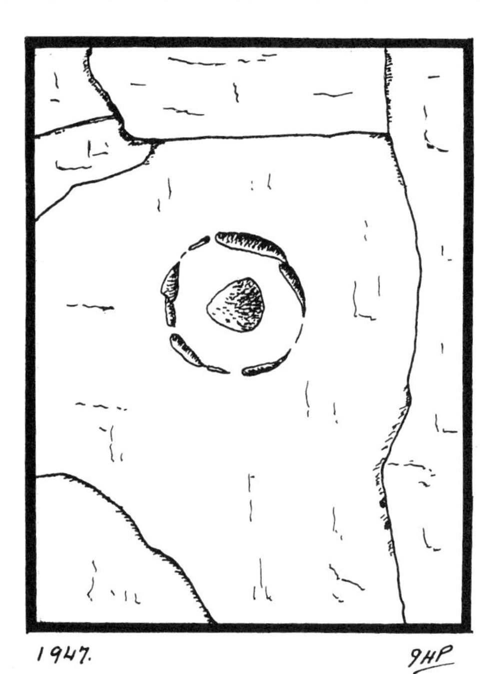

Figure 57. Church Hill Shaft 4: gallery head marking 2 (© Worthing Museum and Art Gallery).

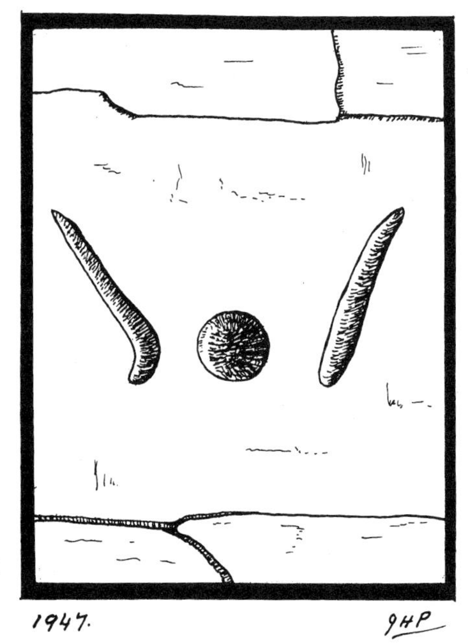

Figure 58. Church Hill Shaft 4: gallery head marking 3 (© Worthing Museum and Art Gallery).

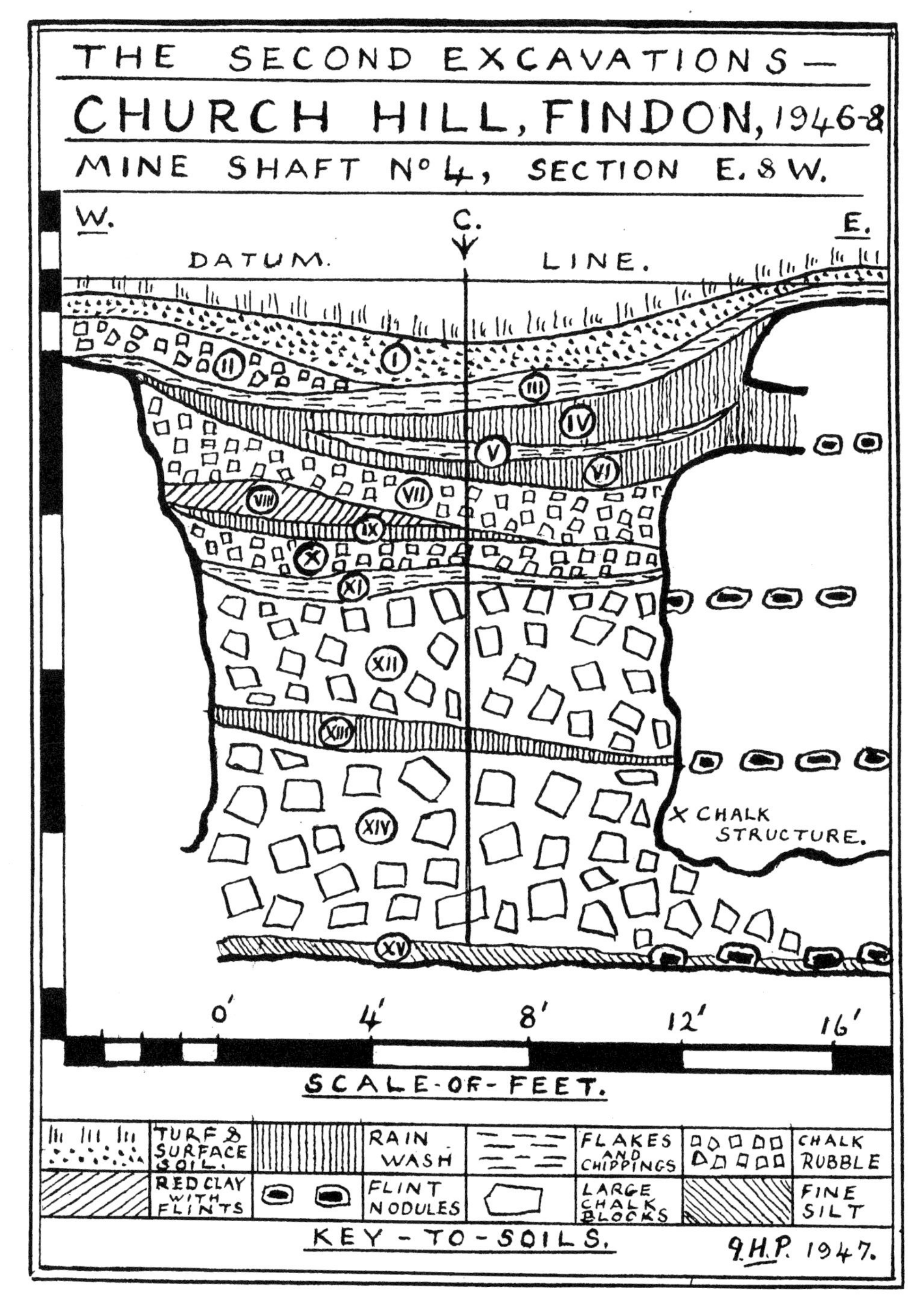

Figure 59. Church Hill Shaft 4: a section through shaft fill. Note that the position of one of the gallery head markings, here referred to as a "chalk structure", is indicated (© Worthing Museum and Art Gallery).

and unfinished flint tools were found in this layer together with a red deer antler flint knapping mallet and a tine of antler which may have served as a punch. This workshop floor was covered in turn by a layer of small chalk rubble (layer x), a little over one foot in thickness, on the south-eastern side which appeared to have been lifted in from that direction. This rubble had been exposed to weather conditions and a fine silting (layer ix) had been tipped onto its surface to a depth of six inches. This layer probably represented a spread of surface soil admixed with chalk rainwash not in situ. Layer viii, a tilt of reddish brown clay with flints, had been deposited on this weathered surface, forming a piled heap one foot in thickness on the western side of the shaft. The presence of this clay with flints definitively marks the sinking of a shaft to the west of our pit. This shaft must have been situated just on the edge of the indefinitely bordered blanket of clay with flints which caps the fill top.

Following the dump of clay with flints a tilt of medium sized, clean chalk rubble (layer vii) had been discharged into the shaft from a westerly direction, marking a further stage in the sinking of the pit to the west. Layer vii may have been up to one foot thicker than found by us for it was covered with a fine silting (layer 6) which may in a large part be the result of the breaking up of the chalk rubble forming the surface of layer vii, which, judging by the information obtained from layer xiii, may mark the passage of a single fairly severe winter. Important finds were made in layer 6: a large sherd of Neolithic A pottery and the charred fragments of a wooden bowl of black poplar, still a favourite material for making 'treen'. Enough was preserved to make a reconstruction possible, with its slightly beaded upright rim and ornament of close vertical incisions. We had long suspected from the design of certain flint tools that a high degree of skill had been developed in the manufacture of wooden objects, but this was the first actual proof discovered. At the same level were two most interesting flint axes. One was the largest, the other the smallest, completed tool found on the site, but both appeared in shape and workmanship to be the product of the same hand. The larger was clearly meant for a woodsman's felling axe, the smaller, identical in all but size, could hardly have been intended for anything but a child's use.

Layer v, a mass of flakes, chippings and broken flint rested on layer vi to a depth of six inches in the centre of the pit. This marks the second use of the shaft as a shelter for flint knapping operations. Above this layer iv had accumulated to a depth of two feet on the east side of the shaft. This was a mass of consolidated chalk rainwash, completely sealing in the chipping floor layer v and extending to the sides of the shaft in all directions. This rainwash must have taken some considerable time to form, and represents the decay of the crumbling edges of the shaft near the surface and a deep drift of broken up chalk from dumps round its edge. In the base of this layer of silt, and sealed beneath the large undisturbed chipping floor which lay above it, were fragments of three Bronze Age urns, with overhanging rims, parts of an Early Bronze Age Beaker and of a Neolithic B type bowl.

The lower portion of layer iv no doubt was formed very rapidly, but the upper portion of the layer had probably taken some considerable time to form.

> Nevertheless, insufficient time had elapsed for any soil to form over it before its surface was covered by the large flint workshop floor layer iii. This floor, consisting of masses of flakes, chippings and waste nodules of flint and a number of finished and partially finished flint implements, including two celts sharpened by the 'tranchet' technique, and pressure flaked flint knives and scrapers, extended from the east, completely covering the rainwash sealed mouth of Shaft 4 in all directions. The flakes and chippings attained a maximum thickness of one foot three inches at a point three feet to the east of the shaft's centre.
>
> Some mining must have taken place to the north-west subsequent to the deposition of the chipping floor, for a dump of large chalk blocks, which rises to the height of four feet above that portion of the natural surface parting Shaft 4 from the large depression in that direction, extended over chipping floor layer v to within 4 feet of its centre, forming layer ii. Since the deposition of layer ii, no further disturbance of the immediate area round Shaft 4 seems ever to have taken place and the surface soil layer i had slowly accumulated over the whole of the site, reaching a depth of one foot three inches in the slight depression over Shaft 4 and a thickness of six inches round its edge. Certain finds were peculiar to the base of the surface soil and occurred nowhere else in the excavation, namely some sherds of Romano-British pottery of about 2nd century AD and the shells of the land snail *Helix aspersa.* (Worthing Museum Acc. No. 1961/1584).

Only a small percentage of the flints noted from either the shaft or the upper working Floors appear to survive in the Worthing and Brighton Museums. Additional elements of the Shaft 4 assemblage were however recently brought to light by Chris Butler from a private collection (Butler 1992), further highlighting the impression that much of the excavated material from Church Hill was at some point dispersed before it could be deposited within a centralised store.

The pottery recovered from layer 6, and interpreted by Pull and Voice as a sherd of 'Neolithic A pottery', could alternatively, and perhaps more plausibly, be viewed as a fragment of Beaker coarse ware (Pye 1968, 30). The 'Neolithic B sherd' from layer 4 has unfortunately been lost since its finding, though this too may have originally been misidentified (Pye 1968, 31). Other pottery within Layer 4 included fragments of cord impressed Beaker (Gibson 1982, 369) misidentified by Gibson as having originated from Shaft 1, and collared urn. Both layers 4 and 6 had been sealed by extensive flint working floors (Layers 3 and 5 respectively), while the uppermost floor (Layer 3) had itself being partially overlain by a large deposit of mining debris (Layer 2). Though it is possible that this final dump of mining debris could represent the slumping of a spoil heap into the upper fill of Shaft 4, it is clear that the pottery within layers 4 and 6 had been sealed by workshop floors, implying that some form of flint extraction and manufacture continued at Church Hill into the Beaker period. Such extraction could, at least in part, be represented by the apparent removal of the first strata of flint on the eastern side of the shaft above Layer 7.

Pull and Voice note the presence of charred fragments of a wooden bowl in layer 6, but unfortunately do not elaborate further as to the nature and extent of survival. Pull later drew a speculative reconstruction of the bowl, akin to an Early Neolithic round-based pot, in an article published in The *Sussex County Magazine* (1953, 16). A series of small charred wood fragments were noted by Pye from the Pull Collection in Worthing Museum (Pye 1968, 32–3), but these appear now to have disintegrated into an largely unidentifiable mass.

The marks recorded from within one of the basal galleries of Shaft 4 appear to be both too large and too regular to have been created by antler picks. Pull and Voice suggest that these could have been produced by the use of 'large wooden bars with rounded ends', hammered into the chalk in an attempt to break up large areas of rock face. Such an interpretation seems hard to dispute given the present evidence available and it is difficult to envisage what else could have produced such impressions (the limited space available would certainly preclude some defined structural element such as a platform or ladder). There is no reason to doubt that experimentation in flint extraction would have taken place during the original operation of the mines and that wooden punches could, if available, have probably been used with some success.

A second series of impressions were noted within Shaft 4 'over the heads' of at least three of the five basal gallery entrances. These are more difficult to interpret than those noted at the flint face, consisting as they do of a series of apparently deliberate patterns of circles and lines, nowhere more than 0.08m across. The three impressions that Pull recorded, a rough circle (or oval) within a broken circle, a circle between two downward-pointing diagonal lines, and a circle with a raised centre, may have been created by the careful application of a flint tool or antler tine directly onto the chalk. The significance of the markings is as yet unclear, especially as similar patterns do not appear to have been observed in any of the other mines. As the symbols occur over gallery entrances they may perhaps represent the identification of a specific gallery or working area with a specific person or group of people, or perhaps with a specific subterranean deity or protecting spirit. Alternatively, given the length of time that the Shaft was left open during periods of excavation between 1946 and 1948 (see Appendix 2), it is possible that the gallery-head markings are of more modern origin, deriving from the activities of some uninvited visitor. Pull noted that one such visitor had left their impression upon the walls of Shaft 1 at Blackpatch, during a period of staff absence, and uncertainty has occasionally been expressed regarding the nature of the engravings recorded upon the gallery wall of Shaft 27 at Cissbury (see below). The form and nature of the Church Hill markings do not, however, automatically trigger alarm, and certainly both Pull and Voice appear to have been convinced of their authenticity.

Shaft 5a and Hearth Site 1

By J. H. Pull and A. R. Voice

On May 23rd 1948 it was decided to try to locate the surface of Shaft 5, the presence of which below ground had previously been ascertained during the exploration of the gallery system of Shaft 4. there was no surface indication of the presence of Shaft 5 whatsoever. Not knowing how large in diameter Shaft 5 was, a point was chosen 42 feet from the north-eastern lip of Shaft 4 with the intention of driving a deep trench toward Shaft 4 in the hope of locating the mouth of Shaft 5.

On lifting the turf we were surprised to find an area occupied by a mass thoroughly burnt flint indicating a hearth. How large this hearth was and what lay concealed beneath it we were yet to discover. The area occupied by the hearth was found on excavation to be an oval measuring 10 feet east and west by seven feet north and south (figure 60). Its western border was 38 feet from the north-eastern lip of Shaft 4 and its eastern border 48 feet from that Shaft. The mass of burnt flints, many of which had been almost reduced to powder, filled in a shallow depression overlaying fine chalk silt to a depth of one foot in the centre of the area. The only charcoal found in this burnt mass was on the north-eastern border and one gained the impression that a large and fierce fire on a hearth of flint nodules had burnt here and that a stiff north-easterly wind had been blowing at the time of its burning. For, except in a windward direction, such a fire of dry brushwood would consume its own charcoal. What purpose this great fire had served, it is impossible to say. It may have been that here was cremated the body of the chieftain whose ashes we found during the 1933 excavations enclosed in the large C Beaker buried in Mine Shaft 1, or it may be that the great fire was just the communal hearth of the miners used for domestic purposes or it may have been a sacred fire connected with some ceremony or ritual.

Round the perimeter of this great fire site, more especially on the north-east, east and south-east, laying on the natural surface of the chalk, below the soil base, a large number of flint flakes, chippings and a quantity of flint tools including a very fine borer, a steep nosed plane, two axes, a very fine pressured flake knife blade broken in two and a disc worked in the Palaeolithic style. All were made from mined flint and by the usual flint mine technique. Some bones and teeth of the ox were also found two feet away from the hearth site on the eastern side. These were unburnt. No pottery fragments of any description were recovered from this area.

Descending below Hearth Site 1, we found, at a depth of three and a half feet below its western edge, the lips of Shaft 5a, the presence of which was completely unsuspected. It could not, from its position, be Shaft 5, which we had originally sought. It was decided to excavate this pit forthwith and our surface fencing, enclosing Shaft 4, was extended to enclose it. Shaft 4 was left open. The various layers of infilling that were encountered in our clearing of Shaft 5a are described as follows. Over all was a foot of turf and mould representing layer 1. On the western side of Hearth Site 1 – layer 2 – rested on a tilt of large chalk blocks – layer 3. This tilt of chalk blocks rested on the natural surface of the chalk to the west and thinned out beneath the hearth two feet from its centre. This tilt of chalk blocks and the remainder of the base of the hearth, rested on a layer of consolidated fine chalk silt – layer 4 – containing a number of dead shells of land mollusca, but not the excessive amount of molluscan remains which were present in the rainwash sealing the shafts at Blackpatch. Here the fine silt layer rested against the wall of the shaft to the west and extended beyond the shaft's edge on the east. This silt layer was one foot six inches thick in the centre and one foot thick at the sides.

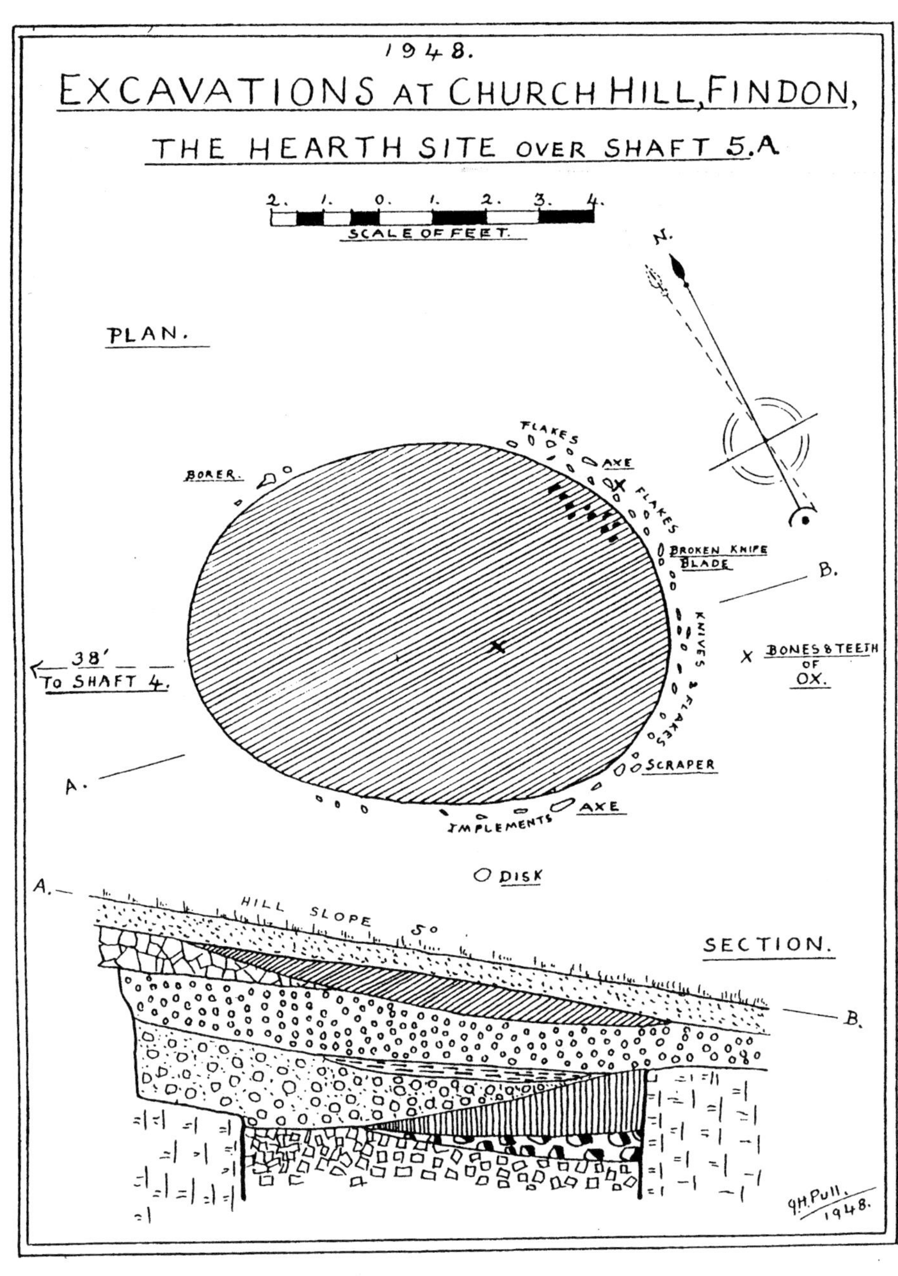

Figure 60. Church Hill Shaft 5a: plan and section of hearth site 1 (© Worthing Museum and Art Gallery).

Below layer 4 was a small chipping floor – layer 5 – consisting of a mass of flakes and fine chipping mixed with broken and waste nodules of seam flint. This floor extended from a point one foot from the eastern lip of the shaft to a point three feet nine inches from the western lip. The floor and the fine silting not covered by the floor, rested on a layer of coarser chalk silting stained yellow – layer 6. This coarse silting was one foot six inches deep on the western side and thinned out to nothing at a point one foot from the eastern edge of the shaft. Below this was a tilt of yellow clay with flints – layer 7 – which had evidently been introduced from the eastern side. This tilt of clay with flints was one foot four inches thick on the eastern side and thinned out to a finish two and a quarter feet from the eastern edge of the shaft. Below it, and occupying the same area as the yellow clay layer, was a tilt of large waste flint nodules nine inches thick – layer 8. Below layer 8, to the bottom of the shaft, fill consisted of a mixture of large and small chalk rubble – layer 9 – the interstices between which were not filled in. this rubble was unstratified and it was not possible to discern from what direction it had been introduced.

Shaft 5a, when emptied of its filling, was nearly circular in plan (figure 61), measuring nine and a half feet in diameter at its surface opening, and eight and a half feet in diameter at its base (figure 62). Vertically it was somewhat irregular. At four feet from the surface it narrowed suddenly on the west and south, but remained roughly vertical on the east and north, its diameter being thus reduced to seven feet. At five and a half feet from the surface, the walls all round were enlarged, increasing its overall diameter to nine feet. From this point to the base, the sides tapered slightly, reducing the basal diameter to eight and a half feet (figure 63). The floor of the shaft was uneven, being ten and a half feet from the surface on the east and 12 feet from the surface on the west. At the centre of the floor was a roughly funnel shaped hole or sump three feet deep and three feet across at the top, tapering to one foot at the bottom, which was 15 feet from the surface.

Three horizontal flint seams had been passed through by the sinking of the shaft itself. The first of these occurred six feet below the surface, the second at eight feet six inches and the third at nine feet six inches. The fourth seam, the one mined for, occurred at 12 feet from the surface and a fifth appeared three feet below this at the bottom of the sump. The floor of the shaft was covered, and the sump was filled with, highly consolidated chalk dust mixed with splinters of broken flint. A curious vertical parting of the chalk ran from north-west to south-east across the shaft and the strata and flint seams were staggered six inches. This vertical strata movement had obviously taken place suddenly and a flint nodule exposed on the shaft side had been sheared through as though, part of it still remaining embedded. The base of Shaft 5a was pierced by two gallery entrances, one on the south-west and one on the south and a deep undercut, the beginning of a third, had also been cut on the north-west. The galleries on the south-western and southern sides led us to the bottom of shaft 5 which we had originally sought, and on the floor of one of these was a much worn, two handled antler pick, which is now preserved in Brighton Museum (Worthing Museum Acc. No. 1961/1584).

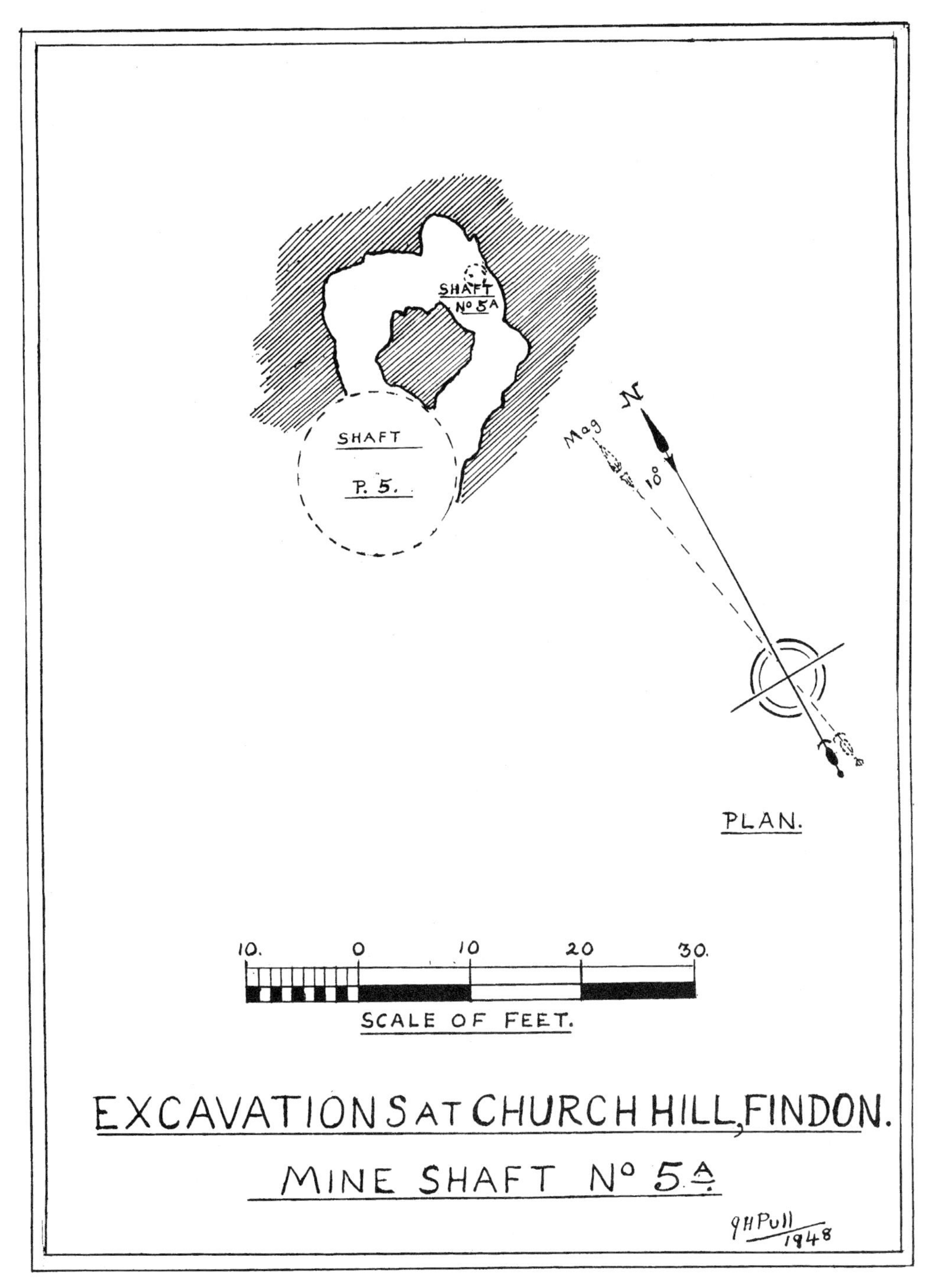

Figure 61. Church Hill Shaft 5a: plan of the subterranean gallery system (© Worthing Museum and Art Gallery).

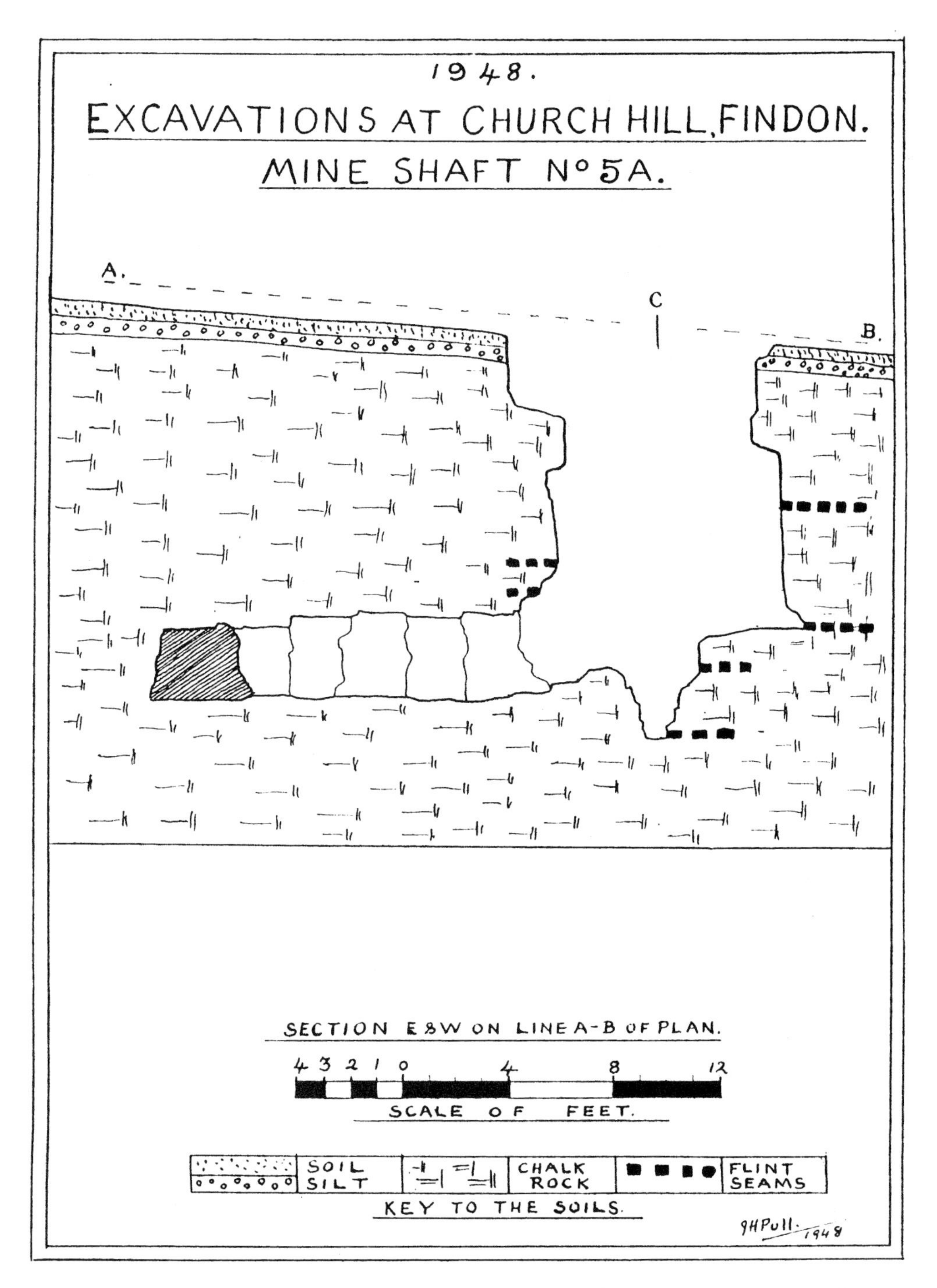

Figure 62. Church Hill Shaft 5a: profile through the excavated shaft (© Worthing Museum and Art Gallery).

Figure 63. Church Hill Shaft 5a: the restricted dimensions of this feature, as well as the difficulties of access, are clearly demonstrated in this picture taken in 1948 (© Worthing Museum and Art Gallery).

Pull and Voice recorded an irregular cut, measuring three feet in depth, at the centre of the Shaft floor, which they interpreted as a sump. Though the feature could well have functioned as a type of water-draining pit, it is also possible that it represents the remains of a pit originally cut to ascertain the depth or extent of a fifth seam of flint (something which it does in fact achieve), and that only later was the decision made to abandon this cutting and to work the fourth seam instead. It is uncertain whether the 'hearth site' that is recorded in the uppermost fill of Shaft 5a represents an area of insitu burning or a dump of secondary refuse into an existing surface hollow. The plan and section drawing produced by Pull illustrates the almost complete lack of artefacts within the 'hearth' itself, the flint flakes and tools massing along the eastern margins. Such an unbalanced finds distribution could be taken to argue against the deposit representing a layer of secondary refuse (where one would perhaps expect a more even artefact distribution), and in favour of it being a zone of insitu burning with other activities being originally conducted at the periphery.

A small number of flint artefacts from Shaft 5a, including two flaked axes, a broken flaked axe and three broken axe roughouts, survive in Worthing Museum. Some 20 flakes, two of which have been retouched, from the area of the hearth, also survive in the Museum Archive.

Shaft 6 and 7

By J. H. Pull and A. R. Voice

The depression indicating these shafts measured 22 feet north – south and 21 feet east west and was two feet deep (figure 64). Immediately around this depression were situated to the south-west Shaft 1 (T19), to the north-east T10, to the south P6 and to the north-west T25. Between the north-east lip of P6 and the south-west lip of the depression was an obvious dump of mining debris, three feet in height,

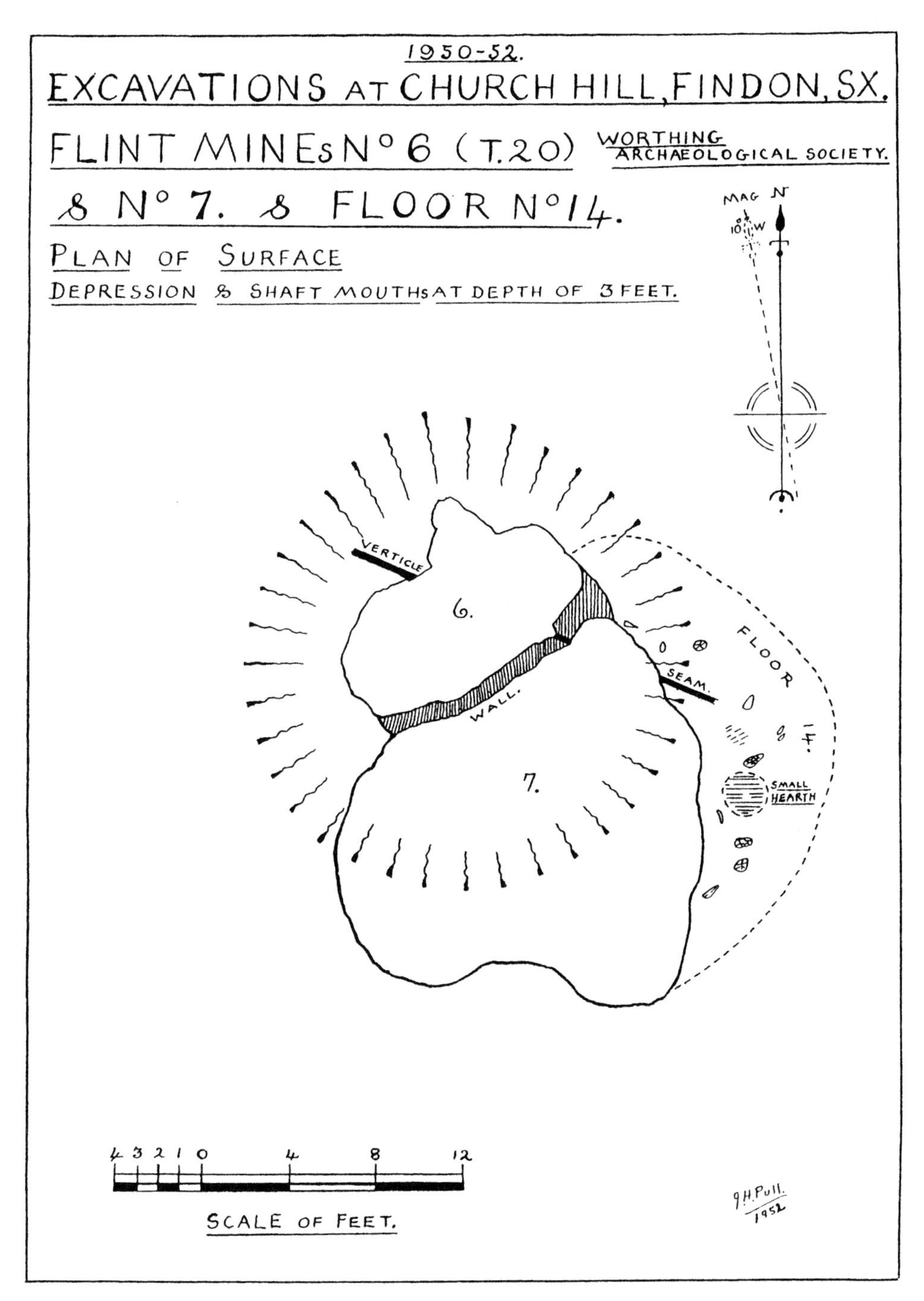

Figure 64. Church Hill Shafts 6 and 7 and Chipping Floor 14: plan of surface hollow with subsurface detail relating to the relative position of the shaft mouths and chipping floor (© Worthing Museum and Art Gallery).

which was presumed to cover the natural surface. On excavating the depressed area indicated as T20 on Tom's original plan, a solid vertical face of, what afterwards turned out to be, the north wall of Shaft 6 was revealed at a depth of one foot seven inches from centre. To the south the southern wall of what was later revealed to be Shaft 7, was located 14 feet from the centre. To the south-east this wall extended another four feet, making 18 feet in all. We thus found that we were dealing with a very large shaft indeed. One foot six inches south of the depression's centre and four foot six inches below the turf line (six feet below the horizontal datum), there was found the top of a narrow vertical chalk wall which proved to be the boundary between the two shafts now numbered Shaft 6 and Shaft 7. The infilling of the depression, which penetrated to this depth, had a general dip from all directions toward the centre of Shaft 6, indicating that this pit was the later of the two to have been sunk and the last to have been filled in.

Shaft 6 was six feet six inches in diameter north and south and 11 feet six inches in diameter east and west. It descended 19 feet in depth below datum and 17 feet below the turf line at its centre, five inferior horizontal seams of flint having been passed through and the sixth one worked (figure 65). These flint seams occurred at three, four and a half, nine and three quarters, 11 and a half, 13 and a half and 17 feet below the surface. At the base, the walls of Shaft 6 were pierced by five short headings chasing the great floor seam (figures 66, 67 and 68). The first of them was on the eastern side and was four and a half feet wide and three feet high at the entrance, five feet wide and two feet high beyond that. It extended from the shaft to a distance of eight feet six inches where it terminated in a round end. This heading had, after it had been worked for flint, been used as a dump for chalk blocks and chalk debris, which was heaped up to within nine inches of the roof. On this pile of debris was a very fine, single-handed antler pick, a broken shoulder blade shovel and two very fine flint knives.

The second heading on the north-east was two and a half feet wide, five feet high and two feet deep terminating in a very square end. This heading was also piled with chalk rubble and contained several large blocks on its floor. On the north-west, the third head was four and a half feet wide, three feet high and four feet deep. This was almost filled with chalk rubble. On the north-west was the beginning of a fourth heading, penetrating only one foot six inches at the floor level and one foot high, being a little undercut to about three feet above this. On the west, was another short heading, three feet deep and three feet wide by three and a half feet high. Common with this was the entrance to a short gallery penetrating the southern wall of this shaft into Shaft 7. This later heading was fairly clear of debris, with only nine inches to a foot of chalk rubble on the floor. Lying on this rubble was a two-handled antler pick, just as it had been left by the miner who drove it.

It appeared as if the penetration of the dividing wall between the two shafts at this point had been the reason for the final abandonment of the pit. When one studies the face of the chalk rock penetrated by the headings, one is impressed by the risks taken by the miners. For instance the north-eastern heading had been driven along the line of a wide vertical master joint in the chalk which gave no

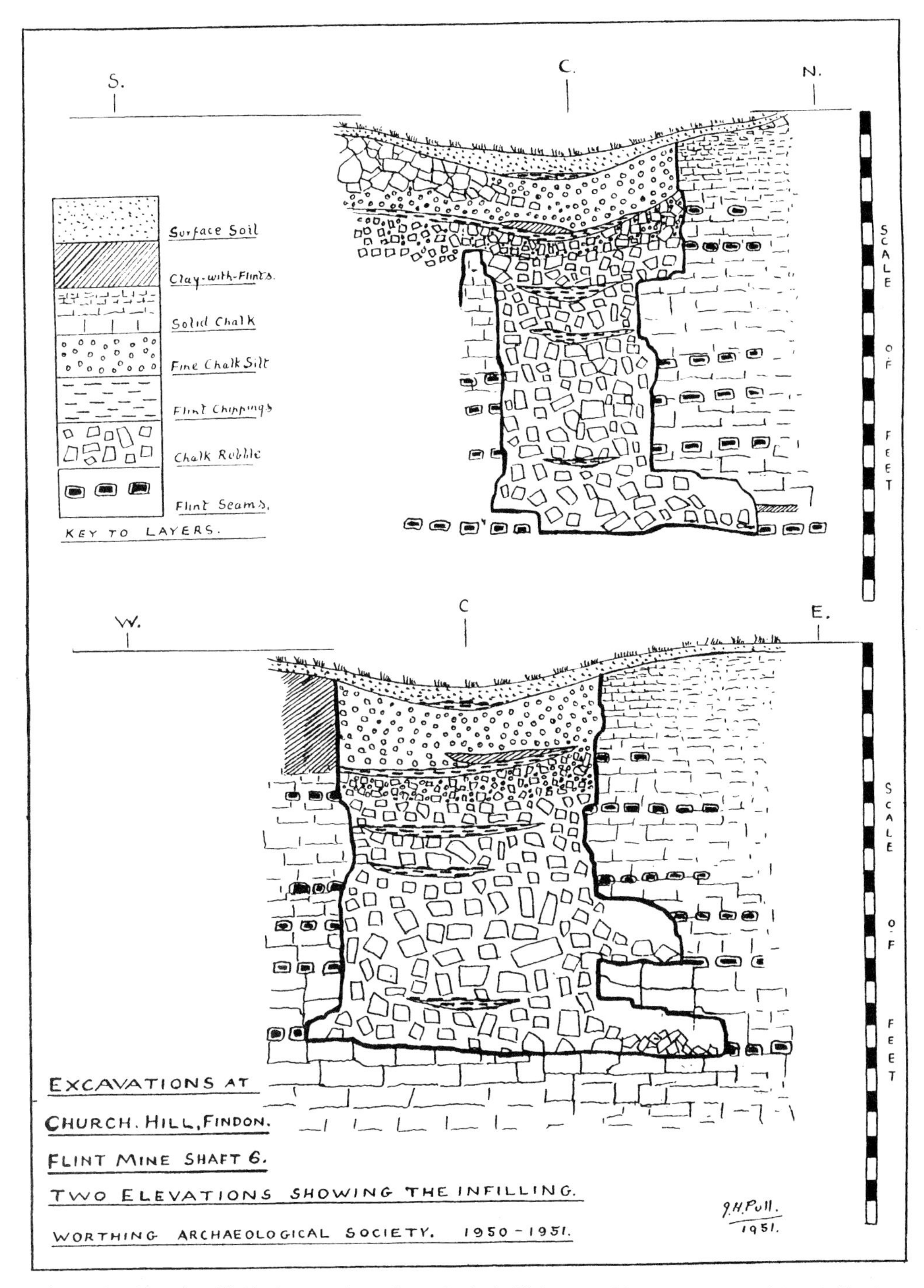

Figure 65. Church Hill Shaft 6: sections through shaft fill (© Worthing Museum and Art Gallery).

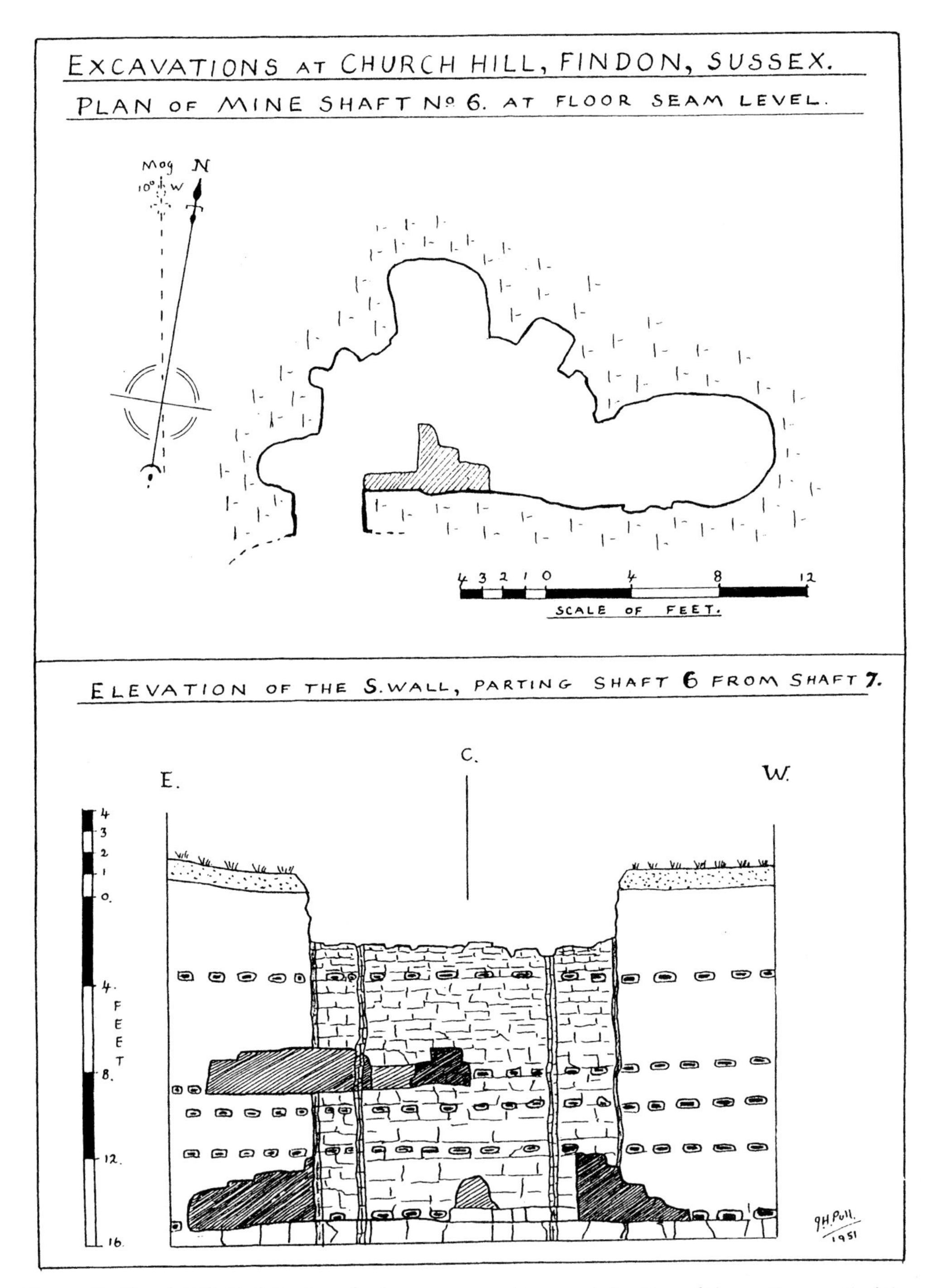

Figure 66. Church Hill Shaft 6: plan of subterranean workings and elevation of the southern wall of the shaft (© Worthing Museum and Art Gallery).

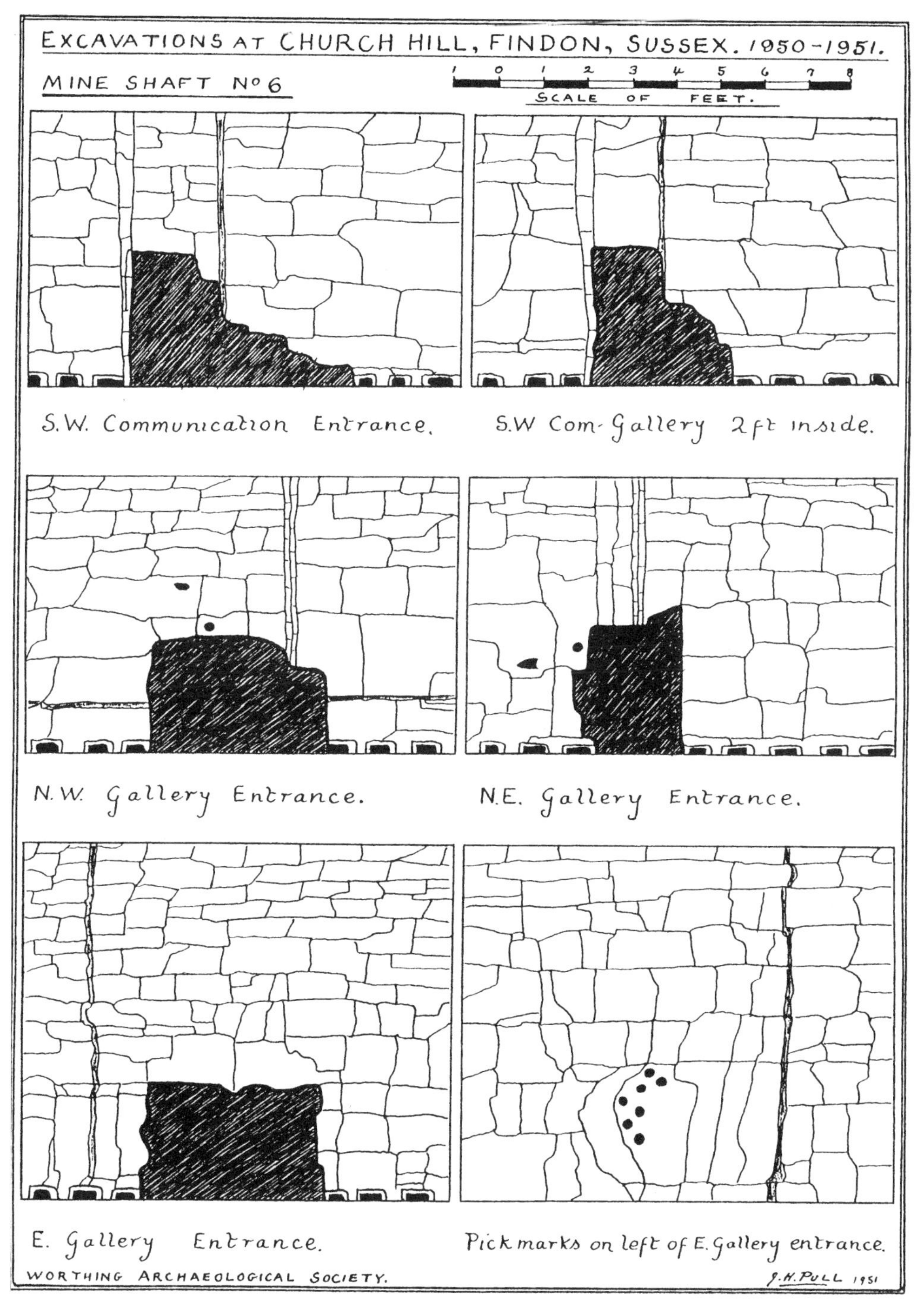

Figure 67. Church Hill Shaft 6: elevations for five of the subterranean working entrances showing the position of certain antler pick marks (© Worthing Museum and Art Gallery).

Figure 68. Church Hill Shaft 6: E. J. Salisbury looking at a series of antler pick marks on the edge of an undercut made into the eastern wall of the shaft in order to extract flint from the second seam. The third and fourth seams are visible to the left of the shot, above Salisbury's right hand, whilst the upper edge of a basal heading, extracting flint from the fifth seam, is visible at the bottom (© Worthing Museum and Art Gallery).

security for the roof. There is no doubt that the heading had been given up because of this. Advantage seems to have been sought from the presence of master joints in the chalk as providing an easy means of extraction, but where these proved to give insecure roofing, the heading was abandoned. The south-west gallery which penetrated the wall between Shafts 6 and 7 was even worse in this respect as the left hand side was along the line of a chalk filled slide joint and the right had side was along the line of a clay filled vertical joint. A great block at the entrance between these two joints had moved downward several inches while the shaft was open and threatened a major roof collapse at any time.

Why the good, sound roofed gallery on the eastern side had not been driven to a greater distance is a mystery we could not solve. True another shaft exists not far away from this, as indicated by a depression other surface, but the flint seam was good and there appears to be no reason why it should not have been pressed

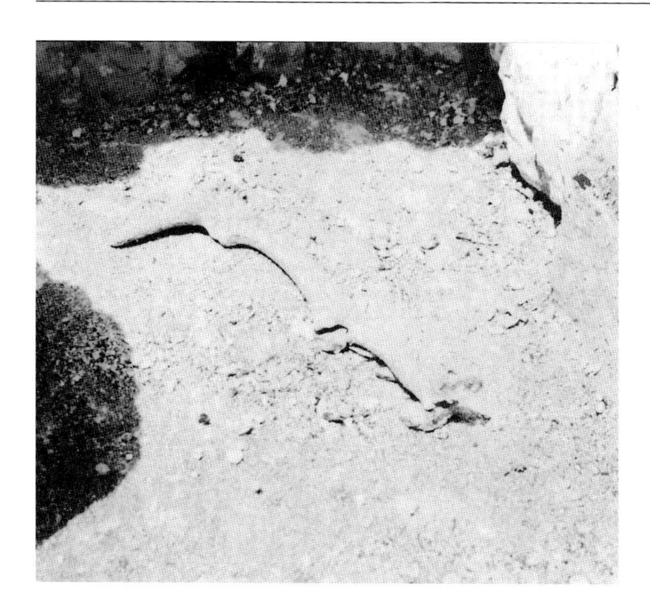

Figure 69. Church Hill Shaft 6: an antler pick photographed in situ at the base of the shaft (© Worthing Museum and Art Gallery).

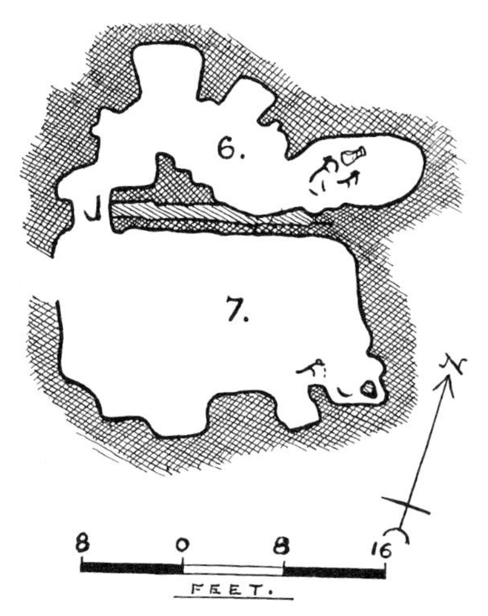

Figure 70. Church Hill Shafts 6 and 7: a sketch plan to illustrate the relative positions of bone and antler tools recovered from the basal levels of both shafts (© Worthing Museum and Art Gallery).

further. When clearing ancient flint mines one often gets the impression that certain pits have been suddenly abandoned by the miners and never worked again. In these lateral headings, apparently just as the miners had left them, were found a variety of antler mining tools (figures 69 and 70), by no means all worn out, a broken ox blade shovel, and several very good flint knives. No reason for abandonment was perceptible – perhaps the flint miners knew more about the instability of chalk rock than we do.

The basal infilling of Shaft 6 consisted of large chalk blocks (layer 8) and chalk rubble of various sizes filling the shaft headings. No appreciable interval had elapsed before the extraction of large chalk blocks from some other pit (layer 7), for no silting had taken place. It was not possible to ascertain from which direction these blocks had come. They filled the shaft to three feet above its floor. A small chipping floor (layer 6) marked a short interval in the chalk infilling. This occupied the centre of the shaft and consisted of a mass, six inches thick and four feet east–west by three feet six inches north–south, of flakes, chippings, waste flint and some unfinished flint implements. Above this, the shaft had been used again as a receptacle for chalk rubble and large blocks with a certain proportion of waste flint nodules which had been extracted from some other shaft. This comprised layer 5 and filled the shaft up to a distance of eight and a half feet above its floor. A short interval had again elapsed before the partially filled pit had been used as a sheltered place in which to manufacture flint implements. This second chipping floor (layer 4) was about six inches thick and consisted of the usual mass of flints, chippings, waste flint and implements in various stages of completion. This was larger than the previous floor, measuring seven and a half feet east–west by five feet north and south.

A further deposit of chalk rubble (layer 3), about two feet in depth, from the working of a neighbouring mine, had been introduced into Shaft 4 above layer 4. Yet again, a chipping floor (layer 2) marked a short interval in the infilling. This extended to within a foot of the shaft's edge on the north, south and west but fell short of the eastern side by two feet. The deposit was six inches thick at its centre. This third floor was covered by layer 1, a mass of large and small weathered chalk blocks, which appear to have been introduced from the north side. Layer 1 filled the shaft to the top of the wall, which separated Shaft 6 from Shaft 7.

Shaft 7 was 16 feet in diameter north and south, by 18 feet east and west. It descended 18 feet below the datum line and 16 feet below the turf line at its centre, the same five inferior seams of nodular flint (met with in Shaft 6) having been passed through and the sixth one removed from its base (figure 71). The base of the shaft was not pierced by any subterranean galleries, other than the connecting gallery with Shaft 6 (figure 72), but was deeply undercut on the south and in two places on the south-east (figure 73). These undercuts were four feet in depth and three and a half feet in height. The undercut in the south-east corner was evidently made from two directions, one along the east wall and one along the south wall. Where the two met, a narrow pillar of chalk had been left and the base of this had eventually been removed by the extraction of the flint seam, leaving the pillar hanging like a large stalactite. On the south wall of Shaft 7 an undercut four feet deep and three feet high had been driven at the level of the third and fourth seam, evidently to extract nodules. Another such undercut had been made at the same level on the south-west wall. More shoulder blade shovels and antler picks were found in the filling of pit 7, as well as a flint pick, a flint axe and two flint knappers mallets made from antlers, these last from a spot where a side heading only partially filled in had provided a sheltered spot for the workmen.

In this shaft a very interesting discovery was made while clearing the chalk rubble with which the shaft had been filled: two slanting holes were found, six to nine inches in diameter, and 15 inches apart, parallel with each other. Careful measurement showed that their lower ends terminated on the middle of the shaft floor, their upper ends on the lip of the shaft on its south-eastern side. They clearly indicated the decay of two stout wooden poles, which might have been either sides of a ladder or of a slide, up which bags of material might be pulled. This is the first direct evidence found as to the miner's methods of descending the shaft or of raising material to the surface.

The earliest layer of Shaft 7's infilling (layer 11), consisted of a mass of large chalk blocks which had been piled about the centre to a depth of about two feet. These blocks presumably represented material from the basal undercuts, which had never been raised to the surface. Following the abandonment of the pit the shaft had evidently been left empty for at least one winter for a certain amount of

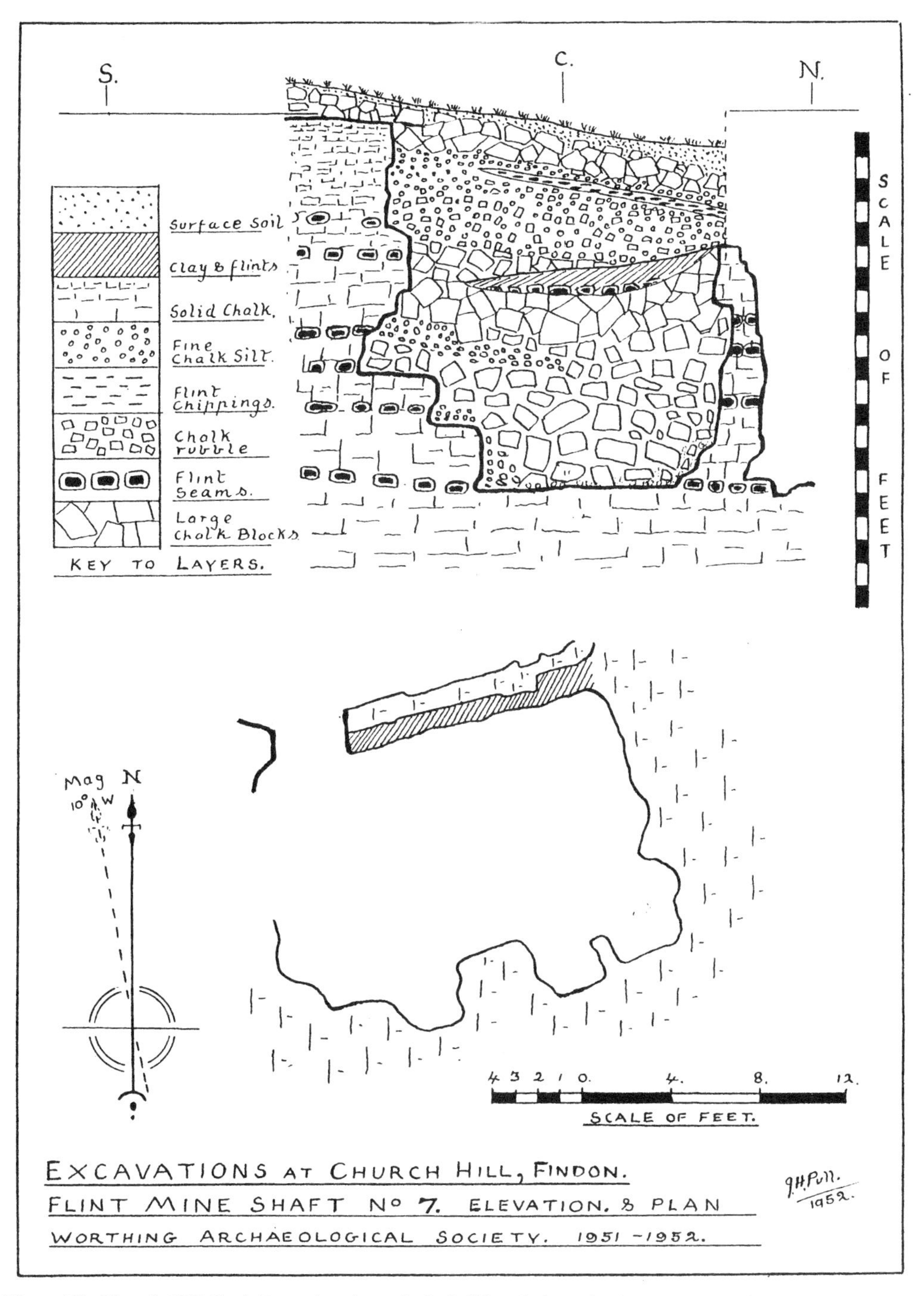

Figure 71. Church Hill Shaft 7: section through shaft fill and plan of subterranean workings (© Worthing Museum and Art Gallery).

Figure 72. Church Hill Shaft 7: members of the excavation team looking through "low level heading no.1" into Shaft 6 for the first time in 1952 (© Worthing Museum and Art Gallery).

Figure 73. Church Hill Shaft 7: Mervyn Hinge clearing rubble from the basal undercut on the southern side of the shaft (© Worthing Museum and Art Gallery).

coarse rapid silting (layer 10), representing material which had fallen from the sides as a result of the first weathering, had accumulated around the sides to a depth of about one foot. Following this, the shaft had been used as a dumping floor for a mass of large chalk blocks and rubble (layer 9) which filled it to a fairly level surface, five feet above the base. The interstices between these blocks were not filled in. it was impossible to determine from which direction layer 9 had been introduced. Many of the larger blocks bore the marks and hollows made by antler picks. One or two bore the marks of the large wooden punches first noted at Church Hill in the galleries of Shaft 4. A certain amount of large waste nodules of mined flint were distributed among the blocks.

Some time had again elapsed before the next layer of artefactual infilling had been introduced into the shaft, for another accumulation of coarse chalk silt, resulting from further weathering of the shaft's lip and walls, overlay layer 9, especially on the south side. This constituted layer 8. Following this second interval in the infilling, layer 7, a tilt of large chalk blocks, had been introduced from the north. These blocks rose level with the lip of the wall dividing Shafts 6 and 7, to a maximum thickness of four feet on that side. This evidently represented material excavated from the basal part of shaft 6. Layer 6 consisted of a mass of large waste flints to which had been added a mass of soft red clay with broken flints and some small chalk. This layer occupied the whole of the centre of the shaft and extended to the western edge where it was nearly two feet in thickness. It did not extend to the south wall by three feet and stopped five feet from the eastern wall. This evidently represented the initial material excavated by the miners in sinking a new pit immediately to the west of Shaft 7 for on that side the deposit of clay with flints overlay the chalk, becoming thicker as one passes westwards. Above layer 6 the infilling of Shaft 7 was common with that of Shaft 6, a level roughly corresponding to the top of the wall between the two shafts.

The twin shafts must have been abandoned for some considerable time following the main period of their artificial infilling, and it is possible that this period saw the weathering, splitting up and demolition of the narrow dividing wall between them which may have reached to a much higher level than when we found it; for a mass of natural infilling occurred above the top of the wall, 10 feet from the base of the shafts (figure 74). This upper filling was common to the whole of the area occupied by the two shafts and consisted of coarse chalk silting, highly consolidated with fine silt. This extended on the south to within one foot six inches of the fill surface and was three feet thick at that point, two and a half feet thick on the northern side. It evidently represented the drifting of weathered and frost powdered chalk from the surrounding walls of the two shafts and a large amount of rainwash from the dumps of chalk debris piled on the surface around the shaft mouths. Upon the surface of this deposit, a large flint knapping floor had been established. This floor, the usual mass of flakes and chippings, up to six inches in thickness, extended from a point four feet from the south wall of Shaft 7 to within two feet of the north wall of Shaft 6. It reached from the western edge of the two shafts to within one foot of the eastern edge. A little to the north of its centre, a small mound of clay with flints, about three feet by five feet, had

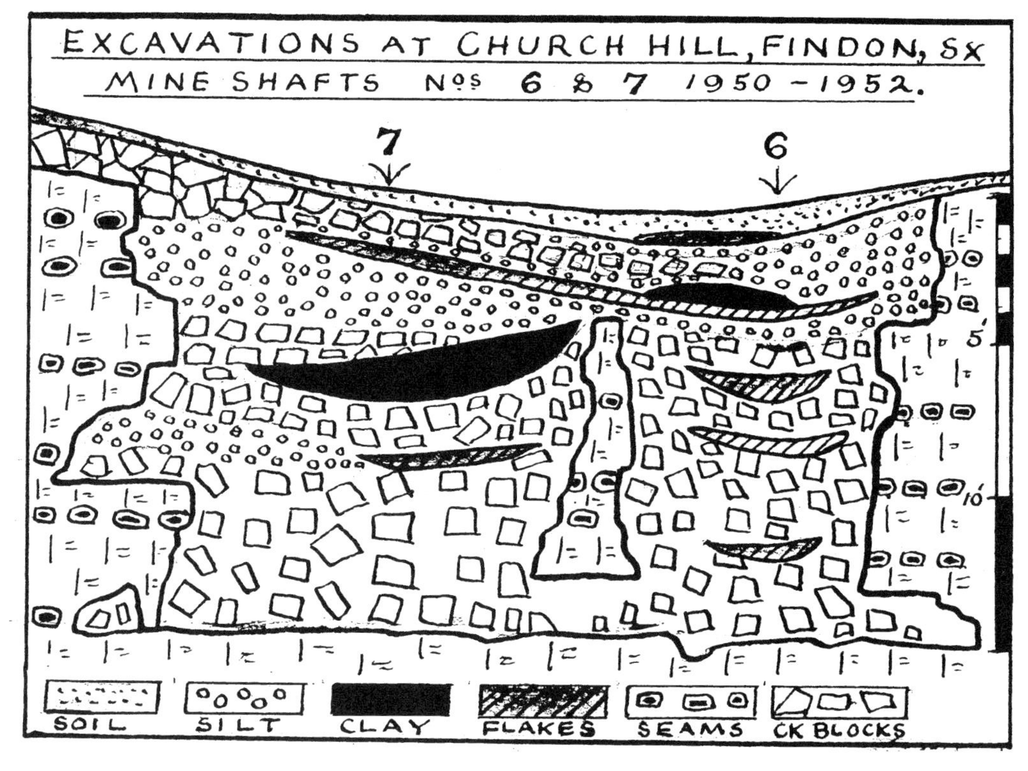

Figure 74. Church Hill Shafts 6 and 7: sketch section by Pull designed to illustrate the relationship between the two features (© Worthing Museum and Art Gallery).

been dumped. This evidently represented material from the upper part of a new shaft being sunk nearby at that time.

Following the working of this floor (Floor 13) further silting had taken place to a depth of one foot, covering the whole. Then it would appear the infilling of the large shaft known to exist immediately to the south of Shaft 7, was well in progress and a large dump of chalk blocks on the surface between this pit and Shaft 7, had overflowed into the rainwash sealed area of Shafts 6 and 7. This completely filled the hollow over Shaft 7 to the surface and extended out to a point six feet six inches from the north wall of Shaft 6. This overflowing of the dump was responsible for the eccentricity of the depression over the two excavated shafts. Following the weathering of this dump of chalk blocks, further silt had accumulated, filling Shaft 6 to the surface. Upon this final silting over the centre of Shaft 6, a small chipping floor had been worked about three feet by four feet. Above this the surface soil and turf had accumulated to a depth of one foot, thus finally sealing the depression above the two shafts (Worthing Museum Acc. No. 1961/1584).

In this archive text Pull and Voice suggest that of the two shafts, Shaft 7 was the earlier, something which Pull later contradicts in the summary of excavation results published in the *Sussex County Magazine* where he notes that '6 had been sunk first and 7 had been dug later' (Pull 1953, 18). This change in interpretation is difficult to unravel. It is possible that the version appearing in the Magazine contains an error and that '6' and '7' were somehow substituted in the text though it is also possible that Pull had reassessed the relationship between the two shafts during post excavation. The section drawings do little to help resolve the problem. True, the upper fills of the two cuts appear to possess a general downwards slump towards Shaft 6, but this need not necessarily prove that 6 was the older of the two, only that its fill had settled more following its abandonment. Shafts 6 and 7 could, of course, have been broadly contemporary, the column of chalk between them serving more as an internal support rather than a chronological divide. This conclusion may explain the homogeneity of the upper fill overlying both shafts, as well as the fact that both were linked by a short gallery which, unlike the others, had been left largely clear of rubble by the miners.

The inked sketch plan of the basal galleries indicates the relative positioning of the 'variety of mining tools' located within Shafts 6 and 7. Whether the grouping of these artefacts, especially at the eastern end of Shaft 6, indicates sudden abandonment, with the tools hurriedly discarded, or whether they were part of a more formal deposit made at the end of a successful mining operation, is unclear. Pull and Voice both appear to favour the former interpretation, noting how the walls of the linking gallery between Shafts 6 and 7 seemed to have been partially collapsing at, or shortly after, the time of abandonment. The single antler pick found at the centre of the gallery joining the two shafts could, in this respect, be taken as an offering left when work within the mines came to a halt or as an artefact deliberately cast aside when the two mines were unexpectedly, and perhaps catastrophically, linked.

The basal gallery entrances of Shaft 6 are illustrated by Pull, giving some idea of their form and of the original method of flint extraction. A series of pick marks above the entrance to the north-western and north-eastern galleries and upon the 'left of the east gallery entrance', are also shown in this drawing. Unfortunately Pull makes no comment concerning these marks in his text or notes and so it is not known whether these were thought to represent impressions created during the original extraction process, or deliberate markings perhaps akin to those noted above the galleries of Shaft 4 (see above). The Shaft 6 impressions, however, appear quite unlike those recorded from Shaft 4, which could perhaps be taken to argue against a form of intentional marking.

A single human fibula was recovered by Pull and Voice from on or close to the floor of Shaft 6. Pye suggested that this may represent part of a disturbed burial which was accidentally incorporated within mineshaft backfill (1968, 28), though it is just as likely to represent a disarticulated body part akin to the type of dismembered deposits noted from Shaft 4 and Barrows 2, 4, 9 and 12 at Blackpatch and the ditches of certain Early Neolithic causewayed enclosures (cf. Whitehawk: Curwen 1931a; 1934a). Few of the antler, bone or flint artefacts from the excavation of Shafts 6 and 7 could be traced at the time of writing.

THE PITS

The remains of three lesser cuts into the natural chalk were recorded and partially examined by Pull at the southern margins of the mining zone.

Pit A

By J. H. Pull

It was in the late autumn of 1933 that our colleague Mr C. E. Sainsbury (now unfortunately deceased) pointed out to us a circular area of turf which showed up green in contrast to the brown and yellow of the short and frost bitten downland turf at that season. This was the only surface indication of the pit marked A on our new survey (1946: see figure 49). This pit is situated 200 feet to the south-east of shaft P1 and 180 feet south of Barrow 4. I may add at this stage that on the new survey it will be seen that a further number of pits, namely those marked B to G, have been added to our score by the same methods of observation made use of by Mr Sainsbury. Also four round barrows, which have been ploughed down almost to the level of the infilling of their ditches (Barrows 5–8).

In the early summer of 1934, we fenced and excavated Pit A. Trial trenches cut round the perimeter of the pit revealed the fact that no overlying clay with flints was present on the fill at this point. Only six inches of turf and soil overlay the chalk. This surface round the mouth of Pit A had been disturbed over a roughly circular area 18 feet in diameter and to a depth of one foot (figure 75). The central portion of this disturbed area was centred over the mouth of the pit, which had been sunk vertically into the chalk rock to a depth of seven feet 6 inches. The infilling of this pit consisted first of surface mould, one foot six inches in thickness. In this surface was found a very beautifully worked disc scraper of flint, a few flint flakes and a flint knife, all patinated dead white on both surfaces.

At the base of the surface mould, and extending almost to the edge of the pit in all directions, was a mass of large flint nodules and broken flints. This flint waste, some of which seemed to have come from a depth and some, judging by their worn and frost bitten surfaces, to have been derived from the weathered out fill surface, rested in turn upon a layer of chalk silt or rainwash some two feet in thickness, completely filling and sealing the core of the shaft. The upper portion of this rainwash was stained brown and yellow with soil from above and was highly consolidated. The base of the rainwash was unstained and looser in structure. Shells of dead land mollusca were prevalent throughout its mass. Certain species of these, namely the Round mouthed snail, *Cyclostoma elegans,* the Bush snail, *Arianta arbostorum,* and the snail *Helix nemoralis,* were markedly predominant in numbers. The rainwash of prehistoric infillings is always a shelly layer, but in this instance it was noted that the shells were not present in such great numbers, as was the case in the pits at Blackpatch. This feature was also notable in the excavation of Shaft P1 here at Church Hill. In addition it was observed that the Bush snail *Adriante arbushtorum* did not attain such a great size in average diameter as those of the giant race found in the shafts at Blackpatch.

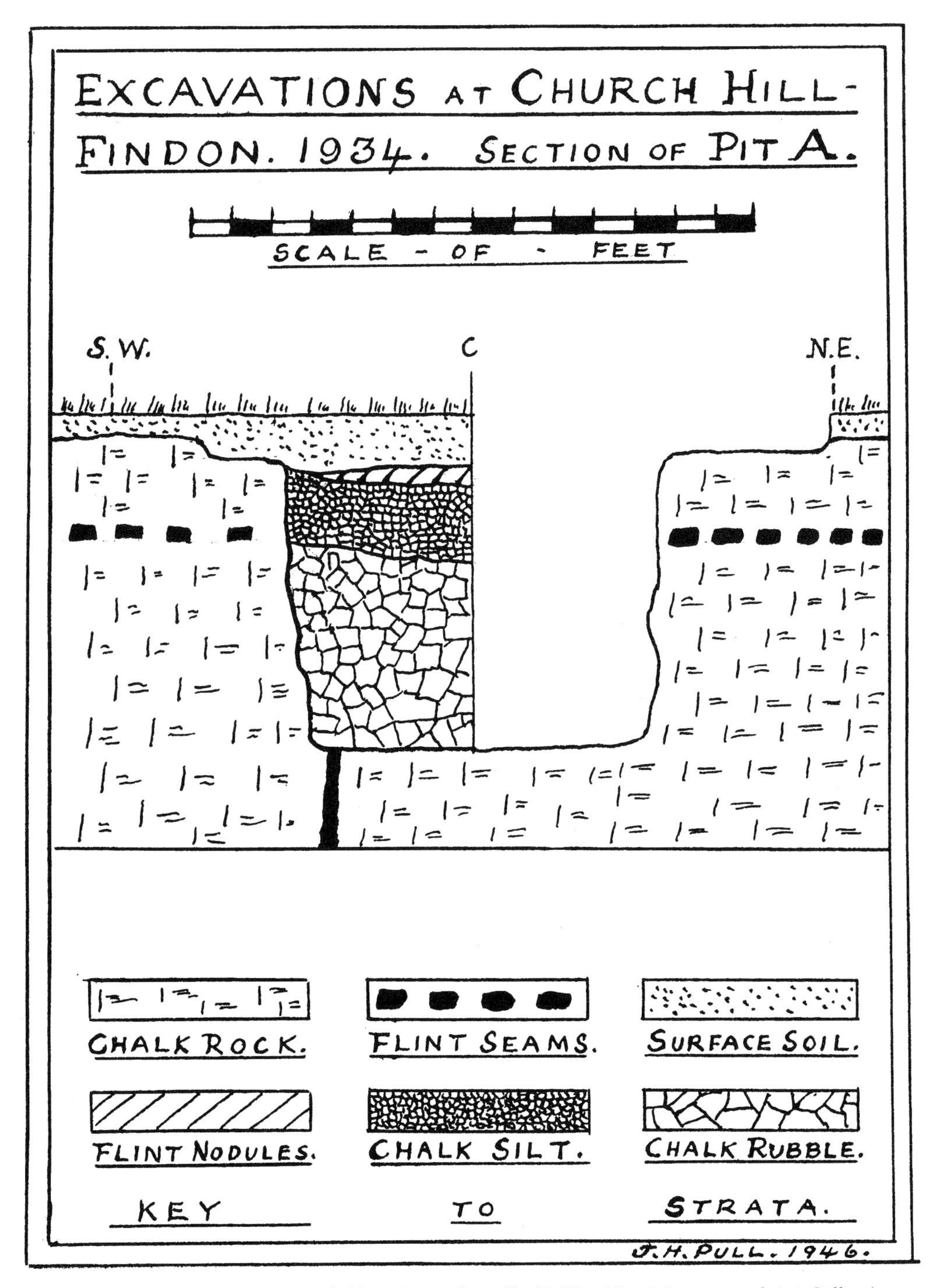

Figure 75. Church Hill Pit A: half section and profile (© Worthing Museum and Art Gallery).

This particular species is, in the opinion of Mr A. S. Kennard FJS FGS, a great climate indicator. It would then seem that judging from the general lessening of snail population coupled with the diminished size of certain indicator species that the excessive wet climate period during which the Blackpatch mines were worked had passed its zenith by the time the Church Hill ones were worked.

The rainwash layer in Pit A was particularly sterile of items of a curatorial nature. Apart from a few scattered flint flakes and chipped pieces of flint, only two good implements were found in it. At the base of the rainwash, three feet from the surface and five and a half feet north of the centre was found half of a very finely chipped celt of small dimensions and broad cutting edge, the workmanship being identical with that of the long thin celt found associated with the remains of a type C Beaker beneath Chipping floor 2. Six inches deeper and two feet to the south of the centre of the pit occurred another celt, perfect and of larger size with roughly parallel sides and broad cutting edge. This is a noteworthy implement because it possesses that curious twist in its longer axis which is so peculiar to certain ovate hand axes of Achuelean age.

Below the rainwash, Pit A was found to be filled from the bottom up with an unstratified mass of chalk rubble and chalk blocks of varying magnitude. Many of these bore the mark of picks of red deer antler which had been originally used to detach them. The interstices between the blocks and the pieces of rubble were open. Fragments of splintered flint and waste nodules were sparsely sown among them throughout. Only one good flint implement came from this rubble. This was found in its upper position four and a half feet from the shafts surface and two and a half feet south-east of the centre of the pit. It was a triangular hand axe of drift form patinated dead white all over.

The empty pit, cleared of its infilling, presented the appearance of a slightly oval shaft with vertical sides and flat bottom. A thin seam of tabular flint, much shattered and fractured, filled a vertical fissure in the chalk which cut across the south-western sector of the shaft. No horizontal seam was present on the pit's floor and only one of very inferior quality, consisting of a thin layer of sparsely sown nodules had been passed through when the pit was originally sunk. This bad seam occurred two and a half feet from the natural fill surface and three feet from the surface of the pits infilling. It seemed that it was impossible to decide whether this Pit A was an abortive mine shaft or whether it had been dug for some other purpose. The absence of charcoal, animal bones and pottery in its infilling excludes it from the category of dwelling sites. As has been already pointed out, the few flint implements found in it were patinated dead white all over and it cannot be proved that they were contemporary with the initial excavation of the shaft. The evidence offered by the land mollusca, the deer form pick marks on the blocks, and the general faces of flakes and chipped pieces from the deepest part of the infilling all combine to show that the pit was of a late date in the Neolithic period and presumably contemporary with the main portion of the mining area on the fringe of which it is situated.

One thing is certain; this pit had not been open for any length of time before the main body of material that had been excavated from it was returned to it. For the unweathered condition of its sides and of the chalk rubble with which it was in the main filled, together with the absence of any silt or soil in its lower depths, demonstrated this clearly. One wonders why the original excavators took the trouble to fill it in at all, much less to have done so almost immediately it had been opened up. The future excavation of Pit G, which was within a few yards of Pit A, may throw some further light upon the problems left over from this excavation (Worthing Museum Acc. No. 1961/1584).

Pit A may, as Pull indicated, represent the remains of a form of lesser quarry or extraction pit, an abortive mine or a cut to ascertain the nature or productivity of the ground at this point. In this respect it may perhaps be related to the smaller pits recorded from Tolmere (see below) that Pull investigated in 1949. Alternatively the feature may have formed some sort of storage facility associated with settlement close to the main area of flint extraction. A Neolithic or Early Bronze Age date for the feature seems probable, given not only the nature of the artefacts recovered but also the observation that antler picks had been utilised in its excavation. Only a small number of the flints recovered from Pit A, including three scrapers and two flakes, survive in Worthing Museum today. None of the axes referred to by Pull could be traced at the time of writing.

Pit B (Site 13)

By J. H. Pull and A. R. Voice

About 1,000 feet south-east of Shaft 4, well down on the hillslope midway between the footpath which comes up from the Findon Road and the field wall which traverses the south-east side of Church Hill, was an isolated depression 12 feet in diameter and one foot deep (figure 76). A pronounced mound measuring 15 feet east–west by nine feet north–south, was noted on the southern side of the depression. This depression and mound, originally listed as Site 13, had long occupied our attention. On December 5th 1948 it was surveyed in detail and the turf removed. The excavation occupied the winter months of 1948–1949.

At the centre of the depression was an almost circular pit, eight feet north–south by seven feet six inches east–west (figure 77). This pit was sunk to a depth of two feet in the solid chalk rock, having vertical sides and a flat bottom. Its infilling consisted of six inches of white, fine chalk silt over the bottom to a depth of one foot six inches at the sides. This silt was quite sterile. Above this the pit was filled to the top with a mixture of chalk and soil with many large rough flints, especially concentrated in the centre. Above this was an accumulation of surface soil, one foot in depth at the centre and six inches deep at the sides. In the mixed chalk and soil on the eastern edge of the pit occurred some fragments, including one large piece of rim, of dark coloured, well fired pottery with fine sand in the paste. These presumably represent fragments of an Early Iron Age vessel of the saucepan-shaped variety, similar to what has frequently been found in the neighbouring hill fort at Cissbury. Also in this same mixed layer occurred half of a roughly bored chalk spindle whorl, some oyster shells and a small quantity of flint flakes patinated dead white, together with a very rough celt.

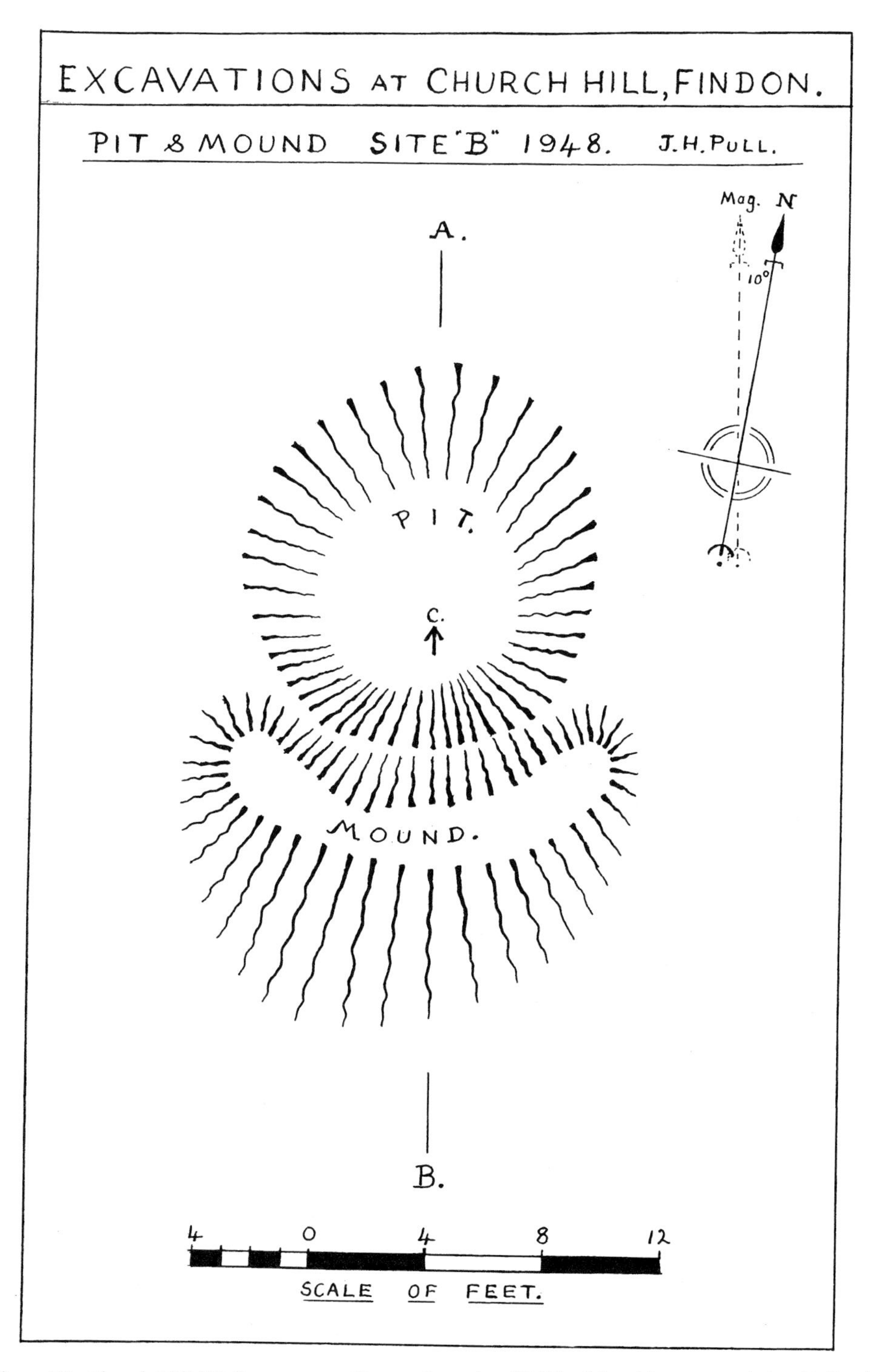

Figure 76. Church Hill Pit B: pre excavation surface plan (© Worthing Museum and Art Gallery).

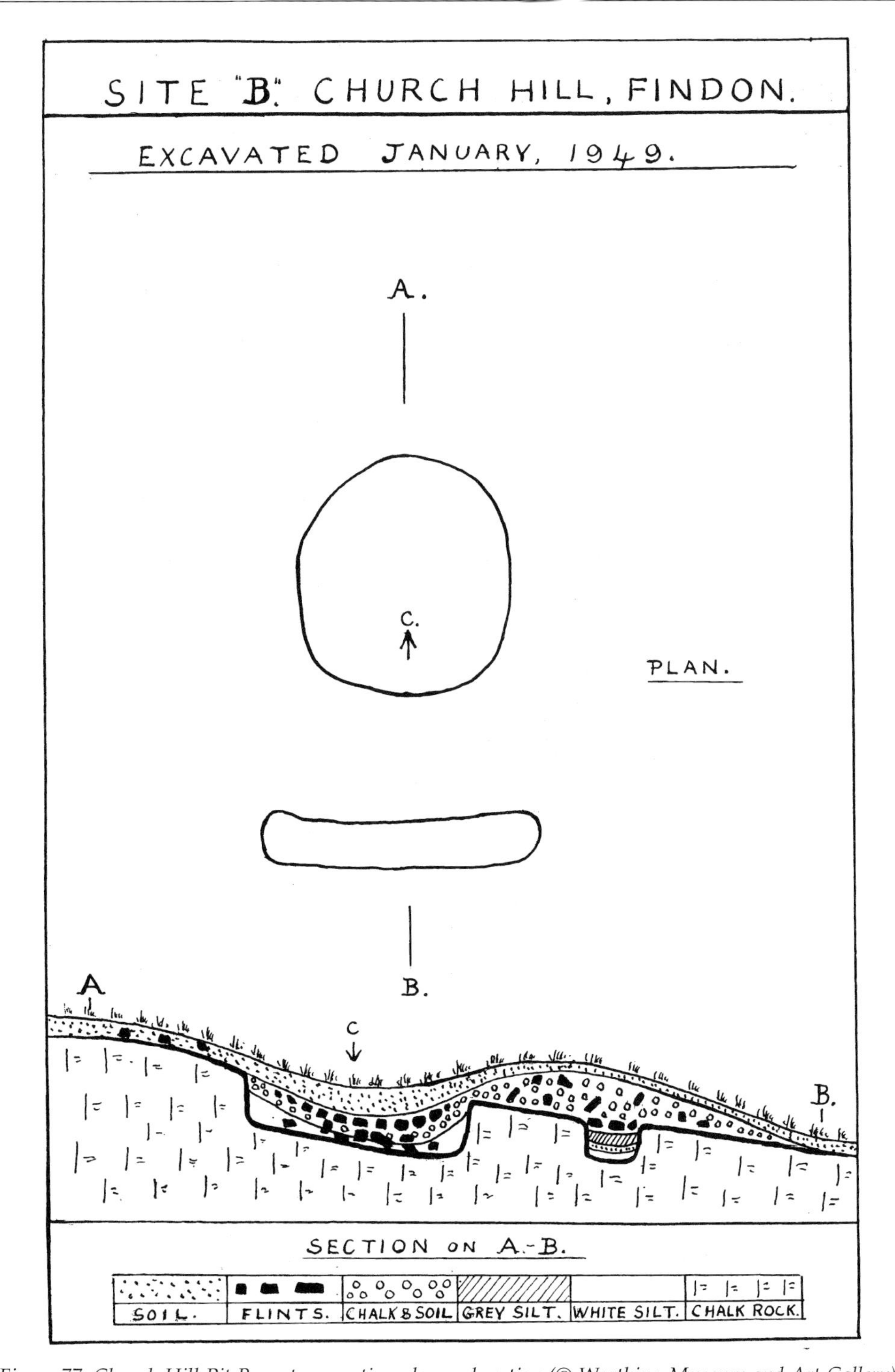

Figure 77. Church Hill Pit B: post excavation plan and section (© Worthing Museum and Art Gallery).

> The shells of land mollusca recovered from below the surface soil were not prolific and were all of a character common to the downland since Early Iron Age times: the damp loving species *Ariana arbostorum* and *Cyclostoma elegans* were entirely absent. *Helix nemoralis* were of a normal form and *Helix aspersa* was common near the soil line. The few worked flints found in the pit were all patinated dead white on both faces and may well have drifted into the pit from the surrounding surface which, even at this level, is sparsely littered with debris from the mining site further up the hillslope.
>
> The crescent shaped mound to the south of the pit, when excavated, was found to be composed of small chalk and soil continuous with that lying in the pit. Admixed with this were large flints, widely scattered. Beneath the centre of the mound was a narrow vertical sided, flat-bottomed trench, which had been cut into the solid chalk to a depth of two feet. The larger axis of this trench lay east–west and measured nine feet six inches. In breadth the trench was two feet. The bottom infilling of this trench consisted of three inches of sterile white silt. Above this was three inches of somewhat bleached soil and above that was six inches of grey silt and chalk dust mixed with ashes but no charcoal. Above this lay six inches of large flints. All the layers of infilling in the trench were quite sterile of archaeological finds, as was also the material of the mound. It would appear from the evidence that the trench had been dug first and that some time had elapsed for it to silt and for soil to accumulate over the silting. Following the filling of the trench, the pit had been dug immediately to the north and the excavated material had been dumped over the trench to form the mound. Some considerable portion of the material from the northern slope of the mound had drifted back into the pit afterwards. The purpose of both the trench and the pit remain obscure, as does the age of the finds, which were too scanty and inconclusive as to enable any definition to be given (Worthing Museum Acc. No. 1961/1584).

The pit and trench that together comprise Site 13 defy precise interpretation. It is clear that the trench was cut prior to the cutting of Pit B, assuming of course that the mound of earth that covered it had originally been taken from the area of the pit during excavation. It is just possible that the linear trench itself represented part of a later feature cut through the spoil mound in an attempt to extract flint rubble (Pull notes in the Tolmere site notebook that some of the barrow mounds around Tolmere may have had their centres removed to provide flint for walling around the nearby farm estates: Worthing Museum Acc. No.1961/1587). One would perhaps expect any such later disturbance to have left a clear impression within the mound and certainly one that Pull himself would have noticed. The Iron Age material retrieved from the upper levels of pit fill may indicate a later period of agricultural activity over the site. Alternatively it may be taken as suggesting that the feature as a whole dates from this later period. If the site may be interpreted as an area of Iron Age activity at the southern fringe of the mining zone (a similar interpretation is also possible for Pit C: see below), then the 'patinated' flint tools also deriving from the feature may be viewed as residual material accidentally incorporated into backfill. Unfortunately none of the recorded finds could be traced at the time of writing.

Pit C

By J. H. Pull

Pit C was situated on the crest of the saddle joining Church Hill to High Salvington at the junction of the tracks and the sunken way. The pit was indicated on the surface by a slightly oval depression measuring 21 feet north–south by 20 feet east–west and with a maximum depth of one foot six inches. When emptied the pit had a maximum diameter north–south of 18 feet nine inches, east–west of 16 feet and a depth of four feet on the western side, three feet six inches on the south-east, with a vertical chalk face on the north and north-east, south and south-east (figure 78). Seams of isolated large flint nodules were noted three and a half feet from the surface.

The infilling on the north-east side showed nine feet one inch of surface mould, one foot six inches of fine silt, one foot of flint nodules and large chalk silting (figure 79). The infilling on the south-west side showed one foot of surface mould, one foot six inches of large flints, clay and soil and one foot six inches of mixed chalk silt and flints. The pit appears to have been originally surrounded on the south-east, south and west sides by walling of large flint nodules packed with turf and clay, which had collapsed into the bottom of the pit. The walling on the north and east had been of flint and chalk blocks. In the surface soil and in the upper part of the flint and clay infilling were found medieval pottery, Romano-British pottery, Hallstatt pottery, Roman nails, charcoal, bones and teeth of ox and the land mollusc *Helix aspersa*. Below this, tusks of wild boar, the skeleton of a wild cat, flint tools and the mollusc *Cyclostoma elegans* were found. At the bottom of the pit a series of crude flint tools made from surface flint and some better examples, an axe and some scrapers, and flakes made from flint of the seam (Worthing Museum Acc. No. 1961/1584).

Pit C is difficult to interpret with any certainty. The field drawings that survive in Worthing Museum, compiled by Mervyn Hinge, appear to indicate a wide feature with shelving edges, quite unlike the prehistoric features associated with the main phase of flint extraction to the immediate north. The amount of Roman and later material recovered from the upper levels of pit fill may indicate a post Roman date for this cut as a whole, with the 'crude' flint tools perhaps representing residual material accidentally incorporated into backfill. None of the recorded finds from Pit C could be traced at the time of writing.

THE SURFACE CHIPPING FLOORS

As at Blackpatch, a large number of flint working floors were identified and examined at Church Hill, both at surface levels close to the mouths of shafts, and within the remnants of the partially backfilled shafts. The working areas within the shafts (4 and 6) have already been discussed within the context of the mines, though an additional 15 surface working areas at least were to have been located by Pull and Voice during

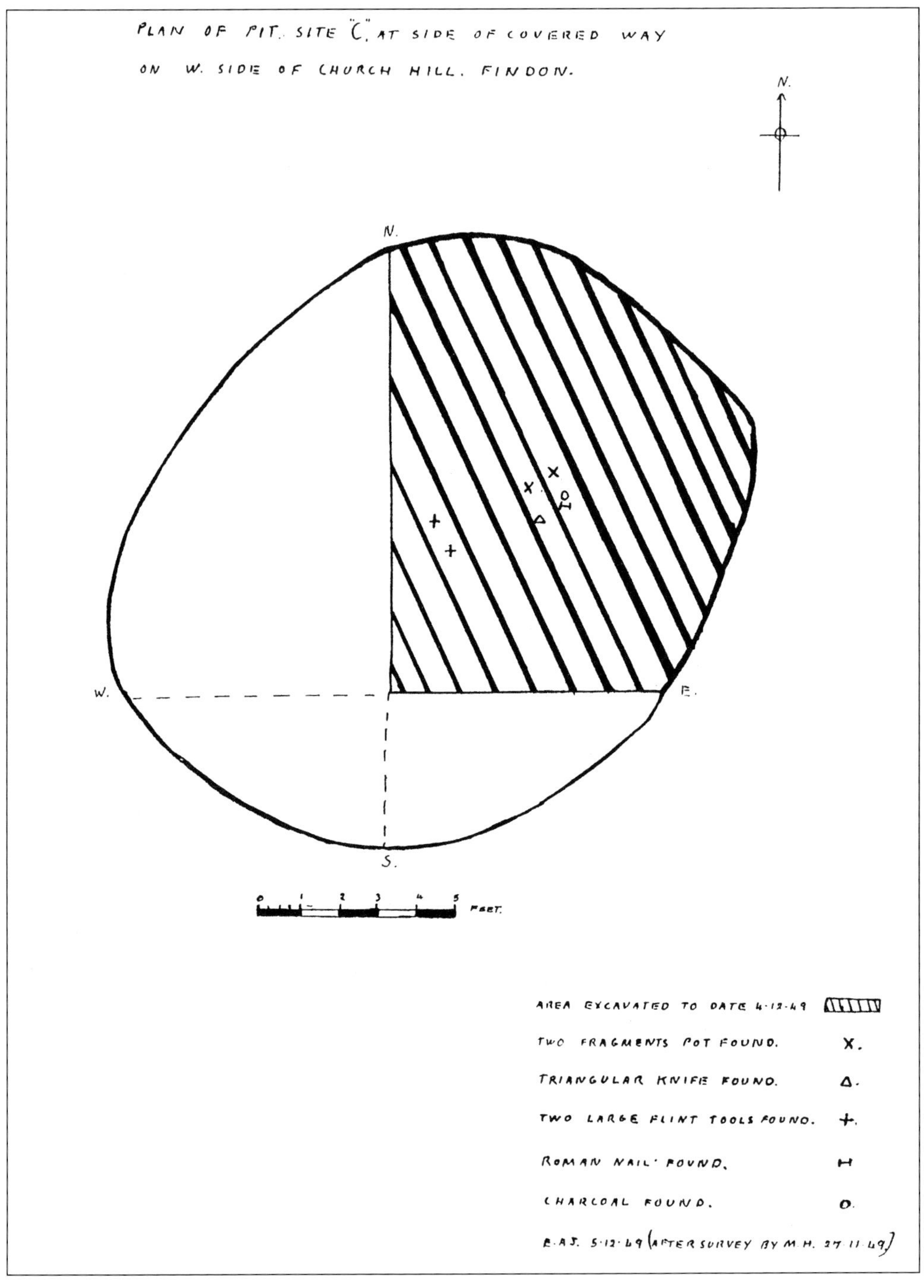

Figure 78. Church Hill Pit C: work in progress sketch plan for 27th November 1949 (© Worthing Museum and Art Gallery).

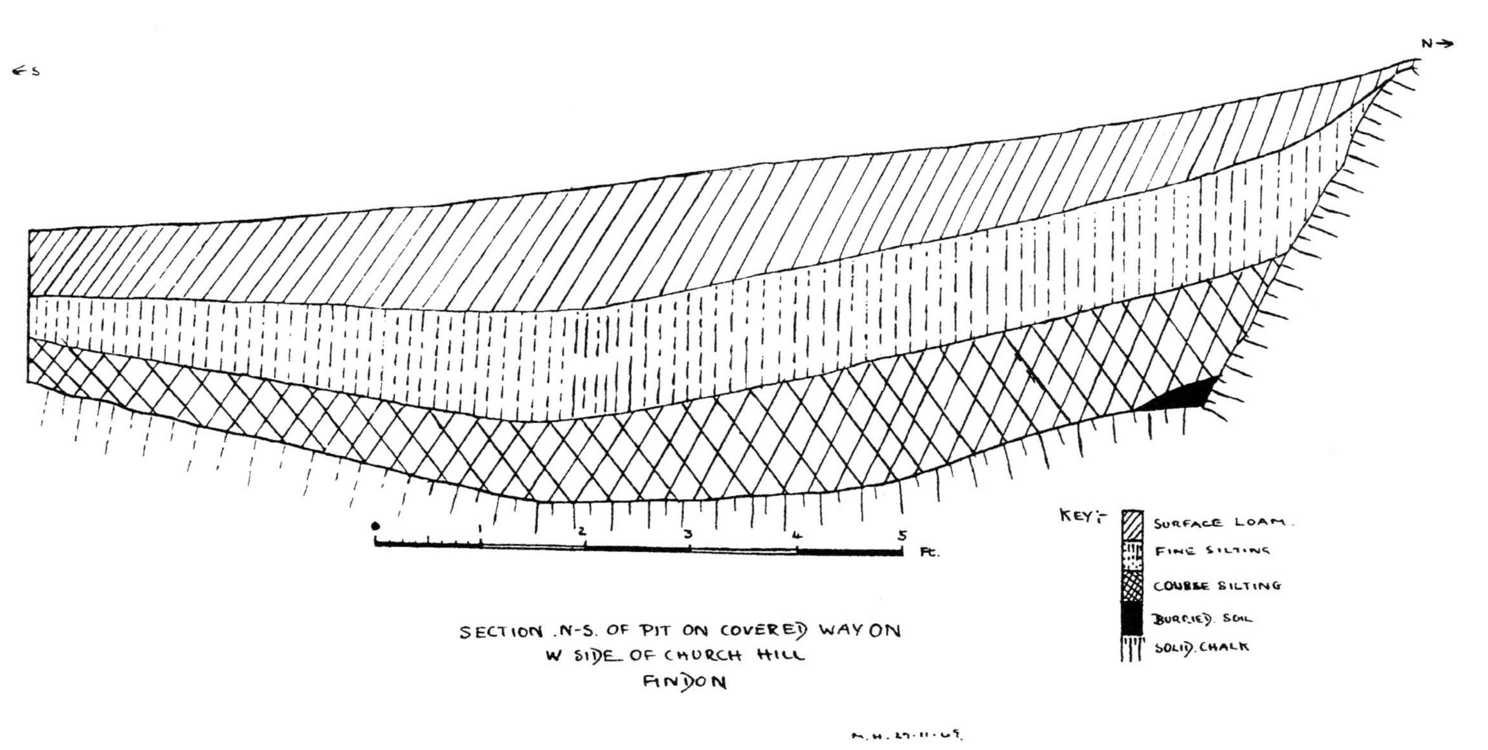

Figure 79. Church Hill Pit C: work in progress sketch section for 27th November 1949 (© Worthing Museum and Art Gallery).

the course of the Church Hill project. Few descriptions of these sites could be traced at the time of writing, though most can be located on the main site plan, specific drawings existing only for floors 2, 12 and 14 within the Worthing Museum archive.

Floors 1–8

By J. H. Pull

Our previous experience has proved to us that the major portion of the flint knapping workshop floors associated with the flint mines are situated upon the ridges between the mouths of the shafts. Eight separate workshop floors have now been located and explored at Church Hill. These all lay on the eastern and southern outskirts of the mining area and on the most downhill portion of the ground pierced by the shafts.

In size, the Church Hill floors varied greatly in the space that they covered, ranging from 100 to 200 square feet. In shape the floors are quite irregular and betray no signs of their ever having been confined within any regular boundary. Hence it is supposed that they were all operated in the open air. The flakes and chippings upon the floors are often packed several inches in thickness with little or no soil between them. Coarse primary flakes that were struck off the outer portion of flint nodules, in the process of reducing them to core implements, form the main portion of these floors. The fine secondary chippings which were the result of the finishing of large implements such as celts, and the manufacture of small tools such as scrapers and drills, usually occur in small patches or form pockets among the main spread of primary flakes, making it appear that as the operators who were engaged upon the flintwork got cramped and stiff through squatting in one position too long, they moved about the floor from time to time.

All of the floors explored were entirely superficial, being worked at one period only. It is interesting to note that the working of the floors and the mines was contemporary. Some of the floors explored were situated on the natural hill surface and had afterwards been partly covered by dumps of chalk rubble thrown up from new pits, which had been sunk either while the floors were being used, or immediately after they were abandoned. Other floors were situated over the top of such dumps, thus showing that they were later than some mining in the area. One floor had been cut away by the sinking of a shaft through it. Another descended at a steep angle into a pit which had been worked out and abandoned. But in no case have we found one floor superimposed upon another, nor did we at Blackpatch. Neither do the types of implements or style of workmanship exhibited by finished artefacts vary sufficiently on the floors to offer the slightest indication of any difference in culture or in flint working technique.

Perhaps one of the most striking features noted as the result of our excavation of the Church Hill floors is the large number of small implements which were made there. Though, as at Blackpatch and Cissbury, the celt was one of the principal implements made, these occur in by far the greatest quantity, large numbers of other tools such as drills, scrapers, knives, engraving implements, saws and planes commonly occur (Worthing Museum Acc. No. 1961/1584).

Floors 1, 2 and possibly 3 partially covered mine shafts, whilst 2 and 3 were themselves covered in later mining debris (mostly chalk rubble). The section produced for Floor 2 (figure 80) shows that the mass of flint debris constituting the working area contained, at its north-eastern end, an axe and at least two discrete areas of what Pull identifies as Beaker pottery (figure 81). Floor 4 seems to have possessed a hearth at its eastern periphery (Pye 1968, 26) though whether this constituted an in-situ deposit, as with 'Hearth site 2', remains debatable. Some burnt human bone was associated with this area. Pye (1968, 28) doubted whether this represented a formal burial deposit, though, considering the quantity of deliberately placed material noted from Chipping Floor sites elsewhere, it seems probable that the human bone, if not a complete burial in itself, may have formed part of a larger ritual or ceremonial deposit. Of the flints noted as deriving from Floors 1–8, only 29 flakes, two borers, one scraper and an axe roughout appear today within the Worthing Museum archive.

Floors 9–11

Floor 9 was detected at the south-eastern margins of Shaft 4. Floor 10 lay to the immediate east of unexcavated Pits E and F. Floor 11 has already been referred to within the context of Shaft 4 where it represents layer 3. This deposit extended out to the south-east of the shaft mouth, being partly covered by mining debris (chalk rubble) from a neighbouring mine. As with Floors 1–8, the whereabouts of the majority of the finds deriving from Floors 9–11 are unknown with only 17 flakes surviving in Worthing Museum.

Floor 12 and Hearth Site 2

By J. H. Pull and A. R. Voice

An excavation of exploratory nature was made on 5th September 1948 at a point 120 feet north-east of Pit 1 and midway between Pits T11 and T12. This resulted in the finding a small flint knapping floor immediately beneath the turf and surface soil. Consisting of the usual mass of flakes, chippings and waste flint, four to nine inches thick, this floor extended 120 feet south-west to north-east and was 10 feet in width (figure 82). Its eastern end rested on three feet of chalk silt and its western end on one foot of the same.

A number of flint implements, both finished and unfinished, were found distributed on the floor, including a fine and rather large cone core, a number of good knife blades which had been struck from some similar core. Three well-finished celts were also recovered. Resting on this mass of flakes at a point four feet from its north-eastern end, was a small circular hearth measuring six feet in diameter. Around the hearth and in it were a number of large blocks of waste flint, some burnt, and a number of bones and teeth of the short-horned ox. Some

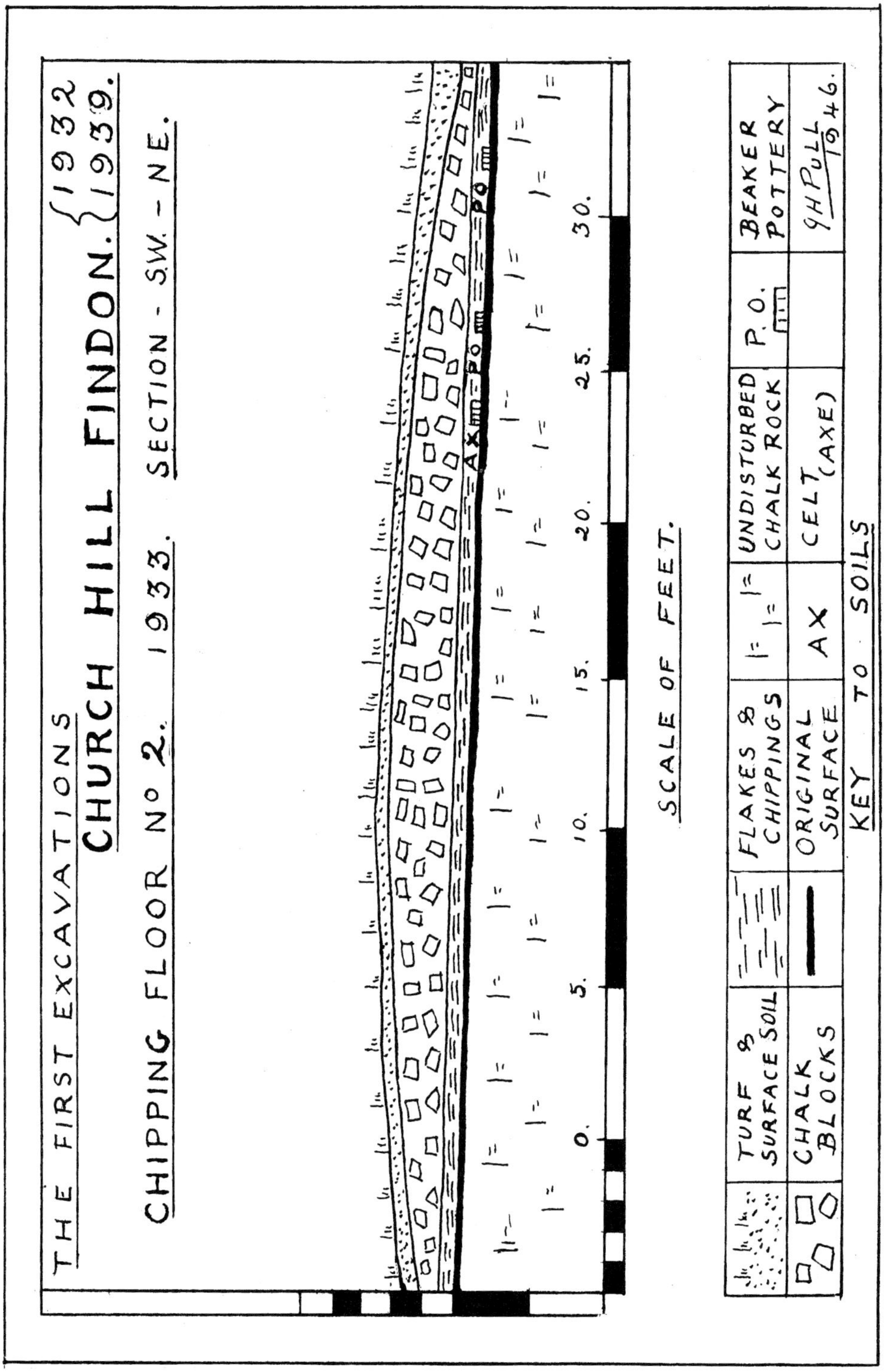

Figure 80. Church Hill Chipping Floor 2: section showing the relative positions of three sherds of Beaker pottery and a flint axe (© Worthing Museum and Art Gallery).

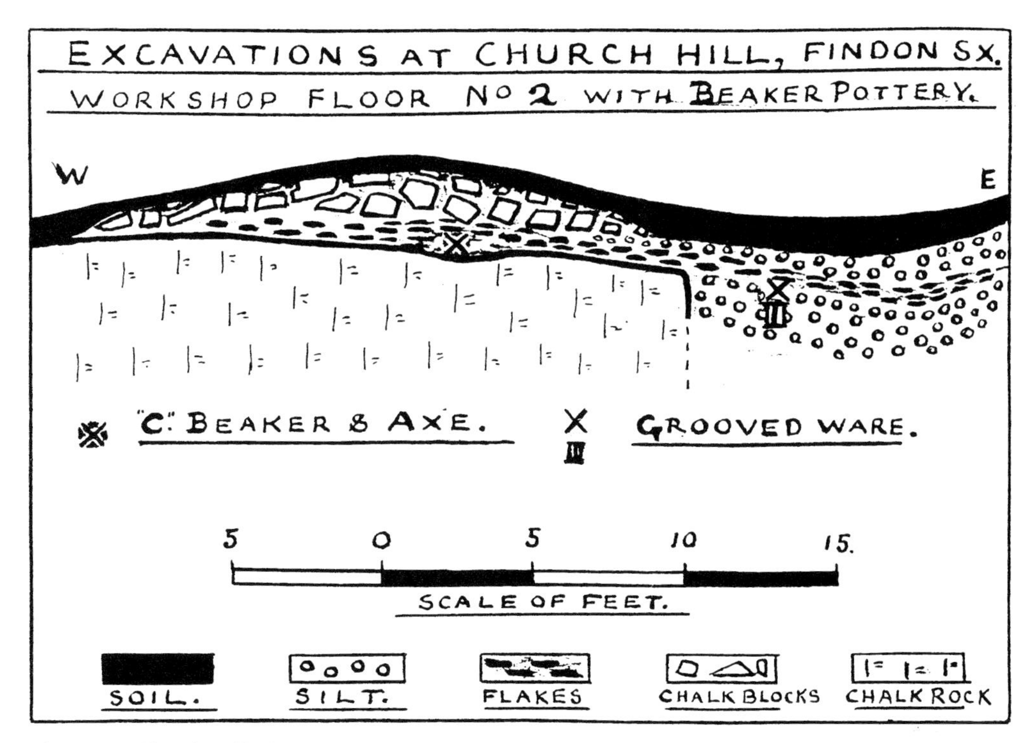

Figure 81. Church Hill Chipping Floor 2: sketch section by Pull to illustrate the relative position of artefacts (© Worthing Museum and Art Gallery).

> of the bones were thoroughly burnt and with them was a quantity of charcoal and, more importantly, the fragments of a Late Bronze Age pot which had possessed an upright rim and fingertip ornamentation below the rim. It would appear, from the above, that we have here a Later Bronze Age camping site superimposed over an Earlier Bronze Age flint knappers workshop. There was no evidence to show that there was any connection between the flints of the Chipping Floor, the pottery and the hearth (Worthing Museum Acc. No. 1961/1584).

A total of 15 flakes, one retouched, and a single axe roughout survive in Worthing Museum from this floor. The present whereabouts of the 'Later Bronze Age' pottery is unknown, so an objective statement of its significance in relation to the floor remains difficult. It is possible, however, given the areas of later activity recorded from within and around Pits B and C (see below), that the material may indicate some form of intrusive later agricultural or settlement activity. The plan of Floor 12 produced by Pull gives a good impression of the relative position of material here, including three centrally placed axes. The large flint nodules which appear at the north-eastern periphery of the chipping floor could represent either part of a floorstone layer, akin to those capping or sealing features at Blackpatch, or a deposit of mined flint which was for some reason never reworked (cf. Shaft 7 at Blackpatch).

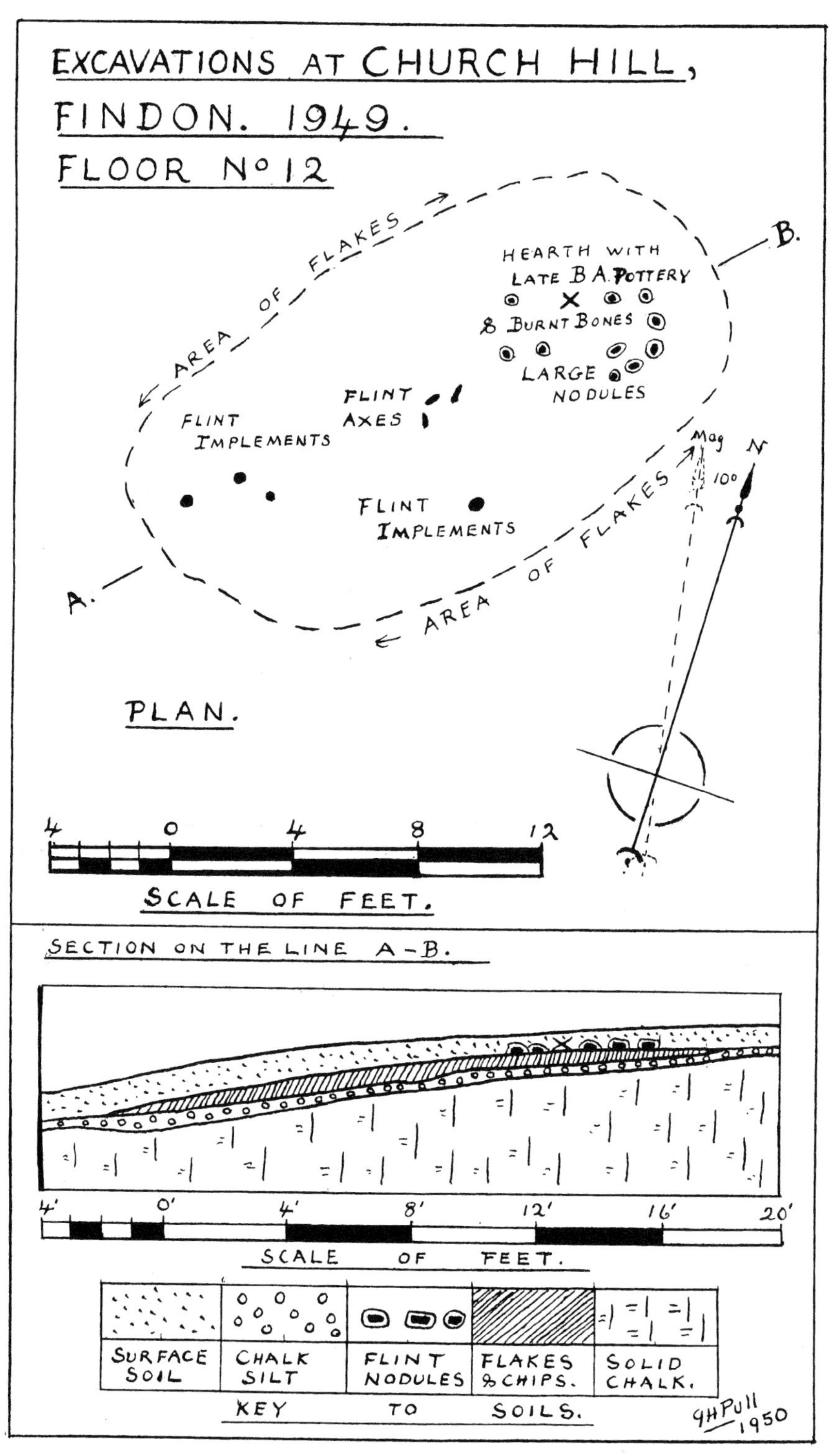

Figure 82. Chipping Floor 12: plan and section showing the relative position of major finds (© Worthing Museum and Art Gallery).

Floor 13

Chipping Floor 13 has already been discussed within the context of shafts 6 and 7 where it was identified as layer 2 within the upper fill.

Floor 14

By J. H. Pull and A. R. Voice

Shafts 6 and 7 had apparently both been sunk through an area of the hill surface already occupied by a large surface flint knapping floor – Floor 14. From a half to two thirds of the area of this floor, representing the whole of its centre and western portion, had been cut through and removed by the later shafts. The remaining eastern portion of this floor occupied a crescent space extending from halfway along the eastern lip of Shaft 6, to the south-eastern lip of Shaft 7, a distance of 16 feet and with a greatest width of six and a half feet opposite the centre of the eastern lip of Shaft 7.

This floor had been deposited upon a layer of yellow stained chalk, evidently a trodden surface, which itself directly overlay the solid chalk. no clay with flints occurs on this side of Shafts 6 and 7. The floor, as we found it, consisted of a compact mass of flakes and fire chippings, three inches thick, mixed with large broken and unworked flint nodules from the deep-mined seam. Here and there upon the floor, and mixed with the flakes, were roughouts for celts and unfinished implements of all classes. As is always the case with these workshop floors, a certain proportion of highly finished tools and a quantity of fine blades and cores, from which they had been struck, were found. Among these were two very fine celts, an exceptionally fine pressure flaked scraper and a fine toothed saw together with a number of beautiful knife blades both large and small. Here, as elsewhere on such floors, we found numbers of butt ends and points of good flint blades, with the central portions missing. On this floor however we also found a number of their central sections and, after careful comparison, realised that they had been deliberately broken out to form the teeth of compound reaping sickles, matched and cemented in a grooved wooden armature, probably with some sort of gum or resin. We have even been able to reconstruct one of these sickles.

The finding of highly finished tools on these flint knapping floors presents a puzzling problem: Were they were and lost among the quickly accumulating waste flakes during the process of manufacture; were they deliberately hidden by the knappers to be smuggled away to some prehistoric 'black market'; was the flint knapping site suddenly abandoned as a result of the approach of some outside enemy in the form of an animal or human; or were certain implements set aside as a sacrifice to some unknown deity of the flint world? Cornish miners, in later days, made offerings of this kind to the 'knockers' – the little people of the mines. We shall probably never know; the human element will always prevent prehistoric archaeology from becoming an exact science.

A small hearth had been established on Floor 14 at some time before it was covered up by a spread of large chalk flints representing debris thrown up from a neighbouring shaft (probably Shafts 6 and 7, which had been sunk through the floor). This hearth was about four feet in diameter and the flakes and chippings, including a very fine flint axe, were well burnt below it. This hearth was evidently somewhat later than the floor itself and represents a fire, which had been lit by the miners sinking some nearby shaft. No animal bones and very little charcoal occurred on or near this hearth. The quantities of land mollusca collected from the silt below the floor and from between the chalk blocks which covered it showed little difference in time and climate as would be expected in such circumstances (Worthing Museum Acc. No. 1961/1584).

The plan of the upper area of Shafts 6 and 7 clearly shows the extent of floor 14 as well as indicating some of the axes recorded from within it and of the area of burning identified as an in situ hearth. Two flint arrowheads, a scraper, an axe-sharpening flake and 78 flakes from floor 14 survive in the Worthing Museum archive.

Floor 15

Nine flint flakes in the Worthing Museum store, are the only artefacts from Floor 15 that could be traced at the time of writing.

THE BARROWS

Barrow 1

By J. H. Pull

The first of the round barrows opened by us at Church Hill was situated 130 feet west of the actual summit of the hill top and just above the 500-foot contour line. The barrow overlooked the great dry valley which separates Church Hill from Blackpatch Hill, and commanded a broad and extensive view of the Downland in the direction of the river Arun. This barrow was a very small one, being but 14 feet in diameter and nine inches in height. In shape it was a flat-topped and almost perfectly circular platform, with no trace of any ditch surrounding its base (figure 83).

On excavation it was found that the whole of the mound was made up of a single layer, about one foot in thickness of closely set flints. These flints represented several tons of large waste nodules and slabs of tabular flint, the greater proportion of which had without doubt been brought from the neighbouring flint mines, which are situated a furlong and a half away. The interstices between these flints were closely packed with dark mould, and the flints themselves had been piled upon the surface of the hill, which had, within the limits of the barrow, been first of all denuded of turf and soil, there being but three inches of red loamy earth, mixed with very small flints between the material of the mound and the stiff red clay beneath it. Red clay at this spot overlies the chalk to a depth of two feet. At a point three feet north-east of the mound's centre

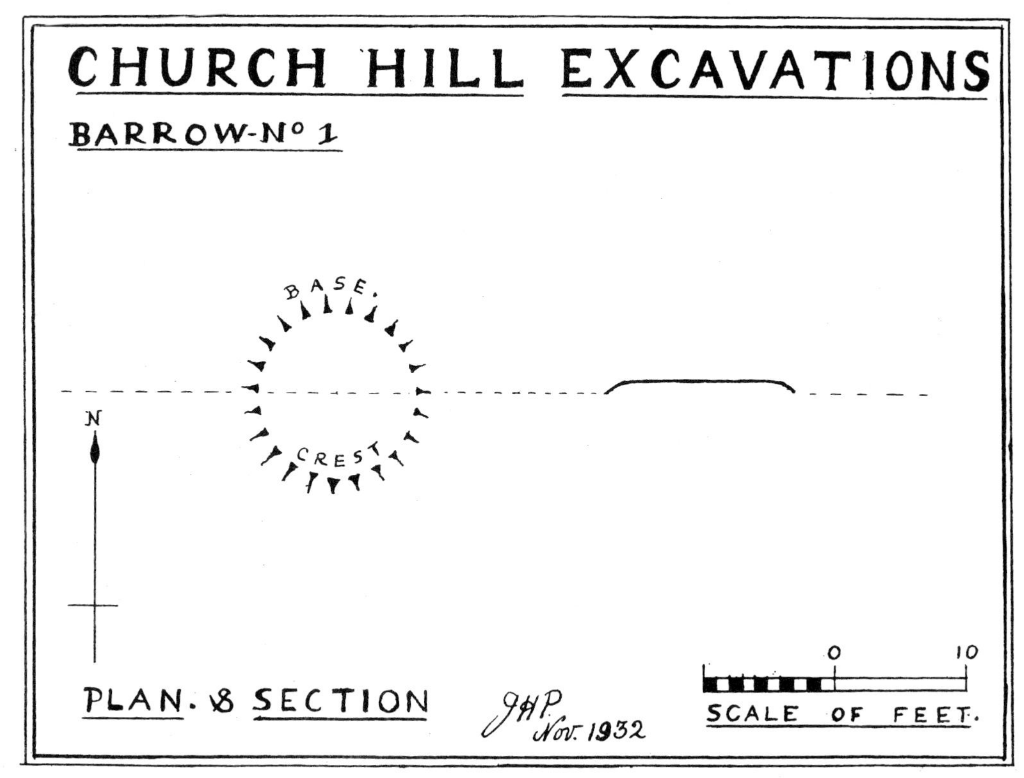

Figure 83. Church Hill Barrow 1: pre excavation surface hachure plan and surface profile (© Worthing Museum and Art Gallery).

and immediately beneath the turf were found many fragments of a Romano-British vessel of pottery. Among the flints, which constituted the material of the mound, were a few large roughly flaked blocks or waste cores of a description commonly found in the infilling of the local flint mines. Quantities of flint flakes also occurred scattered throughout the barrow.

More important finds came from the surface of the red loam upon which the mound rested, a level which had a uniform depth of one foot below the turf line. On this level, within a space commencing three feet north-east of the centre and extending thence a further three feet in the same direction, almost to the edge of the mound, was a mass of broken pottery, comprising portions of four distinct vessels. One of these vessels was a collared urn of cinerary type, which had an ornamental rim, the ornament having been incised with some very thin, sharp instrument. The other vessels were unfortunately too disintegrated to enable their shape to be determined. All had flat bottoms and one appears to have been a very large and thick pot. Fragments of this were widely scattered over the area covered by the barrow, for, besides occurring mingled with the pottery just described, other pieces were found at a point six feet south of the mound's centre.

> With the fragments of the four pottery vessels were some flint flakes, charcoal, a flint knife and the point of another.
>
> At the centre of the barrow and within the east and south-eastern portion of it, and at the same level as the pottery fragments, were scattered many pieces of charcoal and a great number of flint chippings. A number of flint implements were also found, including several knives of simple character made from flakes, a small thick scraper of horseshoe form, several used flakes with serrated edges and an unstruck tortoise core. Three feet east of the centre of the mound was a very fragmentary quantity of slightly burnt fragments of human bone. Lying near these was a flint knife broken in two, the two pieces being separated by a space of six inches.
>
> Below the centre of the mound was a large oval hollow, sunk one and a half feet deep into the red clay. This hollow was about seven feet by five feet and had a direction north-west by south-east. It was filled with alternate layers of red clay and mould mixed with large flints. Near the bottom on the western side lay a thick knife blade of black flint with a finely worked edge. This shallow hollow appears to have been a grave, and although no remains of an interment were found within it, I have no doubt that a body had originally been laid to rest there. The impervious nature of the clay into which it was sunk combined with the presence of much vegetable mould in the infilling would have caused even the harder parts of the skeleton to perish (Worthing Museum Acc. No. 1961/1584)..

As with Barrows 1, 3, 4, 5, 6, 8 and 12 at Blackpatch, Barrow 1 at Church Hill seems to consist predominantly of mining debris, in this instance 'waste nodules and slabs of tabular flint'. Whether this constitutes the floorstone cappings evident from the Blackpatch Barrow sites is unclear. It is also unknown as to whether the flint represents a freshly mined deposit, brought down from main area of mining, or whether it represents a mass of weathered flint gathered from an older spoil heap found adjacent to a disused mine. The distinction is crucial, for if the material had been freshly mined it would imply that some form of flint extraction at Church Hill was continuing on into the Later Neolithic as the collared urns beneath the flints do not, from Pull's description, appear to have been intrusive.

Whether Barrow 1 represents a burial monument, or a mound of structured mining debris containing a number of artefactual assemblages, one of which just happened to be cremated bone, is a matter for debate. The cremation was certainly off-centre in relation to the mound and though Pull explains the absence of human bone from the central pit beneath the mound in terms of decay, it may be possible that the feature was never intended receive a fully articulated body. At Blackpatch we have already noted a number of deliberately constructed mounds of mining debris that do not comfortably sit within the definition of 'barrow' and it is possible that we are seeing a similar type of construct here. The whole structure could in this sense be explained in terms of either a territorial marker, planting the recognisable components of a distinctive social group, including one actual member of that group, into the hill to lay claim to it or a large-scale ceremonial deposition, seeding the hill with ritually charged material to the spirit or guarding deity of the place to give thanks or to ensure the future fertility of the flint-producing earth. Of the finds recorded by Pull as having come from Barrow 1, only two flakes, two scrapers and some fragmentary pieces of pottery, possibly collared urn, survive today.

Barrow 2

By J. H. Pull

Barrow 2 was situated on the extreme summit of the hill about 30 yards east of barrow 1. It was an extremely small bowl barrow with a well-defined outer ditch. The mound was 12 feet in diameter and raised but six inches above the natural surface (figure 84). The ditch, which encompassed its base, was about four feet wide and depressed to a maximum of six inches below the hill surface. The overall diameter of the ditch was 20 feet. The mound was composed of soil and weathered surface flints of all sizes resting upon a bed of stiff red clay sparsely sown with large flints. The ditch proved to be one and a half feet deep. Viewed in cross section it appeared as a segment of a circle, the lower part of which cut into

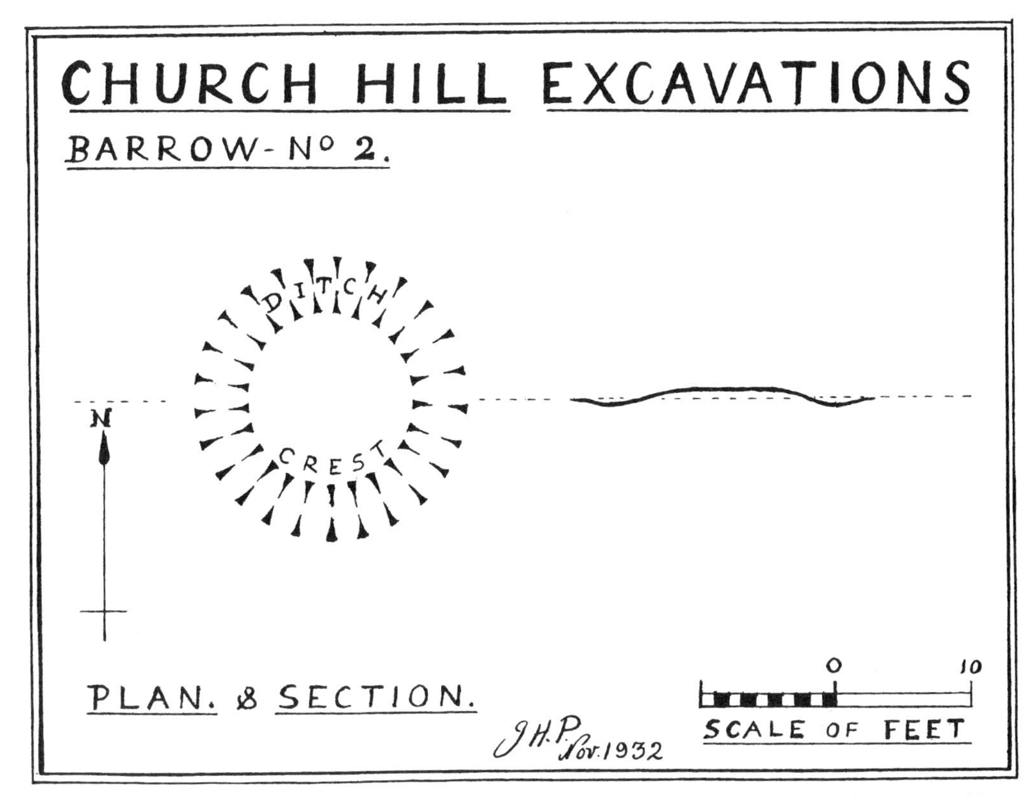

Figure 84. Church Hill Barrow 2: pre excavation surface hachure plan and surface profile (© Worthing Museum and Art Gallery).

the red clay which covers the hilltop. The infilling of the ditch consisted of a mixed mass of flints and soil. The barrow had been constructed by the simple expedient of digging out a circular ditch and throwing the material excavated from it inwards to form the mound. The subsequent infilling of the ditch represents soil and flints which had crumbled from its outer edge, and material which had drifted back from the sides of the mound.

On excavating the mound we found, at a point a little to the west of the centre and two feet below the surface, a large and flat nodule of flint. Roughly chiselled in the soft outer crust of this flint was a broad arrow, the familiar symbol of Her Majesty's Government. This flint marked the trigonometrical station of the Ordnance Survey made in 1873. Thus we came upon the ordnance stone of Church Hill, a strange thing indeed to find interred in a prehistoric burial mound. At the centre of the mound, one foot beneath the turf, were found some fragments of a biconical vessel of thick black pottery and a quantity of fire splintered flints. Two feet north-east of the centre and one and a half feet below the surface were some very thin and finely worked flint instruments. Other flint implements and flakes occurred scattered among the material of the mound. No trace of an interment was discovered in this barrow and we can only conclude, as in the case of barrow 1, that any body which the mound had once covered has gone entirely to decay (Worthing Museum Acc. No. 1961/1584).

Pull observes, in the excavation notebook, that among the finds recovered from Barrow 2 were: a thick-nosed end scraper and three pressure flaked blades 'at a depth of 1'6', 2ft NE of centre'; a blade, a side scraper, three rough scrapers, a large borer and several flakes and burnt flint 'found in the 9' layer'; a steep-ended tool, two thin side scrapers and a fine boring tool from the 'SW corner depth 1'6". Unfortunately none of these finds could be traced at the time of writing, though drawings of the flint tools survive in the Pull Collection. As with Barrow 1, Barrow 2 may not represent a burial monument in its own right (lack of human bone could alternatively be due here, as Pull observes, to decay within the clay-rich soil). The constructional form of the earthwork, a round mound encircled by a ditch, has more in common with conventional barrows than the structured mounds of mining debris recorded from Blackpatch and, unlike 'barrow 1' here at Church Hill, the mound of Barrow 2 was predominantly constructed from spoil taken from an encircling quarry ditch. The clear lack of mining debris within or around the feature therefore makes a direct association with the mining zone difficult to verify.

Barrow 3

By J. H. Pull

Twenty-five feet north-west of Barrow 2 was a third barrow of extremely small dimensions. This barrow consisted of a small bowl shaped mound six feet in diameter and six inches high, surrounded by an outer ditch three feet in width and depressed six inches below the natural surface. Excavation in this mound disclosed that both the material of which the mound was composed, and the infilling of the ditch, were of an exactly similar character to that observed in Barrow 2. Scattered among the material of the mound were a few flint flakes. Two feet south of the centre and on the level of the natural hill surface were some burnt stones and a number of fragments of pottery of a kind that may have formed part of a cinerary urn. The ditch, on excavation, was three feet across and one foot six inches deep and filled with mould and flints. At the centre, one foot below the surface of the mound, a very shallow saucer shaped excavation had been made into the red clay. This hollow was about four feet in circumference and six inches deep. It was filled with large flints, all of which had come from the clay with flints in the immediate neighbourhood (Worthing Museum Acc. No. 1961/ 1584).

Pull records in the excavation notebook for Church Hill that the finds from Barrow 3 included: several worked flints from the 'ditch filling S centre'; fragments of 'Beaker ware pottery', several flint pebbles, a number of burnt stones and a few flakes of surface flint from '3ft S centre at base'; two very long knives and small crude scraper of surface flint from '1ft deep in red clay, 2'3 below apex of mound'; four burnt flints, one small red pebble and a small yellow scraper from 'centre 1ft deep in red clay'; and several worked flakes from 'ditch filling S centre'. Only two flakes, three sherds of pottery and a number of cremated bone fragments survive today in Worthing Museum. The bone fragments may have been miss-identified to source, for Pull does not mention the presence of a cremation deposit in either his text or site notebook. As with Barrow 2, there is nothing from this mound to directly link it with the mining area to the east. In fact the nature of the Barrow 3 flint assemblage, all pieces apparently manufactured from surface flint, would seem to argue strongly against the mound being contemporary or associated with the main period of flint extraction.

Barrows 4–8

By J. H. Pull

Southwards and SW from Barrow 2, and scattered widely over the area encompassed by the 500 foot contour line, were a number of very small circular mounds in shape like miniature barrows. These mounds vary from six to nine feet in circumference and are of such low elevation as to be plainly visible only after a light fall of driven snow or at a time when the sinking sun throws the longest and most pronounced shadows (figure 85). No doubt these mounds have all but lost some of their original height through the levelling action of the plough, for that portion of the hill top, south of the larger and well defined barrows, has at some time in the past, been under cultivation; the boundaries of rectangular fields being still faintly visible. Continual ploughing has not only aided in the obliteration of the former baseline of these mounds, but also in the total filling up of the shallow ditches which appear to have surrounded most of them.

On excavating several of these mounds we found them to have been originally constructed in the same way as the ditched Barrows 2 and 3 but on a smaller scale. That is to say, they were made by the simple process of digging a circular

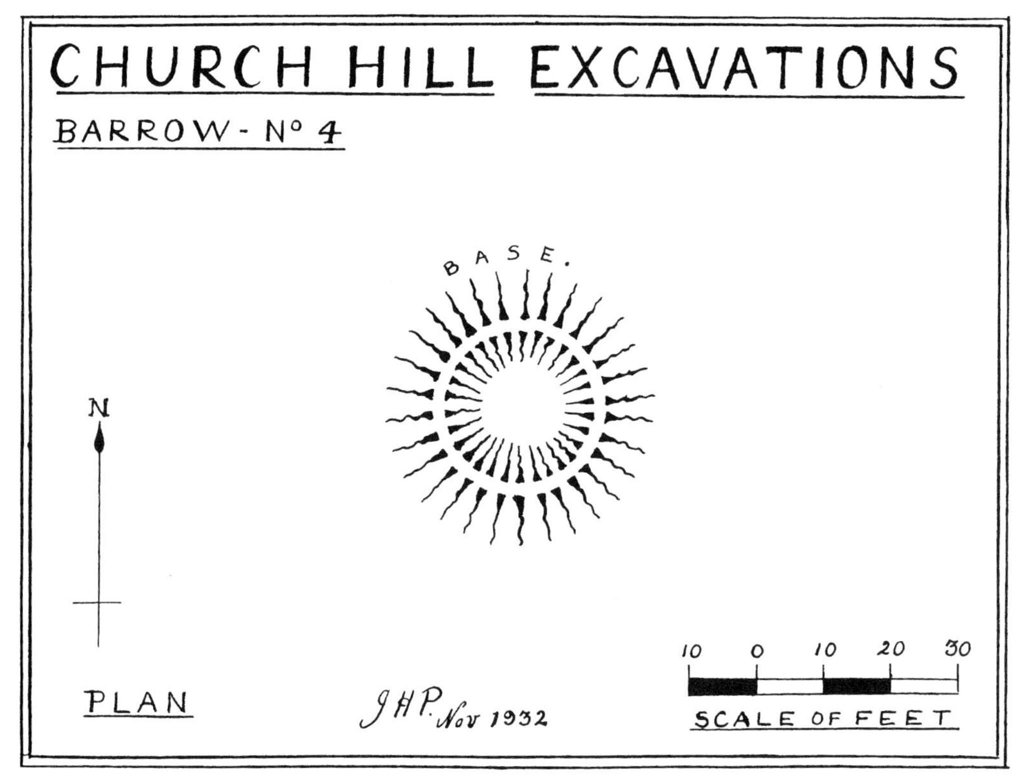

Figure 85. Church Hill Barrow 4: pre excavation surface hachure plan (© Worthing Museum and Art Gallery).

> ditch, and throwing the soil and flints taken from it, inwards to form a mound. Though we found but little evidence in these small mounds to enable us to date them, it seems possible that, standing as they do to definite round barrows, they may be of the same age and constructed by the same people who made the barrows. One is tempted to assume that, while the round barrows on the summit of Church Hill were the burial mounds of departed chieftains, priests, or others of rank and importance among the community, to whose efforts their erection is due, these smaller mounds mark the last resting places of the common folk, who were interred in a simple manner beneath these miniature barrows, without cremation, with little or no funeral furniture, and whose skeletons have all but perished in the soil (Worthing Museum Acc. No. 1961/1584).

Barrow 5, to the south-east of Shaft 4, was initially identified by Pull and Voice during the course of the 1946 survey. Excavation at the site later revealed the earthwork to be of a completely different type of construction, at which point it was reclassified as 'Hut Site 1' (see below). Though no detailed description or illustration (other than upon the main 1946 site plan) of the remaining 'barrow' sites could be traced at the time of writing, it is clear from Pull's description that they were similar in form to

Barrows 2 and 3 at Church Hill, having been created, not from mining debris, but from spoil excavated from a series of encircling quarry ditches. Whether these sites represent burial mounds in the conventional sense is, as usual, uncertain, as is the suggestion that they may have covered the remains of 'the common folk' as suggested by Pull. To be interred within a specific mound one must have presumably possessed a certain degree of social status. Clear lack of mine products from within these mounds, given their extreme proximity to the mining zone, presumably suggests that they were not constructed during a period of major flint extraction. A sickle blade and some cremated bone, a sherd of indeterminate pottery, and a few sherds of collared urn survive in Worthing Museum and are recorded as having deriving from Barrows 6, 7 and 8 respectively. The whereabouts of any Barrow 4 finds are unknown.

Barrow 9

A large, oval mound lying between Shafts T.20, T.10, T.9 and T.8 (Shaft 2), was identified by Pull and Voice during their initial survey of Church Hill in 1946. The mound, clearly more extensive than the series of spoil heaps accompanying mine depressions in the immediate vicinity, was identified as 'Barrow 9'. Excavation of this site, however, proved that it was not in fact a barrow or burial mound, but a large deposit of mining debris containing flint axes, tools, flakes, bone and pottery. Henceforth this particular feature was referred to by Pull and Voice as 'the Large Spoil Bank' or 'the Great Dump', though it retained its original classification 'B9'.

> This was the largest artificial mound in the area. Its larger axis lay NNE by SSW and measured 52 feet at the crest and 77 feet at the base. In breadth it measured 25 feet at the crest and 40 feet at the base. Its greatest height proved to be four feet above the ground surface (figure 86). Early in 1949, in order to find out something about the internal structure of this mound, a section was excavated in it from the centre of the depression marking T10 to the centre of the mound, a distance of 35 feet. This excavation took the form of a trench four feet wide and five feet deep. The turf and soil had an average depth of four inches over the mound and one foot six inches over the centre of T10. Below the surface soil of the mound, from its centre to the edge, consisted of an unstratified mass of closely packed chalk blocks, the interstices between which were filled near the surface with a little soil and silt. Below this they were open. Many of the larger of these chalk blocks bore multiple marks of the use of the antler, tools, which had been originally used in their extraction.
>
> From its centre to a distance of 10 feet towards T10, the chalk block structure of the mound proved to rest on an artificial base of red clay with flints six to nine inches in thickness. This in turn rested upon further chalk rubble up to one foot in thickness. Below this the whole of the mound, to within two feet of T10, rested on the original surface of the hill which consisted of undisturbed clay with flints, six to nine inches thick, resting on the solid chalk. The chalk blocks of the mound beyond the centre of the red clay with flints to the lip of the shaft T10, rested upon the chalk rock.

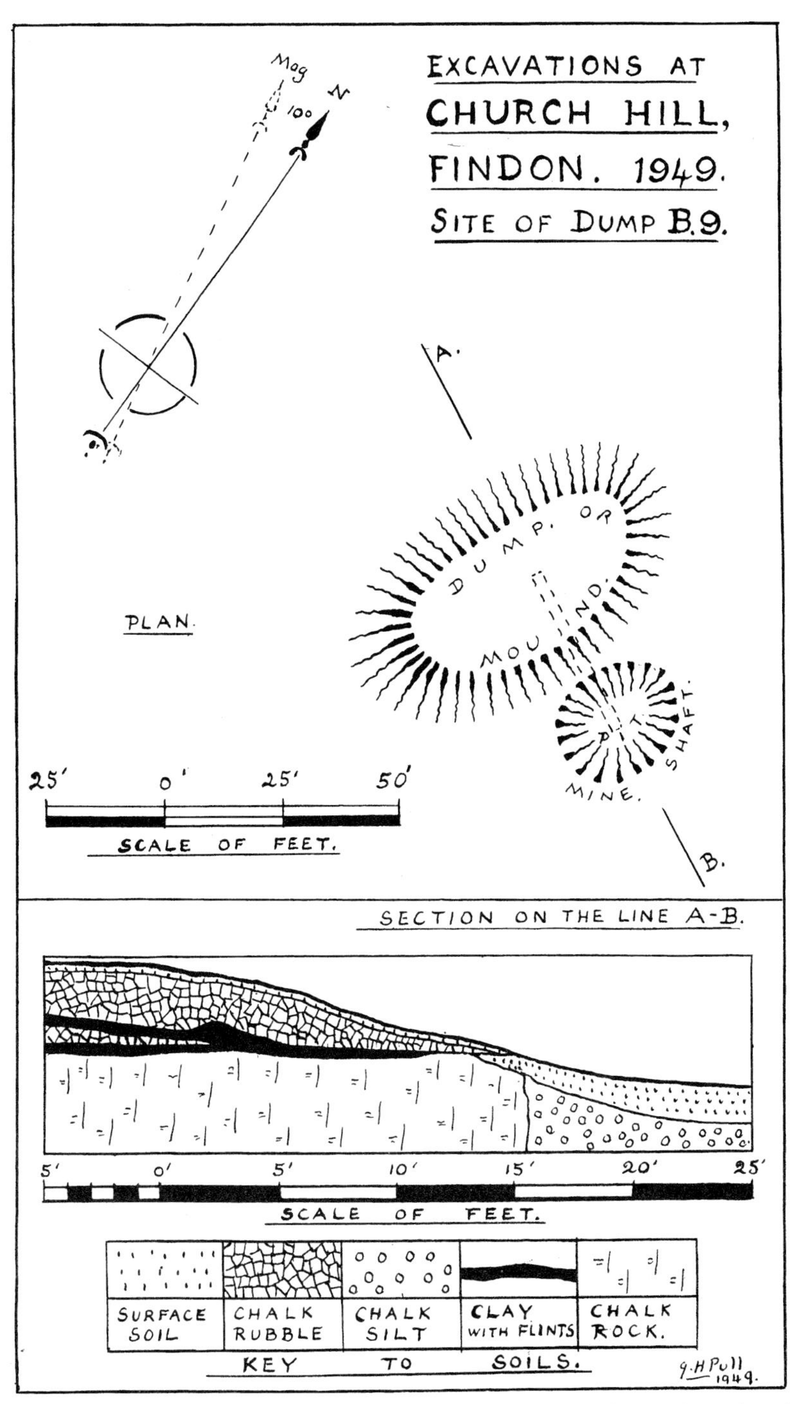

Figure 86. Church Hill Barrow 9 (the "Great Dump"): pre excavation surface hachure plan showing location of main trench and section (© Worthing Museum and Art Gallery).

> When one studies the drawings of this excavation, it would seem that the sequence of events detailing the erection of this great spoil bank might have been as follows: First the old hill surface between Shafts T10 and T8 and T9 had comprised a layer of six to nine inches of undisturbed red clay with flints resting directly on the chalk rock. First upon this surface had been dumped, from the north-west, a layer of chalk rubble, probably excavated from Shaft T8. Following upon this, the excavation of the Shaft T10 was begun. The red clay with flints was first removed from the area of this pit to at least two feet beyond the actual top of the shaft and this clay with flints had been dumped upon the clay with flint surface to the north and west and furthermore upon the earlier boundary of the chalk thrown up from T8. Following this, the chalk blocks extracted from Shaft T10 and possibly Shaft T9, had been piled up over this. It thus would appear that the Shaft T8 was somewhat earlier than Shaft T9 or T10 and that the whole of the Dump B9 represented the accumulation of debris thrown out from the three surrounding pits (Worthing Museum Acc. No. 1961/1584).

As mound B9 was only ever partially trenched, little can be said with regard to its form or function, though, given the sheer quantity of mined chalk rubble within the mound when combined with the clear stratigraphic separation evident in the section, it seems difficult to disagree with Pull's interpretation of it as representing the heaped spoil from at least two separate shafts. The current whereabouts of any of these finds from B9 are unknown.

Barrow 10

No text appears to have survived concerning the examination of 'Barrow 10', though an inked hachure plan and profile of such a feature exists in the John Pull Archive labelled 'Excavations at Church Hill, Findon 1948' (figure 87). The plan shows a roughly circular ditched enclosure with an overall diameter of 14.6m and a surface ditch width of between 2.3 and 1m. Though there is no indication of a central mound on the plan, the profile does indicate a slight rising of ground level within the area enclosed by the ditch. The fact that no artefacts are known to exist for this site, when combined with the fact that the drawing record is of a surface profile and not a stratigraphic section, could be taken to imply that Barrow 10 was merely surveyed, rather than excavated. There can, unfortunately, be no certainty of this for the only records for Barrows 1, 2 and 4 at Church Hill consist also of hachured plans and surface profiles, and these three mounds are known to have been thoroughly excavated by Pull.

One possibility presents itself, however: Barrow 10 has perhaps been misidentified, appearing within the Church Hill notes under a different name, number or lettering system. There is one contender for such a possibility, for in the Worthing Museum store there are a number of finds recorded as having derived from a 'Barrow A'. No drawing exists for this site, though the balance of probability would seem to be that 'Barrow A' was indeed excavated shortly before 1950 (Pull notes that a fence was removed from around it in July of that year prior to the examination of Church Hill

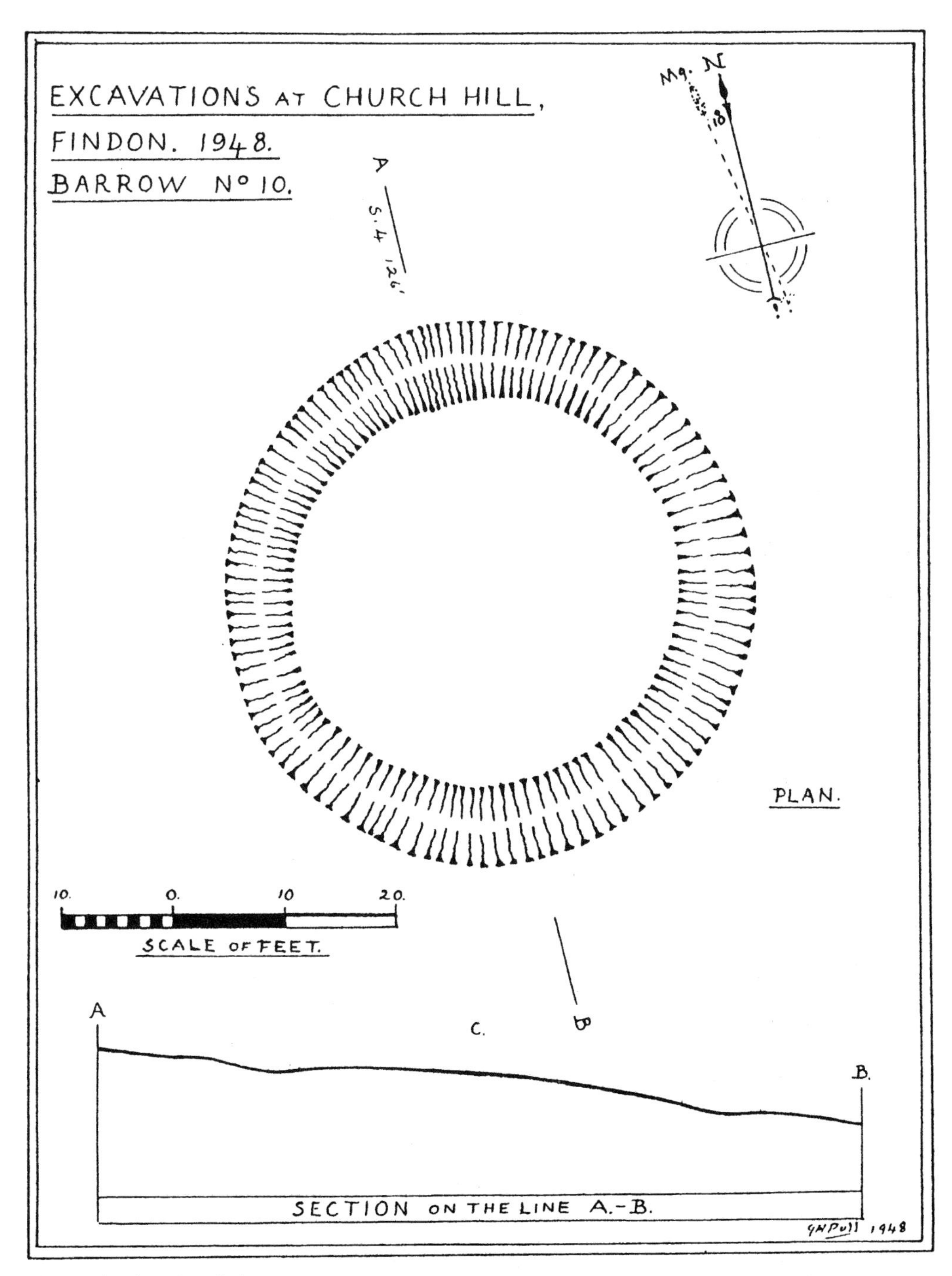

Figure 87. Church Hill Barrow 10: pre excavation surface hachure plan and surface profile (© Worthing Museum and Art Gallery).

Shaft 6: see below). Barrow 10 was surveyed in 1948, and it is not beyond the realms of possibility that A and 10 are one and the same, the designation 'A' perhaps being given to distinguish the feature as belonging to the second season of excavation and survey, in much the same manner as Pits A, B and C.

Barrow A

A large number of flint artefacts, including two borers, an axe roughout, a pick, two scrapers and over a hundred flakes, appear in the John Pull Archive at Worthing Museum as having derived from 'Barrow A'. The location of 'Barrow A', and whether it was ever fully investigated, is, as noted above, somewhat unclear. The recorded finds assemblage could have derived from surface collection over an identified, unexcavated Barrow mound. It is possible that a mound was identified as 'Barrow A', before being renamed or numbered, or that this reallocation occurred at a later date.

This presents the possibility that 'A' could perhaps be correlated with either Barrow 1 (first in the recorded sequence) or the 'Fire Mound' (itself not allocated a number or letter identification). A problem with such an apparently easy resolution is that some of the Barrow A finds are clearly labelled as having derived from 'the ditch', a feature that neither mound 1 nor the fire mound seem to have possessed. Pull mentions Barrow A only once, in the Church Hill excavation notes for 1950 (Acc. No 1961-1584A). Here, when discussing the excavation of Shaft 6, he notes that on July 2nd 'The fencing was brought from Barrow A and Site C and erected round the Shaft 6 depression.' This implies that some sort of activity was being conducted around a 'Barrow A' during the second main phase of fieldwork at Church Hill between 1946 and 1952. Barrows 1-8 and the fire mound were examined in the 1933–9 season, so this would appear to rule these sites out from the discussion. The fact that Barrow A was fenced at some point prior to July 2nd 1950, further compounds the problem, as it implies that 'A' was excavated or that the intention had been to investigate it further, and that such investigation had never occurred. Prior to fencing Barrow mounds elsewhere at Church Hill, Blackpatch, Cissbury and Tolmere, Pull and his team regularly surveyed the site in question, so a surface plot of 'A' should at some time have been made. A correlation with 'Barrow 10', apparently investigated by Pull in 1948 (see above), may provide the answer here and may explain why 'Barrow A' has finds but no illustration while 'Barrow 10' has been illustrated but seems to possess no finds.

OTHER AREAS

The 'Temporary Hut Sites'

A series of shallow surface depressions were noted to the north-west of the main cluster of mines, and just to the east of the 500 foot (152.5m) contour by Pull and Voice

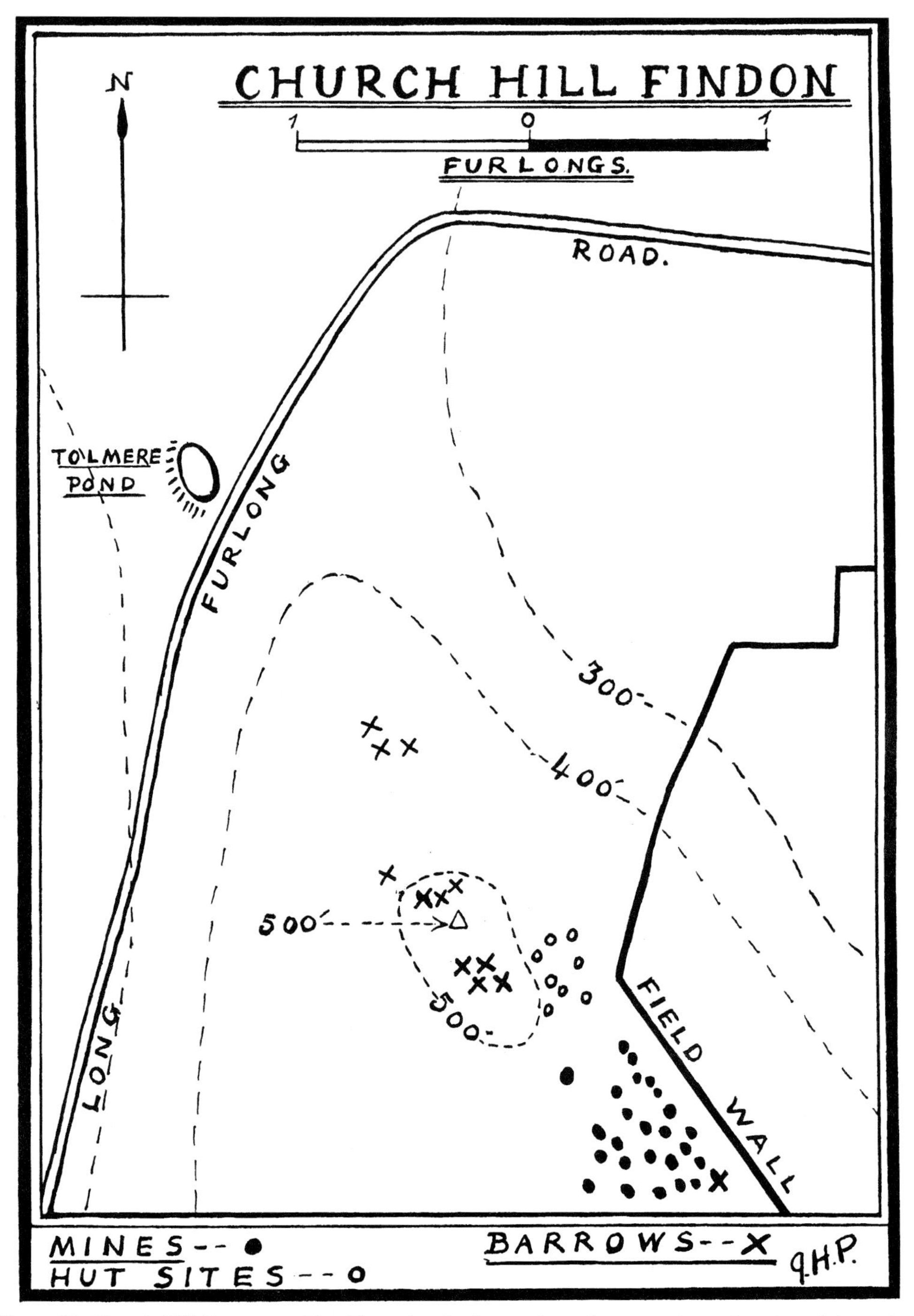

Figure 88. Church Hill Temporary Hut Sites: sketch plan to show the approximate location of the main shafts, barrows and hut sites (© Worthing Museum and Art Gallery).

on a sketch plan of the Church Hill site (figure 88). Pull referred to these features as a type of 'temporary hut site' akin to the examples located by him to the east of the Blackpatch complex (1935a, 438). Just how much archaeological examination was conducted upon these hollows however remains unknown as no detailed text or illustrations could be traced at the time of writing. Pull later noted that:

> special care was taken to search for miners' habitations and an enormous number of trial holes and sections were opened in promising situations over an area of nearly half a square mile in the vicinity of the shafts. Apart from the spade, every conceivable method was tried out in order, if possible, to locate dwelling sites. Percussion of the ground, aerial photography and the diving rod all proved futile (Pull 1935a, 438).

Hut Site 1

By J. H. Pull and A. R. Voice

Situated 83 feet to the south-east of Shaft 4 was an almost circular area measuring 33 feet north and south by 38 feet east and west outlined by a shallow ditch (figure 89). Immediately within the western edge of this ditch was a very shallow circular depression 10 feet in diameter. We at first thought that this might be a ring barrow of some sort but excavation soon proved it to be something of greater importance as we will now proceed to show.

The site was surveyed in detail on March 7th 1948 and the excavation of it began on March 14th and completed on May 16th. It consisted of an outer ditched enclosure which one presumes had carried a fence or unstructured palisade of timber. The ditch itself was four feet in width and two feet in depth with a rounded bottom. It was filled in places with about one foot of silt and above this one foot of large flints. In other parts it was filled almost entirely with large flints. A number of shallow circular postholes, four to six inches in diameter and two to three feet deep, were staggered at intervals throughout its extent. Some of these postholes were filled with consolidated chalk and others with rough flints. In the bottom of the ditch were found a few fragments of pottery that appeared to be of a paste similar to that from which the collared urns found in this neighbourhood are fashioned.

The small circular depression within the western edge of the ditch proved to be a saucer shaped hollow, 10 feet in diameter, sunk to a maximum depth of two feet into the chalk. It was filled with one and a half feet of consolidated chalk silt and one foot of soil covered the whole. This shallow excavation was in turn surrounded by a ring of widely set postholes, one foot to one and a half feet deep in the solid chalk and four to five inches in diameter. In two places these postholes had been duplicated. This small inner enclosure evidently marked the site of a circular hut of light construction with a slightly sunken floor. In the outer ditch, on a line between two of the postholes, which might well have marked the doorway of the hut, was the site of a small hearth about a yard in diameter marked by a mass of thoroughly burnt flints. Near this hearth, on the ditch bottom, were found a number of flint implements, some animal bones and teeth

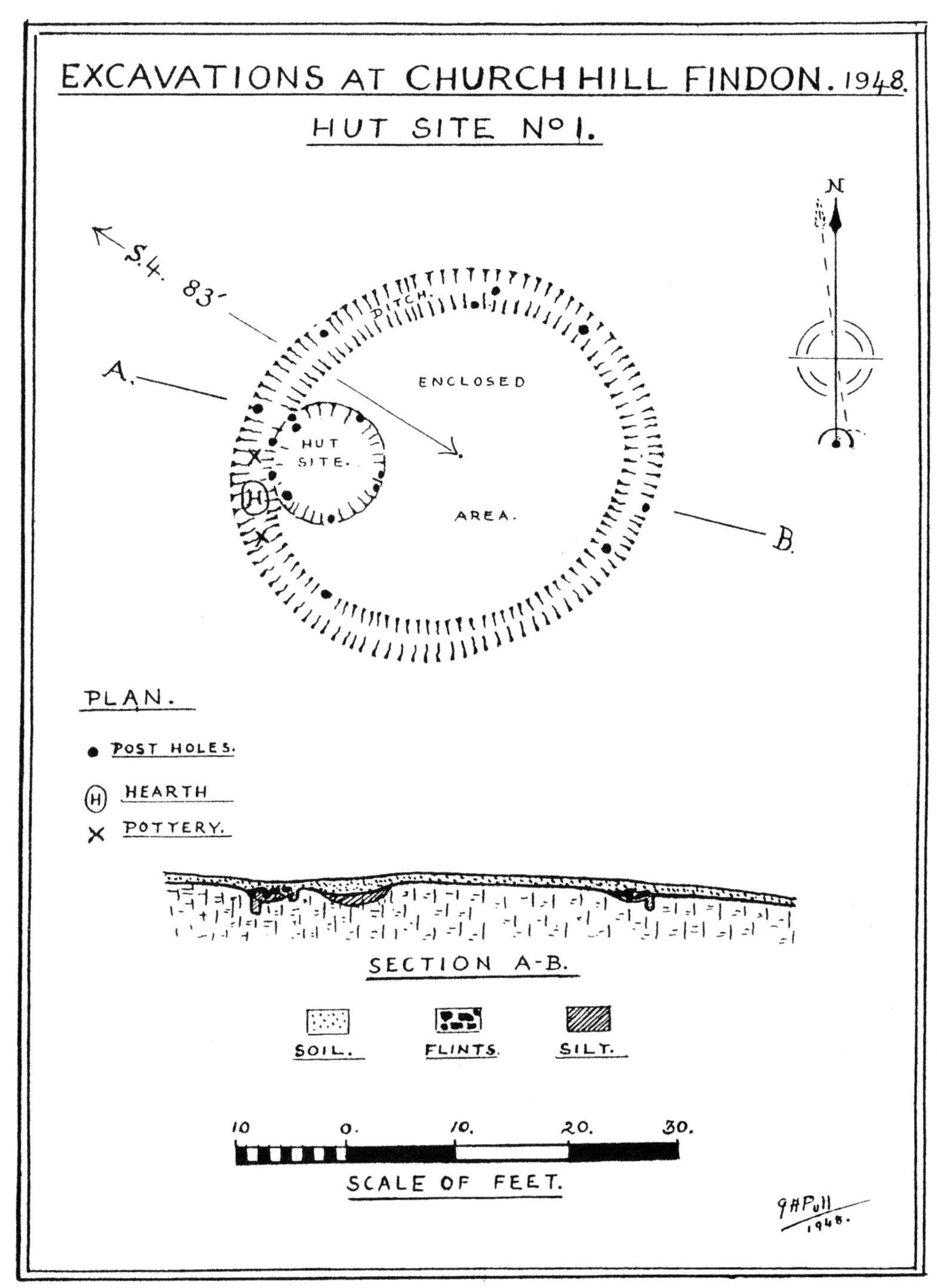

Figure 89. Church Hill Hut Site 1: Surface hachure plan, incorporating subsurface detail regarding postholes and artefact distribution, and site section (© Worthing Museum and Art Gallery).

> (ox and pig) and some fragments of pottery which had flat bottoms and overhanging rims. Upon the inner floor of the hut were also found a number of good flint implements, many of which were worn and blunted with much use. These included a number of scrapers and knives and a long narrow axe.
>
> The exploration of this site clearly indicates that a small hut, or wigwam of circular plan and supported by light timbers with a few main struts or posts, at intervals, of somewhat thicker material sunk into the solid chalk, had been erected over a dished-out hollow in the hillside. This hut had further been furnished with a ditched and fenced compound, evidently to accommodate the owner's cattle or other animals. It appears that this hut site with its outer compound had been occupied by someone at the time the flint mines were being worked, as the finishing of flint implements, all of mine type and workmanship on its floor and on the floor of the outer ditch, indicates. Moreover the occupants of the hut had some small number of animals or other stock which it was necessary to keep within bounds at night or when attendance upon them was not possible, hence the stockade. Probably open and working mines at close quarters necessitated the enclosure of cattle that might run the risk of falling into the deep pits made by the miners.
>
> The period of occupation of the hut is indicated by the small overhanging rim urns. Here it may be pointed out that not only was the flint mining continuing in this part of Sussex into the Bronze Age, but that the collared urn was, as has been shown elsewhere, not especially manufactured as a funerary vessel to enclose the ashes of the dead, as is the usual employment in round barrow interments, but that they were also part of the ordinary domestic pottery of the period as were their predecessors the Beakers. Dr Densham has recently found a small urn of this type, with the rim unornamented, ploughed out with a mass of flakes and chippings and fine flint celts and several flint knives from a chipping floor beneath a mining dump at the neighbouring flint workings at Harrow Hill. The collared urn in this instance having no doubt been used as a drinking cup by the flint knapper working on the site (Worthing Museum Acc. No. 1961/1584).

Hut Site 1 was first recorded as the remains of a potential round barrow (Barrow 5) by Pull and Voice during the course of the 1946 surface survey. Pye records that, as well as the collared urn fragments that Pull and Voice note as deriving from the ditch of Hut Site 1, the internal hollow produced:

> fragments of three urns with decorated rims, one with stroke or stab ornament, one with bird bone impressions and the last with cord ornament; one very small fragment of cord impressed Beaker; animal bones and several flint implements and cores, including scrapers, knives and a long narrow axe (Pye 1968, 34).

Of these finds, only a few pieces of pottery, now too fragmentary to accurately identify, appears within the Worthing Museum archive as having derived from 'Hut Site 1'. Thirty one flint flakes, two scrapers, a borer, an antler fragment, 6 *Bos* teeth and some indeterminate pottery fragments (possibly Beaker coarse ware) are however marked as having derived from 'Barrow 5', the original identification for Hut Site 1, and it is likely that these artefacts represent at least some of the finds referred to by Pull and Voice.

Hut Site 1 is difficult to interpret with any certainty. Pull and Voice were evidently convinced that the excavated structure had originally performed the function of a domestic hut set within the confines of a larger enclosed paddock. The hut hollow at the eastern edge of the larger ditch circuit is odd, however, in that it would appear too rounded and steep to have successfully functioned as a terraced hut platform. Similarly the cut itself seems to be impinge upon the inner edge of the ditch circuit at this point, a relationship that, if observed correctly would imply that the hollow was constructed after the ditch. Problems also exist with regard to the postholes forming the hut structure itself, for these are confined to the outermost lip of the hollow, with no provision made for a series of central roof supports as one should perhaps expect within a round-house. To be fair, if the dating for this construct does place it within the Later Neolithic or Earlier Bronze Age, then, as far as 'domestic structures' are concerned, we are drawing from a sparse corpus. Darvill has recently summarised the evidence for Late Neolithic buildings in England, Wales and the Isle of Man (Darvill 1996, 90-8), and it is true that the structure recorded by Pull and Voice could easily be fitted within what is clearly a diverse range of buildings. Unfortunately house footprints of this period are not standardised to the extent that many of the Later Bronze and Iron Age in Britain are and, as Darvill has admitted, there can be considerable blurring between what constitutes a Later Neolithic house and what is an obviously ritual construct (Darvill 1996, 99-100). This problem is not helped by the fact that a considerable number of Later Neolithic timber buildings have been found within henge monuments (e.g. Richards and Thomas 1984; Wainwright 1989).

Interpretation of the ditch circuit is further confused by the apparent lack of an entrance gap or causeway across it. Absence of a defined point of entrance would obviously have hindered access to any speculative settlement unless some, or all, of the basal postholes originally formed a type of bridge or carrying structure. If however the internal hollow or speculative hut was constructed after the creation and abandonment of the ditch (see below), then lack of entrance may be explained in that the primary cut represented a type of continuously ditched enclosure or monument akin to Barrow 9 at Blackpatch. The placing of posts within the ditch could alternatively imply that the feature was intended to function less as an obstacle to animals, and more as a foundation slot for a visual obstacle such as a setting of timber uprights. The recorded post-plot unfortunately appears somewhat random, though it is possible that not all postholes survived to be recorded by Pull.

The artefactual evidence does not strictly aid interpretation here. The collared urn and possible Beaker pottery could be viewed either as refuse or as ritually charged material, though it should be noted that the flint implements recovered from within the area of the speculative hut were all 'blunted with use', implying perhaps discard within a domestic setting, than the ceremonial deposition of finely finished tools. The discrete area of firecracked flint in the upper ditch fill, over the bones of pig and ox described by Pull and Voice, could plausibly be viewed as the remains of a hearth and therefore be related to settlement activity. Its positioning however, assuming that it is insitu, seems hard to reconcile with the hut interpretation, as it would seem to lie outside the structure in an area interpreted by Pull and Voice as a potential point of entrance. Concentration of artefacts within ditch fill here may imply that the firecracked flint formed part of a larger deposit of secondary refuse which accumulated within the partially backfilled ditch irregularity.

An attempt to resolve the interpretational problems surrounding Hut Site 1 may be made by the examination of the abandonment phase. Here, as at Blackpatch 'Barrow 9', the upper level of ditch fill comprises a dense deposit of large flint nodules, effectively sealing the partially backfilled feature. Pull and Voice do not specify as to whether they considered this layer to represent a deposit of freshly mined flint, similar to the floorstone cappings recorded from Blackpatch, but the fact that the ditch appears to have been so emphatically sealed along its entire length, does suggest a deliberate attempt to terminate the feature. This extensive flint deposit does not seem to have extended into the internal hollow, perhaps indicating that the feature is chronologically distinct from the surrounding ditch. In such a scenario it would be possible to view ditch and hollow as separate entities, the internal hollow being cut following the abandonment of the ditch.

A series of possibilities present themselves with regard to the understanding of 'Hut Site 1'. Firstly the site represents the remains of a roundhouse set at one edge of a larger compound. Secondly the site is a ring ditch or oval enclosure with internal palisade, later reused as a settlement. Thirdly the ditch represents the remains of an oval monument with internal posts enclosing a smaller circle of timber uprights. The presence of collared urns and of implements of 'mine type and workmanship' from the ditch circuit and internal hollow may imply that the feature, whatever its interpretation, was contemporary with a major period of flint extraction though this is by no means certain.

The 'Fire Mound'

By J. H. Pull

Of the three small mounds that occupied the extreme summit of the hill, two were obviously burial mounds. These were subsequently enumerated upon our survey as barrows 1 and 2, the former being towards the west and the latter toward the east. The third, or central mound, now known as the 'Fire Mound', lay exactly 30 feet due south-west of Barrow 2. This little mound, shaped like an inverted bowl, was eight feet in diameter and six inches high. It seemed too small to be a true barrow, and yet it appeared much too geometrically regular and too sharply defined to be likely to cover any natural feature of the ground.

The opening of this mound was the first spade work undertaken by us at Church Hill, and when the digging was commenced we had our first opportunity of observing the nature of the soil and sub-strata with which we would have to deal with at this site. The spadework was commenced on the 18th of December 1932, and it seems almost needless to mention that a good English downpour of rain effectively baptised our somewhat ambitious undertaking. Enthusiasm and dogged determination, however, are capable of overcoming most difficulties, including climatic inclemency. The mound, upon being stripped of turf, was found to consist of six inches of dark, somewhat sandy mould entirely devoid of flints. Below this mould, forming the main mass of the mound and extending to its outer extremities, was a layer about four inches thick, of fairly large and much weathered surface flints, the interstices between which were tightly packed with the mould from above. Among these mixed flints were found several humanly worked flint flakes and chipped pieces, seemingly of great antiquity, exhibiting a very primitive technique.

A little to the north of the mound's centre, below the layer of large flints and mould, scattered over a radius of about 18 inches was a two inch layer of small fire splintered flints, also some very thoroughly burnt ones with which were mixed a quantity of unburnt flints and soil. Among these flints occurred traces of charcoal. This peculiar layer appeared to represent the site of a small fire or hearth which had been scattered and raked over in order to quench its embers. It rested below an undisturbed stratum of stiff red clay associated with large nodular flints. The upper portion of the clay with flints in the vicinity of the scattered hearth exhibited some local discoloration and evidence of the action of fire.

Among the debris of the superimposed hearth were found a few small sherds of a flat bottomed vessel of pottery, the texture and paste of which corresponds with that of the small collared urn found by us in Barrow 5, at Blackpatch, some years ago. On the southern edge of the scattered hearth were found two small fragments of iron sandstone, which may have been portions of a rubber or grinding stone. A number of flint implements also occurred at this spot, all of which may be considered to be contemporary with the remains of the fire. These implements include a knife, a large steep-sided scraper, a steep-nosed tool, two small end scrapers, and a very fine spherical hammer stone, possessing two distinct bruised zones. The hammer stone is a true flint knapper's tool, and, incidentally, is one of the finest specimens I have yet met with in downland. No flakes or chippings indicative of its actual employment on the immediate site were present anywhere within the confines of the mound, so one can only conclude that this hammerstone, together with the flint tools found with it, were some personal belongings of the kindler of the small fire, the remains of which were covered by this peculiar mound, and that these effects had been left behind at the time when the embers of the fire were scattered and effectively covered over. Beyond the remains of the scattered hearth, and the flint tools lying beside it, nothing of note was observed or recovered by us from the material of the mound. The clay with flints below showed no signs of having been anywhere disturbed.

I can give no true reason for the raising of this small circular mound above the remains of a purely temporary hearth. The evidence shows that the degree of burning, which had taken place, was very small, certainly not sufficient for the consuming of a body in the ceremony of cremation. Total absence of animal bones precludes any supposition that a meal was cooked or eaten here. One can only surmise that the fire was connected either with some magical, religious or funerary ritual and the scattering of the embers, and the subsequent raising of a miniature bowl barrow over the site of this possible sacred fire, which at the most

> could have burnt but for a few hours, is a mystery which cannot be solved by the application of the scanty evidence and insufficient knowledge at our command. So far as I am aware, this embarrowed fire, with its associated flint implements and fragments of round barrow pottery, presents a unique feature in connection with the round barrow folk in the neighbourhood (Worthing Museum Acc. No. 1961/1584).

That the burnt material forming the larger part of the mound was an insitu deposit, and had not been dumped here from another part of the site, appears to be confirmed by the fact that the natural clay with flint underlying it had been discoloured by fire action. Pull's statement that the original area of burning had been small scale, is perhaps refuted by the extent of recorded subsoil burning as well as by the nature, extent and quantity of the firecracked flint within the mound. Rather than representing a deliberately embarrowed fire, the mound may alternatively be viewed as the residue of some pyrotechnological activity that has not succumbed to any significant level of later plough attrition. Interpretation is not helped here by the unfortunate lack of illustrative material or artefacts surviving in the Worthing Museum archive.

Though the fire mound was clearly the product of some form of pyrotechnological activity, it may be unwise to use the term 'burnt mound' when describing it, for this has in recent years been a term used to cover a specific type of Later Bronze Age construct consisting of oval or crescent-shaped deposits of charcoal and heat shattered stone, found in close proximity to a stream (or other water source) and covering a defined set of sub-surface features (cf. Barfield and Hodder 1989; Hodder and Barfield 1991). Compared to this type of site, the Church Hill example is decidedly small scale.

A series of interpretations present themselves as to the nature of activity represented by the fire mound (though these should not preclude the possibility of others), namely: cooking area; charcoal burner's mound: cremation pyre; pottery kiln; metalworking furnace. Little is really known about any of these activities in Britain during the Neolithic and Bronze Age, though all were presumably conducted on a localised basis to serve the needs of individual communities. The quantity of flint debris within the mound seems to preclude theories concerning charcoal burning and pottery firing (though the mound may still be seen as the residue of creating sufficient flint tempering for pottery manufacture). Given the absence of metallurgical residue, the metalworking furnace may also appear unlikely. Overall interpretation is not helped by the lack of certainty concerning any subsurface features (pits, postholes, wall-slots etc.) that may have been associated with the creation and utilisation of the fire, for as it is, any discussion of the construct must, of necessity, treat it as an isolated surface feature. Clarification of additional buried remains may, for instance, have demonstrated that the mound originally formed part of a larger hearth set within the walls of a defined timber building.

A mound at Clayton Hill, West Sussex, though larger than the Church Hill example, may provide some comparison to the fire mound. This particular feature, destroyed in 1805, was recorded as consisting of burnt stone (presumably firecracked flint), charcoal and animal bone (Cooke undated, 117). An Early Bronze Age miniature vessel or incense cup of a type usually associated with burial contexts, was recovered from the central area of the mound (Cooke undated, 118; Horsfield 1824, 43). Cooke interpreted the mound as representing the remains of a camp-kitchen or specialised cooking area, though the incense cup, like the collared urn fragments from the fire mound, may suggest the presence of ritual, ceremonial or burial elements.

6

EXCAVATIONS AT TOLMERE, 1949

The series of irregular surface depressions along the north-western side of Church Hill opposite Tolmere Pond (NGR TQ 111088: see figure 48) were first been commented upon by Elliot and Elliot Cecil Curwen in the late 1920s (Curwen and Curwen 1927). The Curwens had completed their examination of one of the Harrow Hill mineshafts in 1924 and, following the Blackpatch publication controversy (White 1995; White chapter 2), may have been looking for an area of prehistoric mining, unclaimed by Pull, on which to concentrate their efforts. The Tolmere scoops appeared to extend in a line along the western contours of the hill to the immediate south-west of the pond and the A280 linking the village of Clapham to Findon in the east.

The Curwens noted that, though the depressions resembled the flint mine hollows of Cissbury and Harrow Hill, they were seen to interrupt the course of an earlier segment of hollow-way, whilst a lynchet, of 'celtic-type' (Curwen and Curwen 1927, 169), and a cross-ridge dyke appeared to skirt around the south and eastern area of the pits. Field has since noted that, though the pits recorded from close to the summit of the hill appear prehistoric in basic form, the more sharply defined nature of the remaining hollows may indicate a more recent origin (Field 1997a, 62). A number of possibilities present themselves with regard to the interpretation of the disrupted hollow-way:

Firstly the trackway is actually later than the pits and the observed stratigraphic relationship, of pits cutting into the track, has been incorrectly recorded. It must be admitted however, that this interpretation seems somewhat unlikely given the Curwen's ability to produce good quality surveys. Secondly it is possible that the hollow-way represents part of a prehistoric track or droveway, into which the later mines were cut. Thirdly it is possible that the mines themselves were, at least in this area, part of a more extensive area of post prehistoric flint extraction, comparable to the Victorian diggings attested on Wolstonbury Hill to the north of Brighton (Curwen 1930b), which disrupted a largely disused downland path. Alternatively the pits could indicate an area of post medieval chalk extraction intended to supply a series of limekilns recorded to the immediate north around Tolmere pond (WSCC SMR 3110; Field 1997a, 62). No clear stratigraphic relationship could be observed between the hollow-way and the other linear earthworks, though the plan produced by the Curwens would seem to suggest that the north-western lynchet was perhaps later than the track (Curwen and Curwen 1927, 169). The cross-ridge dyke to the south

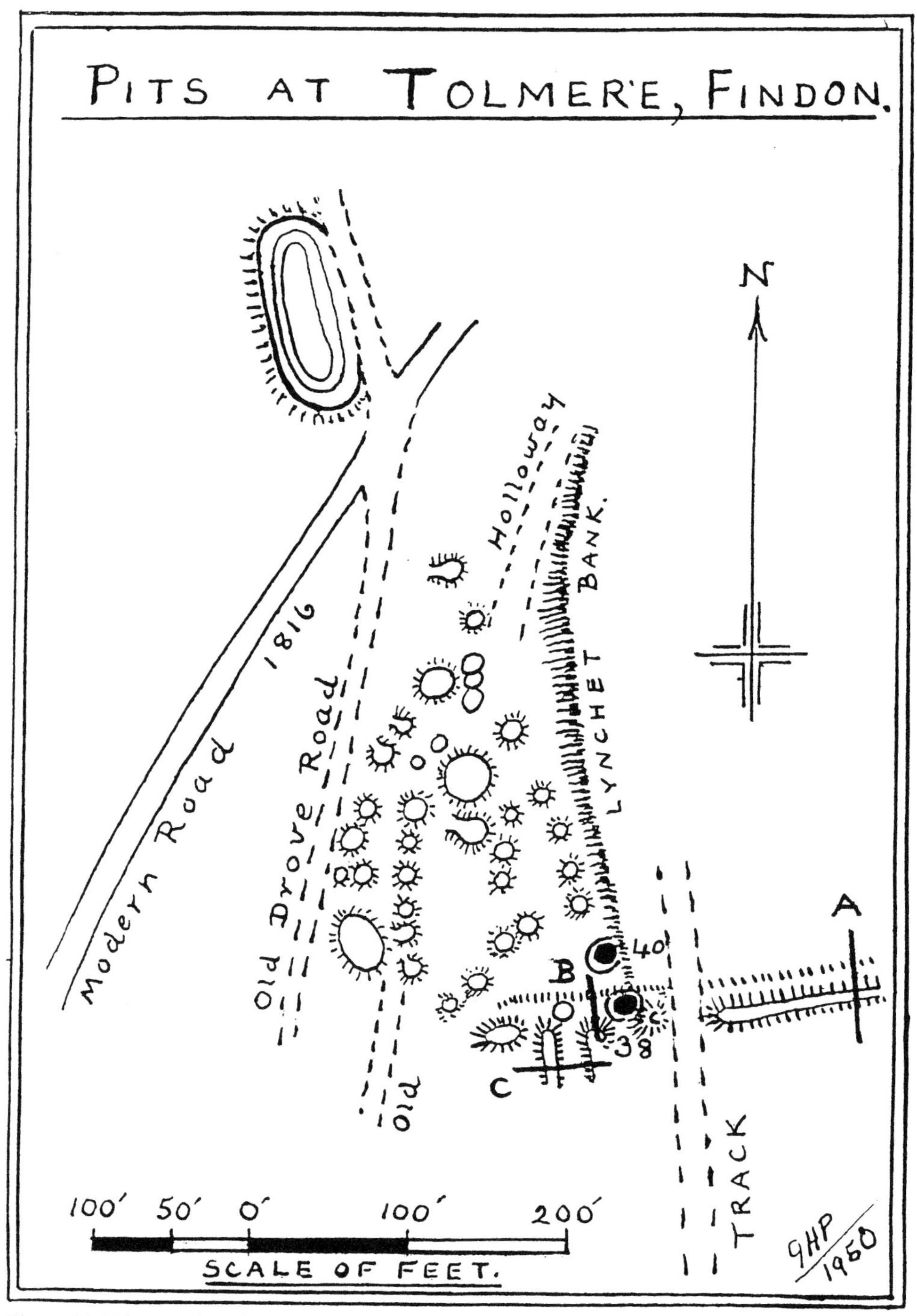

Figure 90. Tolmere: plan showing the location of the 1949 excavation trenches in relation to the main surface features (© Worthing Museum and Art Gallery).

would appear to be later than at least some of the recorded pits, as its northern ditch clearly disrupts the upper levels of pits 38 and 39.

In an attempt to resolve some of the interpretational problems surrounding the date of the Tolmere pits, the Curwens opened a trench across pit 20. Unfortunately, due to a series of unspecified 'circumstances' (Curwen and Curwen 1927, 170) the excavation of the pit was never completed, though the upper levels were recorded as comprising an 18 inch thick deposit of 'mould' overlying chalk rubble. The base of the mould deposit contained 'fragments of an early Romano-British vessel' while the removal of the uppermost area of chalk produced 'a rough flint chopper or wedge of characteristic flint-mine type' (Curwen and Curwen 1927, 170). The Curwens concluded that the site could tentatively be regarded as the fifth zone of prehistoric flint mining in the Worthing area, together with Cissbury, Church Hill, Blackpatch and Harrow Hill.

John Pull began a period of excavation and survey at Tolmere in 1949. At least three pits (38, 40 and 'C') were examined at this time together with a round barrow and a section of the possible Cross-ridge dyke (figure 90). Unfortunately no detailed description, other than the original site notebook, a series of inked illustrations and some photographs, of this period of fieldwork appears to have survived (Worthing Museum Acc. No 1961/1587). It is possible that a detailed report was never written by Pull, who, like the Curwens before him, may have found the immediate results of excavation at the pit-site somewhat inconclusive. Such a view may be supported by Eric Holden, a prominent local archaeologist and friend of Pull, who, in his private journal for November 27th 1949, noted:

> saw Pull who was filling in his abortive flint mine in the Tolmere group. He said he would excavate another mine on Church Hill, Findon, as he was rather disappointed with his efforts on the present site. He has dug two apparent pits and one cutting through a Cross-ridge trench, without any finds and without throwing any light on the history of the earthworks (Holden, unpublished MS).

Pull's own site notebook implies that the excavations at Tolmere were coming to an end by December 1949. Certainly in early 1950 the main area of operations had shifted back to Church Hill with the examination of Shaft Nos 6 and 7.

THE PITS

Pit 38

Pit 38 (figure 91) was excavated between April 13th and May 31st 1949. As with the flint mine shafts at Blackpatch and Church Hill, the fill was emptied in quadrants. The excavation confirmed the surface relationship, first noted by the Curwens (1927, 170), that the feature was almost certainly earlier than the northern ditch of the Cross-ridge dyke (though the plan produced by Pull appears to show exactly the opposite). The section drawings reveal that the pit survived to a maximum diameter of 3.5m

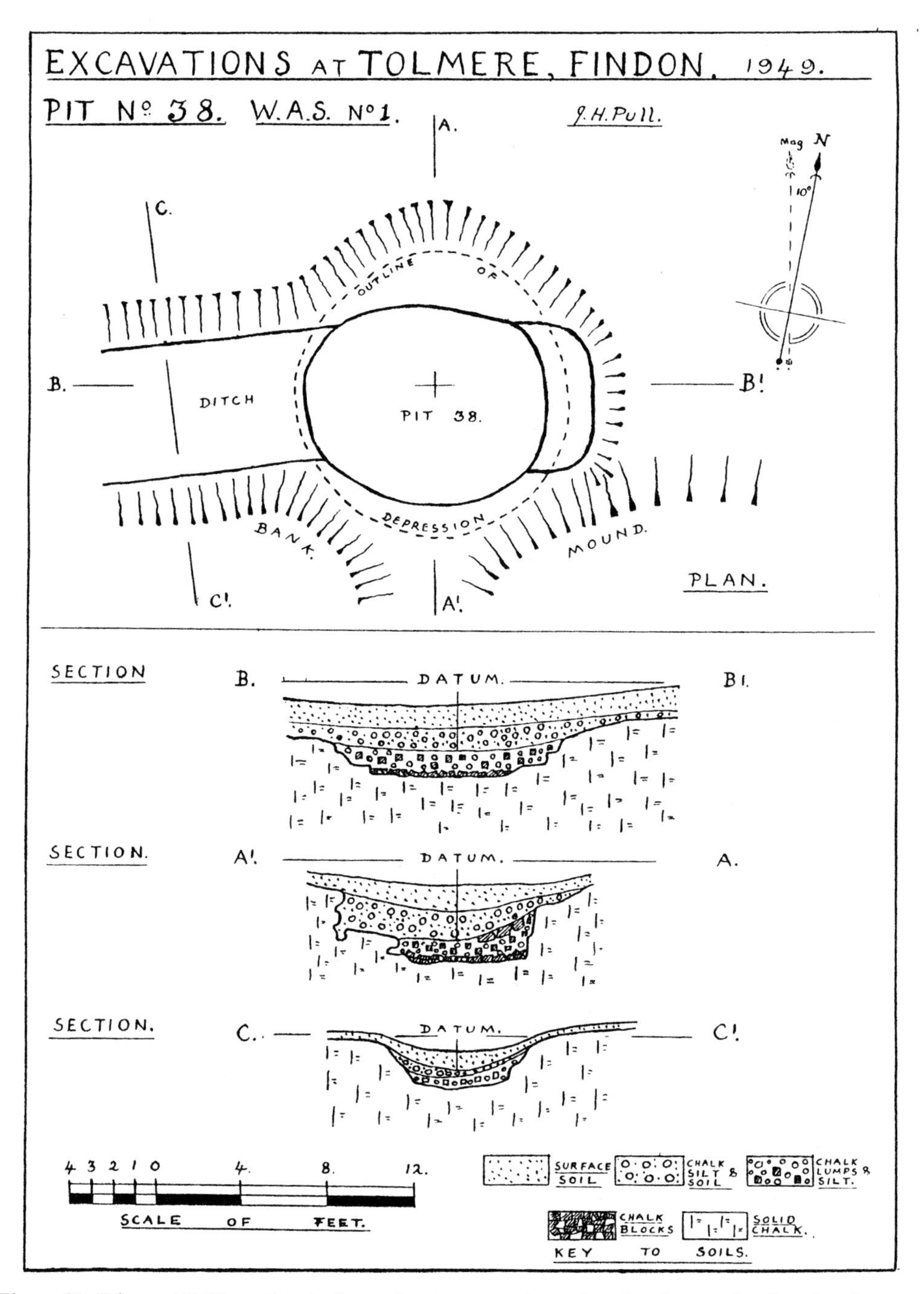

Figure 91. Tolmere Pit 38: surface hachure plan incorporating subsurface feature detail and main excavated sections. Note that Pull's notebook comments would appear to suggest that Pit 38 pre-dated the ditch of the cross-ridge dyke, contrary to how it is shown here (© Worthing Museum and Art Gallery).

east–west by 2.7m north–south, and was 1m deep below modern ground level. Approximately 0.5m of original fill, consisting of 'chalk lumps and silt' and a thin basal deposit of chalk blocks, survived beneath the later ditch cut. This fill contained 'flint implements, flakes, fossils, land mollusca and charcoal fragments' (Pull, site notebook Acc. No 1961/1587). A chalk boulder from the lower fill of the pit retained the impression of an antler pick.

Pull interpreted the feature as being of Neolithic date. Little more can perhaps be said regarding the nature and date of Pit 38, especially since its upper form had been so emphatically removed by the later ditch. Certainly nothing was found within it that would indicate a post Neolithic origin, though, as no flint seams were encountered during the cutting of the shallow feature, it can hardly be viewed as representing the remains of an extraction pit, unless of course it proved to be an abortive one.

Pit 40

Pit 40 (figure 92) was excavated in quadrants between April 19th and May 22nd 1949. The feature appeared to consist of a roughly oval shaped pit, measuring 2.9m south-west – north-east by 2.5m north-west – south-east, and was traced to a maximum depth of 1.9m. Pull interpreted the deeper area at the base of the pit as the remains of a sump, though, as with the feature at the base of mineshaft 5a at Church Hill, this may be viewed as a failed attempt to extend the overall depth of the cut. The majority of pit fill consisted of chalk rubble. Antler pick marks were noted across the sides of the pit and upon blocks of chalk thrown back as pit fill. Pull, in the excavation notebook, recorded that the finds from Pit 40 consisted of 'flint flakes, fossils and land mollusca'.

A bizarre extension to the pit, annotated as an 'entrance trench' on the inked plan was observed and partially excavated to the north-west of the pit. This straight sided, flat-bottomed feature measured 0.8m in width and was 0.6m deep. It was filled entirely with chalk rubble. Nothing was retrieved from Pit 40 to indicate a post-Neolithic or Bronze Age date. In the excavation notebook Pull interpreted Pit 40 as representing the remains of a storage pit, presumably for an as yet unlocated settlement area. Alternatively, as with Pit 38, the feature may be viewed as a small quarry pit or abortive mine.

Pit Site C

Pull, in his field notebook, states that 'Pit Site C', to the immediate east of Pit 38, was surveyed on November 27th, 1949, following the backfilling of Pit 40, while excavation commenced on December 4th , continuing on December 11th. No further mention of this feature is made, and no artefacts or illustrations, indicating the nature of the cut appear to have survived in the Worthing Museum archive.

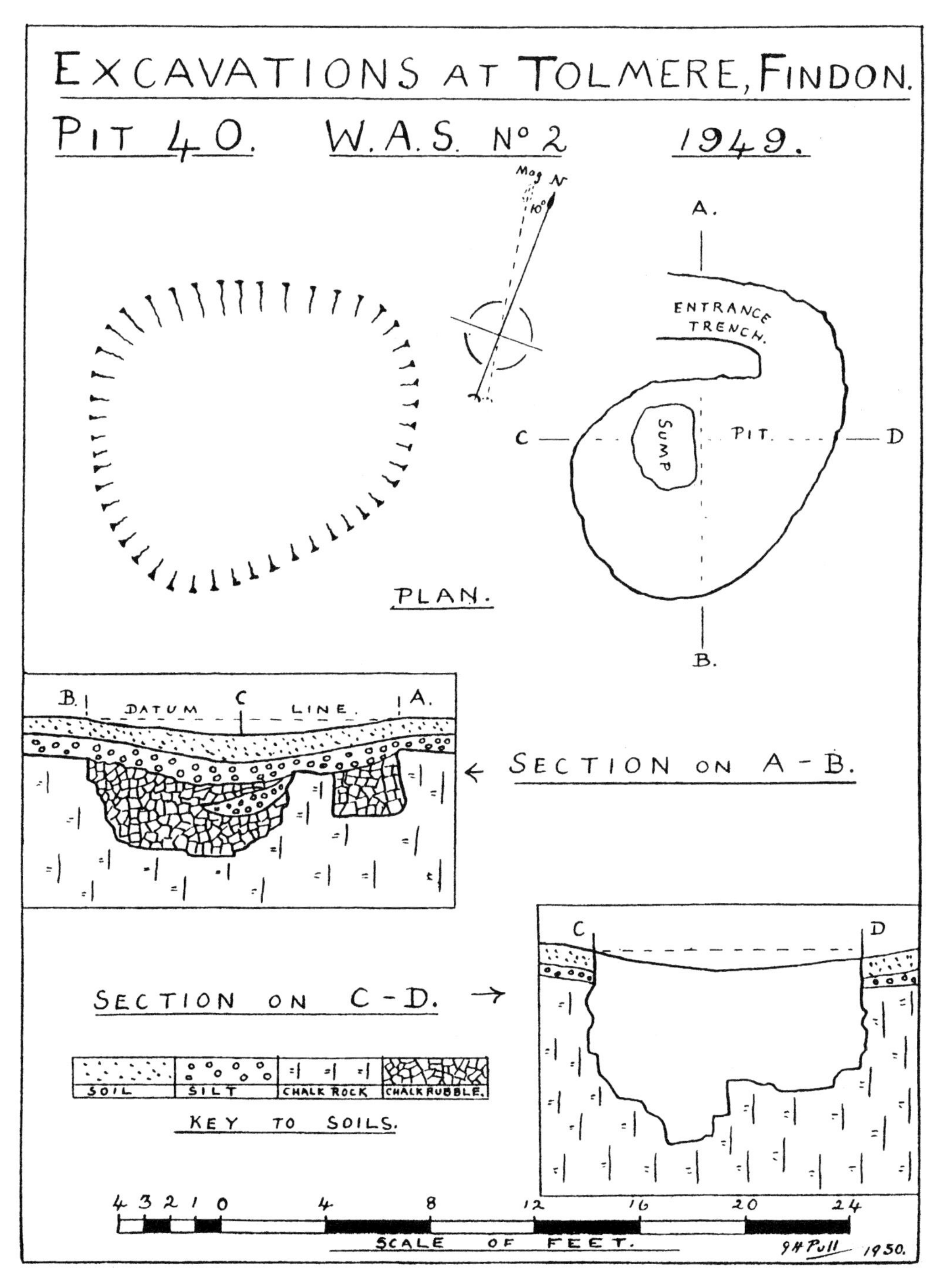

Figure 92. Tolmere Pit 40: (clockwise from top left) pre excavation surface hachure plan, post excavation feature plan, feature profile and section through pit fill (© Worthing Museum and Art Gallery).

OTHER AREAS

Barrow A

Three round barrow mounds were noted to the south-east of the main pit area, half way between the 122 and 152m contour lines. A surface survey of these barrows, labelled A, B and C was conducted on the 29th and 30th of May 1949 (figure 93). Excavation of mound A, employing the strip-method whereby a series of parallel slices, measuring at least 2.4m (eight feet) in width, were cut across the mound in an easterly direction (thus producing a series of progressive north–south sections through the earthwork) began on June 5th (figure 94).

The barrow ditch, which possessed a maximum diameter of 11m, measured 0.9m in width and was 0.25m deep. The feature possessed straight sides and a flat-bottom. A section produced by M. Hinge (Worthing Museum Acc. No 61–1587) shows that at least three types of fill were recorded within the ditch, fine chalk silt, coarse silt and a dense basal deposit of block chalk rubble. Pull records, in the field notebook, that large amounts of flint flakes, cores and implements, including knives, a boring tool together with ox bones and burnt stone (possibly firecracked flint) were found 'scattered' in the eastern portion of the barrow ditch. Flint implements were also

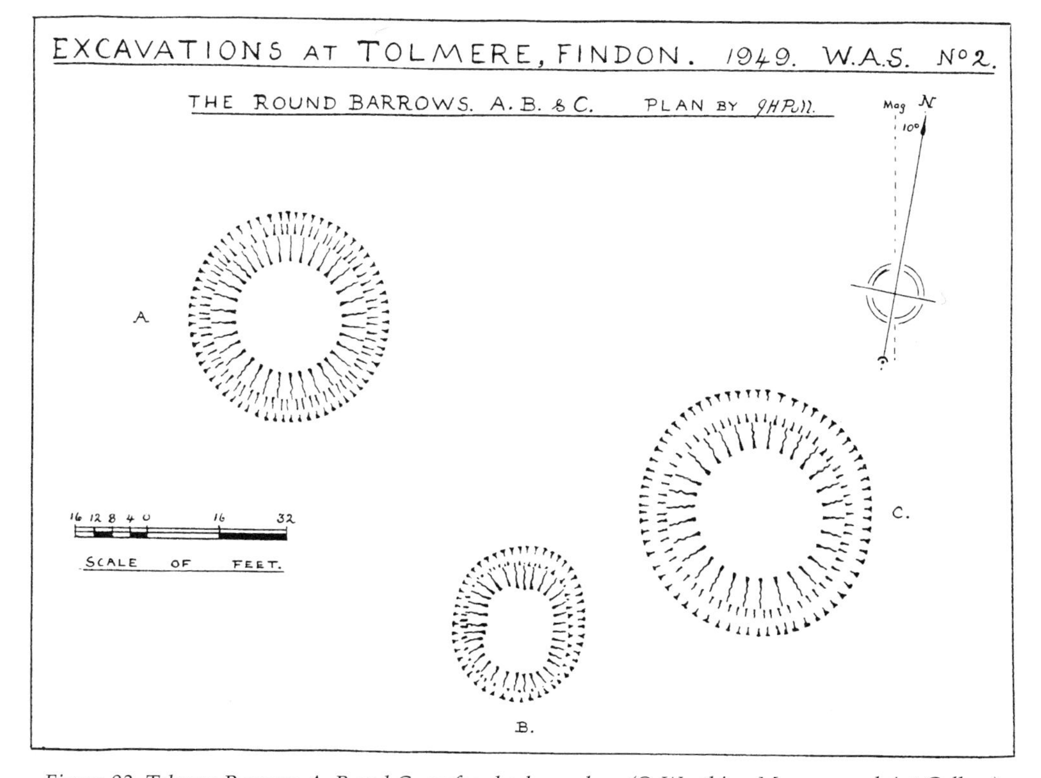

Figure 93. Tolmere Barrows A, B and C: surface hachure plans (© Worthing Museum and Art Gallery).

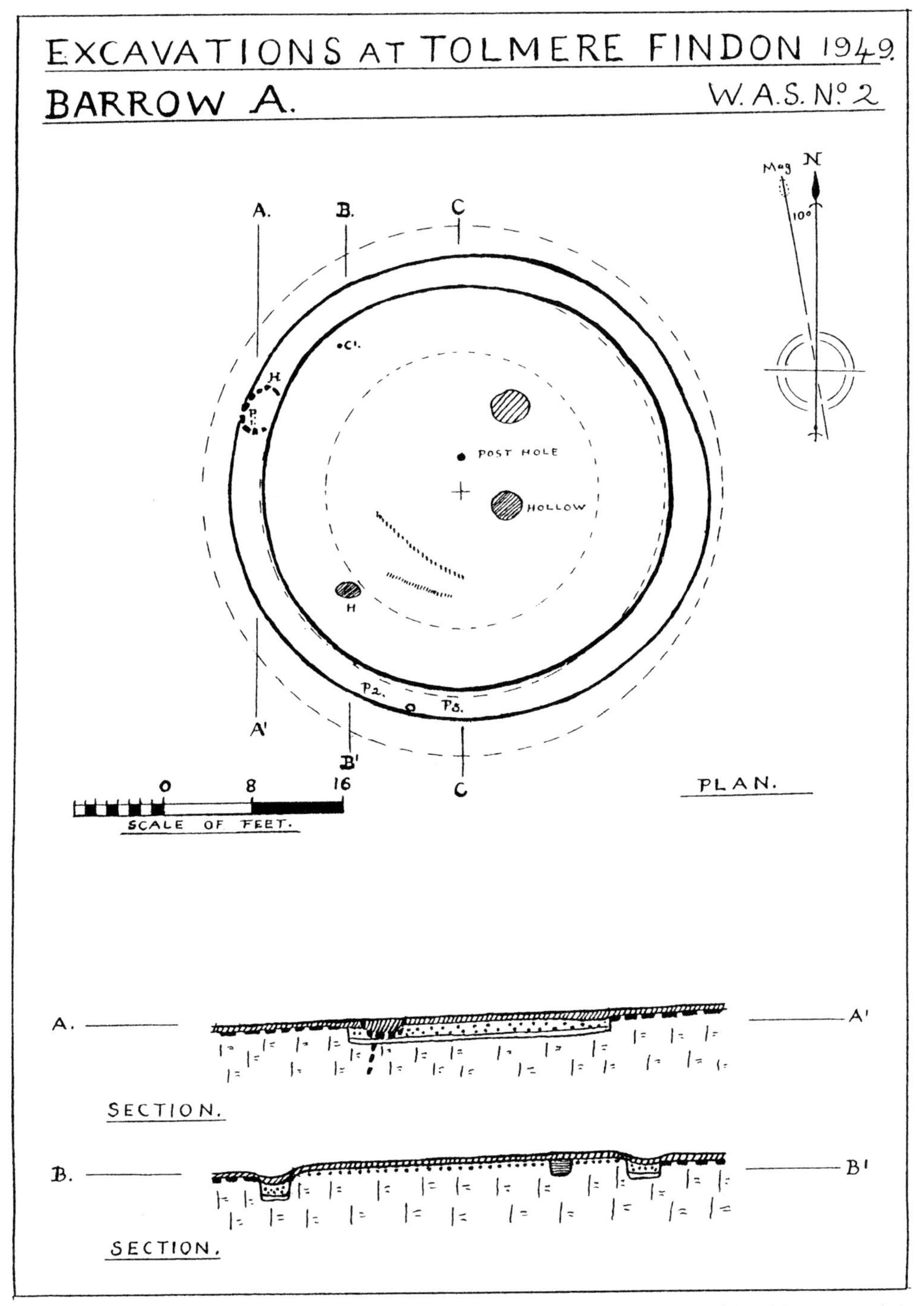

Figure 94. Tolmere Barrow A: post excavation feature plan and sections (© Worthing Museum and Art Gallery).

retrieved from the north-western, south-western and south-eastern areas of ditch fill while an ox jaw and other pieces of ox bone were recovered from the south-eastern and south-western areas respectively. Two antler picks, a fragment of antler tine and some sherds of Bronze Age pottery were also recorded as having derived from the fill of the south-western area of ditch fill. Some Iron Age pottery and a fibulae were also encountered within ditch fill. In the notebook, Pull refers to a hearth, found within the north-western area of ditch, and an 'intrusion' of Early Iron Age date. The hearth is shown in the plan and appears to consist of an oval area of charcoal, burnt stone and pottery. The first section drawing provided for the barrow (A–A1) indicates that the hearth was secondary to the main period of ditch fill, perhaps suggesting that this feature represents the intrusion to which Pull originally referred. A posthole containing an ox bone was noted within the southern portion of the ditch.

The central barrow mound, which survived to no more than 0.3m above ground level, apparently contained 'many large flints', possibly in the form of a capping, together with flint flakes, flint tools including at least one borer and a Cissbury type axe, burnt stone, two pieces of sandstone, some fossils and fragments of cremated bone. Four distinct pottery types (one Bronze Age, the others Iron Age) were reconstructed in sketch form by Pull following the termination of the Barrow excavation (Acc. No 1961/1587). Though not explicitly stated in the notebook, it is presumed that all originally derived from the Barrow. A series of features were located beneath the area of the central mound. These included two areas of north-west – south-east aligned linear disturbance (possibly plough lines), two hollows, an off-centre posthole and an area of cremated bone. The south-western hollow, which according to the section drawing (B–B1), predated the construction of the mound, measured 0.9m by 0.6m in diameter and was 0.4m deep. The larger hollow to the north-east measured 0.8m in diameter. Its depth is unknown. The posthole measured 0.22m in depth and 0.1m in diameter, tapering to 0.06m diameter at its base. This feature was interpreted by Pull as representing the remains of a totem or marker post, perhaps for the recorded deposit of cremated bone.

Barrow A presumably represents a Bronze Age marker mound, set up over the remains of at least one cremation deposit. The position of this deposit may originally have been indicated at ground level by a post or grave-marker. Lack of mining debris or extensive quantities of mine products, such as that noted from the mounds of Blackpatch, would appear to argue against Barrow A being contemporary with a major phase of prehistoric flint extraction. In this context the single Cissbury type axe recorded from the mound makeup may represent a residual find incorporated into the later earthwork during construction. Some form of Early Iron Age activity is indicated across the area of Barrow A in the form of the pottery and possibly the later hearth.

The Earthwork

The linear earthwork, or cross-ridge dyke, consisting of a quarry ditch and southern earth bank, was sampled in three separate places, cuttings A, B and C between May 15th and May 2nd 1949 (figure 95). Section A, 18m to the east of the track, revealed

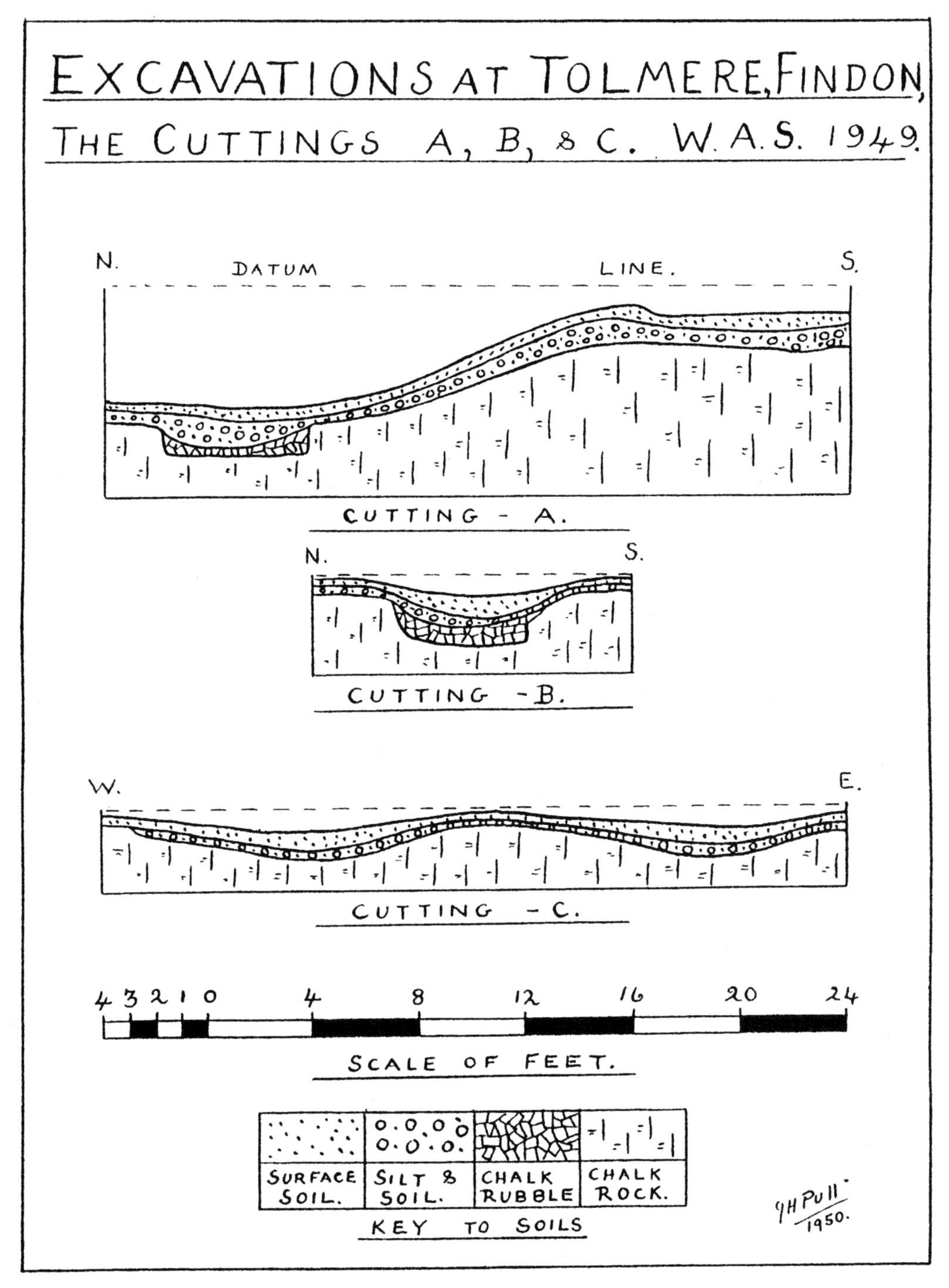

Figure 95. Tolmere Earthwork: three sections cut through the linear feature (© Worthing Museum and Art Gallery).

the ditch to consist of a regular edged, flat-bottomed cut measuring 2.1m in width and surviving to a maximum depth of 0.6m below the modern ground surface. The fill consisted of silt overlying a 0.15m thick basal deposit of chalk rubble. Six flint implements, including a scraper and a saw, and a number of flakes and cores together with a large sphere of iron pyrites, were retrieved from this basal layer. The bank to the south of the ditch cut did not survive to any great degree, the surface feature being represented by 1.2m drop in ground level, rather in the manner of a negative lynchet.

Cutting B, to the immediate west of Pit 38 and the south-west of Pit 40 revealed the ditch here to consist of a flat-bottomed V profiled cut, 2m wide, narrowing to around 1.3m at its base, and surviving to a maximum depth of 0.6m below the modern ground level. The profile of the ditch cut widened considerably as it cut through the upper levels of Pit 38 (section 'A'). At least two pieces of Roman pottery (one described as a fragment of 'Roman blue provincial ware') and a 'Roman nail' were found at a depth of 0.3m within the fill of the ditch. Cutting C examined the apparent continuation of the bank and ditch as it turned to the south. The ditch, as sampled here, is markedly different to the straight-sided, flat-bottomed feature noted within sections A and B. Fossils and land mollusca appear to have been the only finds from this exploratory section.

Pull interpreted the linear earthwork as a type of land boundary. Certainly the feature does not appear to have formed part of a larger enclosure. Stratigraphically it is clearly later in date than pits 38 and 39 (sampled by the Curwens), and may have been constructed before the north–south aligned lynchet bank, running along the eastern margin of the pitted area, that the Curwens first noted in 1927. The date of the earthwork itself is unclear, the Roman finds occurring within secondary areas of ditch fill. This could be taken as indicating a Late Iron Age origin, assuming that the feature did not backfill quickly and the Roman material itself was not residual.

7
Excavations at Cissbury, 1952–6

Cissbury (NGR TQ 140080), at the north-eastern margins of modern Worthing, rises to a height of 184 metres OD. The area of flint mining, which lies to the immediate south-east of Church Hill, is partially enclosed by the remains of an Iron Age hillfort. The earliest excavations at Cissbury, which do not appear to have been recorded in any detail, presumably focussed, in the good antiquarian tradition, upon the opening of barrow mounds. Certainly at least one Beaker, a largely unornamented example, in the Mantell Collection of the British Museum, seems to have been derived from 'a barrow near Cissbury' (Grinsell 1931, 39; 1934, 232, Clarke 1970, 499). Though the find is known to have formed part of Gideon Mantell's private collection by at least May of 1833 (Musson 1954, 108), its exact context and associations remain unknown.

Later investigations at Cissbury centred upon the deep surface indentations visible along the western slopes of the hill, concluding that they were the remains of either 'rude huts', ponds, 'holy consecrated recesses', pig pounds or cattle enclosures (e.g. Turner 1850, 180–1; Irving 1857, 294). Colonel Augustus Lane Fox appears to have been the first to seriously consider the possibility that the depressions had originally been cut 'for the purpose of obtaining flints' (Lane Fox 1869b, 73) following excavation work conducted at Cissbury between 1867 and 1868. Unfortunately neither Lane Fox, nor any of his predecessors, had at this stage fully exposed any of the shafts, exploration being confined to the uppermost areas of chalk rubble fill. Lane Fox did not confine his work at Cissbury to the flint mines however, and a series of small earthwork enclosures to the immediate west of the shafts were also examined in 1868 (Lane Fox 1869b; Toms and Toms 1926).

As at Church Hill, the full nature of additional fieldwork conducted by both Lane Fox and his colleague Cannon Greenwell between 1867 and 1868, remains vague (Burstow 1962). It seems probable, for example, that Greenwell took part in fieldwork of his own beyond the immediate limits of the mining zone, for at least one Beaker, originating from a 'round barrow at Cissbury' exists in the Greenwell Collection, now stored in the British Museum (Kinnes and Longworth 1985, 141). As with Mantell's Beaker, the provenance of this find remains obscure, though Pull, in a sketch plan of the Cissbury earthworks, seems to indicate that the disturbed barrow mound upon the western slopes of the hill beneath the Iron Age ramparts, was perhaps the feature that Greenwell had investigated (figure 96).

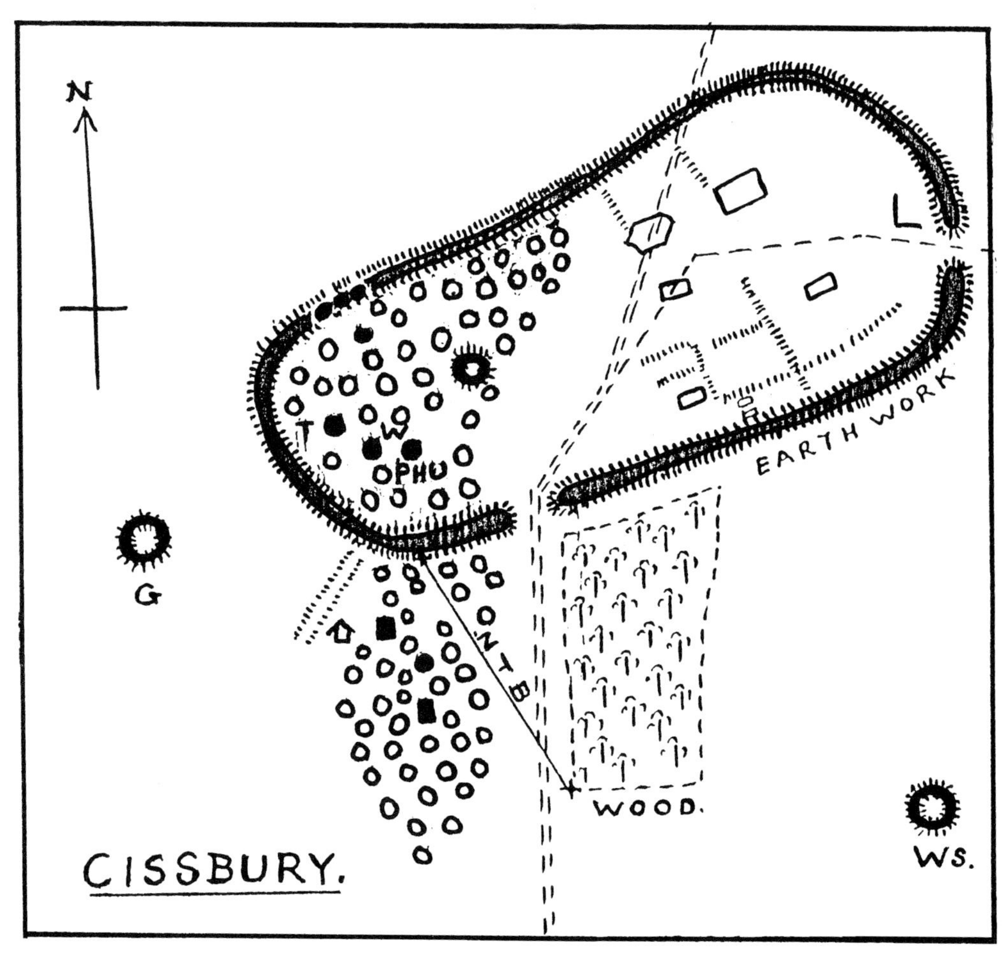

Figure 96. Cissbury: sketch plan by Pull indicating certain areas of earlier examination. W = Willett, PH = Harrison, T = Tindall, G = Greenwell, WS = ? (© Worthing Museum and Art Gallery).

In the autumn of 1873, inspired by Cannon Greenwell's excavations at Grimes Graves in Norfolk, Ernest Willett re-examined one of the Cissbury pits, finding that the area previously recorded was in reality only thc uppermost fill of a much larger feature. This shaft consisted of a 4.3m deep cut possessing at least five basal chambers (Willett 1880, 388). In January 1874 Plumpton Tindall fully excavated a second shaft at Cissbury to a depth of around 12m (Lane Fox 1875, 364–5), though, as Tindall died before he could report on the examination, it is not known whether the shaft possessed basal galleries (Willett 1880, 341). Excavation of a third shaft by Willett commenced the following August. This was revealed to consist of a cylindrical cut, 5.8m in diameter and at least 6m deep with a series of eight 'caves' or galleries, not all of which were fully explored, extending out from its base (Lane Fox 1875, 365; Willett 1880, 339–40, plate xxvii).

Lane Fox returned to Cissbury in 1875 and recommenced the excavation of two shafts that had previously only been partially investigated by Greenwell and himself during the 1867–8 season. Nine shafts were fully examined by Lane Fox during 1875 and, rather crucially, the relative phasing of the site was finally resolved, with at least one shaft being seen to pre-date the Iron Age enclosure (Lane Fox 1875, 373, plates xv and xvi). A series of criss-cross engravings were noted over a number of gallery entrances, while an Early Neolithic carinated bowl and the remains of an inverted human skeleton were some of the more spectacular discoveries that were made at this time (Lane Fox 1875, 375; Holgate 1991, figure 17). Following Lane Fox, work continued at Cissbury under the direction of J. Park Harrison who investigated three additional shafts and their numerous interconnecting galleries as well as re-examining the pit left open by Willett in 1874 (Harrison 1877a; 1877b; 1878). The first detailed survey of the earthworks to the east of the mining area partially investigated by Lane Fox between 1867–8, was conducted by Herbert and Christine Toms in the early 1920s (Toms and Toms 1926). This survey was followed by excavation, through the auspices of the Worthing Archaeological Society, across two sections of hillfort rampart and a series of apparently Romano-British pits and lynchets in 1930 (Curwen and Williamson 1931). In 1952, John Pull, then president of the Worthing Archaeological Society, came to Cissbury with the intention of conducting further excavation of the Neolithic mining area:

> Since the recent excavations which have been carried out on the neighbouring flint mine fields at Harrow Hill, Blackpatch and Church Hill, Findon have yielded much new information on the subject of flint mining, and the flint industries associated with them, it has become more and more necessary to make another attack upon the major mine field at Cissbury in the light of modern knowledge (Worthing Museum Acc. No. 1961/1586).

Pull decided to restrict his work to the previously uninvestigated set of mine shafts continuing beyond the southern margins of the later Iron Age enclosure. Here the need for examination was considered to be additionally important because:

> the activities of the military during the last war had revealed the presence there of a number of surface flint working floors which called for investigation, more especially as the previous excavators had never made any thorough examination of the many chipping floors which exist everywhere round about the pits. Experience has proved that it is from these surface workshops that our greatest knowledge of the tool making industry associated with the mines has been obtained (Worthing Museum Acc. No. 1961/1586).

Work commenced in May 1952 with a detailed survey of the southern mines (figure 97) followed by an application to Worthing Borough Council, upon whose land this particular part of the site lay, for permission to excavate.

> On August 1st the Borough permit to excavate was granted and from then until October 5th the work hereafter described was carried out following the preliminary clearing up and burying of the barbed wire left by army (Worthing Museum Acc. No. 1961/1586).

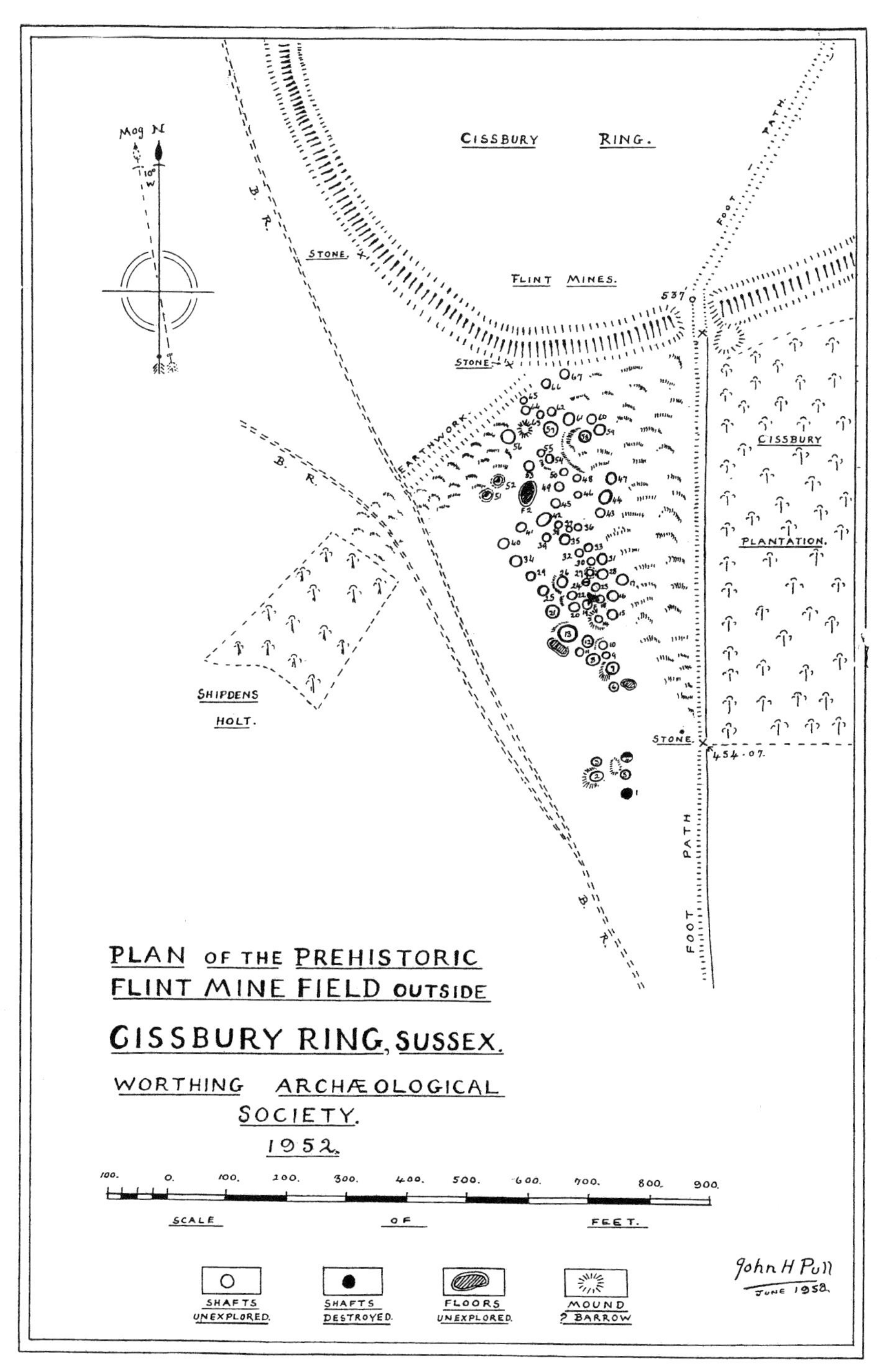

Figure 97. Cissbury: plan of the southern mine series indicating shafts, mounds and chipping floors visible as surface features in 1952 (© Worthing Museum and Art Gallery).

Unlike the excavations conducted at Blackpatch and Church Hill, Pull did not publish summaries of his work at Cissbury within the popular press, though it would appear, from the nature of hand written texts preserved within the Worthing Museum archive, that a detailed publication was seriously being considered. Unfortunately, Pull's untimely death prevented this. The reports that follow are taken from archive texts (Acc. No 1961/1586/A), which, unlike the excavations conducted at Blackpatch and Church Hill, do not all exist as a series of continuous narratives. Hand written summary texts survive for the chipping floors, excavated as the first part of the fieldwork upon Cissbury in 1952, and for Section A through the upper levels of Shaft 18, but, apart from a section on the discovery and removal of a human skeleton from Shaft 27 (reproduced in part as Appendix 3) and a short piece outlining the final stages of the 1956 season (Appendix 4), detailed reports regarding the examination of Shafts 24 and 27 do not appear within the Worthing Museum archive. The texts concerning the investigation of these mine shafts has therefore been taken from notes surviving within Pull's own excavation diaries.

The examination of mine shafts at Cissbury continued until the early months of 1956 when, following a particular harsh winter, the decision was made to backfill all excavated areas. Pull, in his concluding comments for the 1956 season (Appendix 4) noted that:

> in view of the excavation of the newly discovered mining site at Longdown which Mr Salisbury has undertaken, we have decided, with the approval of the Committee of this Society, to transfer the apparatus which we have at Cissbury and our helpers to that site and support Mr Salisbury in what promises to be a long and very important exploration (Worthing Museum Acc. No. 1961/1586).

The excavation of the Worthing flint mines had come to an end.

THE MINES

Shaft 18 (Section A)

The upper levels of Shaft 18 were partially examined during the excavation of Chipping Floor 1 (see figure 116). The trial trench that was dug out from the floor and into shaft 18 was described in the site diary as Section A. A short text by Pull, describing the excavation, exists in the Worthing Museum archive.

> This was a deep section cut into the surface of shaft 18 firstly in order to ascertain if Chipping Floor 1 extended over the infilling of that shaft, which it did not, and secondly to find out something of the nature of the infilling of the pits here. Floor 1 ended four and a half feet short of the north lip of shaft 18 and the hard side of the shaft was located at this point at a depth of one foot below the surface. Section A was extended from the northern edge of Shaft 18 to a point six feet south of this, that is to the centre of the visible depression indicating the presence of this shaft.

> This section proved that the upper most filling consisted first of one foot of turf and topsoil. Below this lay one foot of yellow consolidated rainwash, or fine chalk silt, and this in turn rested upon large unweathered chalk blocks, the interstices of which in the upper part were sealed with the overlying rainwash and below were open and air spaced.
>
> About the centre of Shaft 18, at the base of the surface mould and laying on the upper portion of the silt was a mass of large flints and scattered among these and in the rainwash below were found eighteen flint implements. Although all these have been made from the mined flint and have been primarily flaked by a wood bar or by an antler mallet technique, which is characteristic of the mining industry, yet they do not include any of the celt, or pick types generally made at the mines.
>
> The artefacts present a marked difference to the series of implements recovered from the chipping floor 1 which lay close to the lip of Shaft 18. They obviously had not drifted into the depression over Shaft 18 from that floor. Moreover none of them are in 'mint' condition. They all show signs of use, some of long continued use. No's 166, 167 and 168 recall the Palaeoliths from the drift. No 159 recalls the Neolithic 'A' types of Lake Bierne, No 169, 170 and 171, look a St Gertrude series, No 157, 158 and 160 might have come from any round barrow of the Early Bronze Age. The typology presented by these flints is therefore a mixed one, but the technique employed in the making of them is uniform with that exhibited by the workmanship of the other flint mine areas hitherto explored in Sussex vis, Harrow Hill, Blackpatch and Church Hill, Findon (Worthing Museum Acc. No. 1961/1586).

Seventeen flakes, labelled as having derived from Section A, survive in the Pull archive of Worthing Museum. No further work was conducted within Shaft 18.

Shaft 23

During the course of examining the interlinked subterranean galleries extending from Shaft 27 (see below) Pull identified the talus or basal deposits of an additional two shafts. These he marked Shaft 'A' and 'B' on the site plan. Having completed the investigation of Shaft 27 Pull applied for permission to open Shaft B which he identified as surface depression 23. As with Shaft 27, no detailed text appears to have survived for this feature.

The excavation of Shaft 23 began on March 27th 1955. Spoil was removed in quadrants, the south-eastern quadrant being removed first. Immediately the excavation had begun, it became clear that the shaft was not the one that they had detected within the basal galleries of Shaft 27, its centre being further to the north than had first appeared from the surface survey. This discrepancy was due to the 'convergence of [mining] dumps' which had partially slumped back into the shaft significantly altering its outward appearance. As a consequence of this discovery the sample trench through the upper levels of Shaft 23 was extended in a northerly direction, through Chipping Floor 3, in an attempt to locate the desired Shaft head. By April 12th, with no sign of a second shaft opening apparent, Pull had concluded in his notebook that:

> the talus seen underground is a high collapsed roof at junction of several levels. After checking distances and angles with south drift and plans of underground, decided to fence and excavate Shaft on SW (Worthing Museum Acc. No. 1961/1586).

Consequently, with only the uppermost levels of this feature having been examined (a 'highly consolidated silt 2 feet deep' overlying solid chalk) the excavation of Shaft 23 was abandoned. Two flakes from Shaft 23 survive in the Pull archive in Worthing Museum.

Shaft 24

The investigation of Shaft 24 (figure 98), situated 2.4m to the south-west of Shaft 27 began on April 17th 1955. Unlike the majority of other shafts investigated at the Worthing mine fields, there are no inked sections showing the fills encountered during the clearance of Shaft 24, while the site diary refers only to depths exposed within the shaft, rather than layer descriptions.

An overall list of flint types recovered from Shaft 24 is absent from the Worthing archive, although certain identifications were made in the site diary as the dig progressed. From this we are able to record that 'half [a] Spiennes type pick' together with many flakes, half a roughout, and several 'rough cores' came from the base of the surface soil. From the upper rainwash deposit came a large oval roughout, several large flakes, a piece of antler ('possibly the handle of a knife'), a cow jaw and teeth and an antler pick 'cut from slain animal'. Below this, in the centre soil, two large roughout axes and a fragment bone (possibly ox) were recovered. Between the depths of 1.8 and 2.1m, two ovate flint implements, a number of flint knives, a core, and some animal bone (possibly pig) were recovered. Large quantities of charcoal were noted within the central fill of the shaft at a depth of between 3.6 and 4.2m together with a 'perfect shoulder blade shovel', a mass of flint flakes and blades, an 'unpatinated hand axe quite black' and an antler pick which apparently possessed a wooden handle. None of the flint artefacts recovered from the examination of the shaft appear within the Worthing Museum archive.

When completed, the diameter of the open shaft was recorded as being 2.8m north–south by 2.1m east–west, narrowing in a series of steps at a depth of 3m. The floor of the mine was located at 4.2m on the western side, but was apparently deeper on north-eastern and southern sides. The central point of the feature was measured as being 6.1m from the centre of Shaft 27, 2.4m of solid rock separating the two mines. Six galleries of varying dimensions were noted at the base of the shaft extracting the second seam of horizontal flint. The north-eastern gallery connected with Shaft 27, while the opposing gallery connected, via a window, to an unexplored shaft to the south-west. Two flint knives and part of antler tine were recovered from the western gallery. The gallery noted along the southern wall was about 0.9m high with a 'level ceiling and square sides', measuring 2.4m in width for the first 3m before dividing, both branches continuing for at least another 1.8–2.4m. A great number of 'deep pick and punch holed blocks' were found within these galleries.

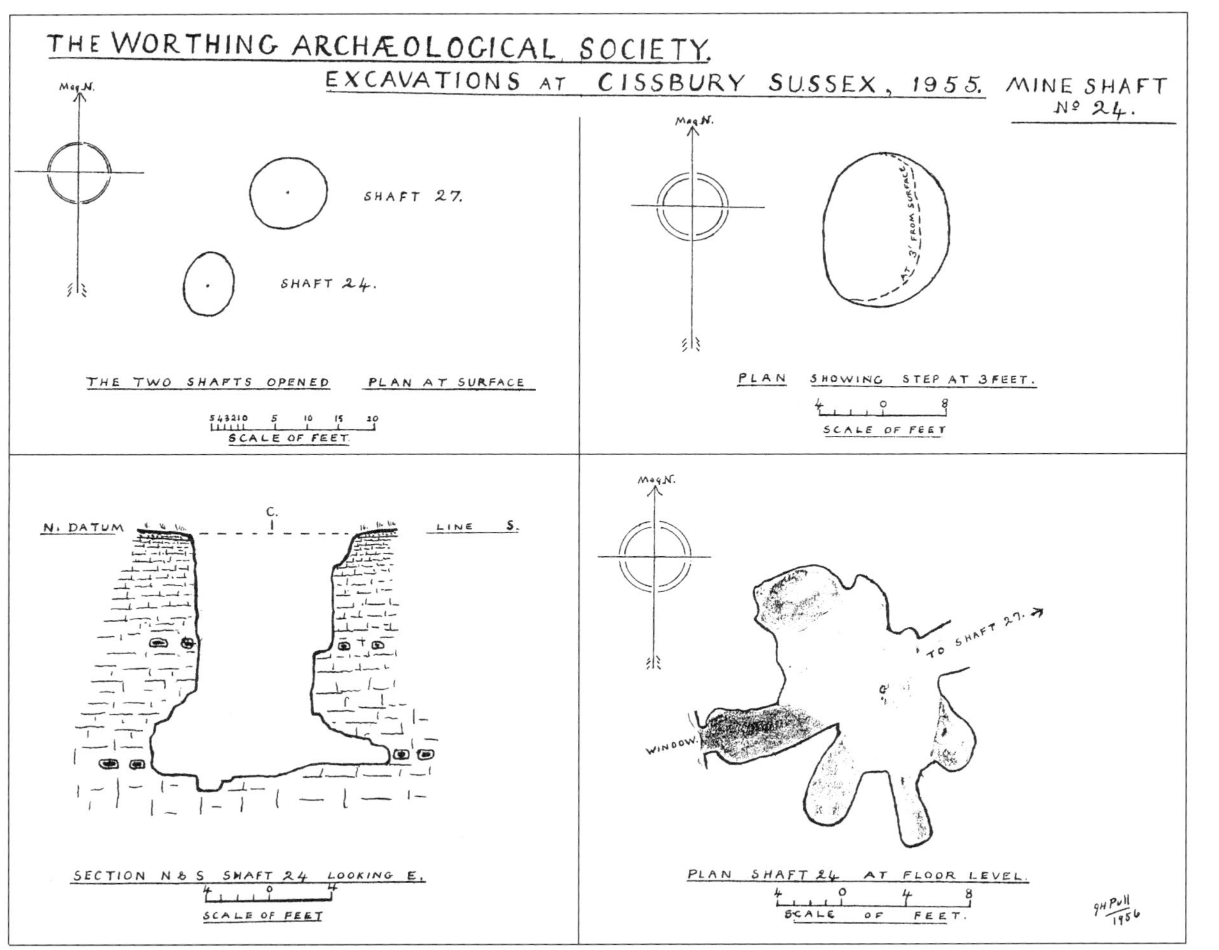

Figure 98. Cissbury Shaft 24: (clockwise from top left) simplified pre excavation plan, post excavation feature plan showing the nature of the shaft wall, plan of subterranean workings, shaft profile (© Worthing Museum and Art Gallery).

Shaft 27

The investigation of Shaft 27, the first piece of mine excavation conducted by Pull at Cissbury, began on Sunday 8th March 1953 (figure 99). As with the excavation of Shafts 23 and 24, no detailed report on the fieldwork exists within the Worthing Museum archive. Given that the concluding work of the 1955 season at Cissbury was reported upon, it is likely that a more complete text for this feature was originally written, but that this became misplaced following Pull's untimely death. The report that follows has therefore been compiled from three sources: a surviving text describing the discovery and removal of a skeleton from shaft 27 (reproduced in full as Appendix 3), the main excavation notebook ('The Diary and Field Notes of Excavations at Cissbury 1953, 54, 55: Acc. No 1961/1586/A) and the surviving inked-in plans and sections.

The diameter of Shaft 27 at the surface measured 3.2m by 3m and soil was first removed in quadrants, with the section drawing being compiled over a considerable period of time (figure 100). Data from Pull's main excavation notebook supplies some information concerning the nature of finds from the upper levels of the shaft fill, the majority of which do not appear to have been handed over to Worthing Museum following the completion of the project (Pye 1968). These comprised three large unfinished roughouts, several pointed knife flakes, numerous rough flakes 'all deeply patinated', a 'shoulder blade shovel', a fragment of burnt bone and a number of flakes and rough nodules from the base of the topsoil. Below this, within the base of layer 1, a large and 'straight-sided' axe, two scrapers, a bone punched 'cone core', a triangular knife, a small roughout axe, a large roughout, many flakes and knife blades, several

Figure 99. Cissbury Shaft 27: visitors to the site in 1953. The shot is facing south towards Worthing and the coastal plain. Note the presence of the chain-link fence, winching tripod and chalk rubble spoil heap (© Worthing Museum and Art Gallery).

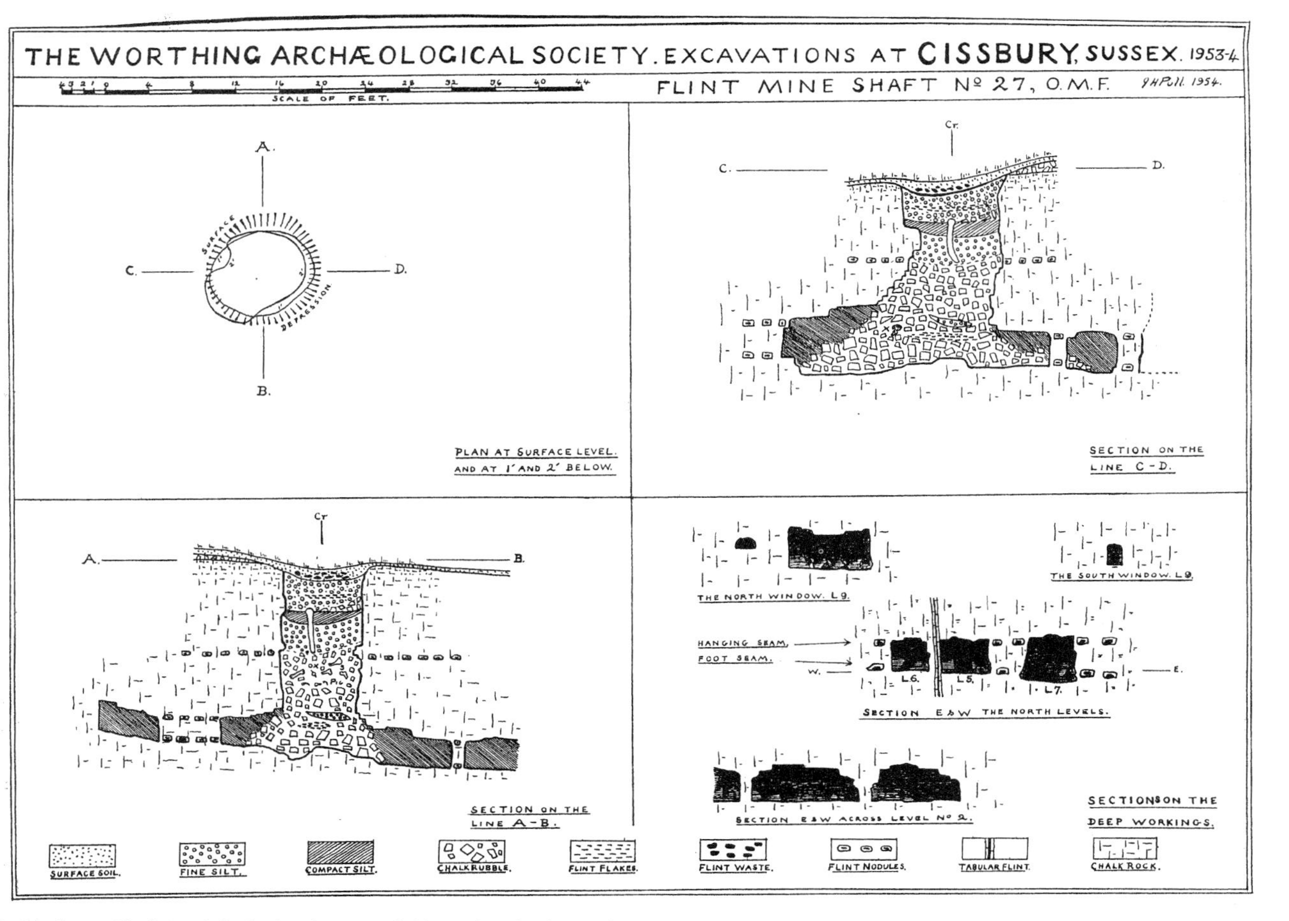

Figure 100. Cissbury Shaft 27: (clockwise from top left) surface hachure plan incorporating subsurface detail regarding the shaft wall, section through shaft fill showing the relative positions of the internal void and human skeleton, gallery elevations, second section through shaft fill showing linear void and the positions of animal bone (© Worthing Museum and Art Gallery).

large knives, a pick marked chalk block and a broken tine of an antler pick were recorded. Layer 2, a deposit described as comprising rainwash, produced a number of small blades, a square end scraper, a mass of secondary flakes, two roughouts, several knives, a number of sickle segments, 'broken animal bones', fragments of charcoal and 'many giant examples of Bush Snail'. The pick-marked chalk rubble recovered from this layer were 'completely rounded as if by water action' perhaps indicating long term exposure to the elements before burial.

Below the naturally accumulating rainwash deposit was a 'highly consolidated layer of silt', 0.3m thick. Once this compacted silt had been removed, the remaining two layers of shaft fill were exposed. These consisted of a series of densely packed chalk debris which 'had been introduced from the workings of other shafts round about at the actual time when mining was going on'. Some 2.4m down into the feature, the sides of the shaft began to narrow. Here Pull noticed a:

> curious hole found vertical in silt between 5 and 8 feet, 5ft N of S wall, lined with redeposited carbonate of lime. A slightly crooked timber, 5 to 8' diameter must have rested here and decayed. No darkening of contact. Found by this hole at 8ft, broken tusk of wild boar and nodule of iron pyrites (Worthing Museum Acc. No. 1961/1586).

The detail of this vertical break in shaft fill appears somewhat vague on the recorded section drawings (figure 100), though a series of photographs taken by E. J. Salisbury and housed within the Worthing Museum archive show the feature to have been a linear void within the 'cement-like' fill of the chalk silt (figure 101). A second, much smaller, void was later recorded to the north, apparently within the wall of the shaft itself. This feature consisted, in Pull's words, of 'a horizontal timber hole' measuring 0.4m by 0.7m in length and lined with 'redeposited calcareous tufa'. Unfortunately the exact position and nature of this particular feature remains unclear. Pye later noted the existence of these two features, but doubted whether they were of any real significance (Pye 1968, 41). Considering the limited amount of data that we possess concerning shaft usage however, these holes are potentially of great importance, especially if they relate to some

Figure 101. Cissbury Shaft 27: the upper fill of the shaft in half section, showing the linear void, interpreted by Pull as representing the remains of a decayed timber (© Worthing Museum and Art Gallery).

form of internal timber construction, such as a platform, ladder or ramp. Removal of chalk and flint debris from the shaft appears to have resulted in the attrition of shaft sides for Pull notes that, at a depth of eight feet, the projection on the south-western edge of the feature had been 'rubbed smooth and round'.

Below a depth of 2.4m into the shaft a large quantity of 'broken tabular flint' was recorded together with 'many bones of very small animals', which had presumably fallen into the shaft whilst it remained half backfilled, and a small, pressure-flaked, leaf shaped arrowhead. Below these levels a series of unusual discoveries were made. Here it is worth repeating the notes from Pull's diary in full:

> Found at 11 ft on N wall to centre and E wall – practically the whole skeleton of an ox with a few bones of another animal (smaller). Much of the ox vertebra in position. Long bones – some broken for marrow, some not. Some bones charred black by fire. At 10 feet, 3 feet from S wall of shaft shoulder blade of ox (used as shovel?). with the ox bones a thin deposit of brown leached soil with many mollusca...Found many more bones, ox and pig, at 12 feet..[and]..down to 15 feet (Worthing Museum Acc. No. 1961/1586).

The base of the shaft was located at a depth of 5.5m (figure 102), though this was not a level surface, two seams of flint, the third and fourth encountered during the cutting of the shaft, being worked and extracted at this point. The final two feet of silt overlying the base of the shaft was found to contain scattered charcoal and a mass of flint nodules and flakes including two knives, a 'fluted core plane', a roughout tortoise core, an axe roughout, half a Cissbury type axe, several pick-marked blocks of chalk and a number of 'small animal bones.'

The entrance to the first gallery was noted on May 13th (figure 103), while an additional two were uncovered four days later. Initial clearance of chalk rubble within the western gallery revealed the buried remains of an articulated human skeleton (figure 104). Pull, in a separate report (reproduced as Appendix 3) notes that 'we had stumbled upon what I had always hoped for, one of the old flint miners, who had met with a fatal accident at his work and whose body had never been recovered by his friends.' The sense of elation experienced by the excavation team at this point can be gauged by the description of the skeleton's removal (Appendix 3) and also within the reports that appeared in the *Daily Express* and the *Worthing Herald* (30th May 1953) under the headlines 'Pit Victim of 4,000 Years Ago is Found' and '2,000 BC Man's Bones Dug up at Cissbury: Archaeologists Discover a 4,000-Year-Old Tragedy'. The entry for the day of discovery in the site notebook is prefaced by Pull's excited comment: 'The Find of the Century!'.

At the time of recovery Pull suggested that the skeleton represented the remains of a miner who, whilst entering one of the basal galleries, perhaps to recommence work with tools left at the workface, had been killed by a sudden collapse of the chalk roof.

> Three large blocks had killed the man. One had smashed his face (figure 105), another had driven his right hand into his chest, and broken the left humerus, a third had broken his back just above the pelvis (Worthing Museum Acc. No. 1961/1586).

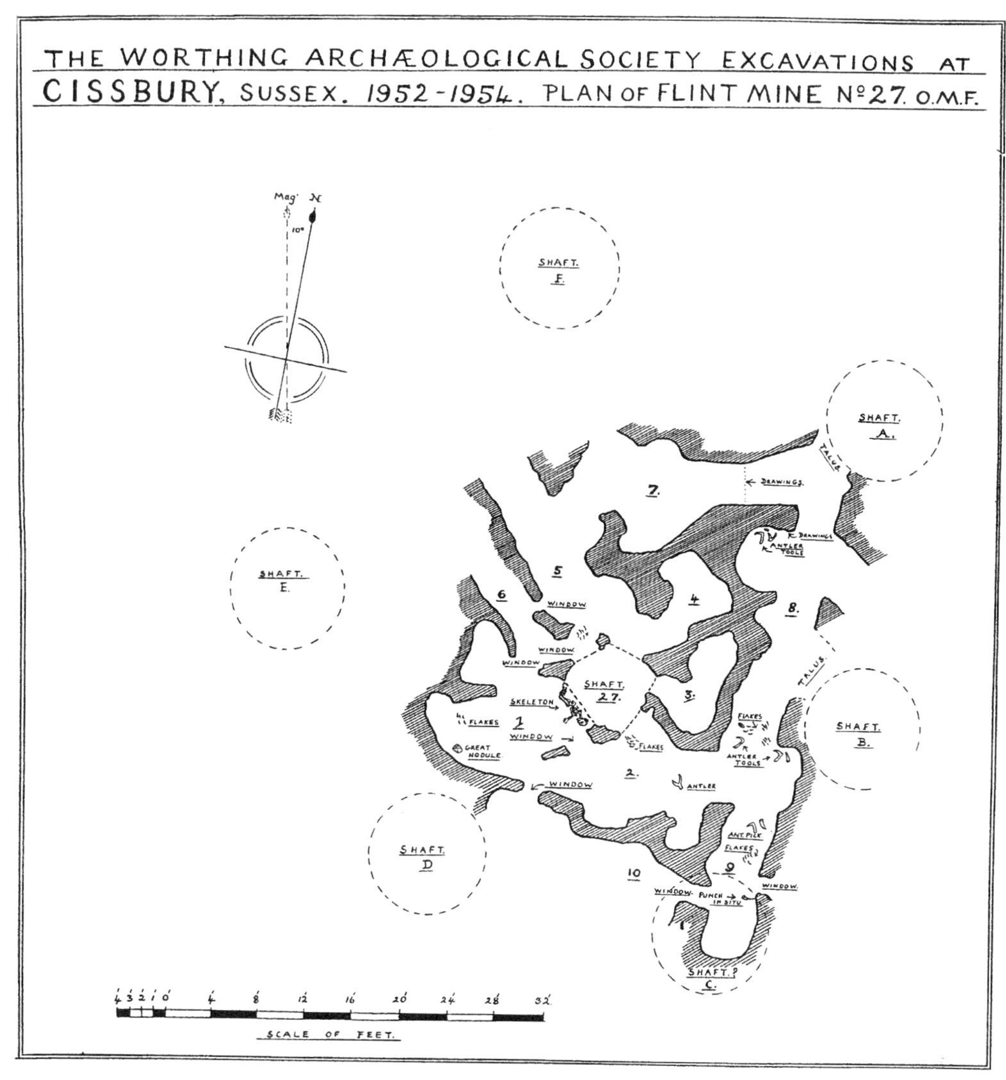

Figure 102. Cissbury Shaft 27: plan of subterranean workings illustrating the relative positions of stone, antler and bone implements, the extended human skeleton and chalk wall carvings (© Worthing Museum and Art Gallery).

The body was later identified as being that of a female aged around twenty (Trevor unpublished MS; Worthing Museum Acc. No 1961/1586/A). Pull dutifully amended his notebook, changing 'he' to 'she' throughout, but discussion over the nature and interpretation of the body appears, certainly in writing, to have progressed no further. Some doubt exists today as to whether the body represents that of a miner killed accidentally by roof collapse or the remains of a formal burial deposit (cf. Holgate pers. comm. 1995). If the body does represent an intentional burial, then it is possible

Figure 103. Cissbury Shaft 27: the entrance to gallery 1, still choked with chalk rubble, prior to the discovery of the human skeleton (© Worthing Museum and Art Gallery).

Figure 105. Cissbury Shaft 27: detail of the upper half of the female skeleton recovered from the entrance to gallery 1 (© Worthing Museum and Art Gallery).

Figure 104. Cissbury Shaft 27: John Lucas (top left) and John Pull (with pipe) standing at the entrance to gallery 1 in 1953. The pelvis and slightly flexed right leg of the female skeleton may be seen to the left of the shot. The body appears to have lain directly across the gallery entrance, the skull facing inwards towards the main area of extraction (© Worthing Museum and Art Gallery).

that its placing, lengthways across the entrance to gallery 1, was designed to deliberately block access to, or seal off the gallery in question.

A small amount of charcoal within the area of the bones comprising the right hand of the deceased were interpreted as the possible remains of a torch or lit taper that the individual had been carrying when the incident occurred. Some days later, on the 2nd of June, further excavation of gallery fill revealed the remaining finger and toe bones of the skeleton. While this material was being carefully removed, a curious piece of

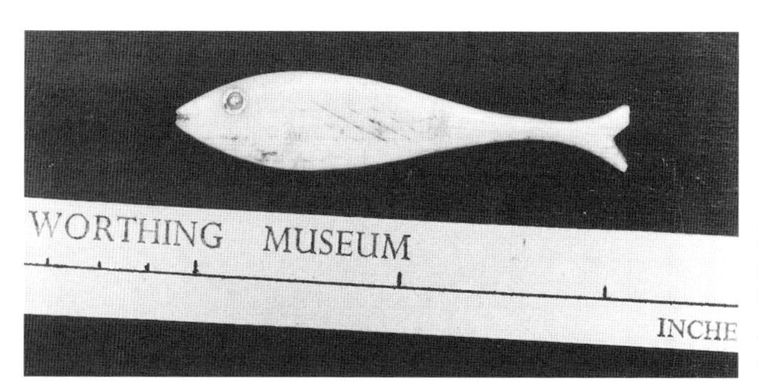

Figure 106. The 'Cissbury Fish', supposedly recovered from close to the human skeleton in gallery 1, Shaft 27 (© Worthing Museum and Art Gallery).

carefully carved and polished bone, the 'ivory fish', was recovered (figure 106). Pull, in a letter to the British Museum dated August 7th 1953 (letter 27, Appendix 5), noted that the find had been made 'near the left hand' of the skeleton, the implication perhaps being that the individual concerned had been carrying the piece at the time of the roof collapse. Since its discovery there has been some considerable doubt over the authenticity of the piece, especially as it compares favourably with a number of post medieval gaming counters noted elsewhere across Sussex (White pers. comm. 1995).

It is possible that the find represents modern contamination, perhaps from an unauthorised visitor to the mines, such visitors being already recorded from Blackpatch (e.g. Shaft 1), though security to this shaft appears to have been fairly sound (see below). It is also possible that the artefact was placed within the gallery as part of a prank intended to temporarily deceive Pull. It is clear throughout the letters and notes surviving in Worthing Museum, that the atmosphere amongst the volunteer team on site was lively and Pull himself was noted for 'a certain impish humour' (Venables 1960). Given the seriousness that the mine excavation work was taken, it would be unlikely that Pull himself had been responsible for such a prank, especially as he would have had nothing to gain from any such deception. In this respect it is perhaps worth noting Pull's earlier reaction to the claim that an artefact found in one of the Blackpatch shafts had been part of a hoax:

> With regard to the engraved flint, 'Antiquary' is absurdly mistaken in supposing that the excavators have removed and examined well over 100 tons of debris at Blackpatch for the purpose of perpetrating jokes upon scientific authorities or the general public. Nor have the excavators done this with the object of recording jokes which may have been played upon them (Letter 3; Appendix 5).

If the fish is modern, as seems likely, its placing in the gallery being intended as part of a practical joke by persons unknown, then it is likely that the joke backfired. Whoever had been responsible for its placement in the mine would probably have been unwilling to confess once the find had been accepted and its discovery been notified to a number of prominent specialists (e.g. Letters 27, 30, 31: Appendix 5) without being made to look foolish. Pull may well have entertained some doubts concerning the authenticity of the find, but, when writing to the British Museum, he

Figure 107. Cissbury Shaft 27: gallery 4 prior to excavation (© Worthing Museum and Art Gallery).

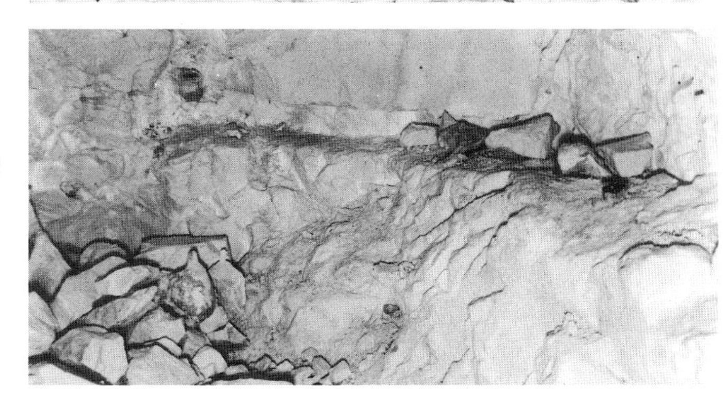

Figure 108. Cissbury Shaft 27: the back wall of gallery 4 during clearance. Note the ledge at the right of the shot, created by the systematic removal of flint nodules, some of which remain embedded in the chalk wall (© Worthing Museum and Art Gallery).

Figure 109. Cissbury Shaft 27: gallery 9 still choked with chalk rubble. Note the presence of an antler pick lying on top of the chalk, at the centre of the picture (© Worthing Museum and Art Gallery).

goes to some length to convince the Keeper, and perhaps by implication convince himself, that forgery was unlikely:

> the excavation is securely fenced with chain link five feet high and bar locked. The keys are kept by me. There is little chance of any planting by any intruder. So that I presume the object enclosed is genuine, moreover it was recovered in my presence by a member of undoubted integrity who is, like myself, a civil servant. Nevertheless I should be very glad of your expert opinion on it (Letter 27: Appendix 5).

Between May 13th 1953 and December 5th 1954 the galleries exposed at the base of Shaft 27 were emptied, explored and recorded (figures 107, 108 and 109). Small but discrete groupings of abandoned flint and antler tools and flint debitage, presumably indicating some limited form of artefact manufacture, were retrieved from within the cleared galleries. Of the flint Pull notes the presence of a knife from the rubble 0.9m inside the entrance to gallery 1, a 'great flint' from close to the southern back wall of gallery 1, flint flakes and a knife from the entrance area of gallery 2, a core, an end scraper and a blade from Gallery 5, a segmented tool, a large core, and several nodules from the junction of galleries 8 and 2 and a large number of flakes from gallery 9.

An additional find, apparently recovered during the course of Pull's excavations at Cissbury (Ainsworth pers. comm. 1993), and comprising of a cylindrical nodule of flint, with a fossil echinoid attached at one end, exists in Worthing Museum. Though the exact provenance of this find remains unknown, it seems likely that the piece originally derived from the Shaft 27 investigation (cf. Pye 1968, 49; Ainsworth pers. comm. 1995). The chief interest of the artefact is in its phallus-like appearance and, if genuine, and not placed within the working area as part of a prank or practical joke like the ivory fish appears to have been, then it may be paralleled with the chalk phalli recovered from Grimes Graves and a number of other Neolithic sites (cf. Varndell 1991, 105-6; Longworth and Varndell 1996, 51).

The antler tools recorded include a three point antler crown from gallery 2, an antler point from gallery 5, picks and crown punches from gallery 8, and two picks, two punches and a three pronged pick from gallery 9. Many of the chalk blocks encountered bore the deep impressions of antler picks and punches while broken tines were observed within the walls of some galleries. The bones of mice within galleries 1, 5 and 9 may possibly indicate some form of infestation whilst the mine was in operation. The majority of excavated galleries appear to have been at least partially filled with chalk rubble derived, presumably, from the working of later gallery systems.

A series of interesting markings were noted upon the chalk cut walls during the clearing of gallery 7. The first to be discovered, on November 22nd 1953, was:

> found in east drift where cutting lowers on the lintel against ceiling, an incised drawing of a short horned bulls head (figures 110 and 111). The 'V' cuts look as if done with a flint tool and are filled with redeposited (fluffy) carbonate. The drawing is more symbolic than naturalistic. It was found by a party of 3 boys of Mr Salisbury's group, Mr Ansell being the first to notice it (Worthing Museum Acc. No. 1961/1586).

A second engraving, facing the first and interpreted as depicting the head of a red deer was uncovered seven days later (figure 110), while a third, again of a red deer (figure 112), was located close by on August 29th 1954. The location of these markings is indicated on at the point within gallery 7 close to its junction with gallery 8. A third series of markings (figures 113, 114 and 115) were discovered on December 13th 1953 within gallery 8:

> In east section right branch on jamb of entrance. Drawings found by Mr Jacobs - a fishes head and star spread indefinite flint cut) below. 'V' miners sign done with antler found – half round groove (Worthing Museum Acc. No. 1961/1586).

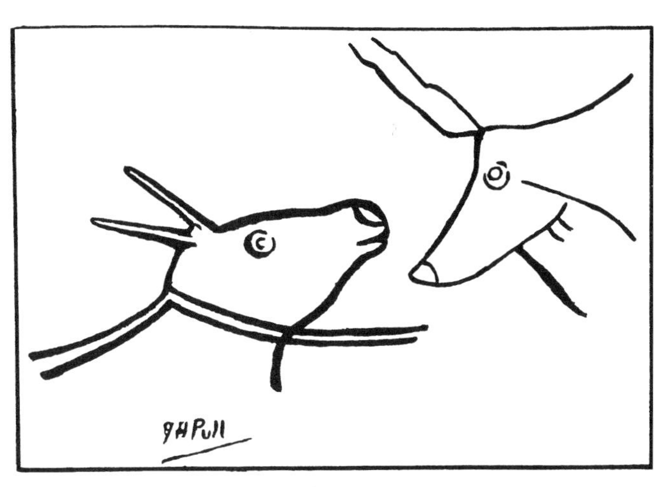

Figure 110. Cissbury Shaft 27: a simplified interpretative sketch, drawn by Pull, of the first two animalistic engravings, the "short horned bull" and the first deer, to be recorded from gallery 7, linked to Shaft 31, in November 1953 (© Worthing Museum and Art Gallery).

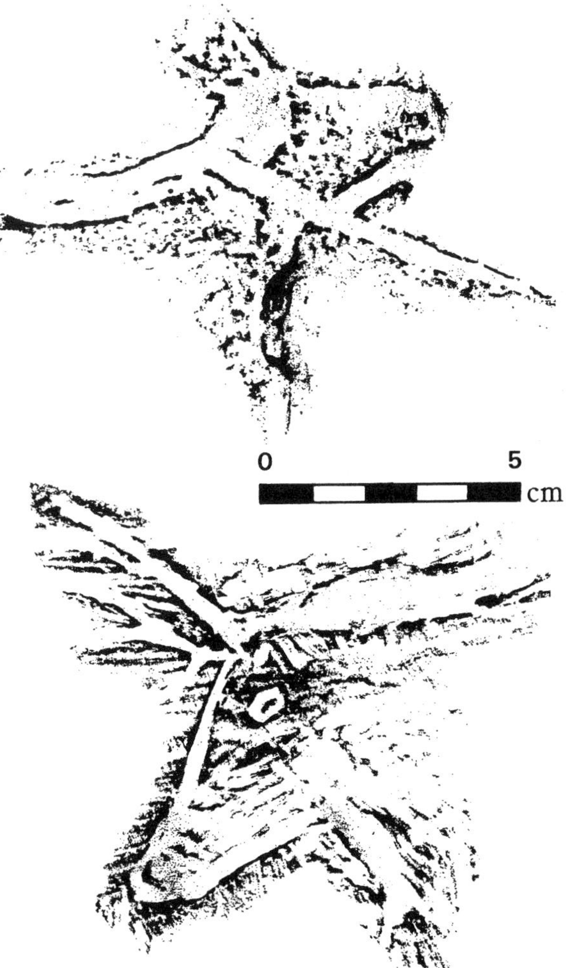

Figure 111. Cissbury Shaft 27: rubbing of the "short horned bull" figure recorded from gallery 7 in November 1953 (© Worthing Museum and Art Gallery).

Figure 112. Cissbury Shaft 27: rubbing of the second deer head to be recorded from gallery 7 in August 1954 (© Worthing Museum and Art Gallery).

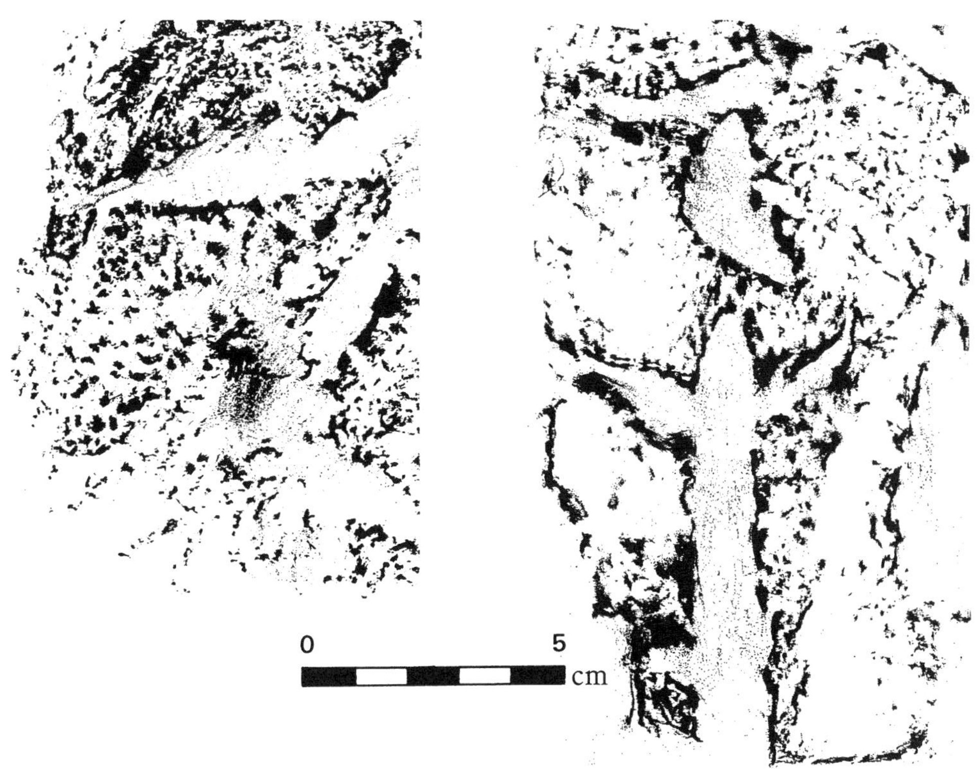

Figure 113. Cissbury Shaft 27: rubbing of the "fish head" or phallus engraving recorded from gallery 8, linked to Shaft 31, in December 1953 (© Worthing Museum and Art Gallery).

Figure 114. Cissbury Shaft 27: rubbing of the "star spread indefinite", "miners symbol", or antler pick, as recorded from gallery 8 in December 1953 (© Worthing Museum and Art Gallery).

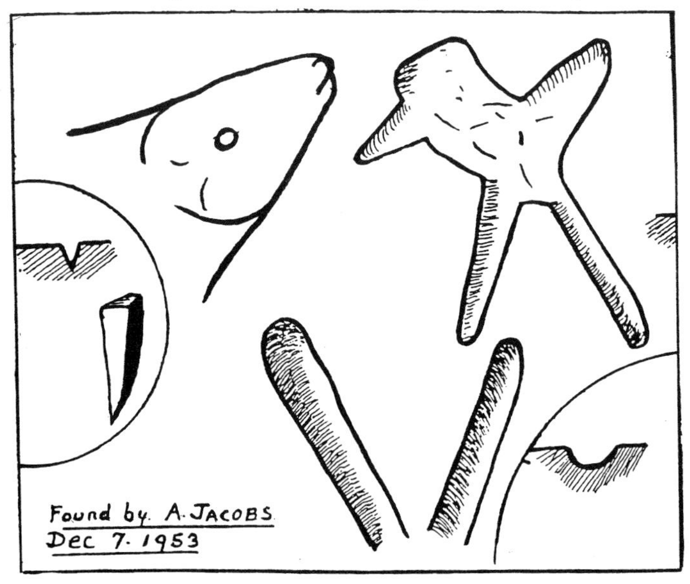

Figure 115. Cissbury Shaft 27: interpretative sketch, showing groove profile, of the "fish head" and "miners symbol" recovered from gallery 8, drawn by Pull in 1954 (© Worthing Museum and Art Gallery).

Additional engravings may previously have been recorded during the initial clearance of Shaft 27, for, in the entry dated May 10th 1953, Pull notes the presence of graffiti on shaft wall at '15 ft on east side', but neglects to provide any additional data as to the nature of these markings or whether it was considered to be contemporary with the original cutting of the mine.

The gallery 7 and 8 markings were sketched and photographed, after they had been highlighted in colour, before rubbings were taken. Copies of the original rubbings exist in the Worthing Museum archive for the short horn bulls head, the second red deer, the fish head and the enigmatic 'miners symbol'. Unfortunately the rubbing of the first red deer to be located within gallery 7 could not be traced at the time of writing, though a partially interpretative sketch drawn by Pull, does appear in the archive. It is possible to ascertain the degree of realistic depiction of this first deer by comparing the bull's head that appears in the drawing with its equivalent rubbing.

The nature of the engravings cause some problems. Firstly it is possible that the features were the product of recent artistic activity in the shaft. Pull was well acquainted with the type and style of modern pieces of graffiti left, on occasion, by unauthorised visitors to the mines and the markings from galleries 7 and 8 were a different thing entirely. Alternatively, bearing in mind the potentially fraudulent ivory fish found within the entrance of gallery 1, it is possible that the markings (especially in this context the fish head) may represent a similar style of prank or practical joke perpetrated by one who was able to make the markings appear genuine. Here it should be noted that doubt continues to surround the authenticity of the chalk-cut female figurine recovered from a Neolithic flint mine at Grimes Graves (Varndell 1991), not to mention the animalistic figures, including red deer, cut into the cortex of flint material from Floor 85 (Armstrong 1922a; 1922b; Mercer 1981, 5; Russell in Press c). Engravings into chalk and chalk objects themselves are both inherently undatable, especially if their creation has been via an obviously non-modern implement such as a flint blade and the possibilities for hoaxing are considerable.

With regard to the Cissbury engravings, the fact that they appeared stained with age, were filled with 'redeposited (fluffy) carbonate' and were only revealed once the excavators were in the process of clearing the galleries of rubble, all appear to indicate that they were not the product of a modern practical joke. It is also interesting that the markings were found by different people working at various times within the shaft. Suspicion would certainly have been aroused if one person were implicated in the discovery or identification of all. Deliberate markings, albeit of a different, more abstract, kind, had already been identified within a number of excavated mines at Cissbury (e.g. Harrison 1877a), and, given the present evidence, the presumption must be in favour of the Shaft 27 engravings being authentic, that is to say they were contemporary with the original use of the mines. Quite what the symbols meant within the context of the mine workings, is a different matter (see conclusions), though one point that should be noted here is that they do not really belong within Shaft 27, being cut upon the walls of galleries that radiate out from the base of Shaft 31 (marked as Shaft A on Pull's plan). As these represent the only parts of Shaft 31 to have been excavated, it is possible that this particular feature and its attendant galleries all possessed a high degree of internal markings. However, until the systems connecting this shaft are investigated further, any such theory must remain speculative.

THE SURFACE CHIPPING FLOORS

At least three Chipping Floors were partially examined by Pull and his team during the 1952-56 season at Cissbury. A series of texts detailing the nature of Floors 1 and 2 exist in the Worthing Museum archive.

Chipping Floor 1

By J. H. Pull

This was located on the southern third of the outer mine area on a ridge of mining debris between three shafts (figure 116). Of the three shafts, 23 was to the north of the floor, 18 to the south-east and 19 to the south-west. The floor comprised a triangular area measuring twelve and a half feet north-south by nine feet east-west and consisted of a compact mass of flakes, fine chippings and nodules of waste flint all of mine quality. On the north, this mass of flint workshop debris was separated from Shaft 23 by a pronounced dump of chalk blocks about six feet in width, which rested on the natural surface. The floor encroached upon and overlay this dump to an extent of two feet and where it did so the flakes and chippings of the floor filled the vertical gaps in between the chalk blocks of this dump.

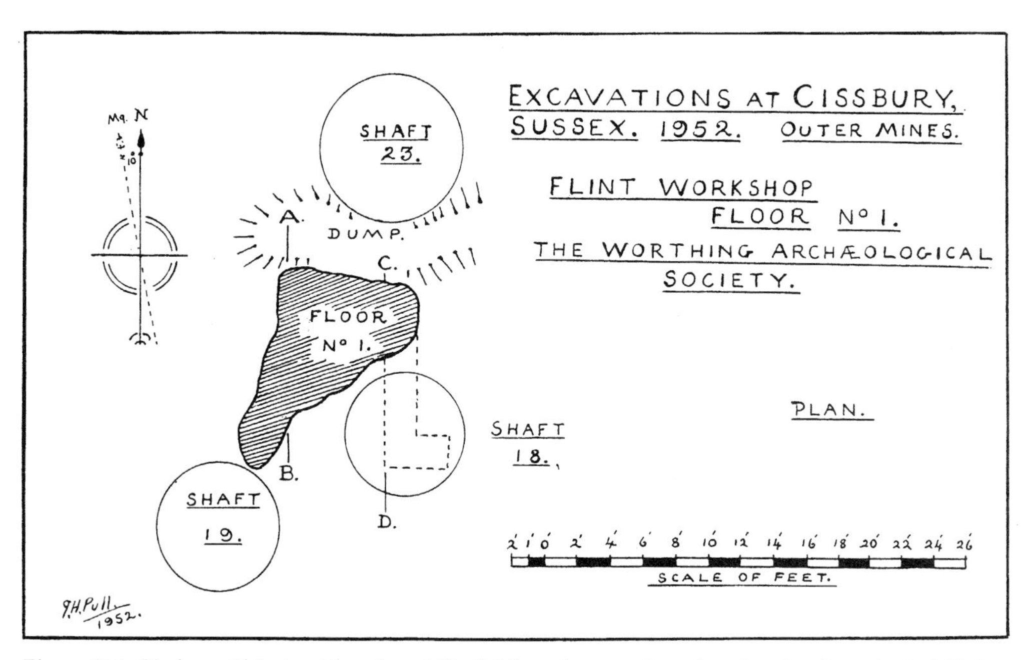

Figure 116. Cissbury Chipping Floor 1 and Shaft 18: post excavation plan showing the extent of flint knapping debris and the relationship of the feature to Shafts 18 (section A), 19 and 20 (© Worthing Museum and Art Gallery).

The dump of chalk blocks evidently represented rubble which had been thrown out from shaft 23 and the floor partially overlying it was therefore a little later in date than the debris over which it partially rested (figure 117). The dump of debris and the floor itself were covered by a thin layer of turf and mould varying from a few inches in depth at the northern extremity to one foot on the southern end. Where the floor was clear of the northern dump it everywhere rested upon six to nine inches of yellow silt which in turn covered the vertical face of chalk rock and from this yellow silt two fragments of ox blade bone were recovered. The amount of flakes, chippings and waste flint removed from the floor amounted to several cartloads. It was obvious that the flint knapping here had taken place at one period only and represented the rapid accumulation of debris which may have been the product of a few days work by one or two operatives.

One hundred and nineteen implements, tools and chipped pieces were recovered from the debris of the floor. These were all patinated white and were in a completely mint condition so far as their edges were concerned, showing no signs of use. Of the implements recovered, 33 were implements, one was an ovate hand axe, three were unfinished hand axes, one was a celt or axe, two were rough outs for celts, one rough adze or hoe, five were scrapers, one was a core, five were

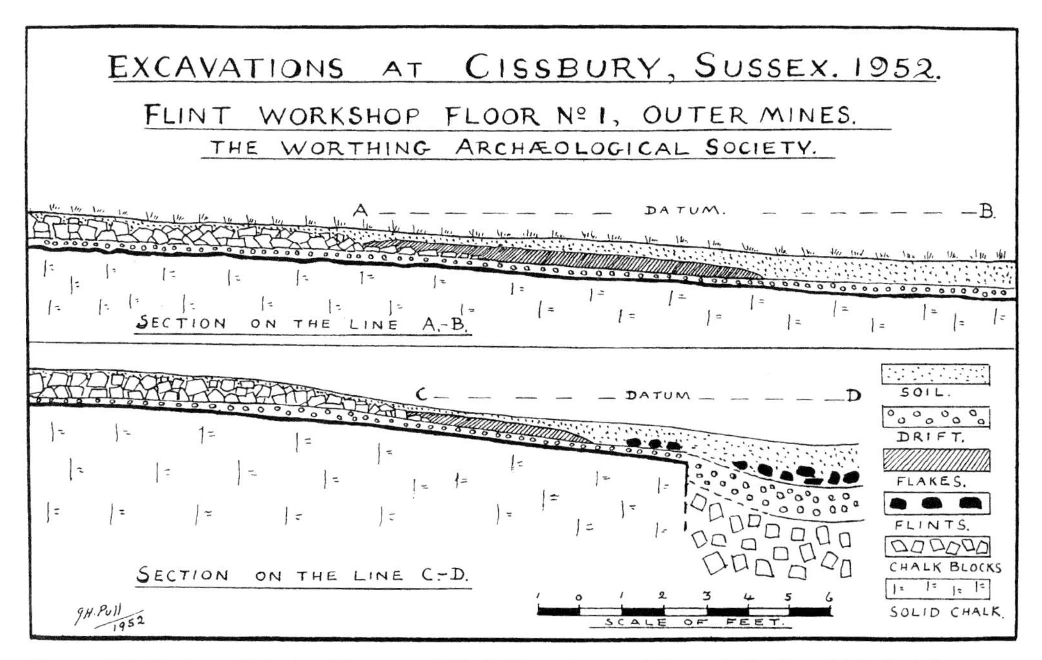

Figure 117. Cissbury Chipping Floor 1 and Shaft 18: sections cut through the floor. Note that the section marked C – D represents section A cut through the upper levels of Shaft 18 (© Worthing Museum and Art Gallery).

> core implements, four were core trimming flakes, three were saws, three were borers and four were implements which had been struck from tortoise cores. The remaining 86 implements were all knives or blades struck from cores. It is therefore obvious that the chief product of this chipping floor was in the form of blades. A minority of core implements were being made. The scarcity of the celt or axe types is notable and the one finished axe found was made from a thick flake. The examination of Floor 1 certainly seems to negate the idea that the main output of the Cissbury industry was celts or axes and the subsequent excavation of floor 2 further stresses the fact that the main output of the flint knappers working here was the production of flake tools and blades (Worthing Museum Acc. No. 1961/1586).

A comparatively large number of flint artefacts from Floor 1, including 146 flakes and 20 axe roughouts, survive in the Worthing Museum archive.

Chipping Floor 2

> *By J. H. Pull*
> This was located on the northern of the outer mine field on the southward sloping natural surface of hill just south of Shaft 52. The floor was entirely superficial and thinly spread covering an oval area measuring 22 feet north and south and 12 feet east and west. The flakes and chippings which constituted it lay on the basal six to nine inches of yellow silt covering the chalk mound and the floor itself was covered by six to nine inches of turf and mould. Twenty-three implements were recovered from the debris of this floor. Of these 20 were blades, some of them very fine, and skilfully struck pieces. No indicators of axe making were found on this floor (Worthing Museum Acc. No. 1961/1586).

47 Flakes, two axe roughouts and a scraper from Floor 2 survive in the Worthing Museum archive.

Chipping Floor 3

Chipping Floor 3 was encountered during the abortive investigation of Shaft 23 in March and April of 1955. Only part of the surface was ever investigated. Pull, in the site notebook for the 1955 season, notes that the floor partially overlay the northern lip of Shaft 23 and that it had petered out 1.8m from centre of the depression. The finds recorded from this floor included a roughly chipped Cissbury-type axe, 'several good knife flakes', three cores, 'several knives' and an unspecified number of flint flakes'. Seventeen flakes survive in the Worthing Museum archive today.

8
Additional Fieldwork

Many areas of archaeological potential were examined by Pull and his colleagues during the course of the excavations at Blackpatch, Church Hill, Tolmere and Cissbury. The details of this work, which survives in varying degrees of completeness, will be published elsewhere as it does not directly impinge upon the main block of mine sites. Four areas surveyed by Pull at High Salvington, Mount Carvey, Myrtlegrove and Strawberry Patch, do however merit discussion here.

HIGH SALVINGTON

The site of High Salvington lies at NGR TQ 119070, to the immediate south of Church Hill, at the northern fringes of the modern housing estate that bears the same name. The report that follows, outlining the discovery and nature of the site, is taken from a series of notes written by Pull and preserved within the Worthing Museum archive. An alternative version of the text was published in the August 1935 issue of the *Sussex County Magazine* under the title The Stone Age Villages of Downland (Pull 1935b).

> High Salvington is an elevation of the chalk bounding the western side of the waterless Findon Valley. Commencing on the north, just above the village of Findon, as a finger-like projecting spur of Church Hill, High Salvington terminates in the bluff upon which an ancient windmill and a newly developed residential settlement are situated. This terminal bluff, now so largely built upon, descends somewhat steeply to the coastal plain at Durrington. The mass of flint bearing chalk rock of which the High Salvington ridge is composed, lies mainly in the geological zone of the type fossil *Actinocomax quadratus*. This chalk, with the horizontal layers of flint nodules which it contains, is well exposed in a long quarry face a short distance southeast of the windmill. The upper surface of the chalk ridge is covered by a fairly thick deposit of reddish-coloured clay with flints.
>
> A good many years ago, a certain Mr Jackson of High Salvington, made a large collection of flint implements from a ploughed and cultivated area situated about a mile south of the flint mining station at Church Hill. Mr Jackson's flints were classified and a representative series of them was arranged and presented by him to the Worthing Museum. Mr Jackson thought that the ploughed land

where he found his flints had at one time been the site of a prehistoric village, but he did not make any systematic or detailed survey of the site, and presently it was forgotten.

Within recent years, Mr Barclay Wills commenced to work on the same ploughed fields between High Salvington and Church Hill, where Mr Jackson had previously found so many good flint implements. Mr Will's careful and patient searching of the field yielded him one of the finest collections of surface flint implements to be seen in Sussex. Mr Wills came to the same conclusion, namely that a village site existed there. Through the kindness of Mr Wills, I have been able to examine the site immediately after it had been freshly ploughed, and I am satisfied that both his and Mr Jackson's opinions are correct.

The prehistoric village site stretches in a diagonal line from the direction of Rogers Clump on the northeast, to the junction of the Honeysuckle and Heather Lanes on the southwest (figure 118). The distance is roughly quarter of a mile, and the maximum elevation about 420 feet above the sea. Along this diagonal line are still to be traced a considerable number of shallow, saucer shaped depressions, now less than a foot deep and varying from 10 to 30 feet in diameter. These depressions mark the ancient hut sites. About midway along their alignment was the site of a large communal village fire, which must have been kept burning for many years. The position of this fire is still clearly indicated by an area some 100 paces across, in which the flints in the soil are burnt almost to powder. The whole of this fire area stands out as a huge circular grey patch on the surface of the field, while the larger hut sites are marked off from the rich ploughed land by a darker tint of brown. Toward the south-west end of the area once occupied by the dwelling sites is a large depression about 100 feet across, and still some six feet deep, which appears to have been a water pond, the once puddled bottom of which has been ploughed out.

Flint implements and fire cracked flints are very common through-out the site, but are most frequently to be found within and round about the rims of the larger hut circles and round the edges of the great fire zone. Since Mr Jackson first drew attention to this area, the number of flint implements collected by surface workers from this village site must run into tens of thousands, and apparently they are still as numerous as ever, for the writer found over a hundred flint implements, in four hours after a recent ploughing. Flint implement manufacture was undoubtedly carried out in this erstwhile village on a very large scale.

So far as the evidence goes, this prehistoric village at High Salvington consisted of a line of irregularly placed, but not widely scattered, dwellings. What form these dwellings took, one is left to surmise. Their circular dished foundations were presumably surmounted by some form of conical or beehive shaped huts, some large, some small, and some constructed, one imagines, of perishable material such as wattle and daub and thatch, or light timbers and hides. There was a central fire for all general purposes and a reservoir for water. The situation of this village was admirably chosen in every way. It was elevated above the misty coombes and swampy coastal plain, sunny and well drained, surrounded by good pasture for cattle and good soil suitable for cultivation. In

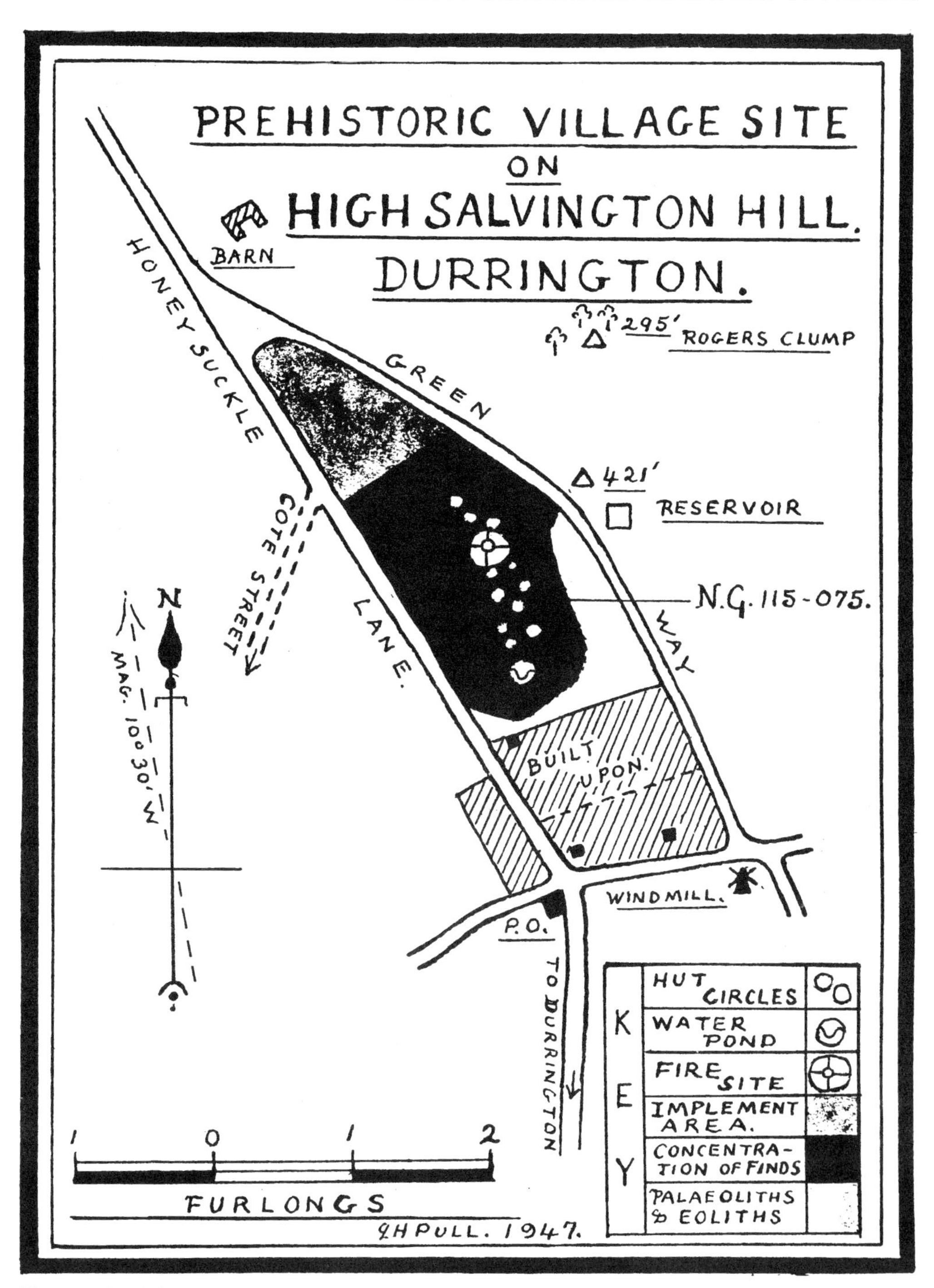

Figure 118. High Salvington: simplified sketch to illustrate the main concentration of surface features and artefacts in 1947 (© Worthing Museum and Art Gallery).

> addition the situation had the great advantage of being in a place where endless supplies of flint were obtainable (Worthing Museum Acc. No 1961/1593).

The flint assemblage from the High Salvington site that exists within Worthing Museum includes two broken polished axes, four fragments of polished axe, 25 flaked axes and 13 axe roughouts as well as an adze, five picks, eight arrowheads (four leaf shaped, one barbed and tanged, one triangular and two oblique), a laurel leaf, five knives (one discoidal), 106 convex scrapers, seven hollow scrapers, nine heavy duty tools, 94 flakes (of which only four were unutilised) and 14 cores (Gardiner 1988, 782–3). It is not known how much of this material represents finds made by John Pull, and how much represents the earlier collections of Jackson and Wills. Neither is it entirely clear what sampling strategy was employed during the original surface collection, though it should be noted that unutilised flakes are remarkably deficient within the total assemblage.

The plan that Pull compiled for the site, seems to indicate that the area bounded by Honeysuckle Lane, Green Way and the modern housing development to the south, was dense in surface artefacts, though the main concentration of finds was located within a band running across the centre of the ploughed field. At least 11 circular depressions are marked on the plan as indicating hut circles, with two larger features to the north and at the southern margins being interpreted as a 'fire site' or hearth and a pond respectively.

Pull seemed adamant, certainly at the time that the site was referred to in print (Pull 1935b), that the surface features represented the remains of a prehistoric village or settlement area, perhaps comparable to the dwellings already partially sampled at Blackpatch. Until detailed excavation work is conducted at the site (and it is unfortunate that ploughing has now almost completely levelled all trace of the surface indentations) an exact interpretation will remain elusive. It is worth noting however that the dimensions of the High Salvington hollows, their linear, dispersed sitting along the crest of the hill descending from Church Hill to the north, the density of working floors and the comparatively high numbers of recorded flaked and roughout axes, could all be taken as indicating an area of flint extraction and artefact manufacture, rather than settlement activity. That additional areas of prehistoric flint mining exist undetected within this particular part of the Worthing Downs seems likely (e.g. Laughlin 1994) and it is possible that High Salvington represents one such site.

MOUNT CARVEY

The site of Mount Carvey lies at NGR TQ 137071, to the immediate south of the Cissbury enclosure and mine field, was fieldwalked by Pull at some point before 1935 and a short report published in the September 1935 edition of the *Sussex County Magazine* (Pull 1935c). The text that follows is an alternative version of that report as taken from the Worthing Museum archive.

The ridge which stretches parallel to High Salvington along the eastern side of the Findon Valley, forming a southward projecting spur of Cissbury, is known as Mount Carvey. The approach to Mount Carvey is made by means of an old track branching northwards from the main Worthing – Arundel road, northeast of Offington Manor. Beyond Broadwater mill cottage, the old track crosses a large portion of the Worthing Golf Links and then ascends to a point about half a mile south of Cissbury Camp. Here the crest of the chalk ridge which the track follows, rises more steeply to an elevation of nearly 500 feet. This is the actual summit of Mount Carvey. From this point onwards to Cissbury the Mount Carvey ridge drops in elevation nearly 100 feet, to form a saddle which sharply separates the two hilltops. It may here be conveniently noted that the chalk elevation embracing both Mount Carvey and Cissbury is part of the same zone of flint bearing quadratus chalk rock as the neighbouring hill of High Salvington and that a similar deposit of clay with flints overlies it.

The land which lies to the west of the old road, where it passes over the summit of Mount Carvey, was, until a few years ago, ploughed arable. The previous owner of the ground, Mr H. R. P. Wyatt of Cissbury, is, and always has been, a keen collector of flint implements. When Mount Carvey was in his possession he acquired a very large collection of worked flints from the ploughed land. Mr Wyatt noted that the majority of these flint implements came from one particular area of the land. Since the land became fallow I have been enabled to make a very thorough search and survey of this ground and was fortunate in being able to trace out the flint implement bearing zone and to map the remains of a prehistoric village very much like the one at High Salvington.

The Mount Carvey village site lies parallel with the Offington-Cissbury greenway which traverses the summit. It is indicated, as at High Salvington, by a number of circular hut sites which stretch in a roughly straight line for about a quarter of a mile along the western side of the thick hedge which once served to part the arable from the beaten track (figure 119). At the northern extremity of this line of dwellings is a large well marked depression, indicating a possible water pond. Half way along the hut alignment is a concentrated area of burnt stones marking the main village fire. Flint implements and chippings are distributed thickly throughout the site, but are most abundant round the rims and about the centre of certain still faintly visible saucer-shaped depressions marking the largest of the old hut floors. The flint implements were undoubtedly manufactured on the site. They include a large variety of fine tools and small types of implements, among which may be mentioned diminutive celts, arrowheads, borers, scrapers, planes and saws. Pottery fragments are rare and seem confined to pieces of coarse unornamented ware with much flint grit in the paste.

In every respect the Mount Carvey village is very like the one at High Salvington. The antiquities found upon its site indicate that it was occupied by a people who were in the same stage of development and who possessed the same habits and culture as those displayed by their High Salvington neighbours (Worthing Museum Acc. No 1961/1588).

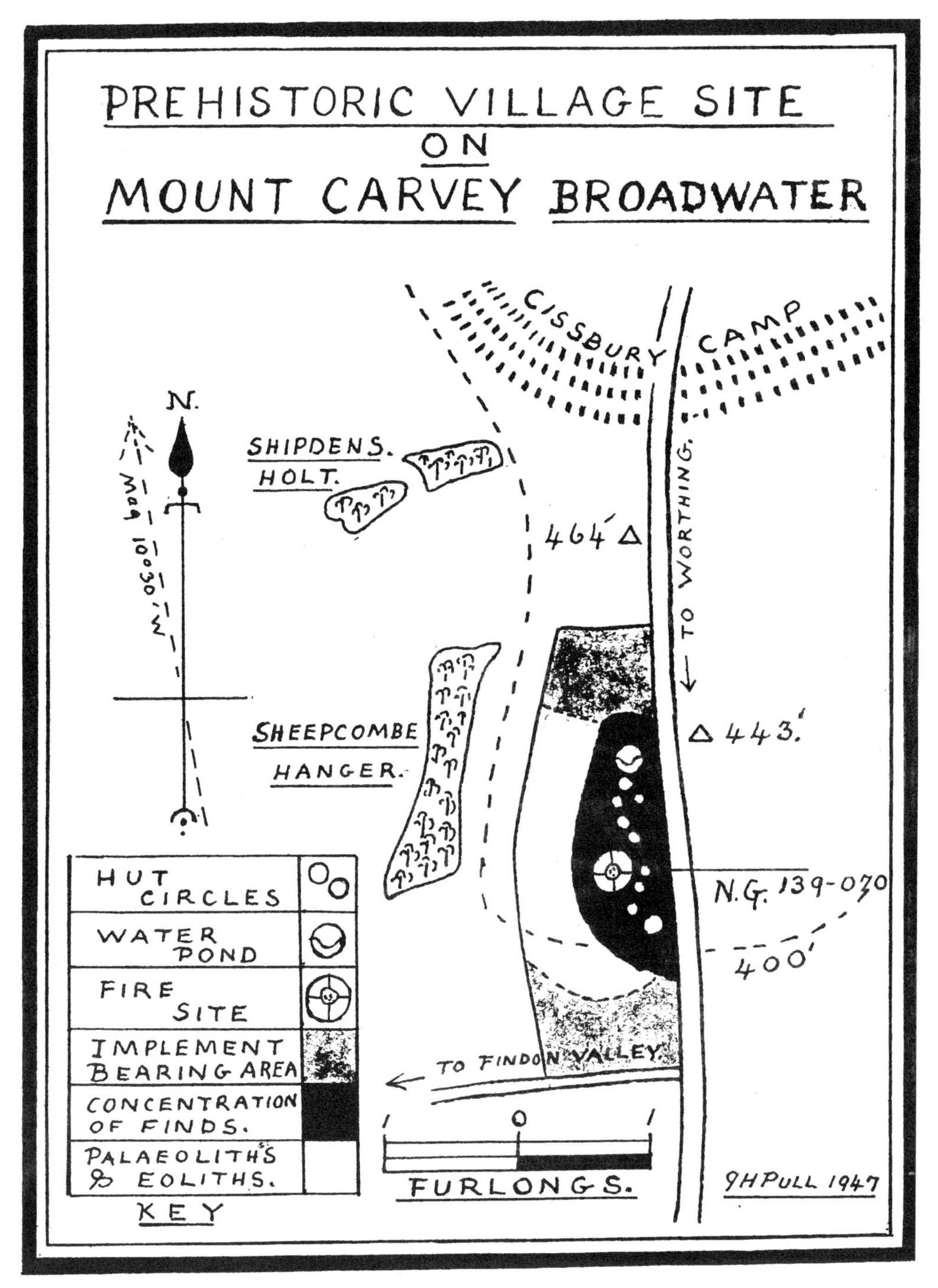

Figure 119. Mount Carvey: simplified sketch to illustrate the main concentration of surface features and artefacts in 1947 (© Worthing Museum and Art Gallery).

The flint assemblage that survives from Mount Carvey within the Worthing Museum archive includes 21 utilised/retouched flakes, a core, one triangular arrowhead, eight convex scrapers, two fabricators, one rod and three piercing tools (Gardiner 1988, 860–1). A detailed plan of the site, put together by Pull in 1947, shows at least nine circular surface depressions of varying size, with two larger features marked as a 'fire site' or hearth and a pond. From this and the comments reproduced above it is clear that Pull viewed the site as representing the remains of an extensive prehistoric settlement. Given the extended nature of the site along the western slopes of the chalk ridge descending from Cissbury and the marked similarity between the surface indentations and those recorded from the southern margins of the minefield to the north, it is possible that the Mount Carvey site, as with that noted from High Salvington, indicates an additional area of flint extraction. If so, and only additional fieldwork can perhaps resolve the issue, then it would suggest that the original area of flint procurement at Cissbury was at least twice the size recorded today.

MYRTLEGROVE

The site at Myrtlegrove (NGR TQ 093090) was surveyed by Pull prior to 1935 and the preliminary results published by him in the *Sussex County Magazine* (Pull 1935c). As with Mount Carvey and High Salvington, the report that follows is an alternative text stored within the archive of Worthing Museum.

> In the parish of Patching, half a mile north of Patching church, is the beautiful vale of Michelgrove, a deep valley entering the downland from the Long Furlong and continuing northwards towards Burpham. The north side of the valley has a deep divide about halfway along its base, which passes northwards between the heights of Blackpatch and Harrow Hill. This branch of the Vale of Michelgrove is known as Myrtlegrove. On the western side of the chalk ridge bounding Myrtlegrove, on what is actually a projecting spur of Blackpatch, at a point about 600 yards north of Myrtlegrove Farm yard, is situated a prehistoric village site which appears to be of considerable size.
>
> The prehistoric village appears to have occupied a lengthy portion of the chalk ridge, and to have consisted of a sort of straggling street of small hut settlements. The depressions marking them are still plainly visible. Several small round barrows are situated along the hut line. The writer opened two of these recently, but alas they had been previously excavated by some person who had left no record of his efforts. Both the barrows covered shallow oval graves cut in the chalk rock in which at some time bodies had been inhumed. From the chalk rubble infilling of these graves, a few fragmentary human bones and one or two flint implements were recovered, together with a broken iron shovel left behind by the previous diggers. Much oak and yew charcoal was also present in both graves.
>
> The excavation of one of the pit depressions yielded different results. The hut site explored proved to be a shallow circular excavation in the chalk about 10 feet

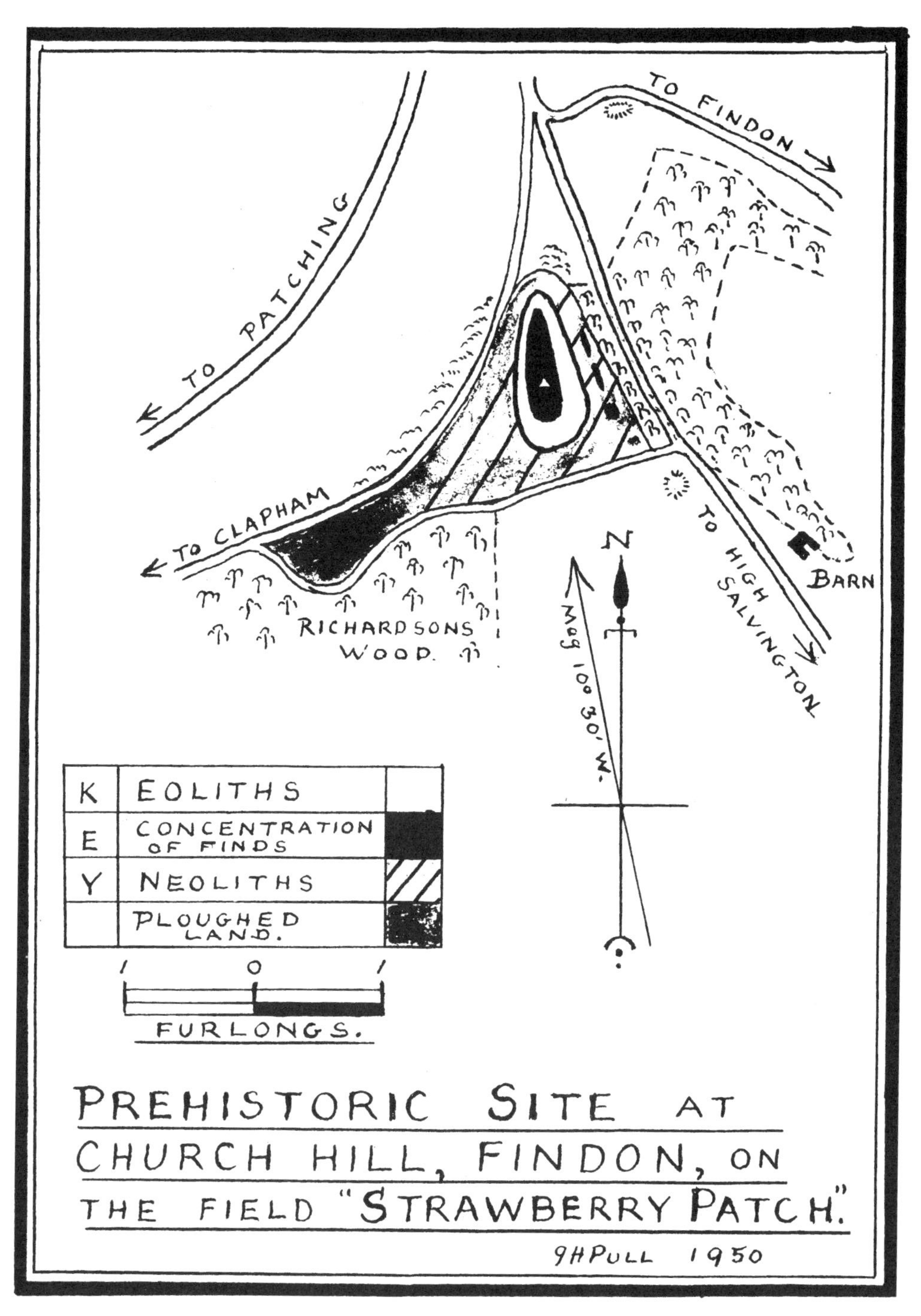

Figure 120. Strawberry Patch: simplified sketch to illustrate the main concentration of surface artefacts in 1950 (© Worthing Museum and Art Gallery).

> across and two feet deep in the centre. The infilling consisted of small chalk rubble surmounted by rainwash and about nine inches of surface mould. Many good flint implements and great numbers of burnt stones, together with some fragments of coarse pottery, occurred at the base of the infilling. A great many flint implements have also been found distributed up and down that portion of the hillslope covered by the hut sites here. It is impossible to say whether this village possessed a communal fire as did the ones at Mount Carvey and High Salvington. No trace of a water pond is visible, but, as the chalk here is not covered by any deposit of clay with flints, the absence of a puddled water hole is not surprising.
>
> The flint implements and tools recovered from the Myrtlegrove Village site are all patinated dead white. They appear to have been fabricated from flint obtained from the nearby mines of Blackpatch and Harrow Hill. Most of the flints are fine, neatly worked tools of patterns which do not frequently occur on the chipping floors which were excavated at Blackpatch (Worthing Museum Acc. No 1961/1595).

Unfortunately none of the recorded flint artefacts derived from Myrtlegrove could be traced at the time of writing and no detailed plan of the site or record of the investigations conducted by Pull could be located within the Worthing Museum archive, making a comparison with the Mount Carvey and High Salvington sites somewhat problematical. The limited fieldwork conducted at Myrtlegrove by Pull does not appear to have helped with regard to interpretation. That no structural features were recorded within the excavated pit depression does not automatically remove it from a discussion on prehistoric house platforms, though its limited depth, 0.6m, does seem to preclude the suggestion that it was originally part of a flint extraction process. Clearly additional fieldwork needs to be conducted here to determine whether this site does represent an area of settlement contemporary with mining activity or an area of quarrying or surface flint extraction perhaps extending from the main site at Blackpatch.

STRAWBERRY PATCH

Strawberry Patch lies upon the western slopes of Church Hill at NGR TQ 111078, to the immediate south-west of the main flint mining area investigated by Pull between 1933 and 1952 at the northernmost margins of Richardson's (Clapham) Wood. A surface collection survey recorded by Pull at some time before 1950 indicated a discrete cluster of worked flint within the area under plough (figure 120). None of these finds could be traced in Worthing Museum, but the annotation on the site plan 'eoliths' and 'neoliths' suggests perhaps a similar range of artefact types that had previously been collected at High Salvington and Mount Carvey. No obvious surface indentations or irregularities were observed within the area of the artefact cluster, though its proximity to the Church Hill sites is worth noting. Further archaeological work needs to be conducted here to ascertain the nature of archaeological elements present.

9

Catalogue of Surviving Flintwork from the Worthing Group of Mines

by Julie Gardiner

This section contains a summary of extant artefacts from excavations and surface collection at the major Sussex flint mine complexes at Blackpatch, Church Hill, Cissbury and Harrow Hill. It is unlikely that a complete catalogue of finds will ever be compiled as material from the sites has been widely dispersed in collections across the country. The following is an attempt to bring together the results of principal investigations of these sites for the sake of comparison and in order that a better picture may be presented of the types and condition of artefacts recovered. This is considered especially relevant as most excavation reports have concentrated upon the vast numbers of axes, at the expense of other material.

In 1968 Elizabeth Pye, then an MA student at the University of Edinburgh, attempted to make sense of the collections of John Pull, held by Worthing Museum. Pull's notebooks were sometimes ambiguous and difficult to work with whilst, as a re-examination of the collections by the present author confirmed, the markings on the flints themselves were often less than helpful. In addition to the problems encountered by Pye, and reflected in her thesis, her own work presents a number of difficulties in itself. Firstly, figures given in her catalogue do not always match up with those cited in the text and, secondly, it is not now possible to be certain that the same material was studied by both Pye and the present author. The numbers of artefacts catalogued do not correspond at all well, but then Pye often used data from Pull's notes relating to finds that were no longer extant, and rather different identifications appear to have been made in some cases. In addition, figures used by Goodman et al (1924) for the Blackpatch excavation material can also be shown to differ.

Under the circumstances there seems little point in adopting an arrogant attitude and assuming that the present author's figures are correct. For this reason the following method of cataloguing has been adopted: for each of the sites discussed below information is provided firstly by collection and secondly by context. Where figures are given by Pye and/or Goodman *et al*, or by Curwen and Curwen (1926) in the case of Harrow Hill, these are also provided for comparison. The format of each entry is therefore as follows:

- Location of site, brief description of extant material, collections and major bibliographical references.
- Summary list of all artefacts recorded by Pye (1968), Goodman et al (1924) and the present author.
- Catalogue of artefacts by collection and context.

It must be repeated that this summary makes no claim to be a complete catalogue of finds from the Worthing group of mines, but is an attempt to draw together widely dispersed information from the old excavations. A few more recent excavations and some more systematic surface collection work has taken place since this catalogue was originally compiled (as part of the author's PhD thesis: Gardiner 1988), for instance at Harrow Hill (Holgate 1989; McNabb et al 1996), but these surveys are not included here since they did not form part of the original study. The total output of flint artefacts from the mining areas is likely to have been staggering and the material listed below can only be a very small part of it, nevertheless, this catalogue represents a considerable amount of work in examining the artefacts and collating the information. It is, however, left to the reader to decide how useful an exercise this has been.

BLACKPATCH

Flintwork from Blackpatch comes mainly from the excavations of John Pull and is housed in Worthing Museum, although a number of artefacts appear to have been dispersed widely at the time of excavation.

Shaft 1	**Pye**	**Goodman**	**JPG**
Cores	35	–	–
Retouched flakes	–	6	–
Axe roughouts	35	35	–
Flaked axes	38	61	–
Type 5 'axes'	–	5	–
'Thames pick'	–	1	–
Scrapers	5	5	–
Hammers	10	5	–
Wedges	3	33	2
Fabricator	–	1	–
'Planes'	–	11	–
Borers	1	–	–
Miniature axe	–	1	–
Knife	2	several	–
Miscellaneous	27	1	–

A group of artefacts are marked with layer numbers only. These probably derive from Shaft 1, but are not mentioned by Pye or Curwen *et al*:

Layer 1	29 flakes
Layer 3	2 flakes
Layer 4	15 flakes
Layer 5	10 flakes
Layer 9	39 flakes
Also 4008 (working floor):	392 flakes and blades,
	5 retouched
	1 axe roughout
Section D:	2 cores
	5 blades
	1 axe roughout
	2 flaked axes
Ploughsoil:	1 fragment of polished axe

Shaft 2	**Pye**	**JPG**
Axe roughouts	–	2

Shaft 4	**Pye**	**JPG**
Flakes	–	7

Shaft 5	**Pye**	**JPG**
Flakes	–	1
Axe roughouts	A few	–

Shaft 7	**Pye**	**JPG**
Retouched flakes	–	3
Flaked axe	1	1
Scraper	1	1
Knife	1	1

Shaft 8	**Pye**	**JPG**
Flakes	–	5
Flaked axe (fragment)	–	1
Laurel leaf (Roughout)	–	1
Slug	–	1

In addition to the Shafts, a number of flint artefacts are marked as deriving from 'Pits 2 and 3'. As Pull sometimes referred to Shafts as Pits it is probable that these are in fact from Shafts 2 and 3, though the possibility that they were originally from two of the three excavated hollows referred to by Pull and Sainsbury as 'dwelling sites', is one which should not be overlooked.

Pit 2	**Pye**	**JPG**
Blade	–	1
Scraper	–	1
Knife	–	1

Pit 3	**Pye**	**JPG**
Retouched	–	2

Floor 1	**Pye**	**JPG**
Flake	–	1
Flaked axe	several	–

Floor 2	**Pye**	**JPG**
Axe roughouts	–	2
Pick	1	–
Chopper	–	1

Floor 3	**Pye**	**JPG**
Flakes	–	2
Axe roughouts	several	2

Floor 4	**Pye**	**JPG**
Axe roughouts	several	–

Floor 14	**Pye**	**JPG**
Axe roughouts	2+	–

Barrow 1	**Pye**	**JPG**
Axe roughout	–	1
Flaked axes	2	–
Knife	1 (fine, oval)	–
'Segmented tool'	1	–

Barrow 3	**Pye**	**JPG**
Axe roughouts	3	2
Flaked axe	1	1
?leaf	1	–
Hammers	several	1

Barrow 4	**Pye**	**JPG**
Knife	1	–

Barrow 5	**Pye**	**JPG**
Leaf	2	–
Hollow scraper	1	–

Barrow 6	**Pye**	**JPG**
Blade	1	–
?leaf	1	–

Barrow 7	**Pye**	**JPG**
Axe roughouts	several	–
Leaf	2	–

Barrow 8	**Pye**	**JPG**
Core	–	1

Flake	–	1
Axe roughout	1	–
Scraper	1	–

Barrow 9	**Pye**	**JPG**
Core	1	–
Flake	–	1
Flaked axe	1	–
Pick	1	–
Scrapers	3	2
Knives	3	–

Barrow 12	**Pye**	**JPG**
Flaked axe	1	–
Wedge	1	–
Knife	1	–

A large selection of unmarked flints from Blackpatch also exists within the Pull Collection:

27	Cores
3	Utilised cores
1	Rejuvenation flake
124	Flakes
5	Retouched/utilised
61	Axe roughouts
41	Flaked axes (many broken including 3 burnt)
1	Sharpening flake
11	Picks
1	Disc knife (unpolished)
10	Scrapers
2	Heavy duties
1	Hammer
9	Choppers
3	Fabricators
1	Chisel
3	Borers
2	Miniature axes
1	Slug
4	Knives

Summary of flint artefacts from the Blackpatch mines and associated features

	Pye	**Goodman**	**JPG**
Cores	35	–	29
Utilised. flakes	3	–	–

Rejuvenation flakes	–	–	1
Waste flakes	–	–	633
Retouched flakes	–	6	16
Axe roughouts	37	35	68
Flaked axes	39	61	45
Axe sharpening flake	–	–	1
Polished axe fragment	–	–	1
Type 5 'axes'	–	5	1
'Thames Pick'	–	1	-
Picks	1	–	11
Laurel leaf (roughout)	–	–	1
Disc. Knife (roughout)	–	–	1
Scrapers	6	5	12
Heavy duties	–	–	2
Cleavers/wedges	3	33	2
Hammers	10	5	1
Choppers	–	–	10
Fabricators	–	1	3
Chisel	–	–	1
'Planes'	–	11	–
Borers	1	–	3
Slugs	–	1	2
Miniature axes	–	–	2
Knives	3	several	6
'Miscellaneous'	27	1	–
TOTAL	**162**	**165+**	**854**

Summary of flint artefacts from the Blackpatch barrows

	Pye	**JPG**
Cores	1	1
Flakes/blades	1	2
Axe roughouts	4+	4
Flaked axes	5	1
Pick	1	–
Leaf	6	–
Scrapers	5	2
Wedge	1	–
Hammers	several	1
'Segmented tool'	1	–
Knives	6	–
TOTAL	**31+**	**8**

CHURCH HILL

Flint material from Church Hill occurs in several collections, including Brighton and Littlehampton Museums, but the larger part is stored within the John Pull archive of Worthing Museum.

Shaft 1	**Pye**	**JPG**
Core	1	–
Flakes	–	2
Blade (in antler haft)	1	–
Axe roughouts	2	–
Flaked axes	4	–
Hammer	1	–
Y-shape	–	2
Knives	–	4
Shaft 2	**Pye**	**JPG**
Flakes	–	2
Shaft 3	**Pye**	**JPG**
Flaked axe		–
Shaft 4	**Pye**	**JPG**
Cores	4	1
Utilised Core	1	–
Flakes	–	55
Retouched	-	1
Roughout axes	5 (1 broken)	3 (1 broken)
Flaked axes	10	9
Scrapers	6	1
Wedge	1	–
Borers	3	2
Serrated flake	1	–
?knives	5	–
Shaft 5	**Pye**	**JPG**
Flake	–	1
Axe roughout	1	2
Shaft 5a	**Pye**	**JPG**
Flakes	–	3
Axe roughouts	1	2 (broken)
Flaked axes	3	3 (1 broken)
Shaft 6	**Pye**	**JPG**
Cores	4	1
Axe roughout	1	1
Flaked axes	5	–
Scrapers	1	2

Hammer	1	–
Knife	1	–

Shaft 7	**Pye**	**JPG**
Blades	3	4
Axe roughout	1	1
Flaked axes	3	1 (broken)
Scraper	1 (double-ended)	–
Serrated flakes	1	2

Pit A	**Pye**	**JPG**
Flake	–	1
Retouched	–	3
Scrapers	–	6
Heavy duty	–	1

Pit B	**Pye**	**JPG**
Flakes	–	8
Retouched	–	1

Pit C	**Pye**	**JPG**
Flake	–	1

Pit G	**Pye**	**JPG**
Flakes	–	2
Retouched	–	2

Unless the use of 'G' is a mistake or a misreading of 'C', then the finds must have derived from the surface of a pit identified as 'G', for no excavation of such a feature appears to have been undertaken at Church Hill.

Pit 9	**Pye**	**JPG**
Flakes	–	4
Retouched	–	1

As with pit 'G', it is possible that the use of '9' to distinguish this feature is a mistake or a miss-reading of an original identification as no pit 9 appears to have been investigated by Pull. Alternatively it could relate to 'Shaft 9', as the terms 'pit' and 'shaft' were often interchanged by Pull. If this is the case the flints must represent surface finds from Shaft 9, which Pull records as lying to the immediate south of Shaft 7, as this feature does not appear to have been investigated by him.

Floor 1	**Pye**	**JPG**
Cores	several	–
Flakes	–	3
Axe roughouts	several	–
Flaked axes	4	–
Scraper	1	–
Serrated flake	1	–

Floor 2	**Pye**	**JPG**
Flakes	–	8
Retouched	–	1
Axe roughouts	numerous	–
Flaked axes	4 + broken ones	–
Scraper	–	1
Hammer	1	–
Heavy duty	–	1
Borer	–	1
Utilised pebble	–	1

Floor 3	**Pye**	**JPG**
Flakes	–	3
Axe roughouts	2	1 type 5 (ovate)
Flaked axe	1	–
Knife	–	1

Floor 4	**Pye**	**JPG**
Flakes	–	10
Axe roughouts	3	–
Flaked axes	2	–
Scrapers	31	1
Serrated flakes	2	–
Borer	–	1

Floor 6	**Pye**	**JPG**
Flakes	–	7
Retouched	–	2
Axe roughouts	1	1

Floor 7	**Pye**	**JPG**
Flakes	–	3
Retouched	1	1
Borer	1	1

Floor 8	**Pye**	**JPG**
Flake	–	5
Scrapers	4	–
Borer	–	1

Floor 9	**Pye**	**JPG**
Flake	–	1

Floor 10	**Pye**	**JPG**
Flakes	–	11
Retouched	–	1

Floor 11	Pye	JPG
Flakes	–	4
Retouched	–	1

Floor 12	Pye	JPG
Flakes	–	16
Retouched	–	1
Axe roughout	1	1
Borers	4	–

Floor 14	Pye	JPG
Flakes	–	78
Axe roughouts	5	–
Flaked axes	2	–
Axe sharpening flake	–	1
Chisel arrowhead	1	1
Oblique arrowhead	1	1
Scraper	1	1

Floor 15	Pye	JPG
Flakes	–	9
Retouched	2	–
Serrated flake	1	–

Hearth Site 1	Pye	JPG
Flakes	2	18
Retouched	–	2
Flaked axes	2	–
Borer	1	–

Hearth Site 2	Pye	JPG
Flakes	–	15
Retouched	–	2

Barrow 1	Pye	JPG
Cores	2	–
Core/hammer	1	–
Flakes	–	2
Axe roughouts	4	–
Flaked axe	1	–
Scrapers	7	2
Wedge	1	–
Borers	7	–
Serrated flakes	5	–
Knives	6	–

Barrow 2	Pye	JPG
Scraper	1	–

Borers	2	–
Barrow 3	**Pye**	**JPG**
Flakes	–	2
Barrow 6	**Pye**	**JPG**
Sickle blade	–	1
Scraper	1	–
Barrow 8	**Pye**	**JPG**
Scrapers	4	–
Hammer	1	–
Borer	1	–
Hut Site 1 (Barrow 5)	**Pye**	**JPG**
Flakes	–	31
Flaked axe	1	–
Scrapers	3	2
Borer	–	1
Serrated flakes	1	–

A selection of unmarked flints from Church Hill also exists within the Pull Collection

2	Flakes
2	Retouched/Utilised
5	Axe roughouts
2	Flaked axes (broken)
1	Chopper

Summary of flint artefacts from the Church Hill mines and associated features

	Pye	**JPG**
Cores	9+	2
Flakes/blades	6	266
Retouched	3	21
Axe roughouts	23+	21
Flaked axes	41+	17
Sharpening flake	–	2
Chisel arrowhead	–	1
Oblique arrowhead	–	1
Scrapers	45	11
Heavy duties	–	2
Choppers	–	1
Hammers	3	–
Wedge	1	–
Y Shape	–	2

Borers	9	6
Serrated flakes	6	2
Knives	6	5
Utilised Pebbles	–	1
TOTAL	**155+**	**361**

Summary of flint artefacts from the Church Hill barrows

	Pye	**JPG**
Cores	2	4
Core/hammer	1	–
Flakes	–	172
Retouched	–	16
Axe roughouts	4	1
Flaked axes	2	–
Pick	–	1
Sickle blade	–	1
Scrapers	116	4
Hammer	1	–
Wedge	1	–
Fabricator	–	1
Borers	10	3
Serrated flakes	6	–
Knives	6	–
TOTAL	**49**	**203**

CISSBURY

Material from the numerous excavations at Cissbury have been well spread around a number of museums and considerable quantities of surface collected flintwork are also extant. Little of this material has been adequately recorded or published and undoubtedly much more exists than is listed here. Cissbury is famed for its beautiful, slender flaked axes, often referred to as 'Cissbury-type' axes, but there is a very wide range of forms extant in collections, suggesting that many more items beside axes were manufactured here. The majority of axes recovered from the site seem to have been broken and all stages of manufacture are represented. Type 5 (ovate) axes are relatively common and lead early investigators to propose a Palaeolithic date for the mines. Principal collections examined are held by Lewes Museum, Worthing Museum, Brighton Museum, the Ashmolean Museum, the Museum of London and the British Museum (see Gardiner 1988, 1227-41 for details).

Shaft 23	**Pye**	**JPG**
Flakes	–	2

Shaft 24	**Pye**	**JPG**
Axe roughouts	7	–
Flaked axe	1	–
Backed knife	1	–

Shaft 27	**Pye**	**JPG**
Cores	2	–
Axe roughouts	9	–
Flaked axes	4	–
Leaf arrowhead	1	–
Scrapers	2	–
'Sickle' fragments	several	–

Floor 1	**Pye**	**JPG**
Cores	6	6
Flakes	–	146
Retouched	–	8
Axe roughouts	12	20
Flaked axes	4	16
Scrapers	9	5
Hammer	1	–
Chisels	–	2
Serrated flakes	5	–
'Points'	10	–

Floor 2	**Pye**	**JPG**
Core	1	–
Core/Scraper	1	–
?Rejuvenation flakes	2	–
Flakes	–	47
Axe roughouts	2	2
Flaked axe	1	–
Scraper	–	1
Chisel	1	–

Floor 3	**Pye**	**JPG**
Flakes	–	17

Floor A2	**Pye**	**JPG**
Flakes	–	17

There is no record of a Floor 'A2' from Pull's excavation notes. It is possible that this refers to Floor 2 or perhaps part of Floor 1 within section 'A'.

P10	**Pye**	**JPG**
Retouched	–	3
Axe roughouts	–	15

'P10', presumably referring to Pit or Shaft 10 at the southern margins of the mining area, was not excavated during the 1952-6 season, so it is possible that the flints so labelled indicate surface finds. Alternatively the finds numbering may have been conducted in error, Shaft '18' being the one intended.

A series of artefacts are also labelled as having derived from Sections A, C and D at Cissbury. Section A is well known, being the trench cut through the uppermost levels of Shaft 18, but the whereabouts of Sections C and D are unknown, unless they too were cut within the immediate area of Shaft 18 in 1952.

Section A	**Pye**	**JPG**
Flakes	–	17

Section C	**Pye**	**JPG**
Flakes	–	4

Section D	**Pye**	**JPG**
Flakes	–	4

Surface	**Pye**	**JPG**
Axe roughouts	2	–
?Sickle fragment	1	–
Scrapers	3	–
Heavy duty	4	–
Borers	4	–

Unmarked	**Pye**	**JPG**
Core	–	1
Flakes	–	32
Retouched	–	6
Axe roughouts	–	35
Flaked axes	–	19
Polished axes	–	2 (1 broken)
Leaf	–	4
Scrapers	–	6
Heavy duties	–	3
Chisels	–	4
Fabricator	–	1
Knife	–	1

OTHER EXCAVATIONS AT CISSBURY

i) LANE FOX'S EXCAVATIONS

'Cissbury pit' (British Museum)

5	Cores
4	Flakes
9	Axe roughouts
5	Flaked axes
1	Pick
2	Laurel leaves (1 roughout)
4	Scrapers
3	Heavy duties
2	Fabricators
2	Chisels
2	Borers
8	Miniature axes
1	Knife

'Large Pit' (Ashmolean, British, Salisbury Museums)

4	Flakes (1 huge)
4	Blades
7	Axe roughouts
2	Type 5 axes
2	Picks
1	Scraper
1	Knife

Pit 1 (British Museum)

2	Flakes
1	Axe roughout
1	Flaked axe

Pit 2 (Ashmolean Museum)

1	Flaked axe

Pit 8 (British Museum)

1	Flaked axe
1	Polished axe

Pit 9 (British Museum)

1	Core
1	Axe roughout
1	Flaked axe (broken)
1	Hammer
1	Borer

Pit 10 (British Museum)

1	Core
6	Axe roughouts
3	Flaked axes
2	Picks
1	Hammer
2	Heavy duties
2	Chisels
1	Knife

Pit 11 (British Museum)

1	Axe roughout
1	Flaked axe
2	Type 5 axes
1	Chopper
2	Knives

Pit 13 (Ashmolean Museum)

1	Core

Pit 17 (Ashmolean and British Museums)

1	Core
1	Retouched
5	Axe roughouts
2	Flaked axes
2	Picks
1	Chopper
1	Knife

Shaft H (British Museum)

3	Flakes
1	Heavy duty

'Workshop' (Ashmolean Museum)

9	Axe roughouts

'Enclosure ditch' (British Museum)

2	Axe roughouts
3	Flaked axes
1	Chisel

'Rampart' (British Museum)

4	Flakes
3	Axe roughouts

Unmarked (Ashmolean, British, Salisbury Museums)

4	Cores
1	Blade core
2	Discoidal cores

1	Core/hammer
26	Flakes
2	Retouched/utilised
19	Axe roughouts
7	Flaked axes
1	Type 5 axe
3	Picks
1	Scraper
2	Laurel leaf (1 roughout)
1	Tranchet tool
9	Heavy duties
1	Fabricator
1	Slug
1	Miniature axe

ii) HARRISON'S EXCAVATIONS

Shaft II (Ashmolean Museum)

1	Core
2	Axe roughouts
1	Pick
1	Heavy duty

Shaft IV (Ashmolean Museum)

1	Axe roughout
1	Type 5 axe

Shaft VI (Ashmolean Museum)

3	Axe roughouts
1	Pick

Unmarked (Ashmolean Museum)

2	Blade core (large)
9	Flakes
21	Axe roughouts (1 very thin)
4	Flaked axes
1	Type 5 axe
2	Picks
1	?Sickle roughout

iii) TINDALL'S EXCAVATIONS

Although Tindall died before he could report on his excavations of 1874 at Cissbury, it was noted that at least some of the artefacts resulting from his work were in the possession of Lord Rosehill (Rosehill in Lane Fox 1875, 389; Willett 1880, 341). In 1924 Lewes Museum bought the 'Rosehill Collection' of flint implements from Christies and, though the context of the finds was noted as being only 'from the Cissbury Mines' (Gardiner 1988, 1229), it is likely that the majority of these finds were actually derived from Tindall's excavations.

Rosehill Collection (Lewes Museum)

18	Cores
several	Flakes
67	Axe roughouts
5	Flaked axes
1	Type 5 axe
7	Tranchets
several	Scrapers
3	Heavy duties
2	Hammers (broken roughouts)
2	Fabricators
1	Borer
4	Miniature axes
several	Knives
1	Stone axe

iv) WILLETT'S EXCAVATIONS

Unmarked (British Museum)

1	Axe roughout
1	Axe sharpening flake
2	Leaf arrowheads
1	Laurel leaf
1	Sickle (roughout)
1	Scraper
1	Chisel
1	Fabricator
1	Rod

v) OTHER COLLECTIONS FROM CISSBURY

Garraway-Rice Collection (Worthing Museum)

4	Cores
15	Flakes
10	Retouched/utilised
20	Axe roughouts
4	Flaked axes

1	Tranchet
3	Picks
1	Scraper

Powell Collection (Horniman Museum)

2	Cores
1	Core/hammer
14	Flakes
3	Retouched/utilised
4	Axe roughouts
1	Pick
1	Heavy duty
1	Tranchet tool
1	Miniature tranchet
1	Slug

Sturge Collection (British Museum)

Floor 2

93	Flakes

Toms Collection (Brighton Museum)

4	Cores
32	Flakes
8	Retouched/utilised
81	Axe roughouts
58	Flaked axes
4	Type 5 axe
2	Adzes
3	Tranchets
4	Picks
1	Laurel leaf
4	Plano-convex knives
1	Scrapers
15	Heavy duties
4	Hammers
9	Chisels
1	Fabricator
11	Miniature axes
10	Knives

Unstratified (Ashmolean, Brighton, British, Guildford, London, Newbury, Reading, Worthing Museums)

23	Cores
6	Blades
7	Rejuvenation flakes
226	Flakes
37	Retouched/utilised

338	Axe roughouts
115	Flaked axes
10	Polished axes (broken)
1	Axe sharpening flake
10	Picks
1	Sickle or knife
24	Scrapers
2	Laurel leaf (1 unfinished)
8	Tranchets
2	Hammers
1	Wedge
14	Heavy duties
1	Waisted core tool
2	Choppers
22	Chisels
2	Borer
11	Fabricators
21	Miniature axes
1	Knife

Summary of flint artefacts from the Cissbury mines and associated features

	Pye (Pull only)	**JPG**
Cores	9	73
Discoidal cores	–	2
Blade cores	–	2
Utilised Cores	1	2
Flakes	–	728
Retouched	–	78
Axe roughouts	32	659
Flaked axes	10	242
Type 5 axes	–	33
Polished axes	–	14
Sharpening flakes	–	2
Tranchets	–	20
Picks	–	36
Adzes	–	2
Leaf arrowheads	1	6
Laurel leaves	–	8
Plano-convex knives	–	4
Sickle	fragments	3
Scrapers	14	45
Heavy duties	4	52

Hammers	1	10
Waisted core tool	–	1
Choppers	–	4
Tranchet tool	–	1
Rod	–	1
Chisels	1	43
Fabricators	–	18
Borers	4	6
Miniature axes	–	46
Slugs	–	3
Knives	1	17
'Points'	10	–
Stone Axe	–	1
TOTAL	**95 (Pull only)**	**2169**

HARROW HILL

Most material from the early excavations at Harrow Hill is now in Worthing Museum, along with some surface finds, although certain pieces are known to have been distributed elsewhere.

Shaft 1	**Holleyman**	**JPG**
Polished axe	1	–
Flaked axes	2	–
Shaft 2	**Holleyman**	**JPG**
Flakes	'nest'	–
Flaked axes	4	2
Choppers	2	–
Shaft 3	**Holleyman**	**JPG**
Axe roughouts	32	3
Flaked axes	1	3
Shaft 4	**Holleyman**	**JPG**
Axe roughouts	–	8
Flaked axes	–	8
Shaft 21	**Curwen and Curwen**	**JPG**
Core	1	1
Flakes	–	44
Retouched	3	5
Roughouts	4	62
Flaked axes	2	16
Type 5 axe	1	–

Pick	–	1
Scrapers	12	1
Choppers	23	1
Wedges	11	–
Spurred piece	1	–
Heavy duties	–	9
Chisel	–	1

A selection of unmarked flints from Harrow Hill also exists in Worthing Museum

5	Cores
1	Axe roughout
5	Flaked axes
1	Scraper
1	Heavy duty

Summary of flint artefacts from the Harrow Hill mines

	JPG
Cores	7
Flakes	54
Retouched	5
Axe roughouts	104
Flaked axes	48
Picks	2
Leaf arrowheads	1
Scrapers	2
Choppers	1
Chisels	2

10
Conclusion: Sussex Mines in Context

> 'That, in some fields of his country there are certain shining stones of several colours, whereof the Yahoos are violently fond; and when part of these stones are fixed in the earth, as it sometimes happeneth, they will dig with their claws for whole days to get them out, and carry them away, and hide them by heaps in their kennels; but still looking round with great caution, for fear that their comrades should find out their treasure. My master said, he could never discover the reason of this unnatural appetite, or how these stones could be of any use to a Yahoo'.
> (J. Swift 1726, Gulliver's Travels)

Before the late 1970s there were few significant works specifically outlining the processes of Neolithic flint extraction that could be drawn upon by researchers. Indeed, when Robert Shepherd was writing *Prehistoric Mining and Allied Industries* he noted that 'even works by eminent prehistorians devote scarcely more than a single page to mining and mostly an odd sentence at appropriate stages in the discourse' (1980, vii). To some extent this situation has been alleviated following the publication of detailed excavation reports for work conducted at the Grimes Graves flint mines in Norfolk (e.g. Sieveking 1979; Mercer 1981; Clutton-Brock 1984; Longworth *et al* 1988; 1991; Legge 1992; Longworth and Varndell 1996) and by the more recent emphasis on understanding the significance, origins and possible meaning of specific artefact types such as the stone axe (e.g. Ferguson 1980; Craddock *et al* 1983; Gardiner 1984; 1987; 1988; Bradley and Edmonds 1993; Edmonds 1995; Pitts 1996). The work of the Royal Commission on the Historical Monuments of England (soon to be merged with English Heritage), which since 1993 has been investigating and surveying the surface evidence of all potential Neolithic flint mine sites in England, should when published (Barber *et al* in Press), further revolutionise our understanding of the nature, form and function of Neolithic flint extraction. In all these works, however, the absence of data relating to the South Downs mine series has been sorely felt. Now that the fieldwork archive of John Pull has been assembled, it is time to assess how this information contributes to our understanding of Neolithic mining as a practice. It is time therefore to put the Sussex flint mines in context.

Mine Sites of the South Downs

A total of 21 sites have now been identified from the chalk ridge of the South Downs as potential areas of Neolithic mining. Of these, six may be described as definite mine sites, one as probable, six as possible, five as doubtful and three as discredited (figure 121). The definite sites comprise Blackpatch, Church Hill, Cissbury, Harrow Hill, Long Down and Stoke Down, where extensive periods of excavation and survey have revealed a considerable amount of Neolithic data (e.g. Barber *et al* in Press; Burstow 1962; Butler 1992; Curwen and Curwen 1926; Curwen 1926; 1927; 1929b; Donachie and Field 1994; Field 1997a; Goodman *et al* 1924; Harrison 1877a; 1877b; 1878; Holgate 1989; 1991; 1995a; 1995b; 1995c; Holleyman 1937; Irving 1857; Lane Fox 1869a; 1869b; 1875; Law 1927; McNabb *et al* 1996; Migeod 1950; Pull 1923a; 1923b; 1923c; 1927; 1932a; 1932b; 1933a; 1933b; 1933c; 1933d; 1933e; 1933f; 1953; Pull and Sainsbury 1928d; 1929c; 1929e; 1930a; 1930b; 1930c; 1930d; 1930e; Pye 1968; Rolleston 1877; 1879; Salisbury 1961; Sieveking *et al* 1972; 1973; Smith 1912; Stevens 1872; Toms and Toms 1926; Topping 1997b; Turner 1850; Wade 1922; Willett 1880).

The only site listed from the South Downs as an area of probable Neolithic mining, is at Nore Down. Here two linear cuts, first identified as comprising the ditches of a Neolithic long barrow (Aldsworth 1979), were reinterpreted following partial excavation, as representing two parallel strips of overlapping mine shafts (Aldsworth 1983b). The site almost certainly indicates a zone of potentially small-scale Neolithic

Figure 121. Probable areas of Neolithic flint mining recorded from the South Downs (diamonds) in relation to Neolithic long mounds (solid circles) and enclosures (open circles): 1 = Nore Down; 2 = Stoke Down; 3 = Long Down; 4 = Harrow Hill; 5 = Blackpatch and Myrtlegrove; 6 = Church Hill, Tolmere and High Salvington; 7 = Cissbury and Mount Carvey (after Russell 1999, figures 5.01 – 5.03).

flint extraction, but the limited area of archaeological examination conducted must ensure that a direct comparison of morphology and chronological sequence with the mine sites of Blackpatch, Church Hill *et al*, remains impossible.

Possible Neolithic mine shafts from the South Downs comprise the plough-disrupted sites of High Salvington (Pull 1935b) and Mount Carvey (Pull 1935c), the possible extensions to existing mining complexes at Myrtlegrove (from Blackpatch: Pull 1935c), West Stoke (from Stoke Down: NMR 245691) and Roger's Farm (from Church Hill: Laughlin 1994) and the possible quarry site disturbed by later digging activity at Tolmere (Curwen and Curwen 1927). Sites viewed as possessing doubtful Neolithic associations comprise Bexley Plantation, Clanfield, Slonk Hill, Wilmington Hill and Windover Hill. Bexley Plantation appears to consist of a series of nineteenth century chalk extraction pits (NMR 245580), whilst the surface indentations from Wilmington and Windover Hills possibly indicate Medieval or later marl pits (NMR 408823; NMR 408826; Field and Barber pers. comm. 1997). At Slonk Hill the mouth of a large circular cut was partially investigated, but as yet there is no evidence of morphology or date (Hartridge 1978, 87). At Clanfield in Hampshire a large number of surface finds, possibly related to flint working, have been recorded, but no conclusive evidence of insitu extraction has yet been found (Sieveking *et al* 1972, 153; Pitts 1996, 363).

Shafts or surface pits where a Neolithic date was originally conferred but which, through excavation or surface examination, may now be redated and removed from the debate, comprise those sites recorded from Bow Hill, Compton Down and Lavant Down. Bow Hill is likely to represent a series of post Neolithic quarry pits (Hamilton 1933; Curwen 1954, 120) whilst Compton Down may be reinterpreted as a single post prehistoric marl pit (NMR 762993). The complex subterranean workings of the Lavant Down site, first revealed in around 1890, would now appear to represent the remains of a medieval or later mine within which Neolithic finds were planted, most probably by Charles Dawson, chief suspect in the Piltdown Man hoax (Russell in Press b).

Considering the quantity of mine shafts and associated activity areas upon the South Downs that remain uninvestigated, it seems clear that we are still some significant way from even partially understanding the range, nature and evolution of Neolithic flint extraction processes. Nevertheless the recording to basal mine levels at Blackpatch, Church Hill, Cissbury, Harrow Hill, Long Down, Stoke Down and Tolmere have all provided evidence of a broad and diverse series of extraction techniques which may be outlined and cross-compared.

The land cuts recorded from the central block of the South Downs above Worthing appear to differ from the other areas of large scale Neolithic flint extraction on the chalk in the extent of shafts excavated during the Neolithic, and presumably the sheer quantity of flint being exploited (Field 1997a). The preliminary results of the RCHME's Neolithic Industry and Enclosure Project, for example, would appear to suggest the presence at Harrow Hill, Blackpatch, Church Hill and Cissbury of at least 160, 100, 26 and 270 shafts respectively (Donachie and Field 1994; Field 1997a, 58; Barber *et al* in Press), with many more having presumably been obscured through later agricultural and settlement activity. The addition of quarry pits from Tolmere and the possible areas of extraction noted from the lower slopes of Church Hill at Roger's Farm

(Laughlin 1994), High Salvington (Pull 1935b), Mount Carvey (Pull 1935c) and Myrtlegrove (Pull 1935c), substantially increases the potential density of prehistoric flint exploitation on this particular section of the central south-eastern chalk.

Harrow Hill
At Harrow Hill, to date the better published of all mine sites on the South Downs, the subterranean flint seams tilt in a north to south direction in contrast to the actual slope of the ground surface (Field 1997a, 61). Here flint first appears to have been extracted by means of open cast quarries at the point of outcrop, and, as the seam descended, extraction progressed by the cutting of increasingly deeper pits, until a second high level outcrop was detected (Field 1997a, 61). Such a methodology may explain the seemingly diverse nature of the Neolithic land cuts at Harrow Hill, Shafts I, III and 13 descending to 3m, 2.6m and 3.2m respectively, whilst Shafts II and 21 descended to 4m and 6.8m. Occasionally more than one seam of flint was exploited within a specific mine. The cutting of Shaft 21, for example, originally involved the exploitation of the first, second and third seams, the second and third being removed through the excavation of small galleries (Curwen and Curwen 1926, 108).

Open cast quarry pits have been detected at a number of places on Harrow Hill, and it is apparent that the quarrying of surface flint was sometimes followed by the cutting of a deeper pit, the earlier area of extraction acting as a useful platform or access point to the deeper seams (McNabb *et al* 1996, 22). This is particularly clear in Shaft 21, where the first seam had been partially removed by cutting a small recess into the wall of the pit (Curwen and Curwen 1926, 108). A series of adit mines to the immediate north-east of Shaft 21 appear to have further exploited this primary flint layer. Such excavated evidence makes it clear that the difference between the exploitation of surface seams through open cast quarries and the cutting of deeper pits with subterranean galleries, is not necessarily chronological (Holgate 1991; Field 1997a, 61).

Subterranean gallery systems at Harrow Hill do not always extend far from the main wall, perhaps because of the close proximity of shafts in certain areas. The limiting of galleries may have been necessary to ensure that the maximum quantity of flint was removed during extraction without having to sacrifice large amounts of flint to unexcavated roof supports (Field 1997a, 61). In areas where the chalk overburden was not extensive, prehistoric miners seemed to have dug shafts in pairs to exploit the desired layer of flint (Shafts 4 and 5, 9 and 12, 24 and 25: McNabb *et al* 1996, 25). Excavations around Shaft 13 in 1982 revealed that this particular cut was surrounded by a series of smaller satellite shafts which were not visible at ground level (McNabb *et al* 1996, 24). Such interlinking of pits may have improved access, lighting and ventilation within the basal working areas.

Blackpatch
At Blackpatch, a variety of extraction techniques were recorded by Pull. Shafts 5 and 6 and the central cut of Barrow 2, located at the north and eastern margins of the main area of extraction, can best be described as quarry pits or adit mines, descending no deeper than 1, 1.8 and 1.3m respectively. Of the shallow workings recorded within

Shaft 5, only two could really be described as galleries, though neither extended more than 1.6m from the wall of the pit. Only a slight undercutting of the southern wall of Shaft 6 appears to demonstrate that any flint other than that exposed within the shaft itself was here extracted.

The central cut within Barrow 2 at Blackpatch did not appear to have exploited any more of the flint than that exposed within the pit, although excavation through the floor of the feature may indicate an abortive attempt to reach deeper seams. The presumed failure of this shaft to locate an adequate source of subterranean flint (cf. Field 1997a, 62), may have prompted its abandonment and immediate backfilling. The soils thrown back into the pit contained quantities of special deposits, which in this instance included human body parts. A similar sequence of abandonment and backfill with special deposits could be suggested to explain the positioning of a structured round mound (Barrow 3) over Shaft 5 if this pit had also been considered unsuccessful in its attempts to extract good quality subterranean flint.

Shafts 1, 2, 4 and 7 at Blackpatch descended to depths of no more than 3.3m, exploiting the first major seam of flint encountered. Seven short galleries extend from the base of Shaft 1, one of which connected with the gallery of a second mine to the immediate north-east. The nature of cutting and later filling of these interconnecting galleries indicates that both shafts had probably been open at the same time. A complex of galleries extended from the lowest levels of Shaft 2, connecting it with at least three other shafts to the east, south and west. Flint extraction within these basal galleries had been sufficiently extensive as to seriously destabilise the overlying chalk rock. Little is known of the nature of workings within Shaft 4, though Shaft 7 possessed nine galleries connecting it to at least four other shafts in a manner reminiscent of some of the more complex basal gallery systems recorded by Pull and others at Cissbury (e.g. Shaft 27).

Church Hill and Tolmere

Shafts 1, 2, 4, 5a, 6 and 7 examined by Pull at Church Hill all exploited generally deeper seams of flint than those encountered at Blackpatch, bottoming at depths of 4.9, 3, 5, 3.6, 5.8 and 4.9m respectively. With the exception of Shaft 2, the details of which unfortunately remain vague, all shafts exploited seams beneath the first to be encountered. Shafts 1 and 2 did not possess basal galleries (cf. Shaft 1 at Longdown, Tindall's Shaft at Cissbury and Shafts 1 and 2 at Stoke Down), though a series of small headings had been cut at the north, west and southern sides of Shaft 1, perhaps in an attempt to remove a greater quantity of flint from the fourth seam. Pull and Voice note that substantial cuttings had been made into the third seam in Shaft 4 and their section drawing seems to indicate that some attempt had been made to remove the primary seam which lay close to the surface. As with Shaft 1, however, it was the fourth seam that was the target of the Neolithic miners, five galleries, one connecting with Shaft 5, being cut from the basal levels. The fourth seam had also been extensively worked within Shaft 5a, with two galleries connecting directly with Shaft 5.

The nature of these inter-linking galleries when combined with the non-appearance of Shaft 5a from the modern ground surface, may suggest that 5a was originally a satellite to Shaft 5, being similar to the lesser shafts recorded around Shaft 13 at

Harrow Hill (McNabb *et al* 1996, 24). Some attempt had been made within Shaft 5a to exploit the third seam, whilst a deepening within the floor of the pit had partially exposed a fifth seam at an overall depth of 4.6m. Shafts 6 and 7 at Church Hill appear to represent paired shafts, presumably being cut, worked and remaining open at the same time. Both pits had passed through five seams of flint before terminating at the sixth, headings being driven into the fourth, fifth and sixth seams. The only true gallery defined within the basal levels of Shafts 6 and 7 was the single one that connected them.

No definite evidence of lesser flint extraction pits, quarries or drift mines, such as noted at Blackpatch, were investigated by Pull at Church Hill, with Pit A, a 2.4m deep cut passing through but not exploiting a seam of surface flint, perhaps indicating the most promising of potential candidates. The other pits recorded from Church Hill, Pits B and C, are almost certainly Iron Age in date and presumably relate to a later period of occupation on the site. In contrast Pits 38 and 40 at Tolmere, to the immediate north of Church Hill, cut to a depth of 1 and 1.9m respectively, are more likely to represent Neolithic constructs, possibly the remains of either abortive shafts or exploratory pits searching for new flint to exploit (Field 1997a, 63). Unfortunately, as archaeological investigation at this site has to date been limited, caution must be emphasised regarding the exact interpretation of these features.

Cissbury

Evidence for Neolithic flint extraction at Cissbury is diverse, with at least 20 shafts having been archaeologically examined between 1873 and 1956 (additional examples having been partially investigated earlier in the nineteenth century). Of the late nineteenth century excavations that we possess detailed records for, it may be seen that the shafts investigated varied considerably in depth, No. 1 Escarp and No.1 Counterscarp bottoming at 2m and 2.2m (Lane Fox 1875), Willett's Shaft 1 at 4.3m (Willett 1880), Willett's Shaft 2, the Cave Pit and Shaft V at around 6.1m (Harrison 1877b; 1878; Willett 1880), Shaft VI at 9.1m (Harrison 1878) and Tindall's Shaft at 12m (Lane Fox 1875, 364–5; Willett 1880, 341). The Large Pit possessed an overall diameter of 20m, descending to at least 12.8m. The full dimensions of this shaft could not unfortunately be gauged, due to the sudden and unexpected collapse of the standing section (Lane Fox 1875, 380).

The nature of subsurface flint workings exposed at Cissbury during the nineteenth century was also varied. As at Harrow Hill and Church Hill, occasional attempts seem to had been made to extract primary and secondary seams encountered during the sinking of deep shafts. Nowhere is this clearer than within the Large Pit examined by Lane Fox in 1875. This particular shaft cut through six seams of flint, the uppermost two layers being exploited through a series of terrace cuts. The first terrace, at a depth of 2.7m, was only 0.3m wide along its northern edge, broadening to around 2.4m along the western and southern faces of the shaft. The second terrace, at a depth of 5.5m, extended to a maximum width of 3m along the west and south-western walls. The flint seam had been further extracted by the digging of 'small caves' or undercuts along the southern and western shaft wall, one of which, measuring 2.4m in length, may more plausibly be interpreted as a gallery. A further four seams were cut through as the shaft descended below the second terrace, the shaft itself narrowing to around 4.3m at its lowest traceable point. Lane Fox speculated that the sheer scale of the shaft may have been due to the fact that it represented a number of open quarry pits and surface workings (c.f. Harrow Hill, Shaft 21: Curwen and Curwen 1926, 108), which had been joined together to become the first terrace, from which deeper cuttings were later made (Lane Fox 1875, 380).

Shelves or terrace cuts observed within other shafts at Cissbury (notably Willett's Shaft 2, the Cave Pit, and Shaft V: Harrison 1878; Willett 1880), may relate to similar attempts to quarry material from multiple seams. In the absence of a clearly defined flint layer, however, an alternative explanation may be that these shelves represent an attempt to lessen the primary workload by narrowing the area of excavation, thus reducing the quantity of material being brought to the surface. A third explanation may relate to the modification of shaft walls during the initial excavation of spoil, in order to create a series of discrete platforms from which ladders could be firmly embedded (c.f. Harrison 1878, 413, 421). Similar narrowing of shaft walls may be seen in Shaft 2 at Blackpatch and Shafts 5a and 6 at Church Hill. A cut in the central floor of Willett's Shaft 2 was interpreted at the time as speculative hole dug to ascertain the depth of the next flint layer (Willett 1880, 341), though it may alternatively be viewed as a sump (as Pull interpreted the feature at the base of Shaft 5a at Church Hill).

Undercuts and galleries were recorded from a number of the shafts examined at Cissbury in the late nineteenth century, though the level of recorded detail is variable. The base of Willett's Shaft 1 was punctured by a series of interconnecting chambers, which Willett noted were around 1.5m in diameter. Unfortunately, though Willett made 'careful notes and memoranda', he was unable to detail the exact form and extent of these cuttings owing to the unfortunate loss of his site notebook (1880, 383). A total of 8 galleries, measuring between 0.9 and 1.5m in width, were recorded from the basal levels of Willett's second shaft (Willett 1880, 399–40). All appeared to have filled to within at least 0.6m of their roofs with chalk rubble. Three galleries (2, 3a and 6) were cleared to almost their full lengths, gallery 2 extending for some 5.m before ending in a rounded terminal, possibly linked via a window to a shaft to the immediate north. Willett notes that a 'strong draught was observed' when a candle was placed at the end of this gallery (1880, 340) demonstrating that, even after extensive backfill, such windows could well have functioned as a source of additional ventilation in the cramped subterranean work space. A similar link to an additional shaft was noted at the end of gallery 6.

Two galleries and two headings were identified at the base of Shaft V, four galleries were identified at the base of No. 1 Counterscarp Shaft, No. 2 Counterscarp Shaft and the Skeleton Shaft, five from No. 1 Escarp Shaft, No. 2 Escarp Shaft and Shaft VI, whilst seven were observed at the base of the Cave Pit. Many of these galleries were accompanied by additional areas of limited undercutting of the shaft wall. Many of these gallery systems interlinked, producing a complex plan of conjoined shafts and tunnels (e.g. Willett's Shaft 1, and Shaft's II–VI: Harrison 1878, plate x). Such a digging regime may reflect a highly organised Neolithic extraction technique whereby the desired seam of flint was systematically removed by the use of multiple interconnected galleries, leaving a network of unexcavated chalk walls to provide structural support.

In this way the repeated digging of vertical shafts down through the bedrock at a series of semi regular intervals may be interpreted as the deliberate creation of a multiple series of entrance points to aid in the extraction process, exit points in case of sudden roof collapse and a way of bringing additional amounts of air and natural light down into the work space.

Certain galleries, such as the northern gallery in No. 1 Escarp Shaft (Lane Fox 1875, 372), possessed internal chambers that widened the working area considerably, whilst others, most notably the southern branch of gallery E in the Cave Pit (Harrison 1877b, 435), terminated in a domed and 'spacious chamber'. The majority of working areas encountered had, on completion, been filled with chalk rubble, presumably derived from excavation in other areas of the shaft. The entranceways into galleries E and F within the Cave Pit appear to have been deliberately sealed by the insertion of two large blocks of chalk which had to be broken apart insitu by the excavation team before exploration of the gallery could commence (Harrison 1878, 418).

No undercuttings or galleries were observed within the shaft opened by Tindall in 1874 (cf. Shafts 1 and 2 at Blackpatch and Shaft 1 at Longdown), though Harrison later comments that a 'basin shaped hollow' was recorded at the base of the feature (1877a, 268). Harrison deduced that the shaft was a well and had not been cut primarily for the extraction of flint. Though this remains a possibility, those working on Cissbury would have required a good supply of water, it must be admitted that as a well, the shaft could have been better placed. That Tindall's feature was Neolithic in date seems, on the basis of the artefactual assemblage, clear enough and it remains likely that either the cut was an exploratory or unfinished mine, or that any speculative galleries were overlooked following the closure of the dig and Tindall's subsequent death (Lane Fox 1875, 364–5; Willett 1880, 341).

Shafts 24 and 27 cleared by Pull at Cissbury bottomed at a depth of 4.5 and 5.8m respectively. Shaft 24 exploited the second seam of flint encountered through a series of six galleries, two of which connected with other shafts, whilst Shaft 27 extracted flint from the third and fourth seams through a series of galleries connecting the feature with at least four other shafts. The plans produced by Pull for Shafts 24 and 27 show a complicated system of subterranean galleries similar to those explored within Shafts I, III, IV, and VI to the north (Harrison 1878, pl X), as well as the galleries recorded from Shaft 7 at Blackpatch. Galleries within Shaft 27 appear to have been further linked by the repeated use of windows. As noted above, such joins may be viewed as the accidental and partial joining of two non-contemporary working areas or part of an attempt to provide more reflected natural light into the galleries, allow a better circulation of air or even as a more efficient means of exit or escape, via an abandoned or disused mine, should the need arise.

The fact that many of the excavated gallery systems at Cissbury were found to be choked with chalk rubble (figure 122) would seem to imply that, as at Grimes Graves (Mercer 1981), miners deliberately filled recently abandoned working areas with debris derived from new gallery systems in order to avoid having to haul a significant quantity to the surface. Much of the chalk debris left within surface spoil heaps around the mine sites must therefore relate more to the initial cutting of the shafts than to the subsequent removal of flint seams. At the termination of mine activity

Figure 122. An unspecified gallery within Shaft 27 at Cissbury prior to examination. Evidence such as this demonstrates that Neolithic miners deliberately filled abandoned gallery systems with chalk rubble derived from later workings in order to avoid hauling considerable amounts of debris to the surface (© Worthing Museum and Art Gallery).

some of the shafts appear to have been backfilled with spoil. Whether this was a economic necessity, designed either to stabilise empty and potentially hazardous mines or to clear the surface of as much unwanted debris as possible before deciding where to sink later shafts, or whether this was an activity of special significance, perhaps intended to 'heal' the wound caused by the sinking of the shaft in the first place, is unclear, as is the degree to which shafts were backfilled, as many large heaps of mining debris still remain at ground level upon Cissbury to this day.

Longdown, Stoke Down and Nore Down
Information surrounding the remaining three areas of Neolithic flint extraction on the South Downs is patchy. Information from the Longdown site consists of a single shaft (Salisbury 1961), measuring over 4.6m in depth, which cut through four seams of flint. The lower levels of the shaft did not appear to contain galleries or evidence of undercutting, though a narrowing of the shaft in two places close to the base, perhaps indicating the deliberate construction of a platform to aid in the extraction process (cf. Harrison 1878, 413, 421), gave the feature a 'rectangular rather than circular shape' (Salisbury 1961, 67). Galleries did not appear to have played a feature in any of the Shafts examined by Wade at Stoke Down, though Shafts 1 and 3 possessed a limited number of undercuts, demonstrating that in at least three areas the flint seam had been followed into the wall of the shaft (Wade 1924, 88–9). The shafts at Stoke Down, numbered 1, 2 and 3, were bottomed at depths of 4.6, 2.9 and 4.2m respectively. At Nore Down, though none of the features have been fully examined, surface indications appear to suggest that the shafts, grouped into two sets of four, were all probably all open at the same time (Aldsworth 1979; 1983).

Inside the mines

Internal Structuration
Few traces of internal structures relating to the extraction process were detected within any of the Blackpatch, Harrow Hill, Long Down or Stoke Down mine shafts, though the curious narrowing in diameter of the south-eastern wall of Blackpatch Shaft 2 at a depth of 0.9m, to create a narrow ledge, may indicate the deliberate creation of a step

or platform, similar intent perhaps to the possible timber platforms noted within the 1971 Shaft at Grimes Graves (Mercer 1980, 20) and interpreted as an aid to both access to the workface and removal of freshly excavated flint. Similar narrowing of shaft walls is evident at Church Hill, perhaps most noticeably within the upper levels of Shaft 5a and Shaft 6, Cissbury, in Willett's Shaft 2 (Willett 1880), the Cave Pit (Harrison 1877b; 1878), and Shaft V (Harrison 1878), and in Shaft 1 at Longdown (Salisbury 1961).

Limited evidence to suggest the former presence of internal timber structures within mine shafts was however recorded at both Church Hill and at Cissbury. In Shaft 7 at Church Hill, two slanting holes measuring between 0.15 and 0.21m in diameter were found at a distance of 0.38m apart in the chalk at the base of the shaft. Pull and Voice suggested that these impressions were probably due to the pressing down of 'two stout wooden poles', which could represent the sides of a ladder or slide, 'up which bags of material might be pulled'. This interpretation has been questioned by Pye who wondered whether such a construct would be left in an abandoned shaft 'unless it was already broken or rotten, in which case it would not leave the positive traces Pull claimed to have found' (Pye 1968, 24). There is no suggestion that the postulated ladder was buried in the mine, however, the only evidence for its existence being the two basal holes observed by Pull and Voice. These features were seen to cut into the floor of the shaft and, as they were not detected within the layers above, would seem to imply that, whatever their interpretation, they were created before any significant fill could develop within the mine. This could strengthen the view that the holes represent the remains of some form of internal structure contemporary with the early use of Shaft 7.

Shaft 27 at Cissbury also produced evidence that may relate to the presence of internal timber features. A horizontal hole, measuring 0.5m in length and 7.6cm in diameter, recorded from the wall of the shaft may possibly indicate the partial remains of an internal platform or structure (cf. Grimes Graves 1971 Shaft: Mercer 1981, 20). Further into Shaft 27, at a depth of 2.4m, Pull observed a vertical break in stratigraphy measuring between 0.1 and 0.2m in diameter and surviving for a length of at least 1.2m. The recorded section drawing for Shaft 27 clearly shows this vertical break in fill, but unfortunately does not provide additional detail. A series of photographs taken by E. S. Salisbury and now forming part of the John Pull archive in Worthing Museum, show the void at the time of its initial discovery with the annotated comment 'this peculiar hole may have been made by the trunk of a small tree used as a ladder by the miners' (cf. Shaft II at Hov in Denmark: Becker 1959, 92). The void has the general appearance of an animal burrow, though its near vertical descent, at the approximate centre-point of the shaft, with no obvious point of continuation within the layers above or below, may, as Pull suggested, indicate where a timber had decayed within shaft backfill.

As with Pye's earlier comments concerning the features observed in Shaft 7 at Church Hill (1968, 24), it could be argued that a potentially useful feature such as a ladder or climbing pole would be reused by the miners elsewhere on site and not left within a shaft, assuming of course that the feature had not already been in some way broken or compromised by use. Many potentially reusable digging tools, such as antler picks, were however also left by the miners within abandoned shafts and gallery systems, possibly because they were a resource that could easily be replenished or because they were being left as an offering or were considered to be 'spiritually contaminated' in some way by their utilisation in the mine. Ladders, ropes and climbing poles, such as the 5m length of 'slender tree stem' with lopped side branches recorded from the fill of Shaft II at Hov in Denmark (Becker 1959), used during the extraction process could also have been thought of in this way.

No evidence to suggest the former presence of roof supports or pit props were located n the radiating basal galleries of the Worthing mine series. Indeed within the Blackpatch shafts Pull noted that:

> No extensive falls of rock appear to have taken place during the thousands of years which have elapsed since they were cut. Judging from this it would seem that there had never been any need for the employment of timbers or pit props such as are used in modern mining operations. No traces of humus from decayed timber or marks resulting from the use of artificial supports were found (Pull 1923a).

Pull may have revised such a perspective at Cissbury, where the poor nature of the overlying chalk in Shafts 24 and 27 necessitated the use of hefty timber and steel pit props.

Tool types utilised

Evidence of the type and range of durable tools used within the flint mines was noted from a number of galleries in the Sussex mines, notably Shaft 2 at Blackpatch, Shafts

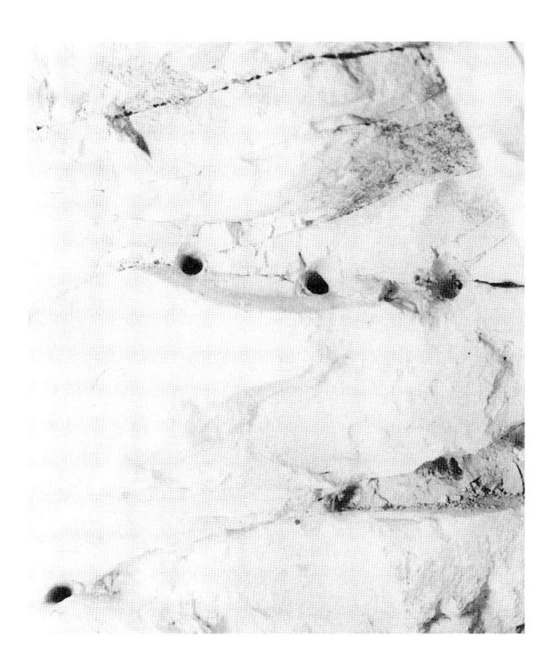

Figure 123. Antler punch marks in the wall of gallery i, Shaft 1 at Blackpatch. Here the extraction technique of the Neolithic miners is clearly demonstrated, the punch or pick having been hammered into the chalk face in two parallel strips, three holes visible at the top and four below, in order to wedge out the intervening block of chalk (© Worthing Museum and Art Gallery).

5, 6 and 7 at Church Hill and Shaft 27 at Cissbury. Here Pull found numerous antler picks, rakes, punches and mallets, ox scapulae and stone axes 'as if freshly discarded by the miners'. Antler picks were used to dislocate flint through the removal of the surrounding chalk (figure 123), whilst the ox scapulae and antler rakes appear to have been used in the shovelling or scraping up of chalk rubble from the working areas. That other types of digging tool were probably being utilised by the miners is evidenced from Shafts 4 and 7 at Church Hill where Pull observed a series of deep and regular impressions implying the use of 'large wooden bars or mauls'. No clear evidence has been found from the Sussex mines to suggest the use of stone axes in the extraction process (as recorded from Greenwell's Shaft at Grimes Graves: Greenwell 1870), though such objects were sometimes found discarded within subterranean gallery systems. Baskets and ropes, if used to remove chalk and flint rubble, have left little trace within the Sussex mines, though Pull claims to have found evidence of rope attrition upon walls of Shaft 5 at Blackpatch and Shaft 27 at Cissbury.

An area of smoke discoloration, perhaps indicating a source of artificial light, was observed on the ceiling of gallery 3 in Shaft 2 at Blackpatch. Pull suggested that, as the gallery in question was flooded with daylight along its entire length, the soot deposit may have derived from the lamp of someone entering the gallery at night, possibly a Neolithic miner returning to retrieve tools left at the workface. Alternatively the soot could relate to a more modern lamp (cf. Goodman *et al* 1924 plates vi and vii) or candle used by an unauthorised nocturnal visitor to the excavation. Similar traces of sooting, recorded from gallery 3 of Shaft 13 at Harrow Hill (Curwen 1930a, plate iv, 2), may also represent an illicit night-time visitation during the course of the 1924–5 excavations. Not only were there no further traces of soot revealed during the re-examination of the gallery in 1982, but the working area would originally appear to have possessed an ample supply of natural light if originally worked during daylight hours (McNabb *et al* 1996, 24).

Whether those working within the shafts would have required a source of artificial lighting to aid in the extraction of flint is debatable (figure 124). Pull noted that none of the recorded galleries were 'long enough to have necessitated the use of artificial light in order to facilitate the performance of the mining operations' (1923a), a view confirmed by Con Ainsworth who worked with Pull at Cissbury (Ainsworth pers. comm. 1999). During the examination of Shaft 2 at Blackpatch, Pull noted that the walls to every gallery, where they turned a right angle, were pierced with large openings designed to 'admit daylight' from the open shaft. In such a way all of the subterranean working areas within the recorded galleries could, in Pull's view, successfully be illuminated. These windows, as already noted, could alternatively be viewed as an additional source of ventilation into the sometimes cramped work place.

Subterranean engravings

Aside from those marks relating to the original extraction process (preserved in the walls of gallery systems) and traces of sooting (found on gallery ceilings), a third type of internal marking has been recorded from within the Sussex mines. At Church Hill, Pull observed a series of distinct impressions above three of the five basal gallery entrances of Shaft 4. These consisted of a rough circle (or oval) within a broken circle,

Figure 124. Looking towards galleries iv and v of Shaft 1 at Blackpatch, a dark and strange subterranean world. How much natural light percolated down to these levels remains a subject for debate (© Worthing Museum and Art Gallery).

a circle between two downward-pointing diagonal lines, and a circle with a raised centre. All may have been created by the careful application of a flint tool or antler tine directly onto the chalk. Nothing quite like the Shaft 4 marks have been observed at any other flint mine site in Britain, though a possible comparison may be made with the 'groups of dots' and 'small cup-shaped marks' observed by Harrison within Shafts III and VI at Cissbury (1878, 418–9, 432). As no detailed record of the Cissbury impressions has survived, this comparison cannot be taken further. The apparent uniqueness of the Church Hill examples may of course be due to their prominent placing over points of entry to subterranean galleries. Similar symbols, if not positioned so dramatically within a shaft, could always have been overlooked or thought to represent pick or gouge-marks deriving from the initial phase of gallery excavation and rubble extraction.

There is little chance of such misinterpretation of the animalistic engravings recorded within gallery 7, linking Shafts 27 and 31 at Cissbury. That these series of markings are both deliberate and contemporary with the prehistoric utilisation of the mine would not appear to be in doubt, though their significance within the mine is by no means clear. A similar series of naturalistic engravings of red deer had earlier been observed upon the cortex of mined floorstone found from Chipping Floor 85 at Grimes Graves in Norfolk by Leslie Armstrong in 1920 (Armstrong 1922a and b). If genuine, these pieces would offer an interesting parallel to the Cissbury animals. Unfortunately the Grimes Graves pieces bear an uncanny resemblance to Palaeolithic carvings recorded from cave sites in France and Spain (cf. Bahn and Vertut 1988, 43, figures 20 and 21) and are likely to represent part of an elaborate hoax designed to establish an early date for the Norfolk mine series (Russell in Press c).

Other forms of internal engravings have been noted from primary contexts within the Sussex and Norfolk mine series, but none approach the more realistic depictions of the Shaft 27/31 examples from Cissbury, consisting mostly of simple combinations of lines. The first group of linear incisions were recorded from the wall of Willett's Shaft 2 at Cissbury by Harrison in 1875 (Harrison 1877a, 264, 268–9). Further vertical and diagonal marks were revealed on the side of the western gallery of No 2 Escarp Shaft by Lane Fox in 1875 (Lane Fox 1875, 374; Lane Fox in Harrison 1877b, 440), whilst others were later observed within the Cave Pit and Shafts III and VI by Harrison (1877b, 434; 1878, 418–9, 432). Further afield, groups of linear cuts have also been recorded from Grimes Graves, in gallery 6 of Pit 2 (Clarke 1915, 73–4), from Shaft 21 at Harrow Hill (Curwen and Curwen 1926, 121–3) and the fill of Shaft 1 at Longdown (Salisbury 1961, 67, 70).

How may these seemingly diverse groups of subterranean engravings be interpreted? Harrison (1877b, 441) suggested that the groups of linear cuts represented 'symbols of ownership', 'religious charms' or perhaps an early form of writing, an idea later discounted by Lane Fox (in Harrison 1877b, 439). Other possible interpretations, including a form of art, tallies to 'denote the number of flints obtained' from each working area and idle scratchings made 'in some moment of fidgety restfulness' (Lane Fox in Harrison 1877b, 271, 440; Rolleston in Harrison 1877b, 438; Curwen and Curwen 1926, 125). It would be tempting to view the recorded groups of linear incisions as a functional tool, intended to aid the extraction process: possibly a primitive map of gallery systems. The discovery of similar groups of linear cuts from chalk recovered from Neolithic ditched enclosures such as the Trundle (Curwen 1929a, 61) and Whitehawk (Curwen 1936, 85–7) would however seem to contradict such a suggestion. Perhaps the linear incisions represented a common form of social identifier, possibly a community marker that was not restricted solely to areas of flint extraction. Perhaps they represented a particular form of marking intended solely for burial within land cuts.

The circular cuts from the entrances to galleries in Shaft 4 at Church Hill could also be interpreted as a tribal identifier or perhaps as a way of linking specific working areas with a particular person or social group. They may also have been intended to work as a form of protective symbol, to placate a subterranean deity (fear of the underworld being a common factor within ethnographic studies of mining activity: O'Brien 1994, 207; Field 1997a, 66–7; Topping 1997b, 130). Alternatively they may have functioned as a form of positioning device or direction finder, the circle in each case representing the position of the central mine shaft, elaboration beyond the area of the circle indicating perhaps the extent, number or direction of particular basal workings.

The diverse series of markings recovered from galleries connected to Shaft 27/31 at Cissbury are more difficult to interpret. The animal heads are unlikely to represent tally-marks, though they could represent the idle sketching of items familiar to the Neolithic artist that created them (being similar in intent to the 'record for future generations' left by Lane Fox's workforce in the Cissbury mines: Lane Fox in Harrison 1877, 269). They could of course have represented deities or spirits thought to be associated with the mine. The portrayal of deer could be due to their perceived importance in the community subsistence base, especially in the production of antler for digging tools. The so-called 'short horn bull' may even represent a deer, its antlers having been truncated or removed. Whatever the interpretation of species for this animal, its importance to the artist may have lain in the apparent depiction of a rope or neck harness. Such a depiction could be taken as an attempt to illustrate domestication and, by implication, of the triumph of human groups over the wild. The markings from the edge of the western recess in gallery 8 are more difficult to quantify, though the star or 'miner's symbol' may represent an antler pick or other digging tool. The 'fish head' could indicate a form of social signature or foodstuff, or, if one is so-minded, may be interpreted as a phallus or fertility symbol (cf. the 'artificially improved' flint nodule possibly recovered from Shaft 27, gallery 7: Pye 1968, 49).

The treatment of human remains

Three categories of human remains have been recorded from the flint mining sites of the central south-eastern chalk: articulated, disarticulated and cremated. Three articulated human skeletons have been recorded from mine fill at Cissbury. In Shaft H (later renamed 'the Skeleton Shaft'), Lane Fox found a complete skeleton of an adult female lying upside down within the fill (1875, 375). Clearance of the western gallery in Shaft 27 at Cissbury revealed an articulated human skeleton, initially interpreted by Pull as the remains of a miner killed by a sudden collapse of the chalk roof. The third articulated skeleton from Cissbury, that of an adult male, aged around 25, was recovered in a contracted position, surrounded by 'a row of chalk blocks and large flints', some 4.9m down in the fill of Shaft VI (Harrison 1878, 431).

Both the Cissbury females were retrieved from more primary shaft contexts than the solitary male, though the question must remain as to whether these represent deliberate depositions or the results of accidental death. Certainly the Shaft 27 skeleton was first thought by Pull to represent the body of a miner accidentally killed. Alternatively, given its position within the mine (figure 125), the body may originally have been placed at the entrance to a basal gallery as a way of conceptually sealing off that particular part of the mine. A similar interpretational problem exists for the body recovered lying head first in the fill of the Skeleton Shaft (Lane Fox 1875, 375). If the position of this body relates to a terminal accident then it would imply that the victim originally fell into the shaft whilst it was already half-filled cut, rather when fully cleared. Alternatively the body could perhaps be viewed as a sacrifice (Pull 1932a, 143; Migeod 1950, 18), or an unusual type of burial deposit.

Other human body parts recovered from Cissbury during the course of antiquarian exploration there comprise two pieces of human skull. The first, a single piece, was observed above one of the basal galleries in Shaft IV at Cissbury (Harrison 1878, 417). The second, a more complete example appears to have been recovered from Tindall's Shaft at Cissbury at some stage in 1874, though the possibility remains that it could have been recovered from elsewhere on the hill (Rosehill in Rolleston 1879, 388). At Blackpatch the extent and nature of bone deposition is more complex with a number of bodies and body parts being retrieved from structured round mounds associated with the mines. Cremation deposits were also noted from the upper fills of Shaft 7, within the flints constituting Floor 2, and within the mounds for Barrows 1 and 3. Cremations were also noted at Church Hill, within Shaft 1 and Floor 4, while a single human fibula came from the fill of Shaft 6.

Figure 125. The extended female skeleton recovered from the entrance to gallery 1, Shaft 27 at Cissbury. It remains unclear whether this individual was originally working in the mines and was killed by the sudden collapse of the chalk roof, was sacrificed at the time the mine was abandoned, or whether she died elsewhere and was buried across the gallery entrance as a form of offering or because this area was considered to possess special or magical properties (© Worthing Museum and Art Gallery).

Human remains occur across Southern Britain within most of the primary and secondary phases of Neolithic enclosure ditches, the primary internal areas of stone-chambered linear mounds, and, less frequently, within earthen long mounds and mine shaft backfill (cf. Pit 1 at Grimes Graves: Clarke 1915, 48–9, 134–41). Links between long mounds and enclosures sites, especially with regard to the occurrence of disassembled human skeletal material, have often been cited (e.g. Piggott 1962; Smith 1965), though the presence and significance of bodies and body parts from within and around areas of Neolithic flint extraction has unfortunately often gone without comment. Interpretation of human remains found in the fill of Neolithic enclosure ditches, usually follow the line that such sites were necropoli or places where human bodies were disassembled prior to the selection and formal deposition of body parts elsewhere (e.g. Mercer 1980; Thorpe 1984, 49–50). The discovery of human bone material within Neolithic mine shafts may, however, suggest that such a clear interpretation is unwarrantable.

Human remains, especially upper body parts such as the skull, occur in ditch and mine shaft fill with significant quantities of other Neolithic cultural debris, such as animal bone, pottery and flint. This could suggest the practice of cannibalism (c.f. Curwen 1936, 81; Piggott 1954, 47–8), with human body parts being discarded with other elements of food residue. Alternatively human bone, together with animal bone, pottery and flint, could reflect part of a representative sample of social attributes which were placed by a specific group into the land via ditches or shafts, so as to indelibly stamp it with their own cultural identity (Russell 1999, 46–9, 116–39). If human bone debris was incorporated within ditch and shaft backfill in an attempt to somehow imprint the monument with a specific social label or identity, then discussion concerning 'burial' in the conventional sense, becomes invalid. The accumulation of human body parts within subterranean cuts (ditches, pits and shafts) could therefore be seen as representing part of a more general process of structured deposition and not the defining element of that process (Russell 1999, 116–39). The fact that within the disarticulated bone assemblages from enclosure ditch-fill, skulls would appear to predominate, may reflect the desire to incorporate the more identifiable elements of certain individuals into the fill of a construct perceived to lie at the ideological or political centre of one or more territorial zones. Discovery of similar deposits within certain flint mine shafts may also have emphasised their importance within the monument frameworks of the southern English chalk.

One other aspect of the human bone data recovered from the Sussex mine series requires consideration, namely the sex of the individuals represented. Thus far there has been perhaps an unconscious view to view those working within Neolithic mines as adult males. This is perhaps due primarily to the male-orientated view of the past as commonly depicted by modern society where there is often a tendency to categorize activities according to sex (Hurcombe 1997, 18–19). Here it should be remembered that at Cissbury, the two bodies recovered from the lowest levels of Shafts 27 and H (the Skeleton Shaft) were female. The Shaft 27 skeleton was, at the time of discovery, interpreted as the remains of a miner killed by a sudden collapse of the roof. This interpretation seems to have quietly disappeared following the identification of the body as that of a female aged around twenty (Trevor unpublished MS; Worthing Museum Acc. No 1961/1586/A). If the Shaft 27 skeleton has been overlooked because of its sex, then this is somewhat worrying, for there is no reason to suggest that flint mining was an exclusive preserve of the adult male. Indeed, to extend this argument, it is unlikely that many of the muscle-bound males depicted in some modern reconstruction drawings would ever have fitted within the small basal galleries and side chambers of excavated shafts. It is certainly clear that many of the modern adult excavators of the Worthing mine sites had severe problems negotiating the narrow spaces within cleared galleries and the possibility that individuals of slighter build, perhaps even immatures (of either sex), worked within such areas is one which should not be overlooked.

At ground level

Flint working floors

On the surface, finds of flint knapping debris around the mouths of the Sussex flint mines, indicate that the working and shaping of freshly extracted raw material originally extended over a considerable area. Analysis of such surface chipping floors at Blackpatch and Church Hill suggested to Pull that though the axe was the principal implement made, other tool types such as 'drills, scrapers, knives, engraving implements, saws and planes' also commonly occurred. Flint flake material retrieved from floors 1, 2 and 3 at Cissbury, studied in depth by Pull at the time of excavation, seemed further to indicate that blades or knives were the product of manufacture here, contrary to the popular view that axes were the primary concern (cf. Craddock *et al* 1983).

Lane Fox, Armstrong, Pull and others have noted the generally high levels of apparent wastage at the flint manufacturing floors. Similarly large amounts of unutilised, though often perfectly serviceable, flint was sometimes incorporated into the backfill of abandoned mine shafts. One explanation for this apparently uneconomical use of the hard worn flint is that an excess quantity of tools and raw material could devalue the price of flint at the marketplace. So as to avoid such devaluation, any surplus material could thus have been deliberately concealed (cf. Longworth and Varndell 1996, 90). Unused flint may also have been deliberately buried so as to limit the effects of weathering upon a material that would later be used to manufacture distinctive tools. Quite why, in this scenario, buried flint was never reclaimed, unless there were certain taboos about doing so, remains unclear. Alternatively the deliberate reburial of excess flint into a shaft or working floor may have been akin to the incorporation of unused floorstone into the structured round mounds of Blackpatch. In other words such activity may reflect large-scale votive deposition, perhaps to give something of value back to the earth, or as an offering to the spirits of the mining area. Whatever the case the material represents something that does not make obvious economical sense from a modern perspective.

It is not known whether the chipping floors recorded by Pull at Cissbury, Blackpatch and Church Hill were originally covered or provided with some permanent form of shelter from the natural elements. Pull did not identify any trace of structures (postholes, stakeholes or timber slots) beneath the floors investigated, though it is worth noting that the semi-regular form of Floor 12 at Church Hill could indicate the former presence of a wall or barrier. The presence of hearths and animal bone debris within the make-up of certain surface flint floors (e.g. Floor 2 at Blackpatch) may strengthen the suggestion that some at least represent the remains of settlement, rather than purely manufacturing, activity.

Settlements

Evidence for structural features from the remaining mine sites of the South Downs is, where identified, often vague and inconclusive (cf. McNabb *et al* 1996, 28). It is of course possible that any form of shelter or covering building may, by reason of being merely a temporary construct, have left little trace in the archaeological record. In general terms, absence of clear structural features around the immediate area of the mine shafts may also be a result of the continual need to reposition shelters in order to accommodate new extraction pits (Topping 1997b, 127). The absence of defined shelters could of course explain why some flint working scatters are concentrated within the hollows of partially backfilled mine shafts, for these would certainly have provided some respite from the extreme forces of nature. This point was noted by Pull at Blackpatch.

> The extreme upper surfaces of filled shafts appear sometimes to have been utilised, usually after the completion of the first or coarse stage of silting. Shaft no 1 gave us an instance of this. A pile of animal bones, burnt flints and implements indicated a hearth site centrally situated in the great saucer-shaped depression over the pit. A similar accumulation of flint working and domestic debris, accompanied by hearth sites centred over other shafts, was located in the depressions. These all gave the appearance of the completely filled shafts having been utilised either for living quarters or at least for domestic purposes (Pull 1932a, 52).

Similar evidence for intensive burning and, possibly in-situ dumping of domestic waste was recorded within the upper levels of the Church Hill shafts, most notably within Shaft 5a.

Pull and Sainsbury were both convinced that a series of hollows examined to the east of the Blackpatch mines represented the remains of dwellings contemporary with the main phase of mine use. The evidence for these features, which were not recorded to the same level of detail as the mineshafts, floors and barrow sites, is unfortunately inconclusive. The finds seem to indicate some form of activity, related more to settlement than to extraction or manufacture, but the absence of any clear structural remains, such as postholes, stakeholes, pits or hearths, makes interpretation difficult. A similar series of features were noted as surface anomalies by Pull and Voice to the north-west of the main cluster of mines at Church Hill. At least two of these hollows were partially examined by Pull (1935a, 438) but no indication is given as to their nature or supposed date. The linear spread of surface hollows at Mount Carvey, High Salvington and Myrtlegrove and interpreted by Pull as the remains of prehistoric villages (1935b and c) may, as already indicated, alternatively represent additional areas of quarrying or flint extraction.

It is worth noting here, as a comparison to the Blackpatch and Church Hill data, the evidence recorded to the east of the flint mines of Easton Down in Wiltshire by J. F. S. Stone. Three 'dwelling pits', measuring around 3m in width and 0.7m in depth, were examined here in 1930 (Stone 1932). Five irregularly spaced postholes were recorded along the north and north-eastern edge of one of the cuts (Pit A1), and Stone suggested that a further three may have lain along the opposing edge. Finds from this feature included sherds from at least five Beaker vessels, flint tools including an end scraper and a burnt leaf-shaped arrowhead, burnt flint and animal bone. Between 1931 and 1932 a total of nine irregular-shaped hollows, measuring between 3m in width and 1.83m in length, bottoming at a depth of between 0.15 and 0.46m, were revealed by Stone at Easton Down and interpreted as the remains of dwellings (Stone 1933). All of the features had, at least partially, been surrounded by stakeholes measuring around 0.14m in width and 0.15m in depth. Stone did not provide a detailed description for each feature, but noted that each possessed a 'habitation layer', containing animal bone, firecracked flint, worked flint and pottery, at a depth of around 0.2m.

The absence of clear structural evidence from the Blackpatch and Church Hill features, as argued above, means that they cannot be viewed as buildings with any certainty. All appear, in their final phases, to have acted as repositories for domestic refuse, though this cannot be ultimately used to define primary function. The features do, however, bear a close resemblance in terms of shape, dimensions, artefact associations, siting and relationship to the mines, to the Easton Down examples which possess a clearer form of structural evidence in the form of an external setting of timber posts. This leaves us with a problem. The shallow features noted at all these sites do not appear to be related to flint extraction (none cut through flint seams), nor would they appear to have functioned well as sunken floor houses, but they do appear to relate to a phase of mining activity, albeit dated to the Later Neolithic. What is needed, at all three sites, is a more scientific and objective analysis of the buried remains in order to ascertain date, form and function. It has to be said, however, that on present evidence, the settlement hypothesis would appear compelling.

Two additional areas of potential contemporary settlement in close proximity to the Worthing mines should also be noted here. The first from New Barn Down, on the lower south-eastern slopes of Harrow Hill has often been referred to as a settlement contemporary with Neolithic mining activity (e.g. Curwen 1954, 112–3; Shepherd 1980, 145). The recorded features comprise an oval cut, measuring 1.8m x 2.6m and 0.6m deep, and a circular cut, measuring 1.2m in diameter and 0.2m deep (Curwen 1934b and c). Superficially the cuts resemble those investigated by Pull and Sainsbury at Blackpatch and Stone at Easton Down, but, without a clear idea as to the full extent and nature of the features, such a comparison can be taken no further.

The second site, at Church Hill and described by Pull and Voice as Hut Site 1, consisted of a shallow circular cut set within a larger oval ditch, both features containing evidence of internal postholes. Given that the smaller cut seems to impinge upon the western inner margins of the ditch, it is possible that the two features are in no sense contemporary. Preference may be given to the theory that the smaller circular cut indicates a phase of Later Neolithic (perhaps even post-mine) constructional activity, set within the area of a disused and partially backfilled enclosure ditch, and that the artefacts recovered from within the fill of the circular cut imply settlement. Whether this makes the feature a house in the traditional sense is therefore unclear. Given that there is no standard footprint for house structures of this period (cf. Darvill 1996, 90–8), the likelihood that the inner cut represents a type of domestic structure, set at the periphery of the mines, is perhaps more likely than not.

Ritual structures

At Blackpatch, a series of eleven round mounds and one ring ditch were investigated by John Pull. Ten of the structures, described by Pull as 'Barrows', were clearly Neolithic in origin, though one (Barrow 10), may well have been Saxon. None of the mounds possessed quarry ditches, material necessary for the construction of Barrows 1, 3, 6, 8 and 12 having been generated from chalk and flint rubble taken from the mines. Barrows 1, 3, 5, 6, 7 and 11 had further been covered or capped with a dense layer of mined flint. A similar deposit of floorstone had also apparently sealed the ditch of Barrow 9, the only non-mound Barrow feature at Blackpatch. Barrows 4, 5, 7, 10 and 11 were all composed of chalk, soil and flint which Pull and Sainsbury suggested had been 'scraped up' from the surrounding surface area. Evidence suggested that some of the Blackpatch Barrows had been constructed during a significant phase of flint extraction, Barrows 1, 3 and 12 being constructed directly over infilled mine shafts, the layers comprising Barrow 1 being indistinguishable from the fill of the shaft beneath it. The eastern layers constituting Barrow 12 had been further disrupted by the subsequent cutting of a shaft, spoil from this feature having been cast out over the margins of the Barrow mound.

A series of round mounds on Church Hill, to the north-west of those excavated at Blackpatch, and again described as 'Barrows', were examined by Pull around the neighbouring flint mining zone of Church Hill. Little detailed information exists concerning the majority of investigations here, but the first excavation at least indicates a basic similarity of form to the Blackpatch examples. Barrow 1 measured 4.3m in diameter and was composed of flints representing 'several tons of large waste' and slabs of tabular flint which had 'without doubt been brought from the neighbouring flint mines'. Beneath the flint rubble, a quantity of pottery, some of which could be identified as collared urn, a large amount of flint knapping debris, a small cremation and a flint knife were recorded.

The constructional form and material composition of the excavated Barrows of Blackpatch, has sometimes led to their dismissal as mere spoil heaps which occasionally contained burial elements (e.g. Drewett 1985, 419; Drewett *et al* 1988, 52). This is unfortunately missing the point somewhat, for although the majority of mounds were clearly created from mining debris, the evidence recorded by Pull suggests that such material had been carefully selected and structured. A second area of interpretational difficulty has been with regard to the diverse nature of human body parts recorded from within the structured mines: articulated skeletons from Barrows 3 and 12, disarticulated body parts from Barrows 4, 7 and 12, and cremated bone from Barrows 1, 3, 5, 6 and 11.

It is possible that marked differences between the deposition of human bodies and body parts at Blackpatch may represent the differing belief systems and ideology of varied human groups drawn to the extraction site by the prospect of flint extraction. Alternatively, it may be that, as with the linear mounds of the Earlier Neolithic, problems surrounding the nature and interpretation of perceived 'barrows' may stem from the automatic assumption that such structures were primarily designed for burial. As has already been noted, information retrieved from a number of Early Neolithic long mounds demonstrates that the disposal of human remains did not necessarily constitute the primary motive for the building of such earthworks. Sometimes the perceived importance of a mound appears to have lain with its construction, composition and location, rather than with any specific association with the dead and it is possible that earthen mounds, whether linear or round, represented a form of structured community archive or marker, in which the material essence of a certain social group was stored in order to lay claim to a particular area of land (e.g. Russell 1999, 94–113, 116–22).

The circular ditch of Barrow 9 at Blackpatch, containing disarticulated human bone, Beaker pottery and flint debitage, represents a feature that is more difficult to interpret with any certainty. The ditch, which encloses an area of 12.2m, originally possessed an external bank, something which could suggest henge affiliations (Russell 1996a, 28–9). Similar problems exist with regards to the outer ditch of Hut Site 1 at Church Hill, situated some 25m to the south-east of Shaft 4. Both Hut Site 1 and Barrow 9 appear to have been sealed, in their final phase, by a dense paving of freshly mined and unutilised flint, demonstrating clear contemporanity with a significant period of flint extraction.

The presence of additional anomalous enclosure sites at the periphery of mining zones may also be indicated at Cissbury by Enclosure II (Russell 1996a, 30–1) and the sites investigated by Mantell and Greenwell in the nineteenth century (Grinsell 1931, 39; Musson 1954, 108; Clarke 1970, 499; Kinnes and Longworth 1985, 141), and at Cock Hill, lying to the east of Harrow Hill (Russell 1996a, 19–20, 31). More convincing evidence of Later Neolithic/Early Bronze Age ceremonial activity on the South Downs has been provided by the excavation of a Beaker burial and post-circle at Pyecombe (Butler 1991), the discovery of a Class II henge monument at Mile Oak, Portslade (Russell in press a), and the identification of at least one Later Neolithic palisade monument of Dorchester-type beneath a Later Bronze Age cairn at Itford Hill, near Lewes (Holden 1972; Russell 1996a). Though work is still being conducted into the nature and extent of such sites, it is clear that the current distribution of Later Neolithic monuments indicates a small but discrete cluster of sites at the interface of the Worthing and Brighton Downs (Russell 1996c, 74–6). Such a clustering of sites may be coincidental, but it is interesting to note that the area is also one where Late Neolithic and Early Bronze Age rich graves (with exotic grave goods such as amber, faience and shale: Drewett *et al* 1988, 80–5), gold and copper (Gerloff 1974; Ellison 1978), flintwork and non-local stone tools (Gardiner 1984; 1990; Woodcock and Woolley 1986) appear to concentrate. This could indicate that either this zone was occupied at the end of the Neolithic by one of the more successful of communities operating within south-eastern England, or perhaps that the mine-clustered hills of the Worthing area continued to be respected or revered as places of ancestral activity, once they had ceased to be major areas of extraction.

Dating the Sussex mines

Radiocarbon chronologies

Problems surrounding the date of the Sussex mines have bedevilled archaeologists since the first recorded investigations in the mid nineteenth century. In an attempt to better place the flint mines within a national and chronological framework, samples of antler were, in the late 1960s, submitted to the British Museum for radiocarbon dating (Barker *et al* 1969). At Blackpatch a radiocarbon determination of 5090±150 BP (4350–3500 cal BC: BM–290) was obtained for an antler pick retrieved from a gallery within Shaft 4 (Barker *et al* 1969). Unfortunately the exact context of the pick within this shaft remains unknown, Shaft 4 being one of the least well documented of all pits examined by Pull during the Blackpatch excavations, with neither drawings nor textual description surviving in the Worthing Museum archive. Of all antler picks recovered from the Blackpatch mining site, this particular piece was therefore probably the least useful for dating. At Church Hill a series of antler picks were radiocarbon dated, providing a determination of 5340±150 BP (4500–3750 cal BC: BM–181). As the picks were derived from unidentified galleries within unidentified shafts (Barker *et al* 1969;

Pitts 1996, 360), their usefulness in dating a particular feature or phase of mining activity at Church Hill is again somewhat limited.

Antler picks from Harrison's examination of a gallery within Shaft 6 at Cissbury (Harrison 1878) were also examined and produced a radiocarbon date of 4730±150 BP (3950–3000 cal BC: BM–185). The exact position of these pieces within the mine had not unfortunately been fully recorded. Two further groups of antler picks from John Pull's excavations at Cissbury were radiocarbon dated, producing dates of 4720±150 BP (3950–3000 cal BC: BM–183) and 4650±150 BP (3800–2900 cal BC: BM-184). As these pieces were unstratified, though they may have derived from galleries within either Shaft 24 or 27 (or both), their usefulness in attempting to produce a secure chronology for specific periods of mining activity at Cissbury could be said to be negligible. A new series of radiocarbon determinations are at present being obtained by the RCHME for Shaft 27 at Cissbury, but are not available at the time of writing (see Barber *et al* in Press for details).

At Harrow Hill a series of radiocarbon determinations have been generated from material collected during all periods of archaeological examination. An antler pick from the Curwen's excavation of Pit 21 at Harrow Hill produced a date range of 4930±150 BP (4040–3370 cal BC: BM–182). Two pieces of antler from the basal deposits of Shaft 13, examined by Sieveking in 1982, have produced determinations of 4900±120 BP (4000–3350 cal BC: BM–2071R) and 5040±120 BP (4250–3500 cal BC: BM–2099R), whilst charcoal samples from the same fill have supplied a date range of 5020±110 BP (4050–3500 cal BC: BM–2075R).

The lack of a clear sampling strategy for the pieces examined to date, when combined with the poverty of accompanying contextual data means that the radiocarbon determinations provided for the Worthing mine series cannot be accepted in any more than a very general sense. In other words we may be reasonably sure that antler tools were being used at the sites by at least 4500 calendar years BC, and by implication that activity within some of the deeper mines was in progress at the same time, but we cannot say anything definitive with regard to the phasing of particular features, let alone make an attempt at sequencing and cross-comparing the four main areas of defined extraction. A far more efficient and systematic sampling strategy for antler and bone samples within the Sussex mine series must be devised before radiocarbon determinations may reasonably contribute to a detailed discussion regarding chronology and phasing (see also Barber *et al* in Press).

Artefactual evidence

Without any useful scientific dates to elucidate the mining sequence, we cannot construct a secure chronological framework for the development of the Worthing mine series or suggest when large scale extraction activity was terminated at each (see also the present arguments surrounding the datelist for the Grimes Graves site: Ambers in Longworth and Varndell 1996, 100–1). The stratigraphic and artefactual observations gathered from John Pull's excavations would, however, seem to suggest that some kind of extensive flint extraction continued at the Worthing minefields for longer than is currently accepted. Pull, in a manuscript now preserved in the Worthing Museum archive, explains the relationship between the mines and the Barrow sites examined at Blackpatch:

> The fact that the flint implements and other articles of grave furniture found in the burial mounds which are scattered among and near the Blackpatch mines, are of the same character and workmanship as similar articles found at the bottom of the pits and also upon the chipping floors is significant. It indicates that the chieftains whose remains these articles accompany were in some way directly connected with the mining.
>
> Barrows 1 and 3 were situated directly over filled in shafts. Their structure and contents coupled with the fact that the shafts beneath were unsilted, demonstrated conclusively that these grave mounds were contemporary with the mining industry. Discovery of the cremation beneath floor 2 and of the cremation in the infilling of Shaft 7, further strengthened the evidence. The exploration of Barrow 12 has added further testimony and has confirmed the conclusions drawn from previous work. For this mound and primary interment were later than Shaft 8 over which it was raised, and was earlier than the huge dump of mining debris heaped upon it on one side and the sinking of a shaft through its base on the other. Barrow 12 was undoubtedly intermine. It is true that it cannot be proved that the secondary interment of a crouched skeleton was made prior to the disturbance of the mound by mining operations which had taken place after its construction. It is, however, reasonable to infer that this secondary interment was made during the period occupied by the mining, for here again, flint implements and chalk carvings placed with the dead were exactly the same character as those from the mines themselves (Worthing Museum Acc. No. 1961/1585B)

At Blackpatch therefore, there are a series of clear stratigraphic relationships linking features containing collared urns and Beaker pottery with areas of large scale flint digging (see also Piggott 1954, 39). Similar observations may also be made for Barrows 1, 3, 5, 6, 7 and 9 at Blackpatch where unweathered and apparently unutilised floorstone flint appear to be integral to the final phases of activity (at Barrow 9 such a deposit emphatically sealed layers containing disarticulated human bone and Beaker pottery). The type of flint material described and recorded by Pull and Sainsbury in such circumstances can only have been derived from freshly excavated shafts and cannot be related to mere reuse of earlier waste dumps (e.g. Drewett *et al* 1988, 79). At Church Hill the evidence from Chipping Floor 2 and the ditch of Hut 1 provides a similar story, albeit on a smaller scale, of flint extraction continuing into the Beaker period. No such evidence has yet been located at Cissbury, where the only material post dating the Early Neolithic would appear to be the Beakers retrieved from nearby barrow mounds by antiquarian excavators (Grinsell 1931, 39; Musson 1954, 108; Clarke 1970, 499; Kinnes and Longworth 1985, 141).

It is clear that there were significant phases of Later Neolithic activity at Blackpatch and, to a lesser degree, at Church Hill during times of major phases of flint extraction. Whether such extraction involved the cutting of deep shafts similar to those of earlier periods, or whether flint was being extracted in lesser quarries or in open cast pits is as yet unknown, but the supposition that the Sussex mines ceased production by 3000 BC would appear untenable. The demise of the large causewayed enclosures upon the South Downs, the latest radiocarbon dates for which are at present 3650–3000 cal BC (I–11846; I–11847: Phase 2 at Whitehawk; Har 3596: Bury Hill), when combined with the apparent absence of any communal or ceremonial monuments of the Later Neolithic and Early Bronze Age has usually been taken to indicate that there was either a change in or a total collapse of, the basic structure of Neolithic society here at some point in the later 3rd millennium BC (Drewett 1977, 228; 1978; 23, 29). The data recorded by John Pull at Blackpatch and Church Hill, however, contradicts this social model, suggesting that, not only did extraction activity continue at these sites well into the 3rd millennium, but also that a new series of monument types were being constructed.

Final thoughts

The shafts from which deeply bedded flint was extracted in the Neolithic have often been simply categorised as economic constructs, associated with the earliest archaeologically detectable forms of heavy industry within the British Isles (cf. Piggott 1954, 36–7; Sieveking, 1979; Shepherd 1980; Drewett *et al* 1988, 60). Recent analysis of the context of stone tools as well as the recorded extraction sites and the material remains associated with them (e.g. Bradley and Edmonds 1993; Edmonds 1995; Whittle 1995; Topping 1997b; Russell 1999), has, however, prompted the suggestion that although the desire to generate sufficient flint suitable for the manufacture of certain tool types presumably provided one of the motivating forces behind the digging of shafts so that 'the range of non-functional features and deposits...suggest that ceremonial or ritual formed a significant part of the extraction process' (Topping 1997b).

It is important to be aware that we cannot judge the Neolithic mine sites by the standards or mindset of today's urbanised society. They cannot be treated as simple industrial monuments or functional constructs in the same way that today one may treat a modern coal, tin or gold mine. These sites were operated within a landscape dominated by non-functional, and, to the modern mind, non-rational activities. Shafts, though often consigned to the footnotes of prehistoric research (Shepherd 1980, vii), may be viewed as being just as important, from the perspective of monumental architecture, as the long mound or the ditched enclosure. Consideration of the less obvious aspects of Neolithic flint extraction, such as the siting of shafts, the experience of being deep underground (figure 126), the symbolic nature of extraction, the significance of carvings, non-functional artefact deposition, human burial etc. may provide us with an alternative way of visualising, conceptualising and understanding the prehistoric mining process (Russell 1999, 29–63, 123–8; Russell in Press c).

The work of publishing the data recorded from excavations at the Sussex flint mine sites will probably never be finished. That may seem a bizarre statement to make at the very end of a book purporting to represent the results of archaeological fieldwork spanning more than 30 years, but, from the point of view that much data, especially relating to the artefactual assemblage, remains lost, misplaced or in the hands of private collectors, then it is probably true. Given this observation, and the likelihood that additional data, drawings, finds and information will continue to emerge (cf. Butler 1992), then our understanding and interpretation of the Worthing group of Sussex mines will constantly be undergoing change. Having set this apparently pessimistic tone, it is heartening to reflect that this text now represents, to date, the

Figure 126. A final view of the mines: looking out from gallery iv into the main area of Shaft 1 at Blackpatch following the completion of the excavation in 1922 (© Worthing Museum and Art Gallery).

most definitive account of the Neolithic flint mines of the South Downs and something which, not only completes a large body of unpublished archive data, but which also underlines and makes accessible the achievements of John Pull and his colleagues.

So much for the backlog; what of the future? Reports upon the artefactual assemblages derived from the Sussex mine sites and the conclusions drawn from them will, as already been noted, be published separately, in a companion volume (Russell in prep). With regard to the mine sites themselves, a comprehensive programme of survey work is currently being co-ordinated by the Royal Commission on the Historical Monuments of England as part of the Industry and Enclosure in the Neolithic Project (Topping 1996b; Donachie and Field 1994; Field 1997a and b; http://www.rchme.gov.uk). This project looks set to revolutionise our current perception of Neolithic mining sites, and, when published (Barber *et al* in Press), should allow a better understanding of how well the sites survive and how they are perceived today. Once complete, further understanding of these flint extraction areas may best be advanced through a new programme of excavation and analysis. In conclusion, I leave the final word to John Pull:

> I think that I am justified in saying that the Blackpatch excavations have made our knowledge of prehistoric flint mining wider and deeper than was the case prior to the investigation of the site, and I trust that the years of work spent upon this field may be of help to students of the history of mankind (Pull 1932a, 147).

Appendix 1

DISCOVERY AND DESCRIPTION OF THE FLINT MINE AREA AT BLACKPATCH

by J. H. Pull (Worthing Museum Acc. No. 1961/1585)

On the 14th May 1922 a hitherto unexamined and unrecorded series of depressions was discovered by Mr H. Bunce and myself as a direct result of an archaeological examination of Blackpatch Hill for traces of primitive occupation. Blackpatch is an elevation of the chalk rising 500 feet above the ordnance datum. It is situated in the parish of Patching, one and a half miles north of Clapham and two and a half miles West of Findon. The hill is united by a low ridge on the north-east to the main escarpment of the Downs at a point a little to the south of Storrington. On the East and south it is bounded by the Long Furlong valley, and on the West by a deep traverse valley which branches from the Long Furlong through Mitchelgrove.

The upper slopes of the down are covered with short springy turf and extensive growths of juniper and bramble. Two deep coombes or short dry valleys cut into the south and west of the hill dividing it into three gently sloping spurs or ridges. Along the crest of the central or south-west spur runs the old, and now for the most part grass grown coaching road from Clapham to Storrington. A little to the West of this road, 1,300 yards north, north-east from its junction with the long Furlong main road, and at an elevation between 300 and 400 feet are situated the prehistoric flint workings which I am now about to describe.

The area covered by what have since proved to be prehistoric flint workings includes saucer shaped depressions in the hillside, ranging from 10 to 40 feet in diameter, and from one to five feet in depth. About the rims of these depressions and between them are low mounds raised above the natural contour of the ground. The whole are grouped closely and irregularly within a space measuring 230yds north and south, by 110 yards east and west. In the centre of this area rises a large mound presumed at the time to be a round barrow. Depressions, mounds and barrow are thickly covered with turf and a large proportion of their area is infringed by a scrubby juniper.

On first inspection of the site it was concluded that the depressions marked the sites of filled in shafts of flint mines. The mounds around them were considered to represent surplus material which had not been returned to the worked out pits. The supposed barrow which is 42 feet in diameter at the base and five feet in height presents the appearance of having been constructed at a date subsequent to the filling in of the pits, as its base infringes and surmounts several depressions. The opinion that the depressions indicated flint mines was one formed by comparison. The depressions here were exactly the same in appearance, and to some extent in dimensions, to those which mark the primitive mining sites of Cissbury and Grimes Graves. Subsequent examination of the surface soil, in and about them, where exposed by mole casts and rabbit holes, produced evidence which considerably strengthened that opinion. Quantities of artificial flint flakes were found, and a large steep-sided implement. The flakes compared favourably with those which litter the vicinity of the mines at Cissbury. They were sharp, unabraded, and patinated universally white. Some of the Primary flakes were very large and indicative of being struck from flint nodules of free flaking quality which do not occur naturally upon the surface. Small secondary chippings indicated skilful, delicate and patient labour. The implement can be matched with one found in a Cissbury flint mine, and which is in my own collection.

The presence of such abundant traces of humanly worked flint in the vicinity of the pits called for deeper investigation. The owners of the ground, the Trustees of the Duke of Norfolk, were informed of the nature of the find and their permission was sought to make an excavation. This was readily granted on their behalf. The director of his Majesty's Geological Survey, also the head of the Department of British Antiquities of the British Museum were advised of the discovery. On June 16th the excavation of one of the largest of the depressions was embarked upon by Mr Bunce and myself. Since that date it has been our privilege to lift a small but very interesting corner of the mantle of green turf which veils the past unwritten history, of a primitive England.

A great deal of new information and evidence on the subject of prehistoric mining has been found as a result, and a good deal of previous information confirmed. I trust that the evidence contained in the report which follows will enable us in the future perhaps to temporarily galvanise the dry bones of prehistoric archaeology into animation and make us competent to reconstruct the outlines of an industry and culture practised and attained by a long forgotten people.

The digging of Shaft 1

The method employed by us in the excavation of the flint mine at Blackpatch hereafter referred to as Shaft No 1, has proved as successful and satisfactory, as the conditions enforced by having only spare time to devote would permit. The depression selected for exploration was, as has been previously stated, one of the largest in the area. Situated north-east of the supposed tumulus, six other large depressions lay immediately near it on the north, north-east, east, south-west, and west. The depression was oval in plan and surrounded by a low mound or rim of irregular height. The ground to the north, west and east was covered by juniper bushes which afforded throughout the excavation some small shelter from the severities of weather.

Work was commenced by Mr Bunce and myself on June 18th and we continued it alone until August 5th. It was first necessary to map the position of the depression. This was accomplished by first fixing the position of the supposed tumulus upon the ordnance survey, and having completed this, recording the position of the pit relative to the mound. The undisturbed cup was then measured from crown to crown of the surrounding rim and found to be 38 feet east by west by 31 feet north by south, its greatest depth being two feet 10 inches. A plan of it was next drawn to scale, a steel rod driven into the centre of the cup, and stakes driven into the north, south, east and west edges served to mark the cardinal points. Lines were next stretched across the diameter, from these stakes dividing the cup into four equal quadrants, NE – SE – SW – and NW.

It having been previously decided to treat the excavation as that of a flint mine until we should find any reason to discard that supposition, our first objective was to ascertain the presence of a shaft beneath. In the case of one existing it was essential to discover if possible how it had been filled in. Consequently it was determined to remove but a quarter of the filling at a time, and to make sectional drawings, as the work proceeded. As we had but little to guide us, as to the extent, and no idea whatever of the depth of our presumed shaft, no previous excavations having been made here, the removal of our first quadrant of infilling was destined to be more or less a step into the dark. South of the line dividing the north and south halves of the cup the turf and surface soil were removed to a distance of 8ft from the centre rod. In doing this a quantity of flint nodules, flakes and chippings, together with finished and partially finished implements, cooking stones and bones were unearthed. This occurred mostly in a pile about the centre. A similar central accumulation has often been noticed immediately beneath the turf in many other flint mining areas.

A deep and narrow trench was next dug from the centre to the East, having for its northern boundary the line east and west. The purpose of this trench being to ascertain the lip of the shaft. The solid chalk lip was reached in that direction 10 feet from the centre, and an important fact established. The surrounding mound of our pit was found to consist of chalk rubble thrown out at the time of the primary excavation. The surface soil and turf, a few inches in thickness, extended over it in every direction, but so difficult was it to trace the old surface beneath, that we concluded that the old surface through which our shaft had been sunk, had been removed for some distance beyond the actual mouth. This is still a point which the digging of many sections alone can confirm.

The chalk edge having been found on the East, a second trench was dug from the centre towards the south, having for its western boundary the line north and south. On finding the chalk lip in that direction, the two trenches, at first only two feet in depth, were depended to 6 feet, and the total infilling of the south-east quadrant removed to a level floor at that depth. After a few days work on this section, it became apparent that we were dealing with a roughly circular shaft, and one not nearly so large as the indicating depression had led us to believe. The portion of the shaft wall exposed was vertical and in good condition, showing no signs of ever having crumbled by exposure. It was noticed from the vertical sections exposed, that it had been filled in with tips of chalk rubble, presumably excavated from neighbouring shafts, and that these tips had been thrown in from several different directions.

On June 21st a preliminary report upon the discovery and excavation at Blackpatch was forwarded to the secretary of the Worthing Archaeological Society. By June 24th the Black Band (layer 4) and the flaking floor (layer 7) had been uncovered. So much had been found, and so conspicuous had become the work by reason of the white chalk thrown out, that it was deemed necessary as protective measure to cover the excavation by a publication. This appeared in London and provincial papers on June 27th. By the time the greater portion of the south-east sector had been removed a ladder was brought into use, and as the surrounding hillside was then being utilised for the purpose of grazing sheep, a wire fence was erected on the sides unprotected by bushes. A public notice board was also erected as a precaution against accidents.

By July 18th a good start had been made on the south-west sector on infilling. Mr H. J. Osborne White on behalf of the Geological survey, first visited the pit on this date, as did also the President and Earthworks Committee of the Worthing Archaeological Society, when material assistance with the work was offered and readily accepted. Mr Osborne White carefully examined the portion of the solid chalk wall of the shaft, exposed on the south-east and having identified the chalk zone, and duly noted that no horizontal vein of flint had yet been encountered, expressed his opinion that one would be met with in the next few feet. As the first flint seam would probably give a key to the depth of the shaft in question, he suggested the advisability of sinking a trial hole below the 6ft level arrived at in search of it. Unlike, perhaps most good advice, his suggestion was immediately put into practice. On July 21st operating alone I sank the trial hole, and 8ft from the surface found the shaft wall undercut considerably. At 9ft the head of the gallery, now known as gallery 4 was uncovered, the floor of which appeared to be about 11ft from the surface. All doubts as to our shaft being that of a flint mine were now at an end, and the exceeding shallow depth promised an excavation of little difficulty.

The gallery entrance was recovered and the trial hole filled in temporarily, it being considered advisable to conceal its presence and to refrain from exploring any workshops until the rest of the infilling of the shaft had been removed to a level floor at 6ft. The process of removing the south-west sector of infilling was next proceeded with, and almost completed by August 5th, though the Western edge of the shaft had not been met with, the large blocks constituting layers 3 and 5 being very difficult to cut through. By August 5th the help promised by the committee of the Worthing Archaeological Society was forthcoming and the work greatly accelerated thereby. The removal of the north-west quadrant was commenced on this date.

On August 9th hoisting apparatus in the form of a large tripod, carrying a wheel, fall, and baskets was erected over the pit. Work progressed steadily, accompanied by continual finds of flint implements, pieces of red deer antler, bones and the like. The north-west sector was the fourth and last to be removed and the whole of the shaft had been cleared to a level floor at 6ft by September 6th, the heads of no fewer than 7 galleries radiating from its base then exposed. On commencing the removal of the north-west sector the central steel rod which acted as our datum point from which to register finds, was supplemented by an additional rod driven into the surface of the south-east lip of the pit. The removal of the next five feet of rubble below the level floor, and the exploration and clearing of the galleries occupied our time until January 6th.

As we were working at the excavation on two afternoons a week only, it became a necessity, if we were to prevent removal, defacement or contamination of evidence by casual visitors, to thoroughly explore each gallery in turn separately, to secure all articles of interest lying exposed on the floors and to note the special characteristics and condition of the walls and roofs. It was also essential to continue and complete the sectional drawings of the infilling of the shaft which had been made on the removal of each sector.

To accomplish these various objectives each gallery was entered by sinking a narrow trench from its opening, toward the centre of the shaft, exploring it immediately enough material had been removed to enable access to be gained, and afterwards extending the sides of the trench until comfortable with the section lines. As most of the galleries were partially filled with chalk rubble and large blocks, the task of clearing them away became a heavy one. The roofs of the galleries were rarely more than 3ft in height and work in such a contracted position as it was necessary to assume could not be carried out with any degree of rapidity. As the work in the open shaft continued however the clearing of the galleries became less difficult. Galley 1 was opened on September 9th and partially cleared of debris, enabling the position and quality of the flint seamed worked to be observed, also the depth of the shaft floor from the surface, presuming it to be on a level with this gallery floor.

Gallery 2 was opened on September 16th, and partially cleared. Mr Reginald Smith of the British Museum visited the excavation on this date and reviewed the flint implements so far found. Gallery 3 was opened on Sept 27th, gallery 4 on October 7th. On October 11th when removing blocks on the East side of the gallery 4 a communication was uncovered leading into gallery 5. Gallery 5 was as a result explored from the communication on this date. On October 18th it was getting late in the year, and chances of bad weather greatly increasing, members of the Worthing Archaeological Society were given facility to view the work, and a brief description of the excavation was given by me. Gallery 7 was opened on October 21st and gallery 6 on November 11th.

From this date the time was occupied in clearing the debris from the workings. Having exposed the whole of the shaft's floor, doubts of its solidity were entertained. Subsequently two holes or sumps filled with rubble and presenting a compacted surface were cleared. One opposite the entrance to gallery 3 and one opposite the entrance to gallery 5. The empty shaft was later photographed and surveyed. Throughout the digging the greatest care was taken not to mark the walls of the shaft or galleries with our tools. As a result the pit on completion of the work presented in every detail the appearance which it had before being filled in by the miners. The only tool marks exhibited on the chalk face were primitive and original, exception only being taken in respect of some made during our absence from the work, over the entrance of galleries 4 and 5 by some youthful and mischievous intruder.

Several drawn sections were made of the galleries showing their infilling. All objects of interest found during the work were recorded in a note book at the time, with particulars as to the layer of infilling in which they had occurred, depth from the datum point and position from the centre rod, and were transported home the same way. The position of the centre rod was originally indicated according to the points of the compass. This method was later substituted by another much easier for the inexperienced helpers to adopt. The north was twelve o'clock, and the points of the compass arranged into hours and half hours. Thus an implement found 7ft NE of the centre was recorded, as occurring 7ft from centre at half past one, and a deer horn pick found at 5ft 6in north-west by west from centre was recorded as occurring 5ft 6in at 10 o'clock. The hours of the clock being much more familiar and easier to remember than the lesser divisions of the compass.

From the outset the material excavated was carefully looked over a second time after having been thrown out. In this way many of the smaller objects of interest which would have otherwise been overlooked were recovered. Samples of the layers of infilling which consisted of any soil other than chalk rubble were taken and preserved. Special attention was devoted to the land mollusca and charcoal fragments. Geological specimens such as fossils, pebbles, iron pyrites, etc., were carefully preserved. Every piece of flint found in the mine was cleaned and examined. The implements were numbered on the spot in pencil and afterwards in indelible ink, a separate record of them being kept. Samples of flakes, chipped pieces and nodules were retained, the remainder being placed in a heap together on the surface. This heap was afterwards resorted with good results. Blocks of chalk bearing primitive tool marks were set aside in the depression of a neighbouring pit, face downwards to protect the markings from the weather. Later they were transferred to one of the galleries, and the best selected and sawn up, into small pieces for convenience of transportation. Plaster casts of tool marks on the walls of the shaft, and galleries, were taken, and in some special instances photographs of such marks were obtained.

Acknowledgements

To Mr A. Mann for his reliable assistance in many directions, but particularly for his excellent photographs of the shaft and galleries. To the President, Committee and Members of the Worthing Archaeological Society for the whole hearted support of the excavation and to all those who assisted with the digging and the work generally.

Appendix 2

REPORT UPON THE SECOND EXCAVATION MADE AT THE PREHISTORIC FLINT MINING STATION AT CHURCH HILL, FINDON, SUSSEX: 1946–1947–1948

by J. H. Pull and A. R. Voice (Worthing Museum Acc. No. 1961/1584)

In November 1945, following the withdrawal of Hill forces from their wartime occupation of the Hill, an inspection of the partially explored area occupied by the flint mines and flint workshops was made by us. It was found that, apart from the sinking of a deep revetted and sand bagged dug out in Shaft 2, and the cutting of a slit trench in the south-west of the area near Shaft 4, little damage had been done to the prehistoric site. No high explosive bombs had been dropped here, nor had any part of the hill been used by our defence units as a range for explosive missiles. A most fortunate state of affairs indeed.

The old survey of the prehistoric station was checked by us at this time. An entirely new map was prepared forthwith and some additional details added. Certain portions of the site were then selected for future excavation. These included the poorly indicated pits marked off on the new map as B, C, D, E, F and G; the large round barrow at the SE edge of the mining area (Barrow No 4), and the two mine shafts in the extreme SW of the area P4 and P5; also the faintly indicated circle marking what has since proved to be a hut site with an outer fenced compound.

It was decided to excavate the shaft P4 first, especially on account of the presence of the open slit trench dug by the army which almost reached the lip of the depression indicating the shafts existence. A preliminary trial hole was sunk into the SW quarter of this shaft's surface at this time. Pottery fragments and flint implements found within two feet of the turf line in this investigation gave great promise of things to come. During the war years the ownership of Church Hill had changed, as also had the farm tenancy, so negotiations were offered with the new owner C. E. J. Hartridge Esq. of Findon Place and also with the tenant farmer Mr J. Langmead of Yapton, for permission to dig upon the site. This permission was most readily granted by both owner and tenant.

The Excavation of Shaft No 4

In the early days of April 1946, the depression indicating Shaft 4, together with the surrounding spoil banks, were surveyed in detail. A scale plan and sectioned drawings were prepared and duly added to as the excavation of the pit in vertical depth proceeded. The area round the pit was next securely fenced, a permanent datum point was established and digging began.

The SW quadrant of the shafts surface filling was first dealt with, use being made of the army's silt trench to undercut the turf and surface soil. The turf and soil were first totally removed from this quadrant and following this were finally removed over the whole of the shafts surface. The turf and soil attained a maximum depth of 1ft over the centre of the shaft, thinning to 3 inches at the sides. Immediately underlying the surface soil at the shafts centre was a flint-chipping floor (layer 3), Floor No 11. This consisted of an uninterrupted spread of flint flakes and chippings both primary and secondary in character, with which were admixed waste flint nodules and flint implements in all stages of completion. This floor was found to extend over the whole of the southern half of the shaft and beyond the shafts edge to the east to a distance of six feet in that direction, it also extended four feet beyond the shafts edge to the south and five feet beyond it to the west.

On the northern edge of the shaft was a large spoil bank which proved to consist of chalk blocks probably thrown out by the miners when sinking the shaft immediately to the north of shaft 4. This dump of mining debris partially overlay Floor 11 on the north and west sides forming layer 2 indicated in the sectional drawing. Floor 11 rested upon the rainwash zone layer 4. This consisted of a mass of highly consolidated chalk silt one foot deep in the centre of the shaft and nearly two feet deep in the north-east quarter. In the base of the rainwash were found fragments of a zoned and cord ornamented B type Beaker and fragments of at least three overhanging rim urns. Two broken picks of red deer antler, a fragmentary shoulder bade shovel and numerous flint implements including a very fine celt, also the tooth of a dog. The removal of the shafts infilling in quadrants was maintained until a total depth of 8 feet from the surface was reached, and the solid walls of the shaft were laid bare. The various layers of infilling met with down to this depth are shown in the sectional drawings and they are described together with the finds made in them in the appendix.

It was now December and the exceptionally severe winter set in which prevented further work for nearly six months. This period of continued frost attended by unusually thick falls of snow turned out to be very instructive. The shaft infilling at the depth reached by us when the winter set in consisted of large loose chalk rubble and chalk blocks, the interstices between which were not filled in. Our excavated material was filled upon the surface all round the rim of the shaft. When we recommenced operations after the cold spell following the melting of the snow and successive heavy rains, it was observed that nearly one foot of consolidated silting had formed in the shaft. Three factors had contributed to the formation of this silt.

1) The breaking up of the exposed surface of the chalk rubble infilling.
2) Chalk and soil which had crumbled from the shaft walls.
3) Chalk and soil that had drifted back into the pit from the sloping piles of debris on the surface round its rim.

Thus we were provided with an excellent illustration of the length of time taken and the conclusions necessary to produce a reasonable quantity of rapid silting in excavations made in the soft upper chalk strata.

In April 1947, serious work was again commenced on the removal of the shafts infilling. The work proceeded slowly until the 15th of May when the base of the shaft was reached on the east side. There were no signs of undercutting or of gallery entrances here. On the 28th of July, Mr A. Voice, working with two others of our digging party, exposed the deep undercut of the high level working on the north-west side of the shaft. Monday August 4th saw the discovery of the first deep seam gallery – No 1. This was entered and exposed on Saturday August 9th at 8pm. On Saturday September 13th, work was taken up by a large digging party which included the Enfield Scouts under Mr John George, and Gallery 2 on the south-east of the shaft was extended and partially exposed. From this date onwards, to the middle of December, the digging was intensified and Gallery's 3, 4 and 5 were opened up on the south-west, west and north-west Shaft. The final removal of the shaft infilling was completed in the early months of 1948.

Appendix 3

SKELETON OF BRITAIN'S MOST ANCIENT MINER FOUND BENEATH A FALL OF ROCK

By J. H. Pull (Worthing Museum 1961/1586)

For over thirty years the writer has been engaged upon the investigation of the Blackpatch and Church Hill mines and is now, on behalf of the Worthing Archaeological Society, conducting excavations on that part of the Cissbury mining area which lies on land belonging to the Borough of Worthing, just outside Cissbury Camp. This portion of the mine field has never been examined. A survey of it was made last year, when some sixty four of the pits were mapped. Preliminary surface excavations were then carried out. A particular depression in the surface surrounded by turf-grown mining dumps was selected for further excavation. The depression was found to cover a vertical shaft of small diameter descending into the hillside.

At two feet from the surface a number of flint implements were found including a beautifully fashioned flint axe head. Down to nearly eight feet from the surface the shaft was found to be filled with consolidated chalk silt which had been sludged in from the surrounding surface dumps by rain, snow and melting ice of the centuries. Below this naturally accumulated material, the infilling consisted of Chalk debris that had been introduced from the workings of other shafts round about at the actual time when mining was going on. In this contemporary filling, at ten feet from the surface, Mr Salisbury, a member of the working party, found a very fine leaf-shaped arrowhead of flint. So far no arrowhead of any description has ever occurred before in any English prehistoric mine. This one, being a type predominant in long barrows and Neolithic camps of the Windmill Hill kind such as the Trundle and Whitehawk, gave an indication of an early date for the flint mine we were working on.

As we proceeded down the shaft with our excavation further references to a date prior to 2000 BC became evident. The shells of the Bush Snail of gigantic size were recovered, indicating a very wet phase of climate known to have existed about that time. At 14 feet from the surface we found bones representing practically the whole of the skeleton of an ox, together with some bones of a pig. These had been thrown into the abandoned and disused shaft from some hearth site near the surface. Some of the bones had been charred in the fire and some split to obtain the marrow. We had by now uncovered the higher portion of a collapsed entrance arch to a horizontal gallery which had been driven by the miners from the west side of the shaft. The excavation of Shaft 27 had been commenced by us on the 1st of March, the work being mostly done at the weekends and sometimes in the evenings, by a band of members of the Worthing Archaeological Society, many of whom had been working at Church Hill in previous years.

On the evening of Wednesday the 27th of May, Mr John Lucas, Mrs Lalor and myself were working in the pit at fifteen feet from the surface. Mr Lucas was digging near the western gallery entrance, where we were just able to see onto that underground working. The rock at the entrance was noted to be shattered and in very bad condition. About 7pm Mr Lucas gave a shout. I was at the entrance, hauling up on the derrick. He had found the feet and lower part of the legs of a human skeleton lying beneath the rubble of the partly broken down archway. I immediately realised that we had stumbled upon what I had always hoped for, one of the old flint miners, who had met with a fatal accident at his work and whose body had never been recovered by his friends.

We carefully covered up the exposed bones and concealed them with large blocks of chalk. The problems presented by our find were considerable and the extraction of the skeleton was pressing and urgent. A careful examination of the underground drift showed it to be part of a maze of lateral workings perforating the chalk rock in the direction of other shafts to the west and south of ours. The rock had been so extensively undercut close to our shaft that the mine pillar had become unsafe and a further serious fall of rock threatened immediately. Moreover, the conditions were now dry, but the glass was falling and I knew that a spell of rain would make the bones very fragile and the whole work of getting them out much more difficult. Also none of us were able to be present at the excavation at the whole time and I was much concerned lest the pit should be entered by any unauthorised person who might negotiate the fence. The next day was spent getting everything ready to get this important skeleton out. Friday afternoon and evening were to be the appointed time.

On Friday the 29th we commenced operations at 4pm. First we inserted what temporary timber struts we could to hold back the shattered rock on the left-hand wall. Then slowly we began to uncover the bones. The large material in the fall of the chalk which had been responsible for this mining tragedy so long ago was removed by us with our hands alone, the smaller material with pocket knives and soft brushes. The skeleton was found to be lying right across the entrance to the drift on the left side with the knees flexed and the thighs crossed. Three large blocks had killed the man. One had smashed his face, another had driven his right hand into his chest, and broken the left humerus, a third had broken his back just above the pelvis.

Photographs were taken at frequent intervals during the uncovering of the bones. By seven o'clock the whole skeleton had been laid bare and Dr Densham was able to examine it as it lay. A very small man with a very long and narrow skull and excellent teeth, probably in his late twenties. A quite different racial type to the Belgian flint miner found near Spiennes. Yes he was of our Neolithic British people, representative of the Mediterranean race of Sergi. The leaf shaped arrowhead previously found in our shaft is a hallmark of his culture. In his right hand was a mass of charcoal, possibly the remains of a torch he was holding when he met his death. What a find. His long bones were perfect and accurate measurements can be made.

Two hours of daylight were now left to us in which to get the bones out, wrapped and packed up ready for removal. We accomplished this final part of our task in an hour and a half, all the time expecting the shaft wall to cave in upon us. The skull was resting on a block of chalk to which there was some adherence. On lifting it the chalk block was found to be stained brown, probably from iron oxide from his blood. The head was lying lower than the feet and most of the bleeding at the time of death must have been from the head. By 10.15pm his bones were safely deposited in Worthing Museum. England's oldest miner and one of Worthing Boroughs first inhabitants had had his first motor car ride. Now his remains will become the subject of a prolonged scientific inquest. The whole task of getting this skeleton out of its precarious position in the mine to a place of safety was one of the most gruelling I have ever experienced. A great tribute is due to the whole of the working party who took part. Everyone executed his job magnificently and I am sure they will never forget the archaeological experience of that evening in May high on the Sussex Downs. Here are their names: Mr L. Bickerton, Dr R. Densham, Mr J. Lucas, Mr K. Walker, Mr E. Salisbury, Mr K. Suckling, Mr V. Bridle, Mr T. S. Sutton, Mr Sprott and Mr A. Jewell.

Appendix 4

CISSBURY EXCAVATIONS 1956

by J. H. Pull (Worthing Museum Acc. No. 1961/1586)

Severe frosts and snow of the winter of 1955–56 did great damage to the two Shafts opened by us. About 8 feet of chalk rubble which had sealed off the sides of the shafts had accumulated in them and the diameter of the shafts had increased by over 3 feet. This was instructive in so much that it gave us a clear idea of the rapid rate with which these shafts in the chalk could fill up by natural agencies.

With our contracted digging party it was nearly midsummer before we got the shafts cleared and communicating south and south-west levels shored up with iron and timbers. The very wet Summer and Autumn gave us poor opportunity for pushing on with the extended exploration of the deep levels, but we did eventually force an entrance into the long and wide southward extension of them. The main southern level was found to go on a further 25 feet into the base of another filled in shaft which is well indicated by a big depression on the surface. A branch to the left of this level obviously communicates with another shaft to the south-east of ours.

A survey of the extremely dangerous state of the whole of the southern area owing to fault shattering in the rock which may well have taken place since the workings were originally operated, convinced us that it would be unwise to attempt to clear this underground area from the shafts opened. So we decided to close the excavation and filling in will, as soon as weather permits, be proceeded with. Had the condition of the chalk rock at Cissbury been as good as it was at Church Hill, we might have had a different story up to tonight, but considering the bad shape that these old mines at Cissbury are in, we have I think been lucky to get away with what we have without an accident of any kind.

The excavation at Cissbury has given us some new information with regard to the mining people of the closing phase of the Stone Age and strongly confirmed other information obtained by us at Blackpatch and Church Hill, particularly the fact that the miners were a mixed people with a very mixed culture. Further, the mining methods were very much the same as those practised on the other Sussex mine fields so far excavated in as much as the whole economy of the mining was obviously based on the fact that they had no means of illuminating their underground workings by artificial light and the shafts were worked in groups of three or four at a time, many of the shafts having been sunk solely for the purpose of letting daylight into the lower levels.

In view of the excavation of the newly discovered mining site at Longdown which Mr Salisbury has undertaken, we have decided, with the approval of the Committee of this Society, to transfer the apparatus which we have at Cissbury and our helpers to that site and support Mr Salisbury in what promises to be a long and very important exploration.

Appendix 5

SELECTED CORRESPONDENCE FROM THE JOHN PULL COLLECTION HELD BY WORTHING MUSEUM *(ACC. NO. 1961/1584–6)*

1 'ANTIQUARY' to the Worthing Herald, November 17th 1923

Sir – without wishing to discourage or disparage in any way the work done by young enthusiasts in connection with Blackpatch, it seems necessary to issue a word of caution in connection with excavations and 'researches' which have recently been made. A careful perusal of the article entitled 'Bronze Age tumulus reopened' makes an experienced archaeologist wonder whether the mound is a tumulus at all; so far, not a scrap of evidence has been produced to show that it is, while to put it down as of the Bronze Age with an entire lack of relics other than a flint flake, is certainly unjustified, and in view of an attempt to date an adjoining mine shaft by calling this mound a Bronze Age tumulus is going to result in the science of archaeology being looked upon as fiction.

In the article in your impression of November 3 it is stated: 'If however these workings do undermine the position of the tumulus this would offer further evidence of the mound being undoubtedly post-mine.' I presume that by 'undermine', 'underlying' is meant, but why the word 'if' when the accompanying sketch distinctly shows that the mine shaft is below the mound? It is unfortunate that a little essay is given to us on the proper way to open a mound, and then to follow this by admitting that what is termed the reopening of this tumulus was merely a trench cut into it on one half day. Surely this is much an attempt at 'looting' as the old method of digging a hole in the centre and filling it in again. If the correct method to open a barrow is to remove the top entirely and then replace it, and this was not possible, surely it would have been better to have left it alone until such time that it could be properly examined, rather than complicate the work of future excavators by making this hurried trench. This, of course, is assuming that the mound is a burial place.

May I suggest that important sites of this character should be opened under the supervision of experienced people, or under the supervision of some society, and not by those who have no experience whatever? I believe I am correct in stating that the people who cut the trench into this alleged tumulus had no previous experience of opening a tumulus of this character and therefore quite likely failed to notice evidences which would have been detected by experienced hands. Reference is made to an engraved flint said to have been described in the 'Herald Magazine' some time ago. This discovery may be of the greatest possible importance, or, on the other hand, it may be the result of somebody's joke. In any case it is essential that more than a mere reference to an engraved flint should be made in view of the scarcity of objects of this sort, and the fact that recent discoveries of a like kind have been questioned.

May I suggest that the specimen should be exhibited in some place where it can be examined? In addition to which an illustrated description would be welcome in your pages. So far I have failed to find anyone who has seen it or knows anything about it, but the fact that it is now made public, necessitates further information being available. What possible comparison there is between the alleged tumulus at Blackpatch and one found near Grimes Graves in 1914 is difficult to see. (I have before me the section given in your paper and the 'proceedings' of the society in question, which can be consulted at the Worthing Public Library.)

2 Herbert Toms to the Worthing Herald, November 24th 1923

Sir – Enquiries prompt me to make it quite clear that I am not the author of the 'Blackpatch' communication printed in your issue of the 17th inst. It is most unfortunate that 'antiquary' has placed himself at the top of such a lofty ('experienced') pedestal in order to shout at 'young enthusiasts' below, for such a tactless proceeding is hardly likely to further the cause of archaeology. Enthusiasm for field work and record, such as Mr Pull and his colleagues have shown, is by no means common; and, if there be in the district archaeologists of wider experience and riper judgement, then from them should emanate encouragement and sincere criticism when necessary, rather than badly veiled snubs and censure. Mr Pull is not the first mortal who, having dug into a barrow like structure and found no evidence of an interment, has announced the thing as a tumulus. One knows even 'experienced archaeologists' who have set 'young enthusiasts' an example by doing the same sort of thing. Mr Pull need have no fear that his contribution to the Herald 'is going to result in the science of archaeology being looked upon as fiction' for that result has been already but too well achieved by the writings of 'experienced archaeologists'.

3 John Pull to the Worthing Herald, 24th November 1923

Sir – May I be permitted to reply to the letter signed 'Antiquary' which appeared in the 'Herald Magazine' of November 17? In the first instance one cannot help deploring the fact that 'antiquary' has not the courage to come out under his (or her) own signature. Had 'antiquary' not remained incognito one would have been able to judge whether or not 'antiquary' is of that type which is more mischievous than the 'young enthusiast'. Also one would have been better able to gauge whether he is experienced in archaeology, the length and extent of such experience, and whether his own writings do not betray much that is not scientific archaeology, but pure fiction.

'Antiquary's' reference to the age of the excavators is entirely uncalled for, and on no account can be cited as fair scientific comment. The fact remains that all archaeologists have the glorious privilege of having been young once, and also the opportunity of taking advantage of the work done by the past generation, thence rising to still greater discoveries, and operating in new fields of research. I maintain that my article dealing with the section in the mound at Blackpatch truthfully recorded the excavation, and that apart from the fact that the opinion of the excavators was given on the matter, it left the reader entirely free to form his or her own opinion. I challenge 'antiquary' with his self voiced great experience to dig a better section and record it in a more scientific manner.

'Antiquary' need entertain no fear that his letter would in anyway tend to discourage or disparage the workers at Blackpatch, as I can prove that they enjoy the wholehearted support, advice, and frequent correspondence of many high authorities who have laboured, and yet will labour, in the fields of archaeological research, and whose names and reputation are not to be ignored in the scientific world. With regard to the engraved flint, 'Antiquary' is absurdly mistaken in supposing that the excavators have removed and examined well over 100 tons of debris at Blackpatch for the purpose of perpetrating jokes upon scientific authorities or the general public. Nor have the excavators done this with the object of recording jokes which may have been played upon them. The engraving will shortly be deposited with the Blackpatch collection in a place where it can be viewed not only by 'Antiquary', but by anyone who is interested enough to go and examine it. I wish to make it definitely plain to 'Antiquary' that the Blackpatch excavations, which I had the honour to direct, will bear the strictest investigation, and that they have had the very high commendations of all authorities who have been concerned.

4 W. Dilloway to the Worthing Herald, November 24th 1923

Sir – After endeavouring, for many weary weeks, to follow the seemingly fruitless controversy which rages round the 'Long Man' of Wilmington, it is with relief that I turn to a letter in your pages on the subject of the now sadly neglected Blackpatch. Although agreeing with 'Antiquary' that the evidence adduced by Mr Pull in his article of November 3 on the reopening of the tumulus is not sufficient to support the assertion that the mound at Blackpatch is a barrow of the Bronze Age, your correspondent's scathing criticism of the excavators moves me to mild remonstrance. One, who was not acquainted with the circumstances, would led to imagine that the five operatives mentioned in Mr Pulls article were naughty boys who had absented themselves from Sunday School for the purpose of digging the tumulus. I assure 'Antiquary' that his young enthusiasts, although not as senile as the archaeologist of the 'movies', are too old, perhaps fortunately for them, to be regarded as possible candidates for the Borstal Institute. Your correspondent, it seems, does not wish to disparage the work done. The young enthusiasts must have skins of abnormal thickness if they regard his letter as one of kindly encouragement. It need not be feared, however, that his remarks will discourage anyone.

Archaeology is like golf. Merciful death is the only cure. I have followed the progress of the Blackpatch excavations since October last, and can claim to have first hand knowledge of all that has been done on the site since that date. The work throughout has been conducted by the gentleman whose article 'The Re-opening of the Bronze Age Tumulus' seems to have incurred 'Antiquary's' extreme displeasure. Authorities have, by visits to the mines, and by perusal of the very comprehensive report, satisfied themselves that the work was conducted on thoroughly scientific principles. In view of this I should imagine that one young enthusiast, at least, is somewhat 'peeved' by the suggestion that digging should be supervised by experienced people. His emotions at the moment must be similar to those of an ambitious young constable who has been asked to fetch a policeman.

I had the good fortune to be present when the test trench mentioned in the article was opened, and noted the thoroughness with which the evidence was observed and reported. Scattered over the Downs in this neighbourhood one finds barrows that have been opened again and again by optimists in search of plunder for the bric-a-brac cupboard. Of many of these excavations there is no account whatever, and of others but scanty references in the proceedings of local societies. The 'young enthusiasts' have at least left a permanent record of the details of their modest effort. It is difficult to understand how the test trench is to complicate the work of future excavators. Surely anyone who intends to dig on a site will first consult the literature on the subject. The engraving found in the trench may be a discovery of the greatest possible importance, as your correspondent says, or it may on the other hand be the result of somebody's joke. The joke, if such it be, is a regular chestnut by now. 'Antiquary' must think that the 'young enthusiasts' are very young. May I suggest that if the exploitation of our local prehistoric antiquities is not to fall into the hands of strangers, our archaeologists, particularly the experienced ones, should, for a season, beat their pens into shovels, and bring their dinners with them.

5 H. Bunce to the Worthing Herald, December 1st 1923

Sir – With regard to Antiquary's letter of the 17th inst., I should, as one of the 'young enthusiasts' referred to, like to fully endorse Mr Pull's reply in your issue of the 24th. I consider that, apart from the scientific side of the question, it is very bad taste for antiquary to attack Mr Pull's methods and archaeological methods without signing his name. It looks as though Antiquary were ashamed of his remarks. Mr Pull I have no doubt would, and does, welcome scientific help and advice from those competent to give it. But to make comments on the fact that Mr Pull and those who have assisted him are still young is not calculated to further the cause of archaeology; neither is it quite the action of an experienced archaeologist who desires to direct and help younger excavators. In conclusion, I should like to say that I have worked with Mr Pull since he discovered the mines in May 1922 and that every stage of his work has been examined by some of the highest authorities on archaeology and they have all complimented him on the care, thoroughness, and general excellence of his work.

6 Antiquary to the Worthing Herald, December 15th 1923

Sir – I am sorry that the well meant advice of an experienced gravedigger should be so resented by Mr Pull and his youthful companions Messrs Bunce, Toms and co. The main object of my letter, however, was to protest against the statement that a heap of rubbish was a 'tumulus' or burial place, and further of the Bronze Age, without a single scrap of evidence. In addition, the age of the flint mine is put earlier than the Bronze Age, because this alleged barrow is above it. This method of reasoning does not help archaeology. In a subsequent article by Mr Pull on Blackpatch, was a drawing of a well known Palaeolithic weapon, figured because it did not occur in Blackpatch. If we begin to illustrate articles in this way, there are a great many possibilities! Certainly the most important object found at Blackpatch, if genuine, is the humanly-inscribed flint. But on this Mr Pull is almost silent. Where is it? I have tried to see it, but have failed. And would not a sketch of a unique thing like this, which has presumably been found in Blackpatch, be more valuable than a sketch of a Palaeolithic implement which has not?

7 L. Salzman to the Worthing Herald, December 22nd 1923

Sir – Allow me to protest against the publication in the 'Herald' of such anonymous letters at that signed by a self-styled 'Antiquary'. Anonymity is rarely justifiable, and never in the case of an attack on named opponents, and such a letter should be contemptuously committed to the merited oblivion of the wastepaper basket. With the merits of the particular controversy I am not concerned; but it is conceivable that wisdom may be found in the mouths, or pens, of the monosyllabic 'babes' and that publication of 'Antiquary's' name might convince us of his implied senility rather than of his equally implied omniscience.

[Mr Salzman seems to lose sight of the fact that although a correspondent may decide to be anonymous for good and sufficient reasons, his identity is known to the Editor through whom he seeks publication. Mr Salzman's letter is, in reality, a criticism of the Editor's prerogative in admitting the letter he criticises to the columns of the 'Herald Magazine'. We can assure him that in this instance 'Antiquary's' reason for publishing a letter under a pseudonym was a sufficient one. – Editor 'H.M.']

8 H. Bunce to the Worthing Herald, December 22nd 1923

Sir – With regard to 'Antiquary's' letter in your issue of the 15th inst., I am very surprised that an 'experienced gravedigger' should hide his identity under a nom de plume when he desires to criticise the work of other people. It is evident that however experienced 'Antiquary' may be, he evidently is not very well acquainted with the names of archaeologists or he would know that Mr Toms is not a 'youthful companion' of ours, but the curator of the Brighton Museum and one of the authorities on archaeology who have been kind enough to help us with criticism and advice. If 'Antiquary' would only reveal his name, and show whether he is the authority he proclaims himself to be, we should welcome his criticisms as we do those of Mr Toms and his colleagues, but we cannot accept them from a person who remains anonymous and who therefore may be an authority, but may on the other hand, be almost completely ignorant of archaeology.

9 John Pull to the Worthing Herald, December 22nd 1923

Sir – In reply to the letter signed 'Antiquary' in your issue of the 15th inst. I wish to say that as director of the excavations at Blackpatch I am in no way adverse to authoritative advice or criticism, in fact such would be heartily welcomed. It is again necessary, however, to point out to 'Antiquary' that advice cannot be accepted on any account from individuals who persist in enveloping their identity in the shroud of mystery. Should 'Antiquary' be the 'experienced' grave digger that he says he is, then he should have no reason to refrain from making his name known, as his reputation as an excavator would undoubtedly be known to archaeological science, possibly to fame, and certainly would live to be handed down to posterity. If one may judge from the last communication signed 'Antiquary', that individual's knowledge of my latter article is poor; further his knowledge of flint implements is imperfect to a degree. He says in his letter: 'In a subsequent article by Mr Pull on Blackpatch was a drawing of a well known Palaeolithic weapon, figured because it did not occur at Blackpatch.'. Referring to my article, 'Antiquary' will note that I said: 'It is worthy of note, however, that no admixture of Palaeolithic forms occurred upon the two superficial floors at Blackpatch, as was the case in the floors examined in the shaft filling. The accompanying illustration will serve to show what is meant by a Palaeolithic form.'

The implement which was illustrated did occur at Blackpatch, on a chipping floor in the filling of Shaft 1. Further, 'Antiquary' will note that I referred to the implement as being of Palaeolithic form or type, which is a totally different thing from a palaeolith. If 'Antiquary' were sufficiently acquainted with the forms of flint implements which occur on primitive mining sites he would know that any implement of Palaeolithic form found in association with a flint mine is not necessarily of Palaeolithic age. The implement in question was only unearthed in August 1922, and my illustration is the first that has been published. How, therefore, this can be pronounced as a 'well-known Palaeolithic weapon' I fail to see. I have already answered 'Antiquary' upon the matter of the engraved flint, and regret that his impatience to examine it is so great. At present it is my care together with the whole of the authoritative information relating to it.

10 W. Dilloway to the Worthing Herald, December 29th 1923

Sir – I am gratified to learn from your issue of December 15 that 'Antiquary' has not abandoned the correspondence on Blackpatch. He is, perhaps unconsciously, rendering a great service to our science in attacking the methods of the excavators. As an untiring advocate of brighter archaeology, I take this opportunity of hailing him as the father (or possibly mother) of vituperative prehistory. For some considerable time I have had a steadily growing conviction that the methods of the visiting archaeologists who exploited our prehistoric antiquities were unsatisfying to the genius of south-country people. The strangers, so I learn, established a dangerous precedent by removing the turf from some of our ancient sites. Happily but few of our local antiquaries followed their example, but some have strayed from the fold. The reports of these misguided ones reveal the fact that digging was invariably followed by revision of opinion. In one case which has come to my notice, Early British hut sites proved to be mine sites, thereby creating alarm and despondency in the ranks of those who thought they had settled the housing problem of the ancient Britons. This instance alone is sufficient to expose the disadvantages of digging as compared to the literary methods employed in the successful confusion of the 'Long Man' controversy.

Archaeology I feel certain would progress quite well in Sussex without excavation. Indeed, had prehistoric man really considered the feelings of his patrons, he would have been careful to fashion his implements of some perishable material. The writers on Cissbury and wanderers of Downland would certainly have appreciated this kindly action. Your correspondent confesses that he is an experienced grave digger, but I trust he has long since abandoned that ghoulish occupation, and now shares with me the conviction that the pen is mightier than the spade, and a great deal easier to handle. It is regretted that the palaeolith figured in Mr Pull's recent article is a Blackpatch product, but it furnishes additional proof that the practice of digging is a serious menace to the progress of our science and to the happiness of our antiquaries. Implements of the drift type, it appears, are as numerous at Blackpatch as elderly ladies at a flint hunt. Those who have not associated the Blackpatch mines in their writings with the Anglo-Saxons have cause to congratulate themselves. With respect to the engraved flint I have to offer a suggestion. There are, I understand, archaeologists who lick pieces of pottery in order to determine their antiquity. Roman ware, it seems, is quite palatable, but not so piquant and appetising as the Hallstatt pots. As 'Antiquary' points out, the Blackpatch engraving may be a joke. I am certain that an experienced Lickologist could not only tell us the age of the joke, but also the point at which we are to laugh.

11 Herbert Toms to the Worthing Herald, December 29th 1923

Sir – May I support Mr Salzman's protest against the publication in the Herald of anonymous letters such as that signed by 'Antiquary'. I do so for two reasons: (1) 'Antiquary's' letters have plainly shown that that individual is a mere amateur in archaeological controversy, and (2) that those letters have raised very grave doubts as to 'Antiquary's' veracity. Surely, if this be so, the editorial sanctum should not be defiled for any reason whatever by the admission of 'terminological inexactitudes' as camouflage, to the columns of the magazine. A close study of 'Antiquary's' letters has revealed to me that the individual is very palpably the one who, under the name 'British' endeavoured to attack my first Cissbury article in the 'Herald', and whose identity is but too well known to me.

12 John Pull, C. Sainsbury, W. Dilloway, W. Watkins and H. Bunce to the Worthing Herald, 1924

Sir – Having with mixed feelings carefully perused the contents of an extraordinary report on excavations at Blackpatch, 1922, prepared on behalf of the Worthing Archaeological Society by an editorial committee and published in a recent issue of the Sussex Archaeological Collections, we feel that despite our admiration of this literary effort we as serious archaeologists should point out that this record is not recognised by the authorised excavators. One can quite appreciate the most worthy motives which moved the Worthing Archaeological Society to make some permanent record of that portion of the work in which its members assisted. However, as this was considered a scientific excavation we are anxious to know why the record before us was not based on the exact notes and measurements made by the director of excavations as the work proceeded. The record of work done prior to the advent of the Worthing Archaeological Society must of necessity be pure fiction, good fiction we admit, but nevertheless – fiction. We yield to no one in our admiration for the editorial committee in producing the undoubted work of art, especially considering the artistic manner with which it ignored all necessary and no doubt troublesome data. A comparison of this record with the official report will be sufficient proof of the artistic and literary value of the former, but as we are not artists, but merely dull archaeologists, we are surprised to observe that this work was accepted by a scientific body. It is common knowledge that the Sussex Archaeological Society takes great pride in the accuracy of data appearing in its proceedings and therefore in view of the fact that the authorised report has already been submitted to them we can only trust that in the interests of scientific truth it will take some steps to expunge all purely artistic efforts of this kind from its collections.

13 Stuart Piggott to John Pull, 3rd July 1946

Dear Mr Pull
Here are your sherds from Church Hill Findon, which I am glad to have seen. My report on them is as follows:
Surface Shaft A – Fragment of Romano-British colander
Shaft 4 Layer 1 – Romano-British Sherds
Surface 20 feet S. of Pit A – Rim almost certainly Late Bronze Age rather than Early Iron Age. Note the carbonised grain of ?Barley in this sherd – it should be examined by a botanist.
Shaft 4 surface – Sherds either Late Bronze Age or Early Iron Age
Shaft 4 Layer 4 – I think two small Middle Bronze Age overhanging-rim cineary urns are represented, one with stab-marks on the overhanging rim and a cordon below. I have noted on the label the sherds I think belong to a second pot.
Please make any use you like of these notes – I look forward to seeing your report on these new mine-shafts which sound very interesting and important.

14 E. Gerard to J. H. Pull, 3rd December 1947

Dear Mr Pull,
I have much pleasure in informing you that at a Committee Meeting held yesterday you were re-elected a member of this Society. We hope to see you at the meeting on Tuesday next. As you will have seen on the Winter Programme we are to hold the Annual Supper on Wednesday, January 14th and following the Supper to have a quiz, which will be kept chiefly to archaeological or allied subjects. Would you help us by being a member of one of the teams? We should be so very grateful if you would.

15 The Director, Royal Botanic Gardens, to John Pull, 16th December 1947

Dear Sir
The fragments of charcoal received with your letter of December 12th have now been examined microscopically. This has shown that it might be Willow, Poplar or Horse Chestnut. Willow (Salix spp.) and Poplar (Populus spp.) can be distinguished from Horse Chestnut (Aesculus hippocastanum) only by microscopical details which are no longer clearly visible in the material which you submitted. It may be significant, however, that the Horse Chestnut was introduced into this country only a few centuries ago, whereas some of the Willows and Poplars are truly indigenous. You give no indication of the probable age of the bowl, but it is presumably of an earlier date than that which the Horse Chestnut was introduced. The fragments are being returned to you under separate cover.

16 John Pull to L. Bickerton (Curator, Worthing Museum), May 12th 1949

Dear Sir
'Excavations at Church Hill, Findon, Sussex'
With the kind consent of C. E. A. Hartridge Esq., the owner of Church Hill, and with the unanimous approval of all who have assisted me with the exploration of the prehistoric flint mining site there, it gives me great pleasure to present to the Borough of Worthing, the antiquities now on loan in Worthing Museum, together with such other material now in store, as may be desirable; always providing that the collection remains on view to the public and accessible to students for all time.

17 John Pull to L. Bickerton (Curator of Worthing Museum), January 17th 1950

Dear Mr Bickerton,
In response to an urgent message from Mr E. Holden I have today visited Blackpatch. The flint mines and barrows have all been completely destroyed, by bulldozing operations previous to general ploughing. New Barn Down has already been ploughed to the top of Harrow Hill. I am contacting all necessary people, these sites were all Scheduled as antiquities of National Importance. In the meantime if any specimens, bones, pottery or flints are brought in to you from these sites, seize them and hold tight please. The extent of the damage may be greater than we know of. I will call and see you as soon as possible.

18 Edward Salisbury (Director, Royal Botanic Gardens, Kew) to John Pull, 25th February 1950

Dear Sir,
The charcoals from Church Hill Findon received with your letter of February 12th have been examined microscopically and identified as follows:

From Hearth. A mixture of Ash (Fraxinus sp.) and Hazel (Corylus sp.), the proportion of Ash being appreciably higher than that of Hazel.
From SW hole with cremation. Mostly Ash (Fraxinus sp.) detected.
From hearth in NW ditch. Mostly Ash (Fraxinus sp.). A small proportion of Hazel (Cotylus sp.) also present, together with a third type which may be Hawthorn (Crataegus sp.)
From SE ditch with ox bones. Only Ash (Fraxinus sp.) detected, apart from one small piece that may be Hawthorn (Crataegus sp.).
The material can be returned to you if required.

19 G. P. Burstow to John Pull, March 1st 1950

Dear Mr Pull
Many thanks for your letter and pottery fragments which I found waiting for me when I called at Norton Road. From your letter I gather that all the pieces were found in one place in the ditch of your Church Hill Barrow. I quite agree with you that they have a Hallstatt-La Tene I flavour. I have numbered them in pencil.
Indeterminate sherd. Iron Age paste. Probably Iron Age AI. I am basing these remarks mainly on Wilson and my article in SAC 87. This sherd falls into our Iron Age AI Class 2. It shows the influence of the round shouldered Hallstatt pottery. Cp. Highdown 1939, SAC 81, fig 3c.
Rim similar to SAC 81, fig 3l etc.
Iron Age AI class 1A in our article. Sharp shouldered piece similar to SAC 87, page 87, pl iv 1a. All class I show the influence of the sharp shouldered Italian Bronze situla.
Base. This paste seems different and there is an absence of flint grit. I should have suggested a later date in the Iron Age, although it is not unlike the base from Park Brow illustrated in SAC 87, p87, plate iv 2a. On looking at it again I think it is much later ware, perhaps overlapping Roman period.

It was very kind of you to allow me to pronounce on the pottery. I appreciate it very much. I should be very pleased to give a talk on 'Prehistoric Pottery' to the Worthing Society on March 17th. It will have to be a rather technical lecture and not one very easy to make interesting, but I shall be delighted to have a try. What I feel about the pottery question is this. Obviously the pottery is the main clue to the dates of ancient sites. Wilson and I, thanks to the work of Hawkes and others, feel we know quite a lot of definite facts about Bronze and Iron Age pottery, but we also realise that there is a great deal more to be learned. I shall be very pleased to talk to you as a humble seeker of truth who has really studied the subject but realises that there are many gaps in his knowledge. I should like a lantern please. I will assemble as much pottery as I can and suggest that we might borrow some from the Worthing Museum.

20 Edward Salisbury to John Pull, 30th May 1950

Dear Sir
The sample of charcoal from 'Site C' Church Hill Findon, which was received with your letter of May 10th has now been examined microscopically. This has shown that

the charcoal is a somewhat mixed collection. A fair proportion of it was identified as Gorse (Ulex sp.) whilst other fragments were found to have been derived from maple (Acer sp.) Elder (Sambucus sp.) and probably Alder Buckthorn (Frangula sp.). In addition one particle was found with the structure badly preserved, but which it is suspected may have been derived from Oak (Quercus sp.).
The material can be returned to you if required.

21 John Pull to G. H. Kempton (Worthing Borough Engineer and Surveyor), July 7th 1952

Dear Sir,
I have to thank you for allowing me to see maps showing the boundaries of the National Trust and Borough properties at Cissbury. As the outcome of my interview with you I wish to make formal application on behalf of the Worthing Archaeological Society for permission to make some excavations on that portion of the land owned by the Borough of Worthing, situated outside the south-west boundary of Cissbury Ring, and also on that portion of the land situated immediately to the east of the boundary line dividing the Borough property from that of the National Trust, that being National Trust owned. So far as that portion which is Borough land is concerned I should like if possible to conduct our proposed excavations there in the months of August and September if possible. The work will initially be in the nature of a surface investigation necessitating the cutting of some sections and the stripping of flint workshop floors marked upon our new survey of the site. These cuttings would be filled in and re turfed immediately, so that no open holes or stripped areas would be exposed for more than one day at a time.

Should this application meet with the approval of your committee I would like to point out that we can, and are indeed anxious to collect and effectively deal with such masses of barbed wire as are at present protruding and we also are prepared to fill in and returf such slit trenches and holes now left open upon the ground which are both unsightly and dangerous. I must mention that Mr E. Salisbury, a member of our committee, who is also a member of the National Trust, would be working with us. We should mention any preview of the ground which we propose to explore and any visits which you or your committee care to make while the work is in progress would also be appreciated. All material of scientific interest found during the course of the proposed excavations will be handed over as a matter of course to the safe keeping of the curator of Worthing Museum. I trust that this application may meet with the approval of the Borough authorities.

22 G. H. Kempton to John Pull, 1st August 1952

Dear Sir,
Further to my letter of the 8th ultimo, and to your request for permission to carry out certain shallow excavations on land owned by the Corporation adjoining Cissbury Ring, this matter was considered by the Council at their meeting yesterday when it was resolved that your application be granted subject, in the case of Cissbury Ring, to

the approval of the National Trust. The Corporation will now be taking up the matter with the National Trust regarding the area on which they are interested. Perhaps you would let me know when you propose to commence the work on Corporation property.

23 John Pull to G. H. Kempton, 20th October 1952

Dear Sir,
'Excavations at Cissbury'
The work which has so far been executed at the site has given most satisfactory results. My Committee are agreed that I should make formal application for the Borough Council's permission to open up and clear out one of the prehistoric mine shafts situated on the Borough land there. Herewith I wish to make this application. The object in view is primarily to obtain a more complete picture of the mining site and secondarily if possible to have one of the mines open for the inspection of the members of the South Eastern Union of Scientific Societies when their annual conference takes place in Worthing in May next. We are prepared to securely fence the deep excavation to your satisfaction and to place suitable warning notices. We have a small hut (8ft by 4ft) of galvanised iron sheeting painted green. This is necessary for our tools and shelter if wet. We should like to erect this hut where it will be as concealed as possible in the bushes near to the excavation.

24 G. H. Kempton to John Pull, 8th December 1952

Dear Sir,
I have to inform you that the appropriate Committee of the Council at a recent meeting considered your letter of the 20th October asking for permission to open up and clear out one of the prehistoric mine shafts on land belonging to the Corporation near Cissbury Ring and for this purpose to erect a small hut 8′ x 4′ for tools and shelter, the hut being placed in a concealed position near the bushes, the excavations being securely fenced and suitable warning notices being erected to my satisfaction. The Committee resolved that that the application of your Society be granted, subject to the reinstatement of the ground to my satisfaction, and this resolution was ratified by the Council at its meeting on the 4th instant. Would you please let me know when you propose to start the works granted by this permission.

25 John Pull to G. H. Kempton (Worthing Borough Engineer and Surveyor), 20th January 1953

Dear Mr Kempton
'Excavations at Cissbury'
Please find a copy of the list of Flint Implements recovered from Section 'A'. The handing over of this series to Mr Bickerton has been delayed until now by reason of the special character of the items. They are of more than usual interest and several have been figured for future report. The whole of the material from the 1952 excavations at Cissbury is now in the hands of Mr Bickerton.

26 G. H. Kempton to John Pull, 19th March 1953

Dear Mr Pull
Many thanks for your letter of the 17th instant, enclosing list of your findings at Cissbury, which I will report to the next meeting of the appropriate Committee. I also note that you have commenced work on the excavations of the main shaft, and I am interested to see your findings which you have so far made. I took the opportunity of visiting the site this afternoon, and was a little concerned to see the very temporary form of fencing which has been erected which does not appear to be in accordance with the arrangements we made on the matter. I assume that you will be putting up a more substantial fence for the protection of the public before the hole is deepened sufficiently to make it dangerous. Perhaps you will let me have your confirmation of this. I have not yet had an opportunity to go through your report in regard to John Selden's cottage, which I will do as soon as possible and probably get in touch with you further on this matter.
Yours faithfully

27 John Pull to the Keeper of the Ethnographical Department, British Museum, August 7th 1953

Dear Sir
The Worthing Archaeological Society are now conducting excavations on that portion of the prehistoric mine field situated on Borough land just outside Cissbury camp. I am in charge of these operations and we have opened one of the mine shafts. Near the bottom, at 16 feet from the surface, we have, as you perhaps already know, found the skeleton of a Neolithic man who had been killed by a fall of roof in the entrance to one of the underground workings. Near the left hand of this skeleton, the enclosed was found. It would appear that the man had descended at night with a torch in his right hand and was laying across the drift (gallery) entrance looking in, propped up on his left elbow. The arch collapsed on him and three large blocks were mainly responsible for his death. One had smashed his face, a second had driven the right hand holding the torch through his ribs, and a third had broken his back. Completely covered with the rubble of the fall, he had never been recovered by his friends and we found him just as he had died. It seems that he was a stranger looking for something in this old mine which had already accumulated two feet of rubble in the abandoned shaft, though the entrances to the galleries were still open.

I must mention that the excavation is securely fenced with chain link five feet high and bar locked. The keys are kept by me. There is little chance of any planting by any intruder. So that I presume the object enclosed is genuine, moreover it was recovered in my presence by a member of undoubted integrity who is, like myself, a civil servant. Nevertheless I should be very glad of your expert opinion on it. It looks as if it might have been carved from walrus ivory. If undoubtedly genuine (I have not washed or cleaned it), it will prove of *immense importance*. I have other reasons for suspecting a contact with the forest folk (Mesolithic survivors) with the mining peoples and it might be that this man was one of them and the carved fish a thing belonging to his culture. Would you be good enough to show it to the Keeper of British Antiquities and let me have some comments upon it, if not a full report, by Wednesday next, if possible, as my committee meet on that day.

28 M. W. McCall (British Broadcasting Corporation) to John Pull, 19th October 1953

Dear Mr Pull
With reference to the telephone conversation that my assistant Mrs White had with you last Friday. This is to confirm that you have very kindly agreed to meet our reporter at 2 o'clock on Saturday 24th October at Cissbury Hotel, Findon Valley, for a visit to the Neolithic flint mine at Cissbury Ring. It will not be necessary for you to make any preliminary arrangements on our behalf, our reporter, whose name will be notified to you later in the week, will be able to explain his requirements when you meet. He will be bringing a small tape-recording machine, and the material he obtains will be for a short descriptive story in our Radio Newsreel. I should like to take this opportunity of thanking you for help in this matter.

29 J. S. Weiner (Department of Human Anatomy, University Museum Oxford) to John Pull, 10th November 1953

Dear Sir,
I much appreciate your letter asking me to undertake an examination of the Neolithic skeleton recently excavated at Cissbury. I regret very much that extreme pressure of work makes it impossible for me to undertake the examination of this interesting skeleton. My colleague who helps me in this work has just left for the Sudan, and as it is I have quit a number of other Neolithic bones which have waited a long time for reporting. As a matter of fact we have in recent years come to the conclusion that (except for Palaeolithic material or anything really exceptional) the course that would best suit all purposes would be for the archaeologist to make as accurate a description as possible of the provenance of any skeletal find, and give a general description of the actual bones and send the material (not to us, as we have not the storage space or the necessary supervisory staff) but to Dr Oakley at the British Museum of Natural History. We have, in fact, placed all our skeletal material at the British Museum and continue to send whatever archaeological material comes our way. We are advising archaeologists to send their material to the British Museum with as much detail as possible, since there is usually little to be gained by the description of isolated finds, and it is only by the accumulation of a very large series of crania, long bones etc., that really informative studies can be undertaken. In the past there have been too many short and superficial descriptions of local archaeological finds and the material has often disappeared. We think that our policy of immediate storage in the British Museum is the better way. If you feel that a physical anthropologist really should look at your material at this stage, Dr Barnicot at University Anthropological Department, London, may have somebody on his staff to help you, or Dr Trevor at Cambridge.

30 Gerald Dunning (Inspector of Ancient Monuments) to L. Bickerton (Curator, Worthing Museum), March 16th 1954

Dear Mr Bickerton
Recently in excavations at Birkbeck College, London, a small fish carved in bone, about 2 inches long, was found in the gravel at some depth below surface. The object may well be prehistoric, but until last week a parallel for it was not easy to find. Now I learn that in a flint mine at Cissbury, a similar small carving of a fish has been found in circumstances dating it Late Neolithic or Early Bronze Age. So that a more direct comparison may be made with the fish from London, I write to ask if you would be so kind as to send me a photo or a pencil sketch of the Cissbury find? This is simply for information, and of course any picture would not be published without your permission.

31 L. Bickerton to Gerald Dunning, March 18th 1954

Dear Mr Dunning
I am most interested to hear of your find at Birkbeck College, and am enclosing a photograph with a scale of the carved bone fish found at Cissbury. As you will see from the back of the print, the Cissbury fish is above the scale and is compared with a fish belonging to Dr Curwen of unknown provenance. We would, similarly, be glad to see a photograph or a drawing of the fish you have found and any details of the site and level at which it was found. Mr Pull, who directed the excavations on Cissbury, and who found the fish, is giving a public lecture very shortly, and any information about the Birkbeck College example would be most useful to him. Dr Childe has been very hesitant about giving an opinion on the Cissbury fish in view of its unique character so far as these islands are concerned, but there seems no reason to doubt that it is contemporary with the infilling of the mine in the Late Neolithic or Early Bronze Age period.

Bibliography

Abercromby, J. 1912 *A study of the Bronze Age pottery of Great Britain and Ireland.* Oxford. Clarendon Press.

Aldsworth, F. 1979 A possible Neolithic oval barrow on Nore Down, West Marden. *Sussex Archaeological Collections* 117, 251–2.

Aldsworth, F. 1983a A circular enclosure within Cissbury Ring. *Sussex Archaeological Collections* 121, 198.

Aldsworth, F. 1983b Prehistoric Flint Mines on Nore Down, West Marden. *Sussex Archaeological Collections* 121, 187–90.

Allcroft, A. 1908 *Earthwork of England.* London. Macmillan and Co.

Armstrong, A. 1922a Flint crust engravings and associated implements from Grime's Graves, Norfolk. *Proceedings of the Prehistoric Society of East Anglia* 3, 434–43.

Armstrong, A. 1922b Further discoveries of engraved flint-crust and associated implements at Grime's Graves. *Proceedings of the Prehistoric Society of East Anglia* 3, 548–58.

Bahn, P. and Vertut, J. 1988 *Images of the Ice Age.* Oxford. Facts on File.

Barber, M. 1997 Landscape, the Neolithic, and Kent. In P. Topping (ed), 77–85.

Barber, M, Field, D. and Topping, P. in Press *The Neolithic Flint Mines of England.* London. English Heritage and the Royal Commission on the Historical Monuments of England.

Barfield, L. and Hodder, M. 1989 Burnt Mounds in the West Midlands: Survey and Excavation. In A. Gibson (ed) *Midlands Prehistory.* British Archaeological Report 204, 5–13.

Barker, H, Burleigh, R. and Meeks, N. 1969 British Museum natural radiocarbon measurements vi. *Radiocarbon* 11 (2), 278–94.

Barrett, J, Bradley, R. and Green, M. 1991 *Landscapes, Monuments and Society: The prehistory of Cranborne Chase.* Cambridge. Cambridge University Press.

Barrett, J, Bradley, R. and Hall, M. 1991 *Papers on the Prehistoric Archaeology of Cranborne Chase.* Oxford. Oxbow Monograph 11.

Becker, C. 1959 Flint mining in Neolithic Denmark. *Antiquity* 33, 87–92, plate xii.

Bradley, R, and Edmonds, M. 1993 *Interpreting the axe trade.* Cambridge. Cambridge University Press.

Burstow, G. 1962 An excavation on Cissbury in 1868. *Sussex Notes and Queries* 15, 98–9.

Butler, C. 1991 The Excavation of a Beaker Bowl Barrow at Pyecombe. *Sussex Archaeological Collections* 129, 1–28.

Butler, C. 1992 Some flintwork from Church Hill, Findon and Cissbury. *Sussex Archaeological Collections* 130, 232–3.

Clarke, D. 1970 *Beaker Pottery of Great Britain and Ireland.* Cambridge. Cambridge University Press.

Clarke, W. (ed) 1915 *Report on the excavations at Grime's Graves, Weeting, Norfolk, March – May 1914.* London. H. K. Lewis.

Cleal, R. 1982 A Reanalysis of the Ring Ditch Site at Playden. *Sussex Archaeological Collections* 120, 1–17.

Clutton-Brock, J. 1984 *Excavations at Grimes Graves Norfolk 1972–1976: Fasicule 1 – Neolithic antler picks from Grimes Graves, Norfolk and Durrington Walls, Wiltshire; A biometrical analysis.* London. British Museum.

Cooke, G. Undated. *A Topographical and Statistical Description of the County of Sussex.* London. Privately Printed.

Craddock, P, Cowell, M, Leese, M. and Huges, M. 1983 The trace element composition of polished flint axes as an indicator of source. *Archaeometry* 25, 135–63.

Crawford, H. (ed) 1979 *Subterranean Britain: Aspects of underground archaeology.* John Baker. London.

Curwen, E. and Curwen, E. C. 1926 Harrow Hill Flint Mine Excavation 1924–5. *Sussex Archaeological Collections* 67, 103–38.

Curwen, E. and Curwen, E. C. 1927 Probable flint mines near Tolmere Pond, Findon. *Sussex Notes and Queries* 1, 168–70.

Curwen, E. C. 1926 On the use of Scapulae as shovels. *Sussex Archaeological Collections* 67, 139–45.

Curwen, E. C. 1927 The old flint mines of Sussex. *Sussex County Magazine* 1, 160–4.

Curwen, E. C. 1929a Excavations in the Trundle, Goodwood, 1928. *Sussex Archaeological Collections* 70, 33–85.

Curwen, E. C. 1929b Downland miners 4,000 years ago. *Sussex Daily News*, August 2nd.

Curwen, E. C. 1930a *Prehistoric Sussex.* London. The Homeland Association.

Curwen, E. C. 1930b Wolstonbury. *Sussex Archaeological Collections* 71, 237–45.

Curwen, E. C. 1930c Neolithic camps. *Antiquity* 4, 22–54.

Curwen, E. C. 1931a Whitehawk Neolithic Camp, Brighton. *Sussex Notes and Queries* 3, 188–9.

Curwen, E. C. 1931b Excavations in the Trundle, Second Season, 1930. *Sussex Archaeological Collections* 72, 100–50.

Curwen, E. C. 1934a Excavations in Whitehawk Neolithic camp, Brighton, 1932–3. *The Antiquaries Journal* 14, 99–133.

Curwen, E. C. 1934b Flint miner's dwelling and Bronze Age farm in Sussex. *Antiquity* 8, 215.

Curwen, E. C. 1934c A Later Bronze Age farm and a Neolithic pit dwelling on New Barn Down, Clapham, nr Worthing. *Sussex Archaeological Collections* 75, 137–70.

Curwen, E. C. 1936 Excavations in Whitehawk camp, third season, 1935. *Sussex Archaeological Collections* 77, 60–92.

Curwen, E. C. 1954 *The Archaeology of Sussex* (2nd edition). London. Methuen and Co.

Curwen, E. C. and Williamson, R. 1931 The date of Cissbury Camp. *Antiquaries Journal* 11, 14–38.

Daily Express 1953 Pit victim of 4,000 years ago is found. May 30th.

Darvill, T. 1996 Neolithic buildings in England, Wales and the Isle of Man. In T. Darvill and J. Thomas (eds), 77–112.

Darvill, T. and Thomas, J. 1996 *Neolithic houses in north-west Europe and beyond.* Oxford. Oxbow Monograph 57.

Donachie, J. and Field, D. 1994 Cissbury Ring: A survey by the Royal Commission on the Historical Monuments of England. *Sussex Archaeological Collections* 132, 25–32.

Drewett, P. 1977 The Excavation of a Neolithic Causewayed Enclosure on Offham Hill, East Sussex, 1976. *Proceedings of the Prehistoric Society* 43, 201–41.

Drewett, P. 1978 Neolithic Sussex. In P.Drewett (ed), *Archaeology in Sussex to AD 1500.* Council for British Archaeology Research Report 29, 41–51.

Drewett, P. 1985 *Settlement, Economy, Ceremony and Territorial Organisation in Sussex, 4th – 3rd Millennium BC*. Unpublished PhD Thesis. University of London.

Drewett, P, Rudling, D. and Gardiner, M. 1988 *The south-east to AD 1000*. London and New York. Longman.

Edmonds, M. 1995 *Stone tools and society: working stone in Neolithic and Bronze Age Britain*. London. Batsford.

Ehrenberg, M. 1989 *Women in prehistory*. London. British Museum Publications.

Ellison, A. 1978 The Bronze Age of Sussex. In P. Drewett (ed), *Archaeology in Sussex to AD 1500*. Council for British Archaeology Research Report 29.

Ferguson, J. 1980 Application of data coding to the differentiation of British flint mine sites. *Journal of Archaeological Science* 7, 277–86.

Field, D. 1997a The landscape of extraction: Aspects of the procurement of raw material in the Neolithic. In P. Topping (ed), 55–67.

Field, D. 1997b The Worthing flint mine complex. In R. Schild and Z. Sulgostowska (eds), 65–9.

Field, D. and Cotton, J. 1987 Neolithic Surrey: A Survey of the Evidence. In J. Bird and D. Bird (eds) *The Archaeology of Surrey to 1540*, 71–95.

Finlay, N. 1997 Kid knapping: The missing children in lithic analysis. In J. Moore and E. Scott (eds), 203–12.

Frost, M. 1929 *The Early History of Worthing*. Worthing. Privately Printed.

Gardiner, J. 1984 Lithic distribution and settlement patterns in Central Southern England. In R. Bradley and J. Gardiner (eds), 15–40.

Gardiner, J. 1987 Tales of the unexpected: Approaches to the assessment and interpretation of museum flint collections. In A. Brown and M. Edmonds (eds) *Lithic analysis and Later British Prehistory: Some problems and approaches*. British Archaeological Report 162, 49–65.

Gardiner, J. 1988 *The composition and distribution of Neolithic surface flint assemblages in Central Southern England*. Unpublished PhD Thesis. University of Reading.

Gardiner, J. 1990 Flint procurement and Neolithic axe production on the South Downs: A reassessment. *Oxford Journal of Archaeology* 9, 119–40.

Gerloff, S. 1974 *The Early Bronze Age Daggers in Great Britain and a Reconsideration of the Wessex Culture*. Munich. Prahistorische Bronzefunde VI, 2.

Gibson, A. 1982 *Beaker domestic sites: A study of the domestic pottery of the late third and early second millennia BC in the British Isles*. British Archaeological Report British Series 107.

Goodman, C, Frost, M, Curwen, E. and Curwen, E. C. 1924 Blackpatch Flint Mine Excavation 1922. *Sussex Archaeological Collections* 65, 69–111.

Greenwell, W. 1870 On the opening of Grime's Graves in Norfolk. *Journal of the Ethnological Society of London* 2, 419–39.

Grinsell, L. 1931 Sussex in the Bronze Age. *Sussex Archaeological Collections* 72, 30–68.

Grinsell, L. 1932 Sussex in the Bronze Age: Addenda and Corrigenda. *Sussex Notes and Queries* 4, 85–6.

Grinsell, L. 1934 Sussex Barrows. *Sussex Archaeological Collections* 75, 217–75.

Hamilton, B. 1933 Suspected flint mines on Bow Hill. *Sussex Notes and Queries* 4, 246–7.

Harrison, J. 1877a On marks found upon chalk at Cissbury. *Journal of the Royal Anthropological Institute* 6, 263–71.

Harrison, J. 1877b Report on some further discoveries at Cissbury. *Journal of the Royal Anthropological Institute* 6, 430–42.

Harrison, J. 1878 Additional discoveries at Cissbury. *Journal of the Royal Anthropological Institute* 7, 412–433.

Hartridge, R. 1978 Excavations at the prehistoric and Romano-British site on Slonk Hill, Shoreham, Sussex. *Sussex Archaeological Collections* 116, 69–142.

Hodder, I. and Barfield, L. *Burnt mounds and hot stone technology*. Sandwell Metropolitan Borough Council.

Holden, F. 1972 A Bronze Age Cemetery-Barrow on Itford Hill, Beddingham, Sussex. *Sussex Archaeological Collections* 110, 70–117.

Holgate, R. 1989 *The Neolithic flint mines in Sussex: A plough damage assessment and site management report*. Unpublished report for English Heritage. Field Archaeology Unit, Institute of Archaeology London.

Holgate, R. 1991 *Prehistoric flint mines*. Shire Publications. Princes Risborough.

Holgate, R. 1995a Neolithic flint mining in Britain. *Archaeologia Polona* 33, 133–61.

Holgate, R. 1995b Harrow Hill near Findon, West Sussex. *Archaeologia Polona* 33, 347–50.

Holgate, R. 1995c Long Down near Chichester, West Sussex. *Archaeologia Polona* 33, 350–2.

Holleyman, G. 1937 Harrow Hill excavations, 1936. *Sussex Archaeological Collections* 78, 230–51.

Horsfield. T. 1824 *The History and Antiquities of Lewes and its Vicinity*. Lewes. J. Baxter.

Hurcombe, L. 1997 A viable past in the pictorial present? In J. Moore and E. Scott (eds), 15–24.

Irving, G. 1857 On the camps at Cissbury, Sussex. *Journal of the British Archaeological Association* 13, 274–94.

Kinnes, I. and Longworth, I. 1985 *Catalogue of the excavated prehistoric and Romano-British material in the Greenwell Collection*. London. British Museum Publications.

Lane Fox, A. 1869a An Examination into the Character and Probable Origin of the Hill Forts of Sussex. *Archaeologia* 42, 27–52.

Lane Fox, A. 1869b Further remarks on the hillforts of Sussex, being an account of the excavations at Cissbury and Highdown. *Archaeologia* 42, 27–52.

Lane Fox, A. 1875 Excavations in Cissbury camp; being a report of the exploration committee of the Anthropological Institute for the year 1875. *Journal of the Anthropological Institute* 5, 357–90.

Laughlin, B. 1994 *An everyday story of country folk? An archaeological survey of Roger's Farm, Findon, West Sussex*. Unpublished BSc Dissertation. Bournemouth University.

Law, H. 1927 Flint mines on Church Hill, Findon. *Sussex Notes and Queries* 1, 222–4.

Legge, A. 1992 *Excavations at Grimes Graves Norfolk 1972–1976. Fasicule 4: Animals, Environment and the Bronze Age Economy*. London. British Museum Press.

Longworth, I. 1984 *Collared Urns of the Bronze Age in Great Britain and Ireland*. Cambridge. Cambridge University Press.

Longworth, I, Ellison, A. and Rigby, V. 1988 *Excavations at Grimes Graves Norfolk 1972–1976. Fasicule 2: The Neolithic, Bronze Age and later pottery*. London. British Museum Press.

Longworth, I, Herne, A, Varndell, G. and Needham, S. 1991 *Excavations at Grimes Graves Norfolk 1972–1976. Fasicule 3 – Shaft X: Bronze Age flint, chalk and metalworking*. London. British Museum Press.

Longworth, I. and Varndell, G. 1996 *Excavations at Grimes Graves Norfolk 1972-1976. Fasicule 5: Mining in the deep mines*. London. British Museum Press.

McNabb, J, Felder, P, Kinnes, I. and Sieveking, G. 1996 An archive report on recent excavations at Harrow Hill, Sussex. *Sussex Archaeological Collections* 134, 21–37.

Mercer, R. 1980. *Hambledon Hill: A Neolithic Landscape*. Edinburgh University.

Mercer, R. 1981 *Grimes Graves, Norfolk. Excavations 1971–72: Volume 1*. Department of the Environment Archaeological Report 11.

Migeod, F. 1950 *Cissbury*. Worthing. Worthing and Littlehampton Gazettes Ltd.

Moore, J. and Scott, E. (eds) 1997 *Invisible people and processes: Writing gender and childhood into European archaeology*. Leicester. Leicester University Press.

Mortimer, R. 1986 Controls on Upper Cretaceous sedimentation in the South Downs, with particular reference to flint distribution. In G. Sieveking and M. Hart (eds), 21–42.

Mortimer, R. And Wood, C. 1986 The distribution of flint in the English chalk, with particular reference to the Brandon Flint Series and the high Turoniam flint maximum. In G. Sieveking and M. Hart (eds), 7–20.

Musson, R. 1954 An Illustrated Catalogue of Sussex Beaker and Bronze Age Pottery. *Sussex Archaeological Collections* 92, 106–24.

O'Brien, W. 1994 *Mount Gabriel: Bronze Age mining in Ireland*. Galway. Galway University Press.

Piggott, S. 1954 *The Neolithic cultures of the British Isles*. Cambridge. Cambridge University Press.

Piggott, S. 1962. *The West Kennet Long Barrow*. London. Her Majesty's Stationery Office.

Pitts, M. 1996 The stone axe in Neolithic Britain. *Proceedings of the Prehistoric Society* 61, 311–71.

Pull, J. 1923a The downland flint mines: system of underground workings explained. *The Herald Magazine*, 7th April.

Pull, J. 1923b Additional discoveries at Blackpatch: Bronze Age tumulus re-opened. *Worthing Herald*, November 3rd.

Pull, J. 1923c Blackpatch: Further discoveries – The chipping floors and surface occupation levels. *The Herald Magazine*, November 24th.

Pull, J. 1927 Flint mining in the Bronze Age: An ancient burial discovered at Blackpatch. *Worthing Herald*, July 23rd.

Pull, J. 1931 Cissbury in the past. *The Herald Magazine*, September 19th.

Pull, J. 1932a *The Flint Miners of Blackpatch*. London. Williams and Norgate.

Pull, J. 1932b The bonds of death: An ancient Sussex burial. *The Herald Magazine*, March 19th.

Pull, J. 1933a Some discoveries at Findon: 1 – The prehistoric antiquities of Church Hill. *Sussex County Magazine* 7, 470–2.

Pull, J. 1933b Some discoveries at Findon: 2 – The fire mound. *Sussex County Magazine* 7, 506–8.

Pull, J. 1933c Some discoveries at Findon: 3 – The burial mounds. *Sussex County Magazine* 7, 597–600.

Pull, J. 1933d Some discoveries at Findon: 4 – The flint industries. *Sussex County Magazine* 7, 653–55.

Pull, J. 1933e Some discoveries at Findon: 5 – The flint implements. *Sussex County Magazine* 7, 727–30.

Pull, J. 1933f Some discoveries at Findon: 6 – The flint mines. *Sussex County Magazine* 7, 810–4.

Pull, J. 1935a The Stone Age Villages of Downland: 1 – The discovery of Neolithic settlements in West Sussex. *Sussex County Magazine* ix, 7, 437–9.

Pull, J. 1935b The Stone Age Villages of Downland: 2 – High Salvington. *Sussex County Magazine* ix, 8, 498–500.

Pull, J. 1935c The Stone Age Villages of Downland: 3 – Mount Carvey and Myrtlegrove. *Sussex County Magazine* ix, 9, 577–9.

Pull, J. 1935d The Stone Age Villages of Downland: 4 – Abinger Rough. *Sussex County Magazine* ix, 10, 636–8.

Pull, J. 1935e The Stone Age Villages of Downland: 5 – The making of flint implements. *Sussex County Magazine* ix, 11, 725–8.

Pull, J. 1935f The Stone Age Villages of Downland: 6 – Everyday tools and their uses. *Sussex County Magazine* ix, 12, 781–4.

Pull, J. 1953 Further discoveries at Church Hill, Findon. *Sussex County Magazine* 27, 15–21.

Pull, J. Unpublished. *The Story of Flint*. Worthing Museum, Acc No 1961/1599.

Pull, J. and Sainsbury, C. 1928a The round barrows of Blackpatch – Article 1: Discovery of many ancient burials. *Worthing Herald*, April 21st.

Pull, J. and Sainsbury, C. 1928b The round barrows of Blackpatch – Article 2: Interesting finds in Barrow no 3. *Worthing Herald*, April 28th.

Pull, J. and Sainsbury, C. 1928c The round barrows of Blackpatch – Article 3: Barrow no 4. *Worthing Herald*, May 5th.

Pull, J. and Sainsbury, C. 1928d The round barrows of Blackpatch – Article 4: The Cissbury Type Celt and its association with barrows of the Bronze Age. *Worthing Herald*, May 19th.

Pull, J. and Sainsbury, C. 1928e The round barrows of Blackpatch – Article 5: The non-marine mollusca. *Worthing Herald*, May 26th.

Pull, J. and Sainsbury, C. 1928f The round barrows of Blackpatch – Article 6: The Beaker folk. *Worthing Herald*, June 9th.

Pull, J. and Sainsbury, C. 1928g The round barrows of Blackpatch – Article 7: The relative age of the barrows and flint mines. *Worthing Herald*, June 23rd.

Pull, J. and Sainsbury, C. 1928h The round barrows of Blackpatch – Article 8: An Early Bronze Age culture. *Worthing Herald*, July 14th.

Pull, J. and Sainsbury, C. 1929a The flint miners of Blackpatch – Article 1: Barrow no 5. *Worthing Herald*, April 20th.

Pull, J. and Sainsbury, C. 1929b The flint miners of Blackpatch – Article 2: Barrow no 6. *Worthing Herald*, April 27th.

Pull, J. and Sainsbury, C. 1929c The flint miners of Blackpatch – Article 3: A burial beneath a chipping floor. *Worthing Herald*, May 11th.

Pull, J. and Sainsbury, C. 1929d The flint miners of Blackpatch – Article 5: The dwellings and hut sites. *Worthing Herald*, June 1st.

Pull, J. and Sainsbury, C. 1929e Servants of the Blackpatch miners – Article 4: The red deer (*Cervus olaphus*). *Worthing Herald*, November 16th.

Pull, J. and Sainsbury, C. 1930a Further discoveries at Blackpatch. *Worthing Herald*, May 31st.

Pull, J. and Sainsbury, C. 1930b Further discoveries at Blackpatch: Second article. *Worthing Herald*, June 7th.

Pull, J. and Sainsbury, C. 1930c Further discoveries at Blackpatch: Third article. *Worthing Herald*, June 21st.

Pull, J. and Sainsbury, C. 1930d Further discoveries at Blackpatch: Fourth article. *Worthing Herald*, July 5th.

Pull, J. and Sainsbury, C. 1930e Further discoveries at Blackpatch: Fifth article. *Worthing Herald*, July 19th.

Pye, E. 1968 *The Flint Mines at Blackpatch, Church Hill and Cissbury*. Unpublished MA Thesis, University of Edinburgh.

Ratcliffe-Densham, H. and Ratcliffe-Densham, M. 1961 An Anomalous Earthwork on Cock Hill. *Sussex Archaeological Collections* 99, 78–108.

Reynolds, A. 1998 Executions and hard Anglo-Saxon Justice. *British Archaeology*, February, 8–9.

Richards, J. and Thomas, J. 1984 Ritual activity and structured deposition in Late Neolithic Wessex. IN. R. Bradley and J. Gardiner (eds), *Neolithic Studies*. British Archaeological Report 133, 189–218.

Rolleston, G. 1877 Note on the animal remains found at Cissbury. *Journal of the Royal Anthropological Institute* 6, 20–36.

Rolleston, G. 1879 Notes on skeleton found at Cissbury, April 1878. *Journal of the Royal Anthropological Institute* 8, 377–89.

Russell, M. 1996a *A reassessment of the Bronze Age cemetery-barrow on Itford Hill, East Sussex, and its place in the prehistory of south-east England*. Bournemouth University: School of Conservation Sciences Research Report 2.

Russell, M. 1996b Problems of Phasing: A Reconsideration of the Black Patch Middle Bronze Age 'Nucleated Village'. *Oxford Journal of Archaeology* 15, 33–8.

Russell, M. 1996c Reassessing Neolithic and Bronze Age Sussex. *Sussex Past and Present* 79, 6.

Russell, M. 1997 NEO-'Realism?': An alternative look at the Neolithic chalkland database of Sussex. In P. Topping (ed), 69–76.

Russell, M. 1999 *Time And Relative Dimensions In Space': Reassessing the origins, nature, significance, impact and evolution of Early Neolithic monumental architecture upon the chalk landscapes of Central South-eastern England.* Unpublished PhD Thesis, School of Conservation Sciences, Bournemouth University.

Russell, M. In Press a Excavations at Mile Oak Farm, 1989-90. In D. Rudling (ed) *Downland Landscape and Settlement: The Archaeology of the Brighton Bypass.* London. English Heritage Monograph.

Russell, M. In Press b Of flint mines and fossil men. The Lavant Caves deception. *Oxford Journal of Archaeology*

Russell, M. In Press c *The Flint Mines of Neolithic Britain.* Tempus Publishing. Stroud.

Russell, M. (ed) In Prep *The Archaeology of Prehistoric Flint Extraction: Essays on the cultural heritage of flint mines.* Bournemouth University.

Russell, M. and Rudling, D. 1996 Excavations at Whitehawk Neolithic Enclosure, Brighton, East Sussex: 1991-93. *Sussex Archaeological Collections* 134, 39–61.

Salisbury, E 1961 Prehistoric Flint Mines on Long Down 1955–8. *Sussex Archaeological Collections* 99, 66–73.

Shepherd, R. 1980 *Prehistoric mining and allied industries.* Academic Press. London.

Sieveking, G de G. 1979 Grime's Graves and Prehistoric European Flint Mining. In Crawford, H. (ed) *Subterranean Britain: Aspects of Underground Archaeology.* John Baker, London, 1–43.

Sieveking, G de G, Bush, P, Ferguson, J, Craddock, P, Huges, M. and Cowell, M. 1972 Prehistoric flint mines and their identification as sources of raw material. *Archaeometry* 14, 151–76.

Sieveking, G de G. and Hart, M. (eds) 1986 *The scientific study of flint and chert.* Cambridge. Cambridge University Press.

Sieveking, G de G, Longworth, I, Huges, M. and Clark, A. 1973 A new survey of Grime's Graves. *Proceedings of the Prehistoric Society* 39, 182–218.

Sieveking, G de G. and Newcomer, M. (eds). 1987 *The human uses of flint and chert.* Cambridge. Cambridge University Press.

Smith, I. 1956 *The Decorative Art of Neolithic Ceramics in south-east England and its Relations.* Unpublished PhD Thesis, University of London.

Smith, I. 1965. *Windmill Hill and Avebury, excavations by Alexander Keiller.* Oxford. Clarendon.

Smith, R. 1912 On the date of Grime's Graves and Cissbury flint mines. *Archaeologia* 63, 109–58.

Stevens, J. 1872 The Flint-works at Cissbury. *Sussex Archaeological Collections* 24, 145–65.

Stone, J. 1932 Easton Down, Winterslow, South Wiltshire, flint mine excavation, 1930. *Wiltshire Archaeological and Natural History Magazine* 45, 350–65.

Stone, J. 1933 Excavations at Easton Down, Winterslow, 1931–32 *Wiltshire Archaeological and Natural History Magazine* 46, 255–42.

Sussex Daily News 1947 Trapped miners of 2,000 BC: Excavations at Findon, October 9th.

Taylor, J. 1980 *Bronze Age Goldwork of the British Isles.* Cambridge. Cambridge University Press.

Thomas, J. 1991 *Rethinking the Neolithic.* Cambridge. Cambridge University Press.

Thomas, J. 1996 *Time, culture and identity: an interpretative archaeology.* London. Routledge.

Thomas, K. 1982 Neolithic Enclosures and Woodland Habitats on the South Downs in Sussex, England. In. M. Bell and S. Limbrey (eds) *Archaeological Aspects of Woodland Ecology.* British Archaeological Report 146, 147–70.

The Times Literary Supplement 1932 Flint Mines, October 13th.

Toms, H. and Toms, C. 1926 The Cissbury Earthworks. *Sussex Archaeological Collections* 67, 55–83.

Topping, P. 1996 Grimes Graves mined 'for ritual reasons'. *British Archaeology* 18, 2.

Topping, P. (ed) 1997a *Neolithic Landscapes: Neolithic Studies Group Seminar Papers 2*. Oxford. Oxbow Monograph.
Topping, P. 1997b Structured deposition, symbolism and the English flint mines. In R. Schild and Z. Sulgostowska (eds), 127–32.
Turner, E. 1850 On the military earthworks of the South Downs, with a more enlarged account of Cissbury, one of the principal of them. *Sussex Archaeological Collections* 3, 173–84.
Varndell, G. 1991 The Worked Chalk. In I. Longworth et al, 94–153.
Venables, M. 1960 Salute to an archaeologist: the late Mr J. H. Pull. Selborne Notes. *West Sussex Gazette*.
Wade, A. 1922 Ancient Flint Mines at Stoke Down, Sussex. *Proceedings of the Prehistoric Society of East Anglia* 4, 82–91.
Wainwright, G. 1989 *The henge monuments. Ceremony and society in prehistoric Britain*. London. Thames and Hudson.
Wainwright, G. and Longworth, I. 1971 The Rinyo-Clacton Culture reconsidered. In G. Wainwright and I. Longworth *Durrington Walls: Excavations 1966–1968*. London. Society of Antiquaries, 235–306.
Welch, M. 1983 *Early Anglo-Saxon Sussex*. British Archaeological Report 112.
White, S. 1995 A most loveable character. *Sussex Past and Present* 77, 11.
Whittle, A. 1995 Gifts from the earth: symbolic dimensions of the use and production of Neolithic flint and stone axes. *Archaeologia Polona* 33, 247–60.
Williams, H. 1997 Ancient attitudes to ancient monuments. *British Archaeology*, November, 6.
Willett, E. 1880 On flint workings at Cissbury, Sussex. *Archaeologia* 45, 337–48.
Williamson, R. 1930 Excavations in Whitehawk Neolithic camp, near Brighton. *Sussex Archaeological Collections* 71, 57–96.
Woodcock, A. and Woolley, A. 1986 Prehistoric Stone Implements from Sussex and their Petrological Identification. *Sussex Archaeological Collections* 124, 9–23.
Young, B. and Lake, R. 1988 *Geology of the county around Brighton and Worthing*. London. Her Majesty's Stationary Office.